MASTERING MULTIMATE ADVANTAGE II

MASTERING MULTIMATE® ADVANTAGE II™

CHARLES ACKERMAN

SYBEX®

San Francisco • Paris • Düsseldorf • London

Cover design by Thomas Ingalls + Associates
Cover photography by Casey Cartwright
Series design by Julie Bilski

MS-DOS is a trademark of Microsoft Corporation.
SuperCalc3 and SuperCalc4 are trademarks of Computer Associates International.
MultiMate, MultiMate Advantage, MultiMate Advantage II, MultiMate GraphLink, and Just Write are trademarks of MultiMate International Corporation, an Ashton-Tate company.
1-2-3 and DIF are trademarks of Lotus Development Corporation.
IBM and Personal Computer AT are trademarks of International Business Machines Corporation.
WordStar is a trademark of MicroPro International Corporation.
dBASE II, dBASE III, and dBASE III PLUS are trademarks of Ashton-Tate.
Norton Utilities is a trademark of Peter Norton Computing.
Mace Utilities is a trademark of Paul Mace Software.
SYBEX is a registered trademark of SYBEX, Inc.

SYBEX is not affiliated with any manufacturer.

Every effort has been made to supply complete and accurate information. However, SYBEX assumes no responsibility for its use, nor for any infringements of patents or other rights of third parties which would result.

Copyright©1988 SYBEX Inc., 2021 Challenger Drive #100, Alameda, CA 94501. World rights reserved. No part of this publication may be stored in a retrieval system, transmitted, or reproduced in any way, including but not limited to photocopy, photograph, magnetic or other record, without the prior agreement and written permission of the publisher.

Library of Congress Card Number: 86-63044
ISBN 0-89588-482-8
Manufactured in the United States of America
10 9 8 7

To my Dad,
because he taught me to enjoy reading, writing, and computers.

ACKNOWLEDGMENTS

    Will the real authors please stand up! You can't see them, but my editors Tanya Kucak and Marilyn Smith stand tallest throughout this book. When you find a part that makes particularly good sense, it's probably their work. Next come the people who helped put it together: Eleanor Ramos, the book designer; John Kadyk, the word-processing coordinator; Michelle Hoffman, the graphics technician; Lynne Bourgault, the proofreader; Gladys Varon, the typesetter; and Greta Mayfield, the technical reviewer.

    Thanks also to Debbie Ritchie at MultiMate International, who patiently provided information, and Tad Dunne, an enthusiast of MultiMate Advantage II, whose suggestions allowed me to "bring something to the party." Finally, the unsung Hannah Robinson, who saved the best cover for me. Indeed, without the contributions of all these people, including Connie Gatto—always with a smile—and the natty Troy Williams—always with a good word—this book would simply not be. Thank you.

TABLE OF CONTENTS

INTRODUCTION .... *xvii*

PART 1 FUNDAMENTALS

CHAPTER 1 LEARNING THE BASICS 1
The Keyboard Arrangement 1
Starting the Program 6
The Main Menu 7
    Create a Document Screen 9
    Document Summary Screen 12
    Modify Document Defaults Screen 14

CHAPTER 2 WRITING A LETTER 17
The Document Screen 17
    Status and Format Lines 18
Writing a Letter 19
Moving the Cursor 20
    Cursor-Movement Keys 20
    Cursor Speed 23
Making Corrections 24
    Escaping Changes 29
Help! 30
Saving Your Document 34
Interface and Mode 34
    The Question of Interface 34

	The Pull-Down Menu Option	35
	Mode of Operation	37
CHAPTER 3	**COPYING, MOVING, AND SEARCHING**	**41**
	Revising the Letter	41
	Entering a Document Quickly	41
	Highlighting	43
	Copying and Moving	45
	Copying within a Document	45
	Deleting Text	46
	Moving Text	48
	Copying from One Document to Another	48
	Document Handling Functions	51
	Copy a Document	53
	Moving a Document	54
	Deleting a Document	55
	Renaming a Document	57
	Search and Replace	58
	Searching for Text	59
	Replacing Text	61
CHAPTER 4	**SPELLING**	**69**
	Checking Spelling	69
	Using a Pull-Down Menu for a Spelling Check	72
	Spelling Edit	72
	Creating a Custom Dictionary	77
	Building a Custom Dictionary	77
	Deleting Words from a Custom Dictionary	78
	Keeping a Written Record of Entries	79
	Using Advanced Utilities to Modify a Custom Dictionary	79
	Create a New File	80
	Delete a Custom Dictionary	81
	Edit an Old File	82
	Using the Thesaurus	85

CHAPTER 5 FORMATTING — 89
- Modify Document Defaults Screen — 89
- Format Lines — 95
  - The System Format Line — 97
  - Current Format Line — 101
  - Page Format Line — 101
  - Deleting the Current or Page Format Line — 102
  - Searching for Format Lines — 102
  - Replacing the Format Line — 103
- Special Printing Characteristics — 104
  - Print Modes — 104
  - Other Screen Codes — 107
  - Hyphenation — 109
- Place Marks — 113
- Underlining — 115
- Page Formatting — 115
  - Page Length — 116
  - Page Break — 117
  - Combining Pages — 117
  - Go to Page — 118
  - Page Numbers — 119
  - Repagination — 120
  - Required Page Break — 121
- Footnotes and Endnotes — 121
  - Creating Footnotes — 121
  - Creating Endnotes — 125
- Headers and Footers — 126
- Comments — 129
  - Creating Comments — 130
  - Printing Comments — 130

CHAPTER 6 PRINTING — 135
- Printers — 135
  - Caution — 135
- Printing One Screen or One Page at a Time — 136
  - Quick Print — 136
  - Hot Print — 137

Preview Printing	138
Printing a Letter	139
How to Stop the Printer	141
Selecting Print Pitch and Fonts from within a Document	144
Changing the Print Pitch	144
Changing the Print Font	144
Customizing Print Parameters	146

PART 2 ADVANCED FEATURES

CHAPTER 7 WORKING WITH LIBRARIES — 157

Creating a Library	157
Attaching a Library	162
Inserting Library Entries	163
Editing Entries in a Library	164
Printing Copies of Library Entries	170
Adding New Entries to a Library	170
Copying Entries from a Document	171
Copying Entries from One Library to Another	173
Deleting Entries from a Library	173

CHAPTER 8 KEY PROCEDURES — 177

What is a Key Procedure?	177
Building a Key Procedure	178
Executing a Key Procedure	182
Pause during Execution	183
Prompt during Execution	187
Building a Key Procedure without Text	188
Replaying a Key Procedure	189
Naming and Renaming Key Procedures	190
Accessing DOS Directly	192
Editing Key Procedure Files	193

Mode Control	198
Key Procedure Display	198
Creating Key Procedures in Advanced Utilities	201
Deleting a File	203
Exiting from the Key Procedure File Edit Utility	204

CHAPTER 9 NUMBERING SECTIONS AND CREATING TABLES OF CONTENTS 207

Section Numbering	207
Flush-Left Numbering	21
Numbering with Tab Indents	215
Editing Section Numbers	218
Numeric Section Numbering	218
Aligning Numeric-style Numbering with Decimal Tabs	220
Creating a Table of Contents	222
Editing the Table of Contents	224

CHAPTER 10 COLUMN APPLICATIONS 227

Creating Columns	227
Creating Bound Columns	228
Creating Snake Columns	233
Editing Text within Columns	235
Highlighting	235
Copying Columnar Text	236
Sorting	239
Moving Columnar Text	241
Decimal Tab	245
Decimal Tabs in Rows	247
Column Calculations	248
Line and Box Drawing	256

CHAPTER 11 ADVANCED PRINTING 263

Merge Printing	263
Creating a Merge Document	264

Creating a List Document	**266**
Printing Result Documents	269
Merge Printing from the Keyboard	271
Special Commands	272
Queue Printing	**276**
Bypassing the Main Menu	278
Typewriter Modes	279
Special Keyboards	282
Printing Document Summary Screens	**284**
Print Document Summary Screens	284
Search Document Summary Screens	286

CHAPTER 12 ADVANCED MERGING *291*

Merge Data Files	291
Designing a Template	291
Creating Records	298
Editing a Template	299
Editing Merge Data Files	303
Sorting Records	307
Selecting and Unselecting Records	308
Merge Printing with Merge Data Files	309
Printing Records and Templates	309
Direct dBASE Merge	311
Merging with Information from Another Database	311
Sequential Data File Merge	311
Random Data File Merge	314
Merge Printing with Merged Data Files	315

CHAPTER 13 ON-FILE *319*

Setting Up On-File	320
Creating Records	322
Searching and Displaying Cards	328
Working Directly from the DOS Prompt	329
Creating a Box from the DOS Prompt	329
Adding a Card from the DOS Prompt	329
Searching and Selecting Cards from the DOS Prompt	330

Moving through a Card Box	330
Displaying, Sorting, Editing, and Deleting Cards	330
Printing Card Information	332
Special Features	333
Templates	333
Creating Templates	334
Editing Templates	337
On-File Utilities	337
Copying Files from One Box to Another	338

APPENDIX A INSTALLING THE PROGRAM   341

MultiMate Advantage II Diskettes	341
DOS Preliminaries	342
Formatting Diskettes	342
Installing on a Two-Floppy System	344
Installing on a Hard Disk	345
Which Files to Load	346
Installing MultiMate Advantage II in a Subdirectory	347
Modifying Console Defaults	348
Converting Custom Dictionaries	352
Dual-Floppy System	352
Hard-Disk System	353
Other Utilities	353
Editing the System Format Line	354
Editing Drive Defaults	354
Editing System Defaults	356
Helpful Hints for Troubleshooting	357

APPENDIX B PRINTER INSTALLATION   361

Viewing Files on the Printer Action Tables Diskette	361
Copying the Right Files	364
Connecting to a Serial or Parallel Port	365
Designing Printer Files	366
Deleting Printer Files	369

APPENDIX C SUMMARY OF COMMANDS AND KEY FUNCTIONS   373

APPENDIX D COMPARING PROGRAM VERSIONS   385

APPENDIX E DISK UTILITIES   389
  Converting Files   389
    Source and Destination Files   391
    Conversion Formats   394
    Editing Format Conversion Defaults   395
  Document Recovery   396
  Automatic Backup Files   398

INDEX   401

INTRODUCTION

MULTIMATE ADVANTAGE II IS A POWERFUL AND versatile word-processing program for microcomputers, and this book will teach you how to use all the features of that program.

History of MultiMate

The history of MultiMate Advantage II goes back to the early years of word processing on computers. The Wang dedicated word processor was one of the first word processors available and was so widely used that the program WangWriter became a corporate standard. In 1981, however, the IBM PC became the most popular computer for word processing. That's when MultiMate was created, and it was deliberately designed to emulate WangWriter on the IBM PC, since so many people were familiar with that program. MultiMate Advantage II, version 1.0, is the most recent version of MultiMate, and it is the version I have used for this book.

What You Can Do with MultiMate Advantage II

As a word-processing program, MultiMate Advantage II can help you with quick jobs, such as writing and printing a short memo, as well as with the more tedious and time-consuming tasks, such as the production of customized form letters merged with database information. MultiMate Advantage II even has its own database to help keep your information all in one place. You can also import files from other databases and from spreadsheets, as well as from documents written by other word processors.

MultiMate Advantage II supports practically every printer on the market, so you should find it little problem to use with your oldest equipment or your newest purchase of a laser printer.

Purpose of This Book

Intended for casual as well as frequent users of MultiMate Advantage II, this book has several distinguishing advantages over the

Multimate documentation. First of all, everything you need to know is contained under one cover. By contrast, the documentation is cumbersome. It consists of many booklets and pamphlets. Although this documentation is fairly well written and well organized, it is not easy to sort through as you learn to use the program, nor is it easy to refer to if you have questions.

In addition, this book has been written as a tutorial. This means that you will learn the basic information first, and then you will learn the more complex features step by step. Since MultiMate Advantage II is a long and complex program, I will focus on just the most important features. They have been divided into two parts: Fundamentals and Advanced Features.

Part I, Fundamentals, will lay the groundwork for the rest of the book by presenting basic information about MultiMate Advantage II: keyboard arrangement, creating and editing letters and simple documents, formatting text, and simple printing. If you are a beginner, you should read each chapter carefully and in sequence. In Part I, it is important that you fully understand the material in each chapter before proceeding to the next chapter.

After you've mastered the fundamentals, you can move on to Part II, Advanced Features. In Part II, you'll learn how to manage libraries of text you use often, how to build and use macros, how to create columns, and how to use merge printing. You will also learn about a program that complements Advantage II's word-processing features: the On-File database for information handling.

At the end of this book, you will find five appendices to help you with technical questions you might have regarding the program. Appendix A will help you install your program diskettes onto a hard disk, as well as help you organize your files. Appendix B will help you select and install the proper printing file to link your printer to your computer. Appendix C is a command summary, and Appendix D is a comparison of Advantage II to earlier releases of MultiMate. Finally, Appendix E includes information about disk utilities.

If you have experience in word processing, you might want to skim the first few chapters before learning the advanced features. Experienced users of earlier versions of MultiMate can dip and skip throughout the text, as suits their needs. If you have experience with MultiMate, you might want to glance at Appendix D so you can see the differences between MultiMate Advantage II, version 1.0, and earlier versions.

The Scenario

To give you practical working examples of MultiMate Advantage II, and to help you understand how all the features work together, I will create a fictitious company, *Wines En Masse,* and develop a scenario **around** it. The story will develop as your skills with Advantage II develop. The examples will be useful to you whether you're dealing with any commodity, or even a service.

System Requirements

MultiMate Advantage II is designed to run on a microcomputer using MS-DOS version 2.0 or later. The program requires a minimum of 384K of RAM to run successfully, and it will operate on all versions of the IBM Personal Computer, from the IBM PC to all models of the PS-2. It will also run on any 100 percent MS-DOS compatible computer, as well as most clones. Although a hard disk is recommended because it offers quicker access and greater file capacity, it is not required. If you are using floppy disks, you should have no problem doing so. There will be times when you need to replace one diskette with another, and I will alert you to these occasions. Fortunately, each of the 11 program diskettes is fairly uniform in purpose, so you will not need to switch diskettes often. In fact, some corporations still prefer to use floppy disks for their documents, so they can keep the information more secure. This book assumes a floppy-disk system, but gives instructions for hard-disk systems as well.

MultiMate Advantage II is not copy protected, so you should have **no** problems either recording the program files to your hard disk or making copies on floppies for your protection.

PART I

FUNDAMENTALS

1

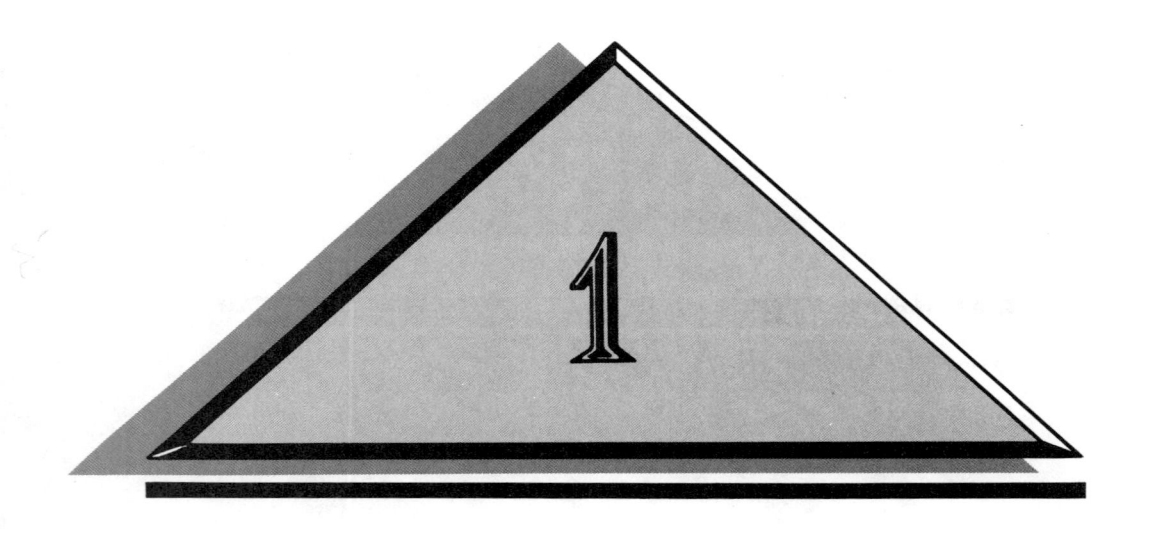

LEARNING THE BASICS

IN THIS CHAPTER, YOU WILL LEARN WHAT YOU NEED to know about MultiMate Advantage II to write your first letter. Everything you do with Advantage II will be controlled by what you type from the computer keyboard, so this chapter will begin with a discussion of the keyboard arrangement and the functions of all the keys. Next, you will learn about the main menu and how menus facilitate your work. Also, you will find out how to access the help functions.

Word processing is a modern and technical method for putting words onto paper. It is intended to make your writing easier and clearer. It is not difficult to learn. Learning to work with a word processor is as easy as learning to use a typewriter, but you can do much more with a word processor than you can do with a typewriter.

Most important, you can write and change what you've written with much greater ease than with a typewriter. You can revise, delete, and insert text as you see fit, and with only a few keystrokes. You can move blocks of copy around just to see how they look elsewhere, and you can incorporate these changes into various documents with only a few keystrokes. And you can do all of this without wasting a lot of paper. Your computer and MultiMate Advantage II do most of the work.

THE KEYBOARD ARRANGEMENT

Mastery of the keyboard is crucial to success with any microcomputer software program. Figure 1.1 illustrates the most common type of keyboard layout for the IBM PC. You can separate the keyboard into four components: function keys on the left, main keyboard in the middle, cursor keys and numeric keypad on the right, and keys sprinkled around the keyboard that access special features. On some nonstandard keyboards, the keys are arranged differently. Regardless of the keyboard layout, all keys with identical labels should work the same way. If your keyboard does not activate the functions as I describe them, you should verify that your keyboard conforms to IBM standards.

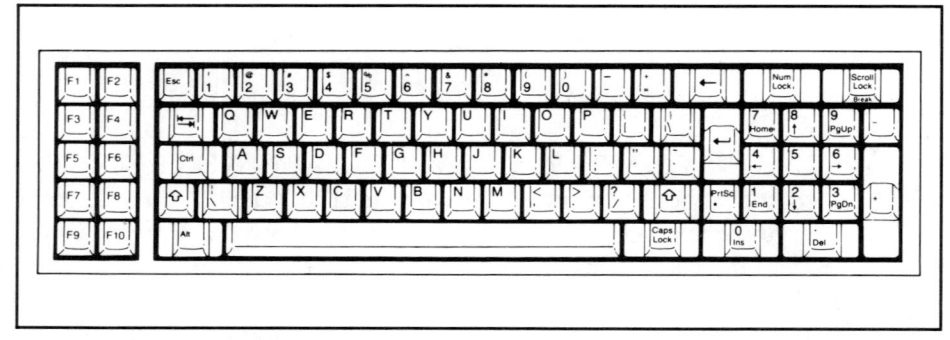

Figure 1.1: The IBM PC keyboard

Function Keys

Look at the left-hand part of the keyboard illustrated in Figure 1.1 to find the ten function keys. The most frequently used procedures in MultiMate Advantage II have been assigned to the function keys so that you can complete each of these procedures with only a single keystroke. In addition, you can use the function keys in conjunction with other keys—Shift, Alt, and Ctrl—for common but less frequently used procedures. The function keys and their uses alone and with Shift are listed in Table 1.1. (Thus, to access help, you would press F1 and Shift simultaneously.)

Main Keyboard

The keys on the main keyboard are similar to the keys on a standard typewriter. These keys allow you to enter text and numbers in your documents, along with punctuation marks. Good typing skills expedite word processing on a computer, so you should practice using this keyboard.

Numeric Keypad and Cursor-Movement Keys

Now look at the right side of the keyboard shown in Figure 1.1 to find the numeric keypad. This keypad has the same layout as the keys on an adding machine, and its keys have two explicit functions: number input and cursor movement. To enter numbers, you can use the number keys on the keypad or on the main keyboard interchangeably. The keypad also allows you to control cursor movement. You'll learn how to use the cursor keys in Chapter 2.

The functions of the keypad are controlled by the Num Lock key, which acts as a toggle. A *toggle* is a switch that flips back and forth

LEARNING THE BASICS 3

Key	Function	with Shift
F1	Go to Page	Help
F2	Page Break	Page Combine
F3	Center	Column Mode
F4	Indent	Decimal
F5	Library	Library Attach
F6	Search	Replace
F7	Move	Soft Hyphen
F8	Copy	Copy External
F9	Format Change	Format Current
F10	Save/Exit	Save

Table 1.1: The function keys in MultiMate Advantage II

between two modes. In this case, the Num Lock key enables you to use the keypad either for entering numbers or for controlling the cursor. When you press Num Lock, it locks out one mode and locks in the other. When Num Lock is switched to the *on* position, only numbers can be entered from the keypad. When it is switched to the *off* position, you can use the keypad only to move the cursor.

Each time you start Advantage II, Num Lock will be in the *off* position. This is the *default* setting, or the setting Advantage II uses unless you change it.

Special Keys

The fourth component of the keyboard consists of 15 keys that perform various functions. Look at Figure 1.2 to familiarize yourself with these keys as you learn about them. These keys can act together or independently to determine specific actions. I will briefly discuss these keys now, and you will learn more of their specific functions at appropriate points in the text.

Num Lock, Caps Lock, and Scroll Lock   The Num Lock, Caps Lock, and Scroll Lock keys are so named because they *lock* into position until you switch them back. You've already learned about the Num Lock key in conjunction with the numeric keypad. The Caps Lock key is a toggle that works like the Shift key on a typewriter: it

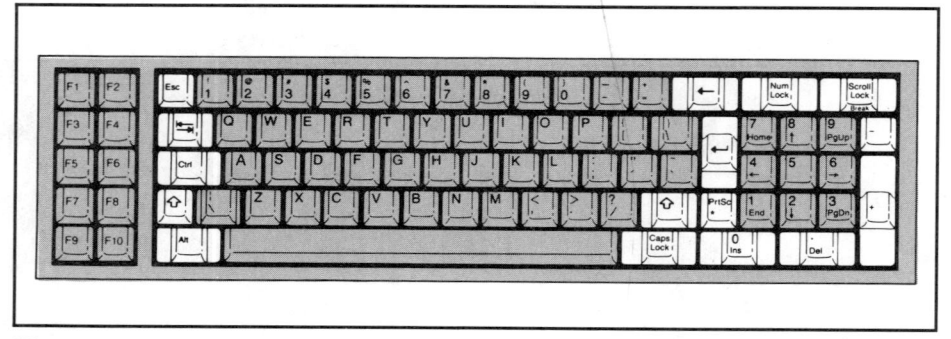

Figure 1.2: The special keys

switches alphabetic keys between uppercase and lowercase. The difference between Caps Lock and Shift is that when you press Caps Lock, you can enter only capital letters until you press Caps Lock again to return to lowercase. The default setting for Caps Lock is in the *off* position or lowercase mode.

Escape The Escape key, marked Esc, serves only one purpose—it stops whatever the computer is doing. In some cases, pressing Escape might only get you out of a procedure you would rather not be in, such as printing a document you suddenly realize is unfinished. In other cases, pressing Escape can shut down the entire Advantage II program. Throughout this book, I will mention those places where it is safe to press Escape.

Tab The Tab key, marked with either the word *Tab* or two arrows facing in opposite directions, acts the same way as the Tab key on a typewriter. It moves the cursor to the next tab position, and it indents the text.

Alt and Ctrl The Alt (alternate) key and the Ctrl (control) key do not do anything by themselves, but work in combination with other keys to perform several dozen functions. You will learn these new functions as they become appropriate. (For a preview, see the command summary in Appendix C.)

Shift There are two Shift keys, one on each side of the main keyboard. Both behave the same way and are marked with either the word *Shift* or an upward-facing hollow arrow. These keys have two functions on your computer.

1. To act like the Shift keys on a typewriter, by shifting the alphabetic keys to uppercase, and the number keys to punctuation, as long as you hold down one of the Shift keys.
2. To work in concert with other keys to perform special procedures; in this respect, the Shift keys are similar to the Alt and Ctrl keys.

Backspace The Backspace key, marked with either the word Backspace or an arrow facing left, moves the cursor one space to the left. In Advantage II, the default setting for this key is a *destructive* backspace, which means it will erase whatever character it moves over. You can change it to a *nondestructive* backspace, which simply moves the cursor backward without erasing anything, through either the Modify Document Defaults screen (for one document) or the Edit System Defaults screen (for all documents). Backspace *autorepeats*—as long as you hold it down, it moves left and erases. You can restore text deleted by the Backspace key with the Undo Delete key (the lowercase asterisk on the PrtSc key).

Return The Return key is a large key between the main keyboard and the numeric keypad. Depending on your keyboard, it is marked with either the word *Return* or *Enter* or with a downward and right-turning arrow. This key works in the same way as the Return key on a typewriter, except that you need not press Return at the end of each line. This is because a feature called *word wrap* automatically moves your cursor to the next line down. When you are writing a document, you need to press Return only when you want to end a paragraph or start a new line.

Insert and Delete The Insert key, marked Ins, allows you to do two things, depending on the position of the Num Lock key. If Num Lock is on and you can enter numbers from the keypad, Insert enters the number zero into your text. If Num Lock is off, then you can insert new text into your document without typing over existing text.

This is an important feature for revising documents.

The Delete key, marked Del, also allows you to do two things, depending upon the position of Num Lock. If Num Lock is on, you can use Delete to enter a period into your text. If Num Lock is off, you can delete characters and text from your document. As with the Insert key, Delete will become an important control for revising documents.

Minus and Plus   To the right of the numeric keypad are two keys marked − and +. The Minus (−) key deletes characters, and the Plus (+) key allows you to insert spaces and characters into existing text. You can restore text deleted by the Minus key with the Undo Delete key.

PrtSc   Holding down the PrtSc (print screen) key while pressing Shift (written as Shift-PrtSc) causes whatever appears on your screen to be printed on your printer, provided that your printer is connected correctly to your computer, turned on, and loaded with paper. What appears on the printed page might or might not accurately reflect what you see on the screen, depending upon the resolution of your monitor and features of your printer, among other things.

Undo Delete   When Advantage II is in document mode, the lowercase asterisk (*) on the PrtSc key serves as the Undo Delete key. Pressing this key causes text that has been deleted in the current editing session to reappear on the screen at the cursor position, with the most recently deleted character or collection of characters appearing first. If you press this key at a DOS prompt, it will insert an asterisk for DOS commands. If you want to type an asterisk in your document, use the Shift-8 key combination.

It will only take you a little practice writing documents to become familiar with your keyboard. Eventually, you will find yourself hardly thinking about which keys to use next.

STARTING THE PROGRAM

Before you can use MultiMate Advantage II for any purpose, you must first run the ID (identification) program. See Appendix A for detailed instructions.

To start—or *boot*—the program on floppy disks, insert the System Diskette in drive A and place a blank formatted disk in drive B. When you see the DOS system prompt

    A>

for floppy disks or

    C>

for a hard disk, type

    WP

for word processing and press Return. This will start the program, and after a few seconds, the main menu will be displayed on your screen.

THE MAIN MENU

The main menu, shown in Figure 1.3, lets you access all the word-processing features of MultiMate Advantage II. This menu gives you nine options, the first eight of which will lead you to other menus. The ninth choice on the main menu will end MultiMate Advantage II and return you to your DOS system prompt.

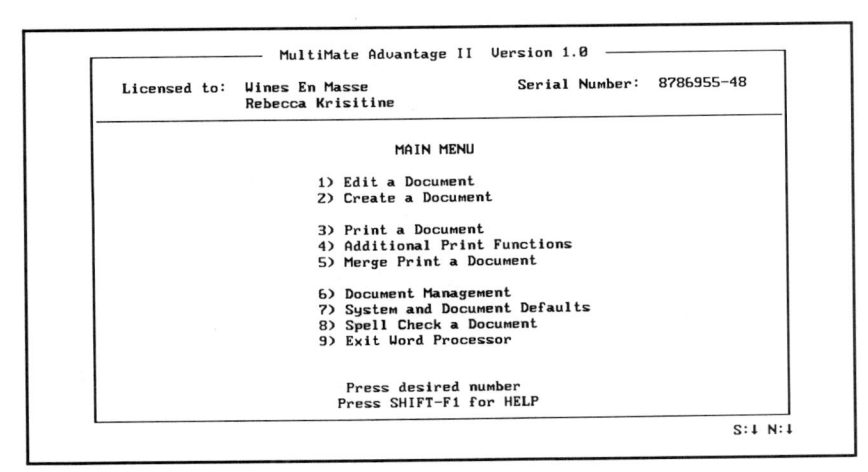

```
┌──────────────── MultiMate Advantage II  Version 1.0 ────────────────┐
│                                                                      │
│  Licensed to:   Wines En Masse           Serial Number:  8786955-48  │
│                 Rebecca Krisitine                                    │
│  ──────────────────────────────────────────────────────────────────  │
│                              MAIN MENU                               │
│                                                                      │
│                      1) Edit a Document                              │
│                      2) Create a Document                            │
│                                                                      │
│                      3) Print a Document                             │
│                      4) Additional Print Functions                   │
│                      5) Merge Print a Document                       │
│                                                                      │
│                      6) Document Management                          │
│                      7) System and Document Defaults                 │
│                      8) Spell Check a Document                       │
│                      9) Exit Word Processor                          │
│                                                                      │
│                         Press desired number                         │
│                         Press SHIFT-F1 for HELP                      │
│                                                           S:↓ N:↓    │
└──────────────────────────────────────────────────────────────────────┘
```

Figure 1.3: The main menu

If you have never worked with a word-processing program before, it will take you only a short time to get up to speed using MultiMate Advantage II. That's because its default interface is driven by full-screen menus (called a *screen-driven, menu-driven* interface). This means that you can select all the basic operations from menus that occupy the full screen. Using the default interface, you will create a new document from a menu selection on one screen, edit it from a menu selection on another screen, and print it from a selection on a third screen. All you have to do to produce finished documents is choose from a list of selections displayed on the full screen.

A second interface available in Advantage II (but not in earlier versions) is called the *pull-down menu* interface. As with full-screen menus, you can select from options presented on pull-down menus, but they occupy only a portion of the screen. We'll discuss pull-down menus and the question of interface in Chapter 2. For now, we'll work with the default full-screen menu interface.

Before proceeding, you should note several features of the main menu (shown in Figure 1.3). The top section of the screen will display the information you logged in when you ran the ID program (as described in Appendix A). This includes your name if the program is a personal copy, the name of the business if that is appropriate, and the serial number of the program. You'll appreciate the display of the serial number if you ever call Ashton-Tate for technical support. The company will not provide any official help or advice until you identify the serial number of your program.

In the lower right corner of the screen, you can see

S:↓ N:↓

S denotes the Caps Lock key, and N denotes the Num Lock key. If the arrow is facing downward, the function of the key is currently turned off.

Go ahead and press Caps Lock and Num Lock to see the arrows flip back and forth between ↑ and ↓. Make sure that when you switch these arrows for the last time, they are both ↓.

Now look at the main menu. You'll see that the first two choices deal directly with documents:

1) Edit a Document
2) Create a Document

Since you have not created a document yet, and therefore have no old documents on record, skip the first choice for now. If other documents are on your disk, I do not recommend that you play with them. You should create your own document first to learn the basics, then edit that document to learn more.

Select *Create a Document* by pressing 2. You will see a series of screens that will help you create a new document.

CREATE A DOCUMENT SCREEN

Once you have pressed 2 from the main menu, you'll see the Create a Document screen, shown in Figure 1.4. You should see a blinking cursor next to the word *Document:*. The blinking cursor is asking for your document name. You are allowed 20 characters for the name, but only the first 8 letters will appear on your disk directory. Therefore, make sure that the first 8 letters of each document name are unique. That is no problem when you are creating your first document, but it may become a problem as you create more documents. In naming a document, you can use uppercase and lowercase letters, numbers, and most punctuation marks. Note that, although you can use uppercase and lowercase letters in a document name, Advantage II does not distinguish between them—Letter1, letter1, and LETTER1 are all considered the same document.

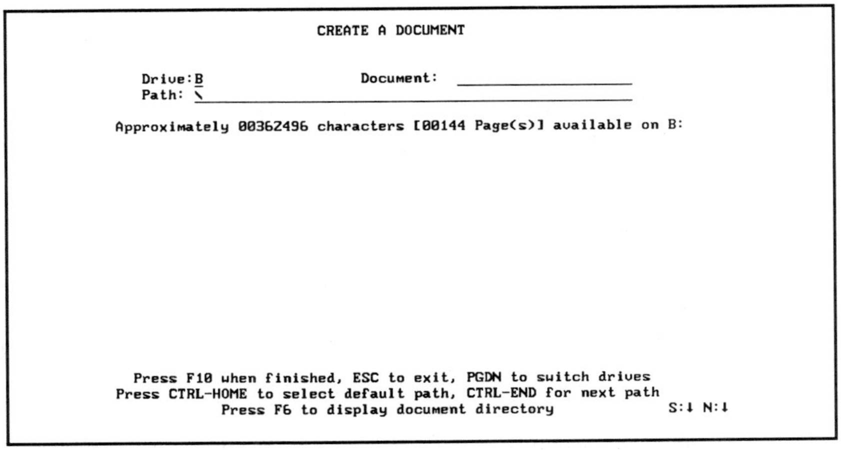

```
                         CREATE A DOCUMENT

        Drive:B           Document: _____
        Path: _____
     Approximately 00362496 characters [00144 Page(s)] available on B:











           Press F10 when finished, ESC to exit, PGDN to switch drives
           Press CTRL-HOME to select default path, CTRL-END for next path
                 Press F6 to display document directory      S:1 N:1
```

Figure 1.4: Create a Document screen

Names cannot contain spaces, either of the asterisks (neither the the uppercase 8 nor the lowercase PrtSc), or keys that contain symbols used in MS-DOS commands. Examples of MS-DOS command symbols are:

* = + ? / \ : ; | . , " > < [ ] { } @ # $ % & – (minus) _(underline)

As long as you are using allowable characters, there are no further restrictions—you can name a document using only underlines, apostrophes, or any other combination of allowable keys.

If you use any of the forbidden characters, the document field, including the characters you entered, will appear in reverse video, with the cursor in the first position of the field. When this happens, Advantage II is telling you that you must change one or more of the characters in the name. Just begin again, entering only allowable characters.

Enter the name *Letter1* next to the word *Document:*. This is called the Document field. (A *field* is an area on the screen in which you can enter information.) The name will appear just as you type it, showing uppercase and lowercase letters. However, whenever the document directory is displayed, the document name appears in all uppercase letters, regardless of the case in which you entered them. Your document directory is the blank area in the middle section of this screen. Since you have not created any documents yet, this area should be blank. Note that whenever a document name appears on any other screen, the name will be displayed exactly as you created it, with both uppercase and lowercase letters.

The two other fields on the Create a Document screen are the Drive and Path fields. The Drive field allows you to switch between disk drives in your computer. The default drive setting will always appear in this field when the screen is first displayed. If you are using floppy disks, Advantage II will automatically try to write your documents to the B drive. If you are using a hard disk, its drive designation will appear on this screen (usually it will be C).

The Path field, a new feature of MultiMate Advantage II, allows you to take full advantage of the disk organization available to users of MS-DOS versions 2.0 and higher. If you are employing subdirectories to organize your documents, this field should contain the pathname to the subdirectory you want to use. Instructions for the correct use of pathnames are given in Appendix A. However, if you are starting out for the first time, leave this field blank for now. If you are working with a hard disk, the default pathname—the one you used to install the Multi-Mate Advantage II program files—will be displayed in the Path field.

You can change the entries in the Drive and Path fields with the following keys:

- Pressing PgDn will switch the entry in the Drive field to the next available drive. You can declare which drives are available in your system in the Edit Drive Defaults screen (more about this screen in Appendix A).

- Pressing Ctrl-Home will display, in the Path field, the default document pathname on the drive showing in the Drive field. You can declare a default document pathname in the Edit Drive Defaults screen. If no such name is declared, the files of the parent directory will show in the document directory.

- Pressing Ctrl-End will display the next available pathname in the Path field. The names of the documents in this path will be shown in the document directory.

- Pressing Ctrl-End again will display the next pathname and its documents, and so on, until you cycle through all the pathnames and return to the first one.

To see a list of documents in the current drive and pathname, press F6. You can switch back and forth between the Document, Drive, and Path by fields using the arrow keys. Pressing Return while you are in the Document field will enter all the information into the system, and if the information is acceptable, you will move on to the next screen, the Document Summary screen. Pressing F10, the Save/Exit key, will also enter the information and move you on to the next screen.

You should be aware that no new information has yet been written to disk. You can cancel an attempt to create a document by pressing Escape at any point in this or the subsequent screen. If you press Escape from the Document Summary screen, Advantage II will take you back to the Edit a Document screen. If you press Escape from there, you'll be taken to the main menu.

After typing the name of the document (and adjusting the Drive and Path fields, if necessary), you can press either Return or F10. The instructions at the bottom of the Create a Document Screen say to press F10, but you might find yourself more accustomed to pressing Return. This is one of the few cases where either key will pass you to the next screen. With most other procedures, pressing F10 is the only way to move through a series of full-screen menus.

DOCUMENT SUMMARY SCREEN

The Document Summary screen, shown in Figure 1.5, works like a reference card you use in the library to look up a book. A library reference card usually contains the title of the book, the author, some publication information, and a few lines about the contents of the book. It may contain other things as well, depending upon the thoroughness of the librarian who wrote the card. So too will this document summary be thorough or sparing of information depending upon how much you enter into it.

A Document Summary screen is attached to every document you create in MultiMate Advantage II. This screen displays 13 fields pertaining to your document. When you open the screen, you should find the cursor blinking at the beginning of the field for *Author*. The name of your document, Letter1, appears automatically in the Document field. Advantage II got the document name from the Create a Document screen. On the same line as the document name is the number of pages in the document. The program will calculate this and fill it in. Since you have not yet created the document, there are 0 pages. You

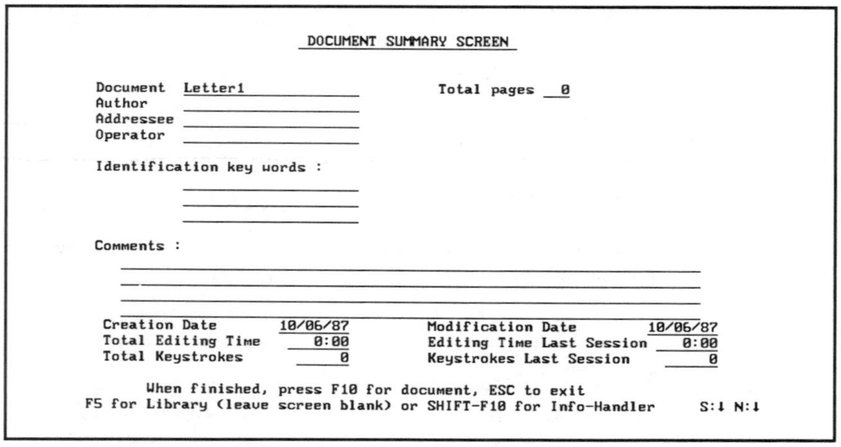

```
                      DOCUMENT SUMMARY SCREEN

       Document  Letter1                 Total pages   0
       Author           _____
       Addressee        _____
       Operator         _____

       Identification key words :
                        _____
                        _____
                        _____

       Comments :
       _____
       _____
       _____

       Creation Date      10/06/87    Modification Date       10/06/87
       Total Editing Time     0:00    Editing Time Last Session   0:00
       Total Keystrokes          0    Keystrokes Last Session        0
              When finished, press F10 for document, ESC to exit
         F5 for Library (leave screen blank) or SHIFT-F10 for Info-Handler   S:1 N:1
```

Figure 1.5: Document Summary screen

need not fill in any of the other fields unless you find it helpful to do so. Briefly, here are explanations of the fields you can fill in.

AUTHOR	*PERSON WHO WROTE THE DOCUMENT*
Addressee	Person for whom the document is intended
Operator	Person who entered the document in the computer
Identification key words	Key words to help the operator relate the document to similar documents, such as a cover letter connected to a contract
Comments	Additional information about the document (up to 50 words)

In addition, the program completes the six fields at the bottom of the screen. If you're creating a new document, and if you have a clock and a calendar as part of your computer system, data from these devices will appear. If your computer does not have a clock, the Creation Date will be whatever date you entered when you started your system. The Modification Date should be the same as the Creation Date the first time you create a document. Each time you return to a document to review or edit it, the Modification Date will be updated to the current system date (or the date you type in when you first start the system). The Creation Date will always remain the same.

Like the Modification Date, the remaining four fields at the bottom of the screen are updated as you work with a document. The first time you create a document, they should show nothing; each time you return to review or edit the document, new figures for total editing time and keystrokes, as well as those for the last session, should appear.

The six fields at the bottom of the Document Summary screen enable you to keep track of your work. They cannot be overridden. If you are handling documents for a business that bills clients for the time spent on their affairs, you will find these date and time fields a convenient way to keep an accurate account of that time. On the other hand, if you are a supervised employee, your supervisor might be interested in these figures as a measure of your productivity.

You will have to pass through this summary screen each time you access a document. You can add more information to this summary and change it as your revisions require. Eventually, when you build up a large number of documents, you will find document summaries helpful in three ways. You can ascertain what information certain documents contain, which documents you want to call up, and in what order to do so.

Now press F10, the Save/Exit key, to save this screen and to go to the Modify Document Defaults screen.

MODIFY DOCUMENT DEFAULTS SCREEN

The Modify Document Defaults screen is displayed automatically only when you create a document. This screen is designed to allow you to change the appearance of your document. The first time this screen appears, it will display settings that reflect the normal arrangement of a standard document—its default settings—as shown in Figure 1.6. A quick look at these default settings will show you that you won't be changing them often.

You can access the Modify Document Defaults screen anytime you wish to change these settings. I'll explain this procedure and discuss the settings in Chapter 5. For now, accept the default settings by pressing F10, the Save/Exit key, which brings you to the screen where you'll type your letter in the next chapter.

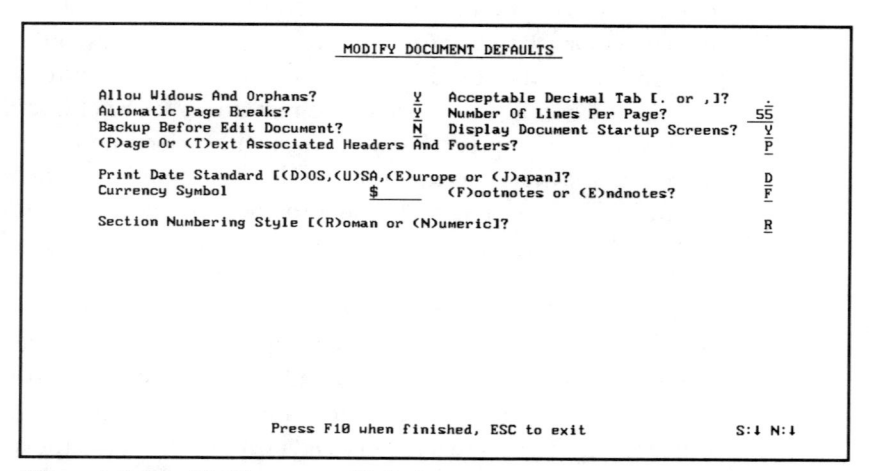

```
                         MODIFY DOCUMENT DEFAULTS

    Allow Widows And Orphans?           Y    Acceptable Decimal Tab [. or ,]?     .
    Automatic Page Breaks?              Y    Number Of Lines Per Page?           55
    Backup Before Edit Document?        N    Display Document Startup Screens?    Y
    (P)age Or (T)ext Associated Headers And Footers?                              P

    Print Date Standard [(D)OS,(U)SA,(E)urope or (J)apan]?                        D
    Currency Symbol              $           (F)ootnotes or (E)ndnotes?           F

    Section Numbering Style [(R)oman or (N)umeric]?                               R




                      Press F10 when finished, ESC to exit         S:1 N:1
```

Figure 1.6: Modify Document Defaults screen

Now you're ready to begin using Advantage II to write a letter in Chapter 2. The more familiar you are with the keyboard, the better you will be at working with MultiMate Advantage II. Practice using the keys; the less you think about which keys to press, the more you can keep your mind focused on your writing. You will also become more familiar with the menus as you work with them to create, edit, and print your documents.

2

WRITING A LETTER

IN THIS CHAPTER, YOU WILL LEARN TO WRITE A letter with MultiMate Advantage II. First you will learn more about the Document screen, where you will write all your documents. You will learn how to interpret the status and format lines, and find out how to move the cursor. Once you have written the letter, you will go back and correct any mistakes. Finally, the Help menu will give you information on any procedure while you are working with Multi-Mate Advantage II.

THE DOCUMENT SCREEN

If you've followed the steps in Chapter 1, you should already be in the Document screen. Let's review those steps.

1. If you are using floppy disks, remember to place the System Diskette in drive A and a blank formatted disk in drive B.

2. At the DOS system prompt $A>$ or $C>$, type *WP* and press Return to get to the main menu.

3. At the main menu, choose

   2) Create a Document

4. At the Create a Document screen, enter the document name Letter1 and press F10 three times (or press Return once and F10 twice): to move into the Document Summary screen, to access the Modify Document Defaults screen, and finally, to accept its default settings and reach the Document screen, which should look like Figure 2.1.

The Document screen is the work area in which you will construct all of your documents. This screen is blank save for two lines at the top and the lock-key messages in the lower right corner, which will appear in every screen of the program. Other screen messages or prompts will appear from time to time at the bottom of the screen to help you through procedures that require a series of steps. The messages will appear only when you need them because Advantage II

```
DOCUMENT: Letter1            ‖PAGE:   1‖LINE:   1‖COL:   1‖
│1--»----»----»--------------------------------------------«_____




                                                      S:↓ N:↓
```

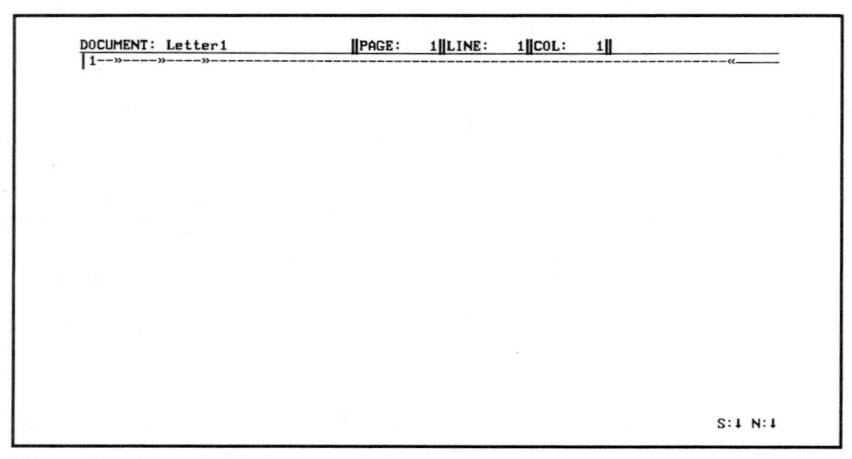

Figure 2.1: Document screen

keeps this screen clear from distractions. Creating your document on this screen is like beginning to write on a clean piece of paper.

STATUS AND FORMAT LINES

When you start out, only the top two lines of the screen have any information, as shown in Figure 2.1. The information displayed can help you write your document, and you will find yourself referring to these lines often. The top line is called the *status line,* and the second line is called the *format line.*

The status line gives you four pieces of information when you create a document. These four fields display the document name, the page number, and the text line and column of the cursor. Advantage II uses the document name from the Create a Document screen.

When you begin to write a document, the blinking cursor is located in the top left corner of the screen. The document begins on the first line below the format line. The cursor position is displayed on the status line in two coordinates: the text line (LINE) and the column (COL). Text lines run horizontally and are numbered from top to bottom. Columns run vertically and are numbered from left to right. Therefore, before you enter a single character for Letter1 in the Document screen, the status line should show

DOCUMENT: LETTER1   PAGE: 1 LINE: 1 COL: 1

As you write, the cursor coordinates will change, and that can be of great help when you are editing.

The fifth field at the far right of the status line will display certain messages pertinent to special editing procedures.

The format line tells you three more things about the document: the line spacing, the tab stops, and the position of the right margin. The format line looks so much like a text line that a marker is used to distinguish it from text lines.

At the left edge of the format line is a number indicating line spacing. When you create a document, you always start with 1 for single spacing. In columns 5, 10, and 15, you will see three identical symbols, which mark the standard tab stops. In column 65, a symbol that looks like the mirror image of a tab symbol marks the right margin.

For the moment, accept the default settings for tab stops and the right margin. You have 23 text lines on the Document screen in which to write your document.

WRITING A LETTER

You can now begin to type your letter. Start with your cursor in column 1, line 1, and type the date

September 24, 1987

using the number keys on the main keyboard. Look at the bottom right of your screen and make sure Num Lock is off

N:↓

because you will soon be moving the cursor. When you have finished entering the date, press Return once to bring the cursor to line 2, column 1. Check these coordinates in the status line.

Notice that a symbol has appeared on your screen directly after the date. This symbol is usually called a *hard carriage return;* MultiMate Advantage II calls it a *return control code,* and you will see this symbol wherever you have pressed Return. Notice that this symbol is identical to the symbol that denotes the right margin in the format line. You will learn several other common control codes or screen symbols in this chapter (Table 5.1 shows the screen symbols for the most common control codes).

Now press Return four more times. Four more return control codes should appear in the left margin. When your cursor position on the status line reads

    LINE: 6 COL: 1

type

    Dear Dave,

and press Return twice. This brings you to the beginning of the text of your letter.

Press Tab to move the cursor to the first tab position. A tab control symbol, which looks just like the tab code in the format line, should appear on your screen. The tab symbol marks the place where you start to write the body of your letter. The text appears in Figure 2.2. Continue typing the letter.

Did you notice how the first sentence automatically spilled onto the second line? This feature is called *word wrap,* and it is designed to make it easier for you to enter text in your documents. You don't have to press Return until you come to the end of a paragraph.

Now finish the letter. Press Return to place an empty line between paragraphs. Don't worry if you make any mistakes; in fact, you should try to make some errors. The more mistakes, the better, as far as learning how to correct them is concerned.

MOVING THE CURSOR

Before you can make any changes in your document, you should know how to move your cursor around the Document screen. Multi-Mate Advantage II not only offers many ways to move the cursor, but also allows you to change the speed at which it travels.

CURSOR-MOVEMENT KEYS

The keys you most frequently use to move your cursor are the four arrow keys ←, →, ↑, and ↓, located on the numeric keypad. Pressing any arrow key will move the cursor one space in the direction of the arrow.

```
September 24, 1987

Dave Bynum

Dear Dave,

    I am pleased to say that my plans are still on course.  I
will be arriving in San Francisco on November 10 on board United
Airlines flight number 256.

    This is a busy time of year for you, I realize, because of
the harvest season.  But I am looking forward to seeing you at
work.  I understand this is a rare sight.

    I am also looking forward to your selection of wines.  I hope
they come up to the level of the excellent ones we bought last
year.

Regards,


Rebecca Kristine
```

Figure 2.2: The text for Letter1

However, they will not move the cursor beyond the last character of text or screen symbol (such as a return control code) in the document. Instead, Advantage II will display the prompt

THIS IS THE LAST PAGE

at the bottom of the screen. (Pressing Return will move the cursor below the last line of text.)

You can also move the cursor in larger increments by using keystroke combinations. For example, to move the cursor to the beginning of the next word, press Ctrl-→, which means "hold down the Ctrl key and press the → key", or "press Ctrl and → simultaneously." To move your cursor to the beginning of the previous word, press Ctrl-←. To move to the end of the line the cursor is on, press Alt-F4. If you want to move to the beginning of the line, press Alt-F3. Alternately, you can move the cursor to the beginning of the line the cursor is on by pressing Shift-Tab.

You can also make larger leaps. To go to the end of the current screen, press End, and to jump back to the beginning of the screen, press Home. To move the cursor down 19 lines, press PgDn, and to move the cursor up 19 lines, press PgUp. When you do this, you should be aware that your screen displays 23 lines of text, but you are moving through only 19 text lines. This allows you to see 4 lines of text that were on the original screen so you can orient yourself to the flow of text.

Ctrl-End moves the cursor to the end of the current page, and Ctrl-Home moves the cursor to the beginning of the current page. If you press Ctrl-PgDn, the cursor will jump to the top of the next page, and if you press Ctrl-PgUp, the cursor will jump to the top of the previous page. If you are on the last page when you press PgDn or Ctrl-PgDn, the prompt

> THIS IS THE LAST PAGE

will appear in the lower left corner of your screen. Similarly, if you are on the first page and press PgUp or Ctrl-PgUp, the prompt

> THIS IS THE FIRST PAGE

will appear. If either of these prompts occur, press Escape, and the prompt

> Do you wish to escape without saving this page? (Y/N)

will appear at the bottom of your screen. Press N, for no. Advantage II will save the current document to disk, and you will remain in the document.

For a summary of the cursor-movement keys, see Table 2.1.

Keys	Action
→	Moves cursor to the right one space, or to next field
←	Moves cursor to the left one space, or to previous field
↓	Moves cursor down one text line, or to next field
↑	Moves cursor up one text line, or to previous field
Ctrl-→	Moves cursor one word to the right
Ctrl-←	Moves cursor one word to the left
Alt-F4	Moves cursor to end of current line
Alt-F3	Moves cursor to beginning of current line
Home	Moves cursor to first character at top of current screen
End	Moves cursor to last character at bottom of current screen
PgUp	Moves cursor 19 text lines up
PgDn	Moves cursor 19 text lines down
Ctrl-Home	Moves cursor to top of current page
Ctrl-End	Moves cursor to end of current page
Ctrl-PgUp	Moves cursor to last character on previous page
Ctrl-PgDn	Moves cursor to first character on next page
F1	Prompts for page to go to; cursor will move to first character on that page

Table 2.1: Cursor-movement keys

CURSOR SPEED

The speed at which the cursor moves on the screen is an adjustable rate. The default setting is halfway between the slowest and fastest speeds available. There are actually two settings: one for the cursor speed, called acceleration rate, which affects the pace of your typing;

and one for the rapidity of autorepeat, called acceleration responsiveness. Autorepeat makes the cursor repeat the most recent entry when you continue to press the key. For example, if you hold down a letter key, that letter will be repeated on the screen until you release it. This feature is particularly useful for moving the cursor. Holding down a cursor-movement key will cause the cursor to race across the screen.

A fast and trained typist will want both quick character input and autorepeat; a slower typist will find the higher settings too fast. I am a quick and accurate typist, yet I find the highest cursor speed settings in Advantage II too fast for me. Characters are entered at the slightest touch of a key, and the cursor runs far past the place where I want it to stop. I've found that an acceleration rate setting of 8 and an acceleration responsiveness setting of 7 work best with my typing rate. You can try out the various speeds to see which ones accommodate your rate, and then, if necessary, adjust the speed for the current session or change the default settings for all documents.

To increase the speed of the cursor, press Shift-+, using the Plus key on the keypad; this is called the Increase Cursor Speed key. The cursor speed will increase slightly each time you press this key combination, until it reaches its highest setting. To decrease the speed of the cursor, press Shift --, using the Minus key on the keypad; this is called the Decrease Cursor Speed key. Each time you press this key combination, the cursor will slow down slightly until it reaches its lowest speed. There are ten different speeds in all.

The setting you select will remain in effect until you change it again, or until you exit the Advantage II word-processing program. The next time you use Advantage II, the midlevel default setting will be back in effect.

If you decide that you always want the cursor to move at a higher or lower speed, you can change the default settings through the Edit System Defaults Screen. See Appendix A, Program Installation, for instructions.

MAKING CORRECTIONS

Correcting mistakes is the best incentive for not making more of them. Since I don't know what mistakes you've made, I will describe how to correct the most common ones. You can make corrections by *overwriting* existing text or by *deleting* and then *inserting* text between characters.

Later in this section, we'll discuss a new feature of Advantage II that allows you to restore deleted text. Many of us mistakenly delete characters (as the Backspace key rapidly autorepeats across the screen), words, or whole portions of text. The Undo Delete function can save you much retyping (and remembering).

Overwriting Text

Overwriting text is a simple operation. Use the cursor keys to place the cursor directly over the character you wish to change. Then type the new character, and it will immediately replace the old character. When you overwrite text, be careful not to unintentionally type over control codes. Whatever new characters you enter will replace the codes underneath, and this can change the appearance of your document. For example, if you type over a return control code between paragraphs, they might not be separated when you print them, and they certainly won't be separated if you repaginate the document.

Deleting Characters

There are several ways to delete text, depending upon whether you want to delete a single character or a series of characters, and whether you want to make the correction immediately after making the mistake or later as part of a revision.

To delete a single character immediately after you enter it, press the Backspace key and enter the new character. The Backspace key deletes the character to the left of the cursor.

To delete a character later, use the cursor keys to place the cursor directly over the incorrect character, press the Minus key to the right of the keypad, and the character will disappear. You can continue to delete characters to the right of the cursor by pressing the Minus key.

You can also use the Delete key, but it will take you two steps to do so. Place the cursor on the character you wish to delete and press Delete. The prompt

DELETE WHAT?

will appear on the right side of the status line. Press Delete again, and the character will disappear. You can continue to delete characters to the right of your cursor by pressing Delete twice for each character.

Deleting Words

Deleting words requires a little more attention. You must first place the cursor on the word you wish to delete. Next, press the Delete key. This is also called the String Delete key in Advantage II because it can delete a string of text as easily as it can delete one character. Pressing this key will bring up the prompt

   DELETE WHAT?

on the status line. The character your cursor is on will then appear in contrast to the rest of your text. This contrast is called *highlighting*. Now move the cursor to highlight the word or words you want deleted, and press Delete again (or press F10) to delete the highlighted text. A quick way to delete a word is to press Delete, then the Space bar—which will highlight the word the cursor is on—and press Delete again. The paragraph in which these changes are made will automatically reformat itself to the original margins. You can delete sentences and even paragraphs this way. Table 2.2 lists the deletion commands.

Deleting Screen Symbols

A common mistake is to press the Return key when you did not intend to. In this case, a sentence might have been cut in half and a new paragraph started beneath it. You can correct this mistake in a manner similar to deleting characters. Move the cursor over the return control code and press the Minus key once, or the Delete key twice, to remove the screen symbol. You might also have to delete extra spaces to bring the halves of a sentence together. You can use this method to delete any of the screen symbols that appear on your page.

Inserting Characters

Sometimes, deleting incorrect text is only half of the problem. If you misspelled a word, you know how to delete the incorrect letters, but you still have to insert the correct ones.

Keys	Action
Any key	Overwrites character at cursor position
Backspace	Deletes character to left of cursor
−	Deletes character at cursor
Delete, Delete	Deletes character at cursor
Delete, Space bar, Delete	Deletes from cursor to following space
Delete, Alt-F4, Delete	Deletes from cursor to end of line
Delete, Alt-F5, Delete	Deletes word cursor is in and following space
Delete, Alt-F6, Delete	Deletes line cursor is in
Delete, Alt-F7, Delete	Deletes sentence cursor is in
Delete, Alt-F8, Delete	Deletes paragraph cursor is in
Delete, End, Delete	Deletes from cursor to end of screen
Delete, Ctrl-End, Delete	Deletes from cursor to end of page
Delete, Return, Delete	Deletes from cursor to first return control code (end of line or end of paragraph)

Table 2.2: Deletion commands

Move the cursor over the space where you want to insert a new character. Press the Plus key, located to the right of the numeric keypad, to create a blank space at the cursor position. Existing text to the right of the cursor will move ahead one space, so you will not lose any characters by inserting this way. All you have to do is type in the new character.

Inserting Words

In Advantage II's default mode, pressing the Insert key will insert text, pushing existing text ahead of the cursor, while continuing to keep the text lines formatted correctly. An alternative inserting mode, called the *drop down method*, drops remaining text off the page, leaving only a few words at the bottom of the screen to remind you what comes after the text you are inserting. In earlier versions of the program, the drop down method was the default mode; now it has been relegated to optional status for those experienced users who feel more comfortable with it. You can change the mode of the Insert key through the Edit System Defaults screen (see Appendix A, Program Installation).

Using the Insert key in the default push mode, move the cursor to the position where you want to insert new characters. Press Insert, and the prompt

INSERT

will appear on the right side of the status line. Now when you type in characters, the existing text moves ahead instead of being replaced. Note that the cursor movement is slightly slower in insert mode, and there may be a delay before the new characters appear on the screen. After you make your insertions, return to typeover mode by pressing Insert again. You'll know you're in the default mode when the insert mode prompt disappears from the status line.

As an example, say we want to add a heading to the letter we just wrote. Press Ctrl-Home to move the cursor to the top of the page. Next press ↓ five times, so that the cursor appears under the letter *D* in *Dear*. Press Insert and enter the following text

Dave Bynum
DAVIS BYNUM WINERY
8075 Westside Road
Healdsburg, CA 95448

Remember to press Return at the end of each line, and once again after the last line. Notice how the text that follows this insertion continues to move ahead to accommodate the new characters. If you are correcting text that contains control codes that you do not want to lose, use the insert mode, and the control codes will move ahead along with any text. Then you can go back and delete any text that you want to remove.

When your cursor is at line 11, column 1, press Insert again to return to the default typeover mode. Letter1 now has a heading inserted in the proper place.

ESCAPING CHANGES

There are two ways to nullify changes you have made to a document during an editing session. One method is to press the Escape key, which is the more general form of escaping changes; the other is to use the Undo Delete key, which restores text accidentally deleted.

Using Escape

If for some reason you wish to cancel all the changes you've made that have not yet been saved to disk, press the Escape key. The prompt

Do you wish to escape without saving this page? (Y/N)

will appear at the bottom of your screen. Enter Y to save your document as it was before you made any changes. This will remove *all* the changes you made to that page in the editing session, unless you pressed Shift-F10 to save any of them. After you press Escape, Advantage II returns you to its main menu.

Undo Delete

All word-processing programs let you delete unwanted text, but most won't restore text that you accidentally deleted. A new feature introduced with Advantage II gives you this capability. The only text you cannot restore is that erased by overwriting. You can bring back text deleted by using the Delete key, the Minus key, or the destructive Backspace key.

To restore such text, place the cursor in the position where you want the deleted text to reappear, then press the PrtSc/* key, called the Undo Delete key. The deleted letters will begin to appear in the cursor position in the reverse order of deletion; that is, those you most recently deleted will appear first. If the text was deleted in a block, the entire block will reappear with one press of the Undo Delete key. If you realize that you made a mistake the moment after the deletion is complete, all you have to do is press this key, and the text will reappear.

When you hold down the Undo Delete key, characters will continue to appear until the memory bank of deleted characters has been completely displayed. Then the prompt

NO DELETED TEXT TO UNDO

will appear at the bottom of the screen. Recalling deleted text does not erase it from the Undo Delete memory. You can recall deleted text as many times as you want to, as long as you do not exit or repaginate the document. Deleted text is remembered only for the current editing session. Unfortunately, accidentally deleted text is lost forever when you exit or repaginate the document.

HELP!

We all need help at one time or another. You can access the full range of help functions whenever MultiMate Advantage II is displaying the Document screen by pressing Shift-F1, the Help key. If you are using floppy disks, a prompt will appear at the bottom of the screen:

INSERT BOOT DISK IN DRIVE A—PRESS ANY KEY

The main Help menu will be displayed on your screen. Once you have inserted the boot disk and accessed help, you will not need to reload help again during the current working session unless you turn off your computer.

The Main Help Menu

The main Help menu, shown in Figure 2.3, will direct you to the best solution for your problem. All you have to do is follow the instructions. To get help for a specific function, press the key or keystroke combination for the function you need help with. If you don't know these keys, press 1 to obtain a list of all functions, listed in alphabetical order. Figure 2.4 shows the first page of the help screen for MultiMate Advantage II functions. There are several screenfuls of help references, which you can move through only one line at a time by pressing the Space bar. If you press PgDn intending to move

WRITING A LETTER 31

```
DOCUMENT: Letter1              ‖PAGE:   1‖LINE:   1‖COL:   1‖
                               HELP MENU
          Press the key for the help required.

          Examples: Press Alt L for help on the Pull-Down Menus.
                    Press Alt F for help on the Footer function.

          To get help on more general topics:

          HELP DESIRED                            PRESS
          ------------                            -----

          List of all help topics and keys           1

          ××××××××××××××××××××××××××××××××××××××××××××××××××××××××××




          Press ESC to exit                                    S:↓ N:↓
```

Figure 2.3: The main Help menu

```
DOCUMENT: Letter1              ‖PAGE:   1‖LINE:   1‖COL:   1‖
The following is a list of all functions and the key(s) to press for help:
FUNCTION         KEY(S)    FUNCTION          KEY(S)    FUNCTION          KEY(S)
--------         ------    --------          ------    --------          ------
ADD. PRINT FUNC..Alt 4     ALT KEYBOARD.....Alt K      AUTO HYPHENATION.Ctrl F2
AUTO PAGE NUMBER.#         AUTO UNDERLINE...Alt -      AUTO UND (ALPHA).Alt =
BACK SPACE.......<<--      BOLD PRINT.......Alt Z      CENTER...........F3
CHAR DELETE......- (Kypd)  CHAR INSERT......+ (Kypd)   CLEAR PLACEMARKS.Alt Y
COLUMN MODE......Shift F3  COLUMN TYPES.....Ctrl Ret   COMMENTS.........Ctrl [
COPY.............F8        CREATE DOCUMENT..Alt 2      CURSOR DOWN......↓
CURSOR UP........↑         DECIMAL TAB......Shift F4   DELETE...........Del
DOC MANAGEMENT...Alt 6     DOCUMENT REORG...Ctrl F2    DOS ACCESS.......Ctrl 2
DOUBLE UNDERLINE.Ctrl _    DRAFT PRINT......Alt D      EDIT A DOCUMENT..Alt 1
END..............End       ENDNOTES.........Ctrl ]     END OF PAGE......Ctrl End
ENHANCED PRINT...Alt N     EXIT WORD PROCES.Alt 9      EXTERNAL COPY....Shift F8
FOOTER...........Alt F     FOOTNOTES........Alt U      FORMAT CHANGE....F9
FORMAT CURRENT...Shift F9  FORMAT PAGE......Alt F9     FORMAT SYSTEM....Ctrl F9
GO TO (Page).....F1        GO TO PLACE MARK.Ctrl F1    HARD SPACE.......Alt S
HEADER...........Alt H     HOME.............Home       HORIZONTAL MATH..Ctrl F3
HOT PRINT........H         HYPHEN (Soft)....Shift F7   IMPRT ASCII FILE.Ctrl 6
INDENT...........F4        INSERT...........Ins        KEY PROC-BUILD...Ctrl F5
     Press ESC to exit, RETURN to go to previous menu, SPACEBAR to scroll   S:↓ N:↓
```

Figure 2.4: Help screen showing program functions

down a full screen, you will obtain help information on the PAGE-DOWN function instead. (See Appendix C for a complete description of all function keys and their actions.)

For example, say you want to indent a section of your text.

1. Press Shift-F1 to go to the main Help menu. (If you are using floppy disks, replace the System Diskette with the Boot Diskette in drive A at the prompt.)

2. Press 1 to get the list of functions.
3. On the alphabetical list of functions, look for INDENT.
4. Press F4, the Indent key.

Figure 2.5 shows the resulting instructions for indenting text.

Context-Sensitive Help

Help can also give you more detailed information in complicated situations. Ten major functions in MultiMate Advantage II, listed in Table 2.3, require a series of steps. You follow the same procedure for accessing help—press Shift-F1 and then the key for the function you need help with—but the program responds with a detailed list of instructions. Similarly, if you forget any of the steps while you are working in the Document screen, you can press Shift-f1 and then the specific key to obtain a list of steps to follow.

Say you wish to copy text from one part of your document to another. Copying text is a common procedure, and it has been assigned to the F8 function key. When you are in the main Help menu and you press F8, your screen will show the information for copying text, as shown in Figure 2.6. You have to perform six steps to complete the copy function.

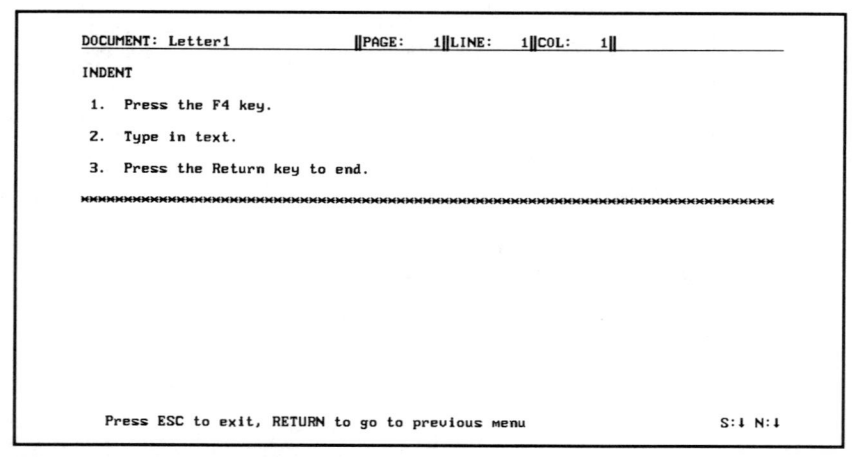

```
DOCUMENT: Letter1           ‖PAGE:    1‖LINE:    1‖COL:    1‖
INDENT
   1.   Press the F4 key.
   2.   Type in text.
   3.   Press the Return key to end.
   ►◄►◄►◄►◄►◄►◄►◄►◄►◄►◄►◄►◄►◄►◄►◄►◄►◄►◄►◄►◄►◄►◄►◄►◄►◄►◄►◄►◄




           Press ESC to exit, RETURN to go to previous menu          S:↓ N:↓
```

Figure 2.5: Instructions for indenting text

Keys	Function
Delete	Delete
Insert	Insert
F6	Search
Shift-F6	Replace
F7	Move
F8	Copy
Shift-F8	External Copy
F9	Format Change
Shift-F9	Format Current
Ctrl-F9	Format System

Table 2.3: Context-sensitive help functions

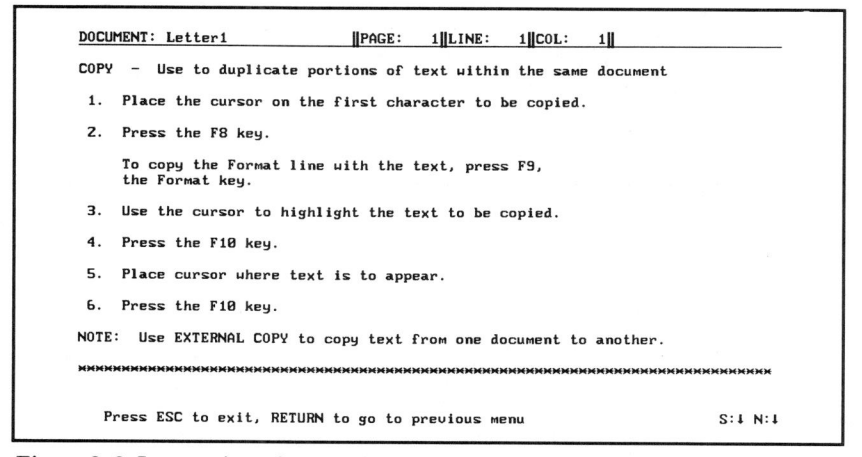

```
DOCUMENT: Letter1              ‖PAGE:   1‖LINE:   1‖COL:   1‖
COPY  -  Use to duplicate portions of text within the same document
    1.  Place the cursor on the first character to be copied.
    2.  Press the F8 key.
        To copy the Format line with the text, press F9,
        the Format key.
    3.  Use the cursor to highlight the text to be copied.
    4.  Press the F10 key.
    5.  Place cursor where text is to appear.
    6.  Press the F10 key.
NOTE:   Use EXTERNAL COPY to copy text from one document to another.
××××××××××××××××××××××××××××××××××××××××××××××××××××××××××××××××
       Press ESC to exit, RETURN to go to previous menu             S:1 N:1
```

Figure 2.6: Instructions for copying text

Exiting from Help

You can exit from all help screens by pressing the Escape key. If you are in the main Help screen, pressing Escape once will take you back to where you left off. If you are in a context-sensitive screen—for example, copying text—you will need to press Escape twice.

SAVING YOUR DOCUMENT

Saving your document is a crucial step. MultiMate Advantage II can record your document to disk at regular intervals, but this might not be often enough to ensure that you don't lose valuable work when an accident causes your computer to fail. Just because your text appears on the screen does not mean it is a permanent creation. All that you have done is record your text into *RAM*, which is an acronym for random-access memory. This memory is active only when your computer is turned on and the MS-DOS operating system and Advantage II program are functioning correctly. If there is a failure in any one of these three components—and inevitably there will be—some or all of the data stored in RAM will be lost.

The only permanent memory in a personal computer is disk-based (either hard disk or floppy disk). Unless you save the characters you see on the screen to disk (or have Advantage II do this automatically, as explained later in this chapter), they will be gone as soon as you exit the program or turn off your computer.

To save your data to disk, press Shift-F10, the Save key. The prompt

<<<PLEASE WAIT>>>

will appear at the bottom of your screen while Advantage II saves to disk the document you are working on. Nothing else will change on your screen, and as soon as the document is saved, you can continue where you left off. To save your document and return to the main menu, press F10, the Save/Exit key.

INTERFACE AND MODE

MultiMate Advantage II users are offered a choice of program interface and mode of operation. Earlier versions of the program provided only the default full-screen menu interface and page mode of operation. Now you can use pull-down menus instead, and document mode is the new default setting, with page mode offered as an option.

THE QUESTION OF INTERFACE

A program's interface is both its most obvious feature and the least noticed. The interface can be more simply called the "face" of the program, alluding to its appearance on your screen. It also refers to the manner with which you, the user, communicate with the program. An example of Advantage II's interface is the full-screen menus we've been seeing. It is through this interface—these menus—that Advantage II shows you what you can do. The prompts that appear intermittently, asking you to insert a disk, highlight characters to delete, or please wait, are also part of Advantage II's interface. Another facet of the interface is the way that you send commands from the keyboard, such as pressing Shift-F10 to save a document and remain in it.

Although you may be very aware of a program's interface the first time you use it, as you become familiar with it, you will hardly notice the interface at all. Indeed, ask experienced users to describe the interface of a program they use frequently, and they will be hard-pressed to come up with the details.

THE PULL-DOWN MENU OPTION

Advantage II now offers a pull-down menu interface. As the name suggests, pull-down menus can be pulled down from the top of your screen (like window shades) to display a range of features you can use. The pull-down menus occupy only a small section of the screen, leaving most of the text of the current document in view, which can be very helpful.

The full-screen menu style has been standard with all versions of MultiMate, and it remains the default interface when you start up Advantage II. Ashton-Tate, the manufacturer, has included a pull-down menu interface in its other products, including the very popular dBASE III Plus. New users find pull-down menus easier to work with, while more experienced users still prefer the full-screen ones and use pull-down menus only for certain operations. In this book, we've used the default full-screen menus for most examples. I'll point out the situations in which I've found a pull-down menu to be the most expedient way to get things done.

You can access the pull-down menus by pressing Alt-L, the Pull-Down Menu key. The status line at the top of your screen will be replaced with a horizontal list of seven options. These options offer the same range of functions that are available through the full-screen menus, as well as through the key combinations. Figure 2.7 shows the horizontal option bar with the first pull-down menu active.

```
┌─────────────────────────────────────────────────────────────────┐
│  LAYOUT   TYPESTYLE   CUT&PASTE   LIBRARY   SPECIAL   PRINT   EXIT │
│ ─────────────────────────────────────────────────────────────── │
│ ┌───────────────────────────────┐                               │
│ │ Modify Current Format Line    │                               │
│ │ Insert Copy Of Current Format Line │                          │
│ │ Insert Copy Of Page Format Line │                             │
│ │ Insert Copy Of System Format Line │                           │
│ │ Decimal Align                 │                               │
│ │ Center                        │                               │
│ │ Indent                        │                               │
│ │ Page Break                    │                               │
│ │ Page Combine                  │                               │
│ │ Document Reorganization       │                               │
│ │ Preview                       │                               │
│ └───────────────────────────────┘are still on course. I         │
│ will be arriving in San Francisco on November 7 on board United │
│ Airlines flight number 256.«                                    │
│ «                                                               │
│     »I am also looking forward to your selection of wines. I hope │
│ they come up to the level of the excellent wines we bought last │
│ year.«                                                          │
│ «                                                               │
│     »This is a busy time of year for you, I realize, because of │
│ the harvest season. But I am looking forward to seeing you at   │
│ Press F10 to select.  Use TAB to set tabs, RETURN to set right margin.  Press │
│ F10 when finished.                                      S:↓ N:↓ │
└─────────────────────────────────────────────────────────────────┘
```

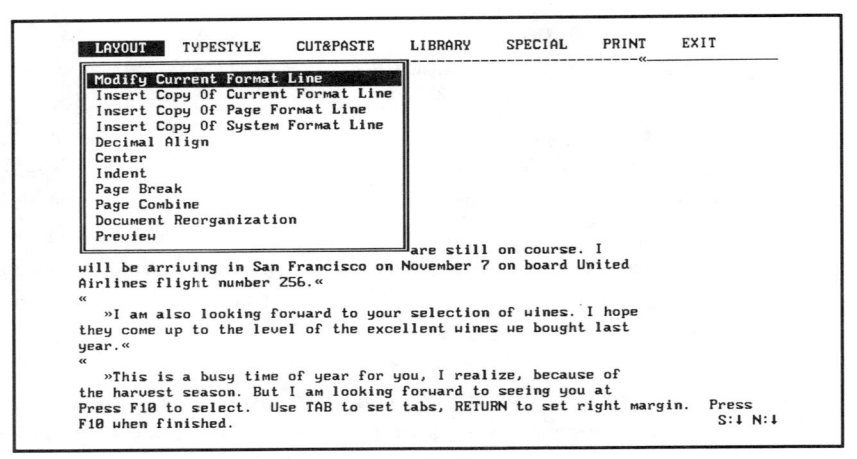

Figure 2.7: Using pull-down menus with Letter1

    The first option is called Layout, and the pull-down menu attached to it contains 11 selections relating to page layout. The Layout option will always be the first one to appear when you press Alt-L during a working session. Table 2.4 lists the seven horizontal options and the selections available in the pull-down menus beneath each option. You can move among the options on the option bar by pressing → or ←.

    When an option is active, it will be highlighted on the horizontal bar, and the menu attached to it will display the selections available. You select a function by moving the light bar over it, either by pressing ↑ or ↓ or by typing the first letter of the selection you want, and pressing Return. When the light bar highlights a selection, you will see a prompt at the bottom of the screen describing what that function does.

    As an example, activate the pull-down menu interface while Letter1 is on your screen by pressing Alt-L. The Layout option pull-down menu will appear. Now press the letter C for Center. The light bar immediately jumps to that option, and you can now center text directly following the cursor by pressing Return. You should be aware that you cannot do any actual text editing while working with the pull-down menu interface. When the pull-down menus appear, the cursor disappears. If the position of the cursor is crucial to the function you want to perform (as when centering text), make sure that it's where it should be before you press Alt-L.

Option	Selections
Layout	Modify Current Format Line
	Insert Copy of Current Format Line
	Insert Copy of Page Format Line
	Decimal Align
	Center
	Indent
	Page Break
	Page Combine
	Document Reorganization
	Preview
Typestyle	Superscript
	Subscript
	Strikeout
	Draft
	Enhanced
	Bold
	Shadow
	Underline Text
	Underline Alpha
	Underline Double
Cut&Paste	Move
	Copy
	Delete
	Move a Column of Text
	Copy a Column of Text
	Insert a Column of Text
	Delete a Column of Text
	Undo Delete
Library	Attach
	Copy Text To a Library

Table 2.4: Pull-down menu options and selections

Option	Selections
Special	Insert Library Entry into Document
	Sort
	Import ASCII File
	Line & Box Drawing
	Footnotes
	Thesaurus
	Spell Check an Entire Document
	Spell Check Portion of Document
	Spell Edit Flagged Word
Print	Current Document
	Current Page
Exit	Save Text
	Save Text/Edit
	Exit Without Saving Text
	Edit Another Document
	Create a New Document
	Exit Word Processor
	DOS Access

Table 2.4: Pull-down menu options and selections (continued)

One thing you should watch for, when selecting a pull-down menu function by entering its first letter, is how many selections in the menu begin with that same letter. For example, press Alt-L to return to the Layout menu. The Layout menu should appear with the Center selection highlighted, just as you left it. If not, highlight the Center selection now. Next press the letter P for Page Combine. You'll notice that the light bar did not move to that selection; instead it went to the next selection down beginning with a P: Page Break. Pressing P a second time will move the light bar to Page Combine, the next selection beginning with that letter. Of the seven horizontal option menus, all of them except Library contain selections that share the first same letter.

You can exit the pull-down menu option by making a selection and activating it by pressing Return. Also, you can press Escape to return to the place in your document where you were when you last pressed Alt-L, without making a selection.

MODE OF OPERATION

The mode of operation refers to the manner in which a word processor handles its documents and records them to disk. The two traditional modes are document mode and page mode. Advantage II is the only word processor that offers both options.

Document mode means the entire document is handled as a single file. The user can cross visible page breaks and move around the document with little hindrance. Although this mode allows you greater freedom, it is more dangerous because you can lose unsaved changes to the document.

Page mode means that a document is handled page by page, with each page handled as a separate file and saved to disk before the user can move on to the next page. Most word processors can operate in only one kind of mode, and document mode is by far the more popular.

As its default, MultiMate Advantage II uses a modified form of document mode. Page breaks are shown on screen, and you can see text both above and below the page-break line. But whenever the cursor crosses the page break, or moves from one page to another, the program saves to disk all data on the preceding page. This slows down scrolling through pages of text; however, it speeds up the program's performance when you first enter the document file (because only one page has to be loaded) and when you exit a long file (because only the current page needs to be saved). All this amounts to a unique combination of features for optimal operation. You can view a file as if you were in document mode, but you retain document security as if you were in page mode.

You can only change the mode of operation through the Edit System Defaults screen. You can change it at any time during the program, but the mode you select remains in effect for all documents until you change the setting on this screen again.

You have now written your first document using MultiMate Advantage II. Although subsequent documents will be more complex, you will find them easier to create because what you have learned in this chapter will apply to all documents. In the next chapter, you'll learn how to revise a document.

# 3

COPYING, MOVING, AND SEARCHING

REVISING A DOCUMENT IS JUST AS IMPORTANT AS creating it. Now that you've written your first document, you can probably find certain aspects of it that you would like to change. Since a computer can do so much to enhance the appearance of a letter, more is expected of a document written on a computer.

There are several things you can do to enhance a simple letter. In this chapter, you will learn how to

- Enter a document quickly
- Highlight text
- Copy, move, and delete text within documents
- Copy, move, and delete entire documents
- Search for and replace text

REVISING THE LETTER

To revise a document, begin at the main menu and choose

1) Edit a Document

to bring up the Edit a Document screen, shown in Figure 3.1. Type the name *Letter1* and press F10 to go to the Document Summary screen. Press F10 again to see the letter displayed on your Document screen. (Notice that Advantage II skipped the Modify Document Defaults screen that you saw in Chapter 2). This screen is only displayed when you first create a document. If you want to change any of the settings for an existing document, you can call up the Modify Document Defaults screen by selecting System and Document Defaults from the main menu.

ENTERING A DOCUMENT QUICKLY

MultiMate Advantage II provides two methods for entering a document more quickly than the standard method just described. One

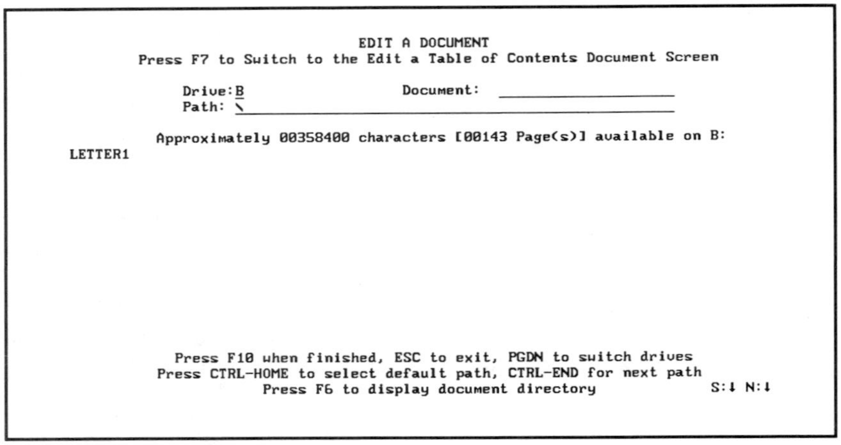

```
                        EDIT A DOCUMENT
         Press F7 to Switch to the Edit a Table of Contents Document Screen

              Drive:B              Document: _____
              Path: _____

              Approximately 00358400 characters [00143 Page(s)] available on B:
     LETTER1




              Press F10 when finished, ESC to exit, PGDN to switch drives
           Press CTRL-HOME to select default path, CTRL-END for next path
                      Press F6 to display document directory         S:1 N:1
```

Figure 3.1: Edit a Document screen

of these methods allows you to bypass the Document Summary screen, and the other allows you to enter a document directly from the DOS prompt.

You can go directly from the Edit a Document screen into the document itself by changing the Display Document Startup Screens setting on the Edit System Defaults screen. See Appendix A for instructions on how to make this adjustment.

To enter a document directly from the DOS prompt (with the DOS prompt in view), you must begin on the drive and in the directory that contains the MultiMate Advantage II program files. Type the starting initials for Advantage II (wp), enter a space, and then type—following DOS conventions—the correct drive and pathnames for the document that you want to enter, followed by the name of the document. The form is

    C>wp *drive:\path\document name*

Then press Return. If you are not familiar with DOS conventions, refer to the section that discusses them in Appendix A, Program Installation.

Now you are ready to learn the editing functions. Before we begin, let me remind you that when a document first appears on your screen, the cursor will be operating in the default typeover mode. Be careful not to overwrite valuable text!

Because all the topics in this chapter depend on highlighting, we'll discuss highlighting and dehighlighting techniques next.

HIGHLIGHTING

Highlighting is a graphic function that marks text to contrast with the rest of your text. Highlighting can show up either as brighter letters, or as a block of characters in reverse video. If a highlight does not show up on your screen, check the controls that change your video display contrast.

Highlighting is essential to performing all *block* moves—copying, moving, and deleting. Each function requires the same sequence of steps.

1. Place the cursor on the first character of text to be highlighted.
2. Press the appropriate function key or keys:

Copy internally	F8
Move	F7
Copy externally	Shift-F8
Delete	Delete

3. Move the cursor to the last character to be highlighted.
4. Press the appropriate function key a second time to highlight the block.
5. Perform the specific function (copying, moving, deleting) by following the prompts on the screen. (Note that if you are deleting, the deletion occurs just after you've highlighted the block.)
6. When you've finished making changes, simply press F10 or Shift-F10 to save your revisions.

You can define the limits of your highlighted block in two ways. You can move your cursor character by character with the cursor keys, if the block is short. You can also jump ahead in the text if the block is longer, and if you know where the block ends, by pressing any of the jump keys listed in Table 3.1.

You have great flexibility in changing the limits of your highlighted block. You can jump ahead several pages, highlighting everything in-between automatically. You can then increase and decrease the size of the block, using the keys shown in Table 3.1, until you are satisified with the text you have highlighted.

For Highlighting	Keys
Next character	→
Single word the cursor is on	Alt-F5
Current line, from cursor to right margin	Alt-F6
Current line, from cursor to same position on next text line below	↓
Complete sentene the cursor is on	Alt-F7
Complete paragraph the cursor is on	Alt-F8
Current screen, from cursor to end of screen	End
Current page, from cursor to end of page	Ctrl-End
Current word, from cursor to next space	Space bar
Current page, from cursor to top of next page	Ctrl-PgDn
Current document, from cursor to top of specified page	F1
For Dehighlighting	Keys
Previous character	←
Previous word	Ctrl-←
Current line, from cursor to left margin	Alt-F3
Current line, from cursor to same position on text line above	↑
Current screen, from cursor to top of screen	Home
Current page, from cursor to top of page	Ctrl-Home
Current page, from cursor to end of previous page	Ctrl-PgUp
Current document, from cursor to top of specified page	F1

Table 3.1: Cursor jumps for highlighting

COPYING AND MOVING

Copying and moving are helpful features to use when editing and revising documents. The difference between copying and moving is that when you copy text, you duplicate it in another position. This gives you two occurrences of the same text. Moving text, on the other hand, means that you pick up a section of text and relocate it in another position. No trace of the moved text is left behind.

Copying and moving are similar in the way they are handled. In both cases, the section of text to be transferred is highlighted first, and then the appropriate keys are pressed to perform the transfer.

COPYING WITHIN A DOCUMENT

Most of the time, when you want to revise a document by transferring text, you will want to move that text rather than copy it, so that it does not appear twice. I recommend that you learn to copy text first, however. This allows you to see what the text looks like in its new position. Then you can decide whether the transfer was correct. Since there is a small chance you will lose text while transferring it, using the copy function provides security. The problem is that you will have to take an extra step to erase one of the duplicate occurrences. As you grow more skillful with the program and with your own editing judgment, you will end up moving text more often than copying it.

As an example, say you've decided to move the third paragraph in Letter1 so that it appears right after the first paragraph. To start transferring text in Letter1, place the cursor over the first character in the third paragraph. This is the tab mark. When you press F8 for copy, the tab mark will be highlighted, and the prompt

COPY WHAT?

will appear on the right side of the status line. Move the cursor to the hard carriage-return symbol at the end of the third paragraph by pressing Alt-F8, the Paragraph Highlight key. When the complete paragraph is highlighted as shown in Figure 3.2, press F8 to activate the copying function. You will see the prompt

TO WHERE?

```
DOCUMENT: Letter1              ‖PAGE:   1‖LINE:  22‖COL:   6‖      MOVE WHAT?
 1--»----»----------------------------------------------«
October 7, 1987«
«
«
«
Dave Bynum«
DAVIS BYNUM WINERY«
8875 Westside Road«
Healdsburg, CA  95448«
«
Dear Dave,«
«
    »I am pleased to say that my plans are still on course. I
will be arriving in San Francisco on November 7 on board United
Airlines flight number 256.«
«
    »This is a busy time of year for you, I realize, because of
the harvest season. But I am looking forward to seeing you at
work. I understand that is a rare sight.«
«
    »I am also looking forward to your selection of wines. I hope
they come up to the level of the excellent wines we bought last
year.«
                                                          S:1 N:1
```

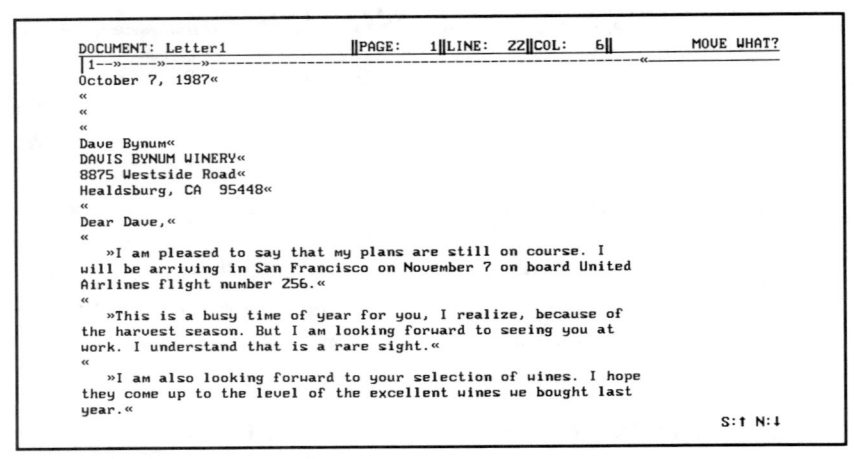

Figure 3.2: Highlighting a paragraph

on the right side of the status line. The highlighting will disappear from the block of text, but don't worry about it. You can now move the cursor without changing the limits of the block.

Move the cursor to the first character in the second paragraph and position the cursor on the tab symbol. Pressing F8 will put the third paragraph right after the first paragraph, while moving the second paragraph down to third place. You will also see a fourth paragraph—the original occurrence of the text you copied—which you'll learn how to delete in a moment.

One cosmetic flaw in your letter is that there is no blank line separating the second and third paragraph. To correct this, place the cursor on the first character, or tab symbol, of the third paragraph. Press Insert, Return, and Insert, and a blank line will appear between the two paragraphs, arranging the letter so it looks like Figure 3.3.

DELETING TEXT

Deleting completely erases text from the document. In this example, you will delete the redundant fourth paragraph of Letter1, so you will retain a copy of what you are erasing.

To delete the redundant fourth paragraph, follow these steps.

1. Move the cursor to the first character of the fourth paragraph in Letter1.

```
September 24, 1987

Dave Bynum
DAVIS BYNUM WINERY
8075 Westside Road
Healdsburg, CA 95448

Dear Dave,

     I am pleased to say that my plans are still on course. I
will be arriving in San Francisco on November 7 on board United
Airlines flight number 256.

     I am also looking forward to your selection of wines. I hope
they come up to the level of the excellent wines we bought last
year.

     This is a busy time of year for you, I realize, because of
the harvest season. But I am looking forward to seeing you at
work. I understand that is a rare sight.

     I am also looking forward to your selection of wines. I hope
they come up to the level of the excellent wines we bought last
year.

Regards,


Rebecca Kristine
Senior Wine Buyer
```

Figure 3.3: Letter1 after moving the first paragraph

2. Press the Delete key. The prompt *DELETE WHAT?* will appear on the right side of the status line.

3. Highlight the entire fourth paragraph by pressing Alt-F8.

4. Press the Delete key a second time. This will delete the highlighted block, and the fourth paragraph will disappear.

MOVING TEXT

After looking at this new arrangement, you might realize that the way it stood before is better. After all, there is another cosmetic change to make. You will have to remove the word *also* from the second paragraph and insert it in the third, in order to restore the proper sequence of things you are looking forward to.

To move the second paragraph back into the third position, follow these steps:

1. Move the cursor to the first character in the second paragraph of Letter1.
2. Press F7, the Move key. The prompt *MOVE WHAT?* will appear.
3. Highlight the second paragraph by pressing Alt-F8.
4. Press F7 again to invoke the move function.
5. Move the cursor to the second line after the last paragraph. Press F7 a third time. The move is accomplished. This time, there is no redundancy.

COPYING FROM ONE DOCUMENT TO ANOTHER

When you write letters, memos, and reports often, you will find there are many times when you want information that was created in one document to appear in another document. It is tedious and time-consuming to re-create this text each time you want to use it, so Advantage II provides you with a method of copying text from one document to another. This method is called *external copy*.

Copying text to another document is a little more complicated than copying text within a document. There are two crucial differences. First, you must work with two documents in place of one; and second, instead of starting out by highlighting the block of text you want to copy, you begin by marking the place where you want the text to appear.

Since you have created only one document at this point, you will have to create a second before you can copy text from the first, which is Letter1. This second document, when used for external copy, is called the *destination document*.

COPYING, MOVING, AND SEARCHING   49

To create this second document, start at the main menu and select

1) Create a Document

Call the destination document Memo1. After typing the name of the document, press Return and then F10 twice to accept the default settings in the Modify Document Defaults screen and reach the Document screen. Starting with the cursor in the top right corner of this screen, type the text as it appears in Figure 3.4.

```
           September 24, 1987


           from the desk of
           Rebecca Kristine


                  I will be out of the office from November 7-17 visiting
           wineries in Northern California. I will submit an itinerary
           before I go, but if this trip is anything like the others, I will
           be hopping around with last minute schedule changes. I will be
           calling in periodically for messages, however, if an emergency
           arises, or you must get in touch with me quickly, use the
           following contact:
```

Figure 3.4: Text for Memo1

When you reach the end of the text, press Return twice. This should put the cursor in the position marked on the status line as

    LINE: 18 COL: 1

At this point, you can begin the external copy of text from Letter1 to Memo1. Press Shift-F8, the External Copy key. Immediately, the prompt

    EXTERNAL COPY

will appear on the right side of the status line. In addition, the following information will appear at the bottom of the screen:

    Drive:B Document:
    Path:\
    Press F10 when finished, ESC to cancel, F6 for Directory, F7 for TOC

For revision purposes, you can ignore the instructions *F6 for Directory* and *F7 for TOC*. Pressing F6 will display the files on the current directory, and pressing F7 will create a table of contents (see Chapter 9). If your document diskette is not in drive B, use the cursor to highlight the drive symbol and change it. If the document you want to copy to is on another diskette, insert that diskette now. Then press Shift-F1 to obtain the directory of your document disk.

Now you can begin to copy the heading from Letter1 into Memo1. This is the heading you want to copy:

    Dave Bynum
    DAVIS BYNUM WINERY
    8075 Westside Road
    Healdsburg, CA 95448

To begin this procedure, fill in the space after *DOC Name* on the information line by entering the name of the source document, *Letter1*. You can use up to eight characters. If the document is in a pathway, enter the pathname in the path field. Press F10 to save this entry, and in a few moments *Letter1* will appear on your screen.

Now highlight the block of text you wish to copy in Letter1. You do this by placing the cursor over the first character in the heading, the capital D in Dave. Press Shift-8, and the prompt

COPY WHAT?

will appear on the right side of the status line. Next, move the cursor to the last character in the heading, the 8 in the zip code 95448. Press Shift-F8, and you will see the Document screen of the destination document, Memo1. The heading you copied from Letter1 should now appear in the upper left corner of the Memo1 screen.

To summarize, these are the steps to follow for external copying:

1. Start from the destination document (the document to which you want text copied).
2. Place the cursor in the position where the copied text should appear.
3. Press Shift-F8.
4. Enter the source document name (and pathname, if applicable) you want to copy from.
5. Press F10 to go to the source document, then press Shift-F8 to highlight text to be copied.
6. Press Shift-F8, and the text you want to copy will appear in the destination document.

You can move, copy, and delete entire documents as well as parts of documents.

DOCUMENT HANDLING FUNCTIONS

A selection on the main menu, Document Management, can help you perform certain copy, move, and delete functions, if you want to perform the function on a complete document. At the main menu, select

6) Document Management

Press Return, and you will see the screen shown in Figure 3.5. There are seven options on the Document Management Screen. The first four options and the last one act upon a complete document in some manner. Only the first four will be explained in this chapter, since these relate to the copy and move functions. (Options 5 and 6, dealing with Document Summary screens, will be explained in Chapter 11. The last option will be explained in Appendix E.)

You will want to use one of the first two options on this menu to copy or move one complete document into another document. You will want to use the second two options when you wish to change the nature of a specific document, either by giving it a new name or else deleting it from your document disk. In all four cases, you can perform the function on any file on your disks, not only documents.

COPY A DOCUMENT

You might want to copy a document completely to do one of the following:

1. Include a smaller document in a larger one.
2. Make a backup copy of a document onto another disk for security.
3. Make a copy of a document on the same disk, and edit the copy so the original remains untouched.

```
                    DOCUMENT MANAGEMENT

                 1) Copy a Document
                 2) Move a Document
                 3) Delete a Document
                 4) Rename a Document
                 5) Print Document Summary Screens
                 6) Search Document Summary Screens
                 7) Restore a Backed-up Document



                    Press desired number
                    Press ESC to exit
                                                        S:1 N:1
```

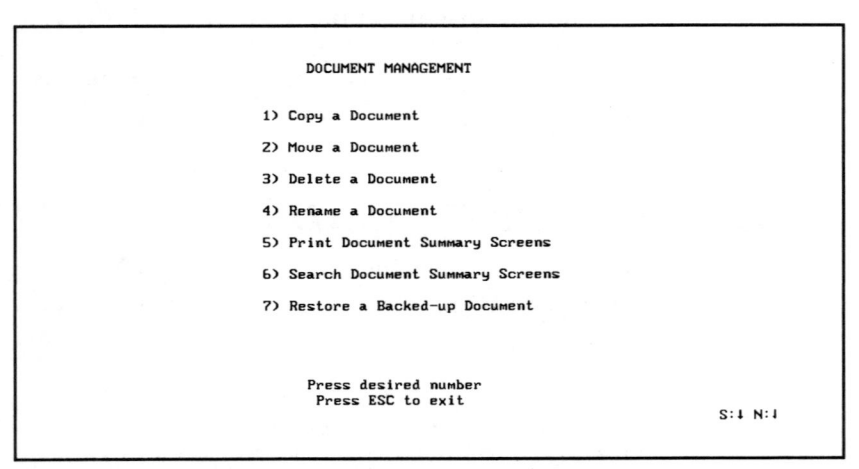

Figure 3.5: Document Management

The steps for copying complete documents are controlled by the Copy screen, shown in Figure 3.6, which you obtain by selecting

    1. Copy a Document

from the Document Management screen.

File names on the disk in the drive shown on the screen will appear in the middle of the Copy screen. The cursor will be blinking in the *COPY FROM Document:* field. If you wish to copy from a drive different than the one shown in the COPY FROM Drive: field, enter that drive letter and press Return to set this change. Enter a pathname if appropriate.

Now enter the document name you wish to copy from in the COPY FROM Document: field. The cursor will move to the COPY TO Drive: field. Enter the drive you wish to copy to, press Return, and the cursor will move to the COPY TO Document: field. Enter a pathname if you are using one. You should remember that if you are making a copy of the document onto the same disk where the original resides, you will have to use a different document name. Note that if you are copying to a different disk, but using a file name that already resides on that disk, the old document will be replaced with the new one. This means you will lose your old document.

When all the fields are set correctly, press F10. If you are using a

```
                              COPY A DOCUMENT
         FROM : Drive:B             Document: _____
                Path: \

         TO  : Drive:B              Document: _____
                Path: \
                Approximately 00358400 characters [00143 Page(s)] available on B:
LETTER1




                Press F10 when finished, ESC to exit, PGDN to switch drives
                Press CTRL-HOME to select default path, CTRL-END for next path
                       Press F6 to display document directory          S:1 N:1
```

Figure 3.6: The Copy screen

hard disk and you are going to copy to the hard disk, the copy procedure will start at this point.

If you are using floppy disks, or you want to copy a document from the hard disk to a floppy, the prompt

> INSERT DISKETTE(S), STRIKE ANY KEY WHEN READY

will appear at the bottom of your screen. Once the proper document disk is ready, press any key. The prompt

> OPERATION IN PROGRESS
> - DO NOT INTERRUPT -

will appear at the bottom of your screen. When the operation is finished, the prompt

> - OPERATION COMPLETE -
> <ESCAPE> to abort, any other key to continue.

will appear at the bottom of your screen. In this case, pressing Escape will not abort the operation. The document or file will have been moved. If you copied the incorrect document or file, you can erase the first copy and then copy the correct file. If you press Escape when the *OPERATION COMPLETE* prompt appears, you will move back to the Document Management screen, and pressing Escape a second time will move you back into the main menu.

MOVING A DOCUMENT

You might want to move a document rather than copy it, either for archival purposes or to make more room on a document disk. This is because moving *removes* the document from the original document disk. This procedure is customarily performed outside of the word-processing program with a DOS command, but MultiMate Advantage II provides you with a method of moving a file without exiting from the program.

If you want to move a document rather than copy it, select

> 2. Move a Document

on the Document Management screen. Figure 3.7 shows the Move screen.

The steps for moving an entire document are identical to those for copying an entire document. The cautions also apply.

It is possible to use the Move screen to rename a document. All you have to do is enter the name of the document you want to rename in the *FROM Document* field, and then enter the new name you want to use in the *TO Document* field. Remember to enter a pathname if one is invaved. You can rename a document when you move it, or you can rename a document and leave it on the same disk. There is also a separate procedure for renaming files, which is discussed later in this chapter.

DELETING A DOCUMENT

Although deleting a document is also customarily performed with a DOS command, you can delete a file while remaining within the Advantage II program. To delete a file, select

   3. Delete a Document

on the Document Management screen. Figure 3.8 shows the Delete screen.

```
                           MOVE A DOCUMENT
       FROM : Drive:B              Document: _____
              Path: \

       TO  : Drive:B              Document: _____
              Path: \
                 Approximately 00358400 characters [00143 Page(s)] available on B:
    LETTER1




                 Press F10 when finished, ESC to exit, PGDN to switch drives
                 Press CTRL-HOME to select default path, CTRL-END for next path
                      Press F6 to display document directory         S:1 N:1
```

Figure 3.7: The Move screen

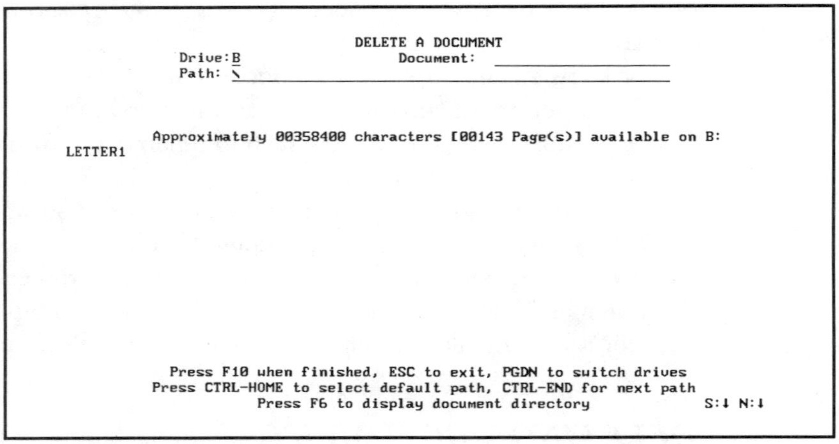

```
                              DELETE A DOCUMENT
              Drive:B            Document: _____
              Path: \

                    Approximately 00358400 characters [00143 Page(s)] available on B:
     LETTER1




              Press F10 when finished, ESC to exit, PGDN to switch drives
           Press CTRL-HOME to select default path, CTRL-END for next path
                     Press F6 to display document directory        S:1 N:1
```

Figure 3.8: The Delete screen

    This screen, unlike the Copy and Move screens, only asks for one drive designation and one document title. The steps for deleting a document are therefore fewer than those for copying or moving documents. When the Delete a Document screen first appears, the cursor will be blinking in the Document field. If the drive showing is correct, all you have to do is enter the name of the document you want to delete and press F10. Immediately, the prompt

    INSERT DISKETTE(S), STRIKE ANY KEY WHEN READY

will appear at the bottom of the screen. *There is no special warning when you delete files or documents with this function.* This prompt is the only chance you get to double-check what you are doing. As soon as you press any key, the prompt

    OPERATION IN PROGRESS
    - DO NOT INTERRUPT -

will appear at the bottom of the screen. Pressing Escape will return you to the Document Management screen. Press Escape a second time to return to the main menu.

RENAMING A DOCUMENT

Renaming a document is also customarily performed with a DOS command, but Advantage II allows you to perform this function within the program.

From the Document Management menu, select

4. Rename a Document

and you will see the screen shown in Figure 3.9. As soon as this screen appears, you will see the cursor blinking in the FROM Document field. This is where you enter the name of the document you want to change. The document drive should be entered in the FROM Drive field. If the document you want to change is on a different drive, change that drive designation. Remember to enter any pathnames involved.

As soon as you have entered the name of the document you want to change, press Return, and the cursor will appear in the TO Document field. There is no drive designation for this new name, since Advantage II assumes you only want to change the document name. If you want to change the name of the document and move the document to another disk, use the Move function.

```
                         RENAME A DOCUMENT
         FROM : Drive:B         Document: _____
                Path: \
          TO  :                 Document: _____
              Approximately 00358400 characters [00143 Page(s)] available on B:
       LETTER1




                Press F10 when finished, ESC to exit, PGDN to switch drives
              Press CTRL-HOME to select default path, CTRL-END for next path
                       Press F6 to display document directory       S:1 N:1
```

Figure 3.9: Rename a Document screen

SEARCH AND REPLACE

An invaluable tool for revising your documents is the ability to search for specific words or phrases, and then systematically replace them. You can use this feature to update the name of a product or to correct a misspelled name, for example. We will use a new document, the query memo shown in Figure 3.10 to practice using the search and replace function.

```
October 10, 1987

from the desk of
Rebecca Kristine
Senior Wine Buyer

        I will be out of the office from November 7-17 for my twice
yearly trip to California. At this point in time, most of the
people I hope to see will be busy, since it is the harvest
season. This means I know where to find them, and I like to see
how they make their wine. This information helps me buy more
wisely and explain my purchases more intelligently to the buying
committee.
        One thing I am intending to do is buy more red wine. At this
point in time, we are sold out of all Pinot Noirs. It is my
intention to purchase more of these, particularly from Davis
Bynum, with whose wines we have had great success.
        If there are any members of our company who can recommend
new wines and wineries they have run across, you have until
November 1 to tell me about them. Most winemakers are willing to
see me at any time; however, I do not want to visit a new one
without setting up an appointment first. At this point in time, I
see nothing that will change my schedule, so please get your
information to me before the 1st if you expect me to investigate
it. Davis Bynum always gives me an earful of industry chit-chat
when I show up, so even if I can't visit the wineries you might
mention to me, Davis no doubt will be able to tell me more about
them.
        I will be busy with last minute details until I leave, so
this is the only time I can ask you for your help. At this point
in time, I have more to do than I have time to do it in. Since I
often hear colleagues complain that I do not give them enough
notice about my trip and buying inclinations, this memo is meant
to correct that perception.
        Remember, red wine, particularly Pinot Noir, Merlot, and
Cabernet Sauvignon, are the ones I am most interested in.
```

Figure 3.10: Query memo

SEARCHING FOR TEXT

There are two things you should know beforehand to search with success. First of all, it is helpful to know the approximate location of what you are searching for. If you want to locate every occurrence of a word or phrase in your document, this is no problem. The search process can move forward or backward through your text and will locate all the occurrences. If you wish to find a specific occurrence, you can save time if you try to avoid wading through irrelevant sections of your document by starting near the proper place and searching in the right direction.

A second important thing you should know before you start your search is what text you are looking for, as closely as you can define it.

You can enter a *string* of up to 49 characters. This string can contain anything you enter from the keyboard, including spaces, punctuation marks, numbers, and screen symbols. Just remember that Advantage II will search for exactly what you tell it to. The longer the string, the greater the risk of making an error—but also, the greater the chance of finding exactly what you want.

Now, let's try an example. Using the query memo, we'll search for the word *wine*. Start this search at the beginning of the text in the memo. Press Home to place the cursor on the *O* in *October*. Next press F6, the Search key. The prompt

SEARCH MODE

will appear on the right side of the status line, and the search window will be in the lower half of the screen, as shown in Figure 3.11. This window lets you define your search in three different ways: by text to be searched for, case sensitivity, and direction of search.

The cursor will appear in the first position of the Search For field on the bottom line of the screen. Enter the word *wine* and press F10 to begin the search. The cursor will move to the first occurrence of the word: in the job title, three lines down from the top. But this is the word *Wines*, not *wine*.

The search function did not discriminate between the lowercase and uppercase *w* because we accepted the default setting of Not Significant for the case-sensitivity option. If you wanted Advantage II to discriminate between cases, you would press Alt-1 before beginning the search to change the case-sensitivity setting to Significant.

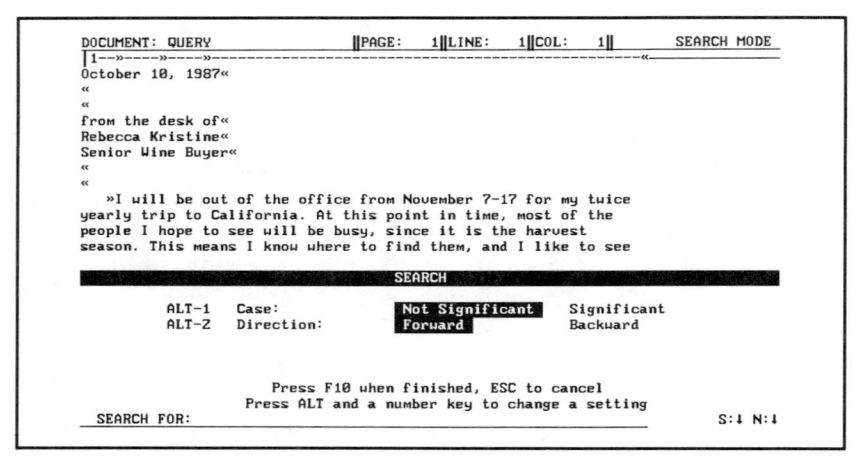

```
DOCUMENT: QUERY              ‖PAGE:   1‖LINE:   1‖COL:   1‖      SEARCH MODE
┌1─»────»───────────────────────────────────────────────────«─
October 10, 1987«
«
«
from the desk of«
Rebecca Kristine«
Senior Wine Buyer«
«
«
    »I will be out of the office from November 7-17 for my twice
yearly trip to California. At this point in time, most of the
people I hope to see will be busy, since it is the harvest
season. This means I know where to find them, and I like to see
                              SEARCH
            ALT-1    Case:        Not Significant    Significant
            ALT-2    Direction:   Forward            Backward


                    Press F10 when finished, ESC to cancel
                  Press ALT and a number key to change a setting
   SEARCH FOR:                                                      S:↓ N:↓
```

Figure 3.11: The search window in the query memo

We also accepted the default setting of Forward for the direction of the search. Pressing Alt-2 will switch to a backward search, beginning at the current cursor position. Both of the search options toggle between the two settings; press Alt-1 to switch case sensitivity off and on and Alt-2 to switch to a forward or backward search.

At this point in our example, we could cancel the search and make it case sensitive, but let's leave the default settings to see the other words that are considered a match. Press F6 to continue the search, and Advantage II will continue to locate all occurrences of the search text, including *wines*, *wineries*, and *winemakers*.

The search function found all these matches because we were not very specific in our search specification. If all we really wanted to locate was the single word *wine*, we would have had to specify case sensitivity and enter a space before the letter *w* and after the *e* to separate the word wine from all other words that contain those letters in that sequence (our example search would also have found *swineherd* if that word was in the memo).

If you enter text in the Search For field and then want to change it, you will need to use the Delete key to delete the characters. In search mode, the Backspace key does not erase text, and the Plus and Minus keys on the keypad will insert + and –, regardless of whether Num Lock is on or off. Pressing Return enters a hard-carriage return symbol as one of the characters to be located in the search. However, you can still switch between insert and typeover modes.

To summarize, follow these steps to search for specific text:

1. Place the cursor at the spot where you want to begin the search.
2. Press F6 to enter search mode and open the search window.
3. Make case sensitivity significant or not, and specify the direction of the search.
4. Enter the text you wish to search for, including any spaces or screen codes.
5. Press F10 to begin the search, or Escape to cancel the search.
6. Press F6 to continue the search.

REPLACING TEXT

Replacing text is similar to searching for text (the function is actually called search and replace). Search and replace is a more powerful command than search because, instead of just locating specific text, it will act on the text according to your instructions. You can instruct Advantage II to correct spelling, to change from boldface to underlined, or to delete the text entirely. And you can perform these changes on text as short as one character or as long as 49 characters.

Search and replace is also more dangerous than search because the function makes changes to text flawlessly. This means you should be careful when you use search and replace. Incorrect instructions can have disastrous results. When you use this replace function to make changes in a document, you should have a clear idea of exactly what you want to do.

To have Advantage II replace text, begin by pressing Shift-F6, the Search and Replace key. The prompt

REPLACE MODE

will appear on the right side of the status line, and the search and replace window will appear in the lower half of your screen, as shown in Figure 3.12.

This window is similar to the search window, but it provides two additional options, for a total of four. Along with case sensitivity and

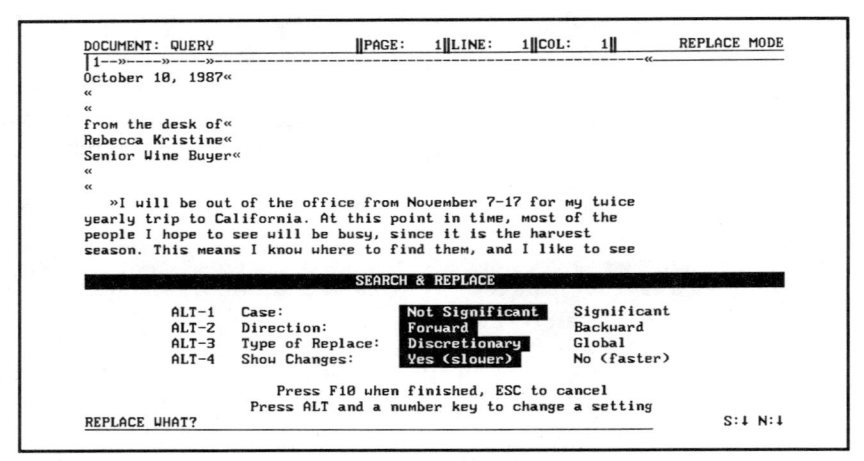

```
DOCUMENT: QUERY              ||PAGE:   1||LINE:   1||COL:   1||      REPLACE MODE
|1--»-----»----»----------------------------------------------«
October 10, 1987«
«
from the desk of«
Rebecca Kristine«
Senior Wine Buyer«
«
    »I will be out of the office from November 7-17 for my twice
yearly trip to California. At this point in time, most of the
people I hope to see will be busy, since it is the harvest
season. This means I know where to find them, and I like to see
                         SEARCH & REPLACE
         ALT-1   Case:            Not Significant   Significant
         ALT-2   Direction:       Forward           Backward
         ALT-3   Type of Replace: Discretionary     Global
         ALT-4   Show Changes:    Yes (slower)      No (faster)
                Press F10 when finished, ESC to cancel
                Press ALT and a number key to change a setting
REPLACE WHAT?                                              S:↓ N:↓
```

Figure 3.12: The search and replace window in the query memo

search direction, you can specify the type of replacement—global or discretionary—and whether or not the replaced text should appear on the screen. The prompt on the bottom line of the screen asks you what text string you want to replace. You can enter a text string up to 49 characters long. After you enter the text you want to replace, press F10, and the prompt now asks you to enter the text that will appear as the replacement. You can change the four replacement options by using their toggle keys, Alt-1 through Alt-4. Press F10 one more time to begin the search and replacement process.

Let's begin the practical lesson by discussing the two additional options.

As an example, Rebecca Kristine has written a memo to her colleagues (Figure 3.10) telling them about her upcoming trip and querying them for their recommendations on wines and wineries to look up. Upon rereading this memo, we find there are three changes we want to make. First, Davis is too formal for Dave, whom everyone else in the office also knows. Second, *at this point in time* sounds awkward. Third, the generic term *wine* should be replaced by *wines,* which refers to specific types of wine. First, let's try a global replacement.

Global Replacement

The most frequent kind of replacement you will perform is a global replacement. This is the situation where you want to replace a word or phrase wherever it appears in your document. You can use this feature to correct mistakes as well as save keystrokes.

We'll use this type of replacement to change Davis to Dave in the query memo. Begin by pressing Home to place the cursor on the first character in the document. Press Shift-F6, the Search and Replace key, and the search and replace window appears. Press Alt-3 to toggle the type of replacement from the default of Discretionary to Global. Next enter the name to replace at the first prompt

REPLACE WHAT? Davis

and press Shift-F6. Type the replacement name at the second prompt

REPLACE WITH? Dave

Press F10 again, and the prompt

REPLACING

will appear on the bottom of your screen for a moment while the replacements occur. You can cancel the procedure at any time by pressing Escape; however, all replacements made up to that point will remain in your document unless you change them again. In a few moments, the cursor will appear blinking at the bottom of the document, and all occurrences of Davis will now be replaced with Dave.

Note that you can also use the global replacement to make a global deletion—replace with "nothing"—simply by pressing only Shift-F6 in response to the REPLACE WITH? prompt.

Discretionary Replacement

The second item we want changed in the query memo is the phrase *at this point in time*. This phrase occurs three times in the report, and it sounds awkward. Unfortunately, the phrase is used to mean one thing the first time and another thing the second and third times. This is the sort of situation where a discretionary change is called for. With discretionary replacement, the program searches a document for all occurrences of the word or phrase you want to replace, but enables you to decide whether to change each occurrence.

Start by placing the cursor at the beginning of the memo. In longer documents, you might want to work in sections. Perhaps you started using a name or a phrase halfway through a document, or only in a middle section of the document. In those cases, you would begin the search and replacement function where the replacement should occur.

Now press Shift-F6, and when the search and replace window appears, press Alt-3 to toggle back to Discretionary. Enter *At this point in time* as the section of text you want to replace, and press F10. Now type *At this time of year* as the replacement text. Pressing F10 again will begin the discretionary replacement. The prompt

REPLACING

will appear at the bottom of your screen until the search finds the first occurrence of the text. The cursor stops on the first letter of the word or phrase you are looking for, and the prompt

REPLACE? Y/N/ANY OTHER KEY TO CANCEL

appears at the bottom of your screen. Entering Y will invoke the replacement of the old phrase with the new, and almost immediately the cursor will skip to the second occurrence of the phrase you want to replace. To leave the phrase as written, press N, and the cursor will jump to the next occurrence.

To continue the replacement, you could continue pressing Y or N, and Advantage II would continue to present you with replacements at your discretion. Press any key other than Y or N to cancel the discretionary replacement.

The remaining two instances of the phrase *At this point in time* can be replaced with *For the present,* and you can replace both instances globally.

In the example, there still remains the problem of changing the generic *wine* to *wines,* stressing varieties. If you do this by requesting a global change of *wine* to *wines,* you will see some interesting changes you did not expect, as shown in Figure 3.13. First of all, the title will be changed to *Senior wines Buyer,* and further along there appears *winesries* and *winesmakers.* This is much worse than before, and the mistakes occurred because of two specific instructions you must remember when you indicate text to be replaced. The search is both case-specific and character-specific. If you do not specify that the text

```
October 10, 1987

from the desk of
Rebecca Kristine
Senior Wine Buyer

        I will be out of the office from November 7-17 for my twice
yearly trip to California. At this point in time, most of the
people I hope to see will be busy, since it is the harvest
season. This means I know where to find them, and I like to see
how they make their wine. This information helps me buy more
wisely and explain my purchases more intelligently to the buying
committee.

        One thing I am intending to do is buy more red wine. At this
point in time, we are sold out of all Pinot Noirs. It is my
intention to purchase more of these, particularly from Davis
Bynum, with whose wines we have had great success.

        If there are any members of our company who can recommend
new wines and wineries they have run across, you have until
November 1 to tell me about them. Most winemakers are willing to
see me at any time; however, I do not want to visit a new one
without setting up an appointment first. At this point in time, I
see nothing that will change my schedule, so please get your
information to me before the 1st if you expect me to investigate
it. Davis Bynum always gives me an earful of industry chit-chat
when I show up, so even if I can't visit the wineries you might
mention to me, Davis no doubt will be able to tell me more about
them.

        I will be busy with last minute details until I leave, so
this is the only time I can ask you for your help. At this point
in time, I have more to do than I have time to do it in. Since I
often hear colleagues complain that I do not give them enough
notice about my trip and buying inclinations, this memo is meant
to correct that perception.

        Remember, red wine, particularly Pinot Noir, Merlot, and
Cabernet Sauvignon, are the ones I am most interested in.
```

Figure 3.13: Interesting changes during replacement

to be replaced is case-sensitive, Advantage II will locate all instances of the text, in both uppercase and lowercase letters.

The second mistake occurred because you instructed Advantage II to search for all instances of "wine", using four characters. If you specify " wine ", with spaces before and after the word *wine,* the program will search for only those instances where *wine* stands alone as a single word.

Showing Changes

Another way that you can be aware of incorrect changes is by using the fourth option in the search and replace window, called Show Changes. The option instructs Advantage II to display all instances of replaced text on your screen. Such a display can be particularly helpful during a global replacement, but you may even want to use it during a discretionary replacement just to be sure that each change is appropriate. However, there is a price to pay for this help, and the cost is speedy performance. It takes time to register the changes to screen, so selecting Yes for Show Changes will slow down the replacement procedure dramatically.

Escaping Replacements

If you've pressed Shift-F6 to begin the replacement procedure, but then decide you don't want to use that function, you can easily cancel the command by pressing Escape.

To review, here are the steps for replacing text:

1. Press Shift-F6 to begin the search and replace procedure.
2. Specify the nature of the replacement you are going to perform: case, direction, type, and whether or not changes will be shown on the screen.
3. Enter the text to be replaced and press F10.
4. Enter the replacement text and press F10.
5. Press Escape to cancel.
6. Press Shift-F6 to continue the search and replace process.

You've now learned most of the editing procedures that will make revisions easy to do. In the next chapter, you'll learn about one more function you'll want to use before you print your documents: the spelling checker.

4

SPELLING

ENGLISH SPELLING IS ONE OF THE MOST DIFFICULT aspects of the language. Some people are better at it than others, but few are perfect. Yet we all pause when we recognize someone else's misspellings. The growing popularity of spelling-check software practically requires that a document contain no misspellings to be considered professional. This is why the spelling-check capacity of Advantage II can be a great help to you.

MultiMate Advantage II's spelling checker is located on the Speller/Dictionary Diskette. This is the one part of the program where you might find a floppy-disk system to be cumbersome. You'll need to switch disks whenever you want to check the spelling function or use the dictionary. Thus, if you are using floppy disks, pay special attention to the prompts that instruct you to insert the appropriate disk.

The most important part of the Speller/Dictionary Diskette is the dictionary of 110,000 words; however, there is also room for you to create your own personal dictionary. This custom dictionary can consist of legal, medical, or technical phrases not in common usage. You might also want to use shop talk or trade jargon that applies to your line of business. You can even include brand names and trade names in your personal dictionary.

CHECKING SPELLING

Now that you have written and edited a document, you will learn how to check it for spelling mistakes. Start the spelling check from the main menu by choosing

> 8) Spell Check a Document

and press Return to enter the selection. The Spell Check a Document screen, shown in Figure 4.1, will be displayed on your monitor. This screen is similar to the Edit a Document screen. You will find the cursor blinking in the Document field. The Drive field should already contain the letter B, the default setting. (If you are using a hard disk, or

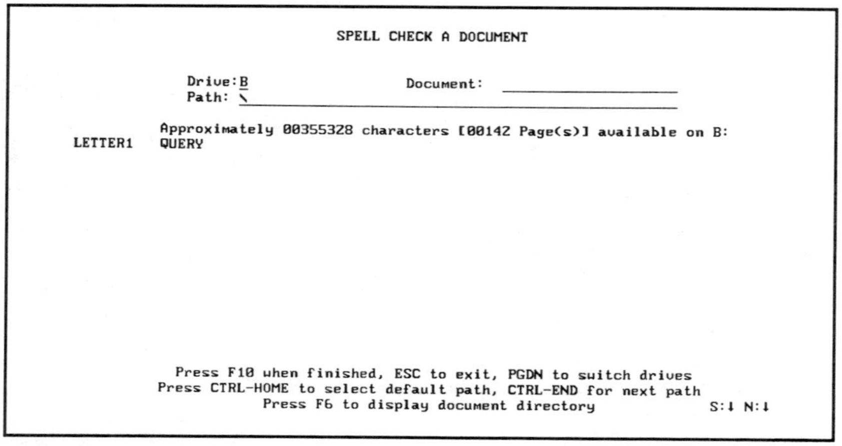

```
                    SPELL CHECK A DOCUMENT
            Drive: B              Document: _____
            Path:  \
            Approximately 00355328 characters [00142 Page(s)] available on B:
   LETTER1  QUERY




            Press F10 when finished, ESC to exit, PGDN to switch drives
           Press CTRL-HOME to select default path, CTRL-END for next path
                    Press F6 to display document directory         S:1 N:1
```

Figure 4.1: Spell Check a Document screen

if your document is on some other drive, you can change the default drive designation on the Drive Default Modification screen, described in Appendix A. Otherwise, enter the letter of the drive where your document is located.)

In the Document field, enter the document title Letter1 and press Return. The prompt

   Start page [001] End page [999]

will appear on the screen under the Path field, along with the prompt

   Enter Page numbers, Press F10 when finished, ESC to exit

at the bottom of the screen. You can select the section of your document you want checked for spelling by entering the appropriate page numbers. In this case, you can accept the default values: to start on page 1 and end on page 999, since the letter is only a page long. Press F10 to begin the spelling check.

If you are using floppy-disk drives, Advantage II will display the prompt

   OPERATION IN PROGRESS

near the bottom of the screen for a few moments, and then the additional prompt

> **INSERT DICTIONARY DISK CONTAINING WEBSTER.CLX IN DRIVE A, PRESS ANY KEY**

will appear at the very bottom of the screen. You should remove your System Diskette from drive A and replace it with your Speller/Dictionary Diskette, and then press any key.

If you are using Advantage II on a hard disk, it will display the prompt

> **OPERATION IN PROGRESS**

Once Advantage II starts to check the spelling of your document, the following information will also be displayed:

> **[00000] WORDS MISSPELLED [00000] WORDS TOTAL**

These fields will register increasing counts as Advantage II progresses through the text. The numbers displayed will depend upon how many misspellings were found, and how many words were checked. When the spelling check is complete, the program will beep and display the prompt

> **OPERATION COMPLETE - PRESS ANY KEY TO CONTINUE**

Pressing any key will return you to the beginning of the document that was just checked so that you can see which words have been identified as misspelled.

Escaping from Spelling Check

If for some reason you wish to cancel the spelling check before it is complete, press Escape. This will halt the check and bring up the prompt

> **SPELL CHECK DISCONTINUED ON PAGE X**

where X is the number of the page where the spelling check stopped. You can press any key to return to the main menu. If any misspelled words were found before you ended the spelling check, these words will now be flagged in the document. You can proceed to check these words, or you can remove the flags. Both procedures are described later in this chapter.

USING A PULL-DOWN MENU FOR A SPELLING CHECK

Checking the spelling of a document is one of the common functions for which I recommend using a pull-down menu. This allows you to check the spelling in a document while you are working with it. Let's try an example.

With the query memo displayed on your screen, press Alt-L to access the pull-down menus and then pull down the Special menu, as shown in Figure 4.2. The sixth selection is

Spell Check an Entire Document

Press S and Return to begin the process. You will immediately be taken to the Spell Check a Document screen for the query memo. Proceed with the instructions for spell checking. As soon as the checking is complete, the text of the memo will return to your screen. You will be taken directly into the spelling edit procedure, which you can complete after swapping disks, if you have a floppy-disk system.

SPELLING EDIT

The spelling checker flags potentially misspelled words by setting *flags*, or *place markers:* you will see the first letter of each suspect word blinking. You should be aware that the words Advantage II flags as misspelled might or might not be misspelled. You might have used words that don't appear in the Speller/Dictionary Diskette. If the dictionary does not find a match for a word in your document, Advantage II assumes the word is misspelled.

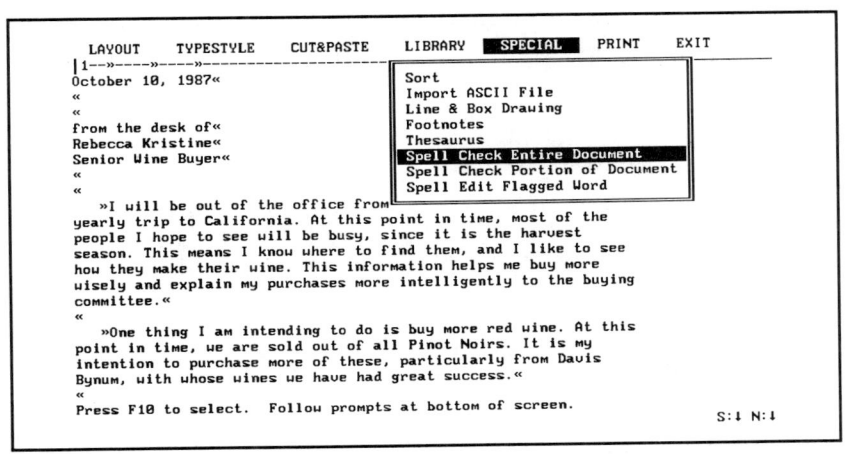

```
           LAYOUT    TYPESTYLE    CUT&PASTE    LIBRARY   SPECIAL   PRINT   EXIT
        |1--»----»----»-----------------------
        October 10, 1987«                     Sort
             «                                Import ASCII File
             «                                Line & Box Drawing
        from the desk of«                     Footnotes
        Rebecca Kristine«                     Thesaurus
        Senior Wine Buyer«                    Spell Check Entire Document
             «                                Spell Check Portion of Document
             «                                Spell Edit Flagged Word
             »I will be out of the office from
        yearly trip to California. At this point in time, most of the
        people I hope to see will be busy, since it is the harvest
        season. This means I know where to find them, and I like to see
        how they make their wine. This information helps me buy more
        wisely and explain my purchases more intelligently to the buying
        committee.«
             «
             »One thing I am intending to do is buy more red wine. At this
        point in time, we are sold out of all Pinot Noirs. It is my
        intention to purchase more of these, particularly from Davis
        Bynum, with whose wines we have had great success.«
             «
        Press F10 to select.   Follow prompts at bottom of screen.      S:1 N:1
```

Figure 4.2: The pull-down menu for checking spelling in the query memo

Press Alt-F10 to begin the spelling edit. If you are working with a hard disk, you can go directly into editing the spelling check. If you are using floppy disks, the prompt

PLEASE INSERT SYSTEM DISK AND PRESS ANY KEY

will appear at the bottom of your screen. Once you have inserted the System Diskette and pressed any key, you will see the prompt

INSERT DICTIONARY DISK CONTAINING WEBSTER.CLX IN DRIVE A, PRESS ANY KEY

Pressing any key will instruct the spelling program to go through your document a second time, within the limits of the page numbers you originally entered. The cursor will move through the text of your document until it finds the first word that the dictionary has flagged as a misspelling. At each occurrence of a flagged word, the Spell Edit menu, shown in Figure 4.3, will be displayed in the bottom half of your screen.

To correct the words that have been flagged, enter the number of the action you wish to perform. You'll learn more about options 0 and 5 later in this chapter, in the section on the Custom Dictionary.

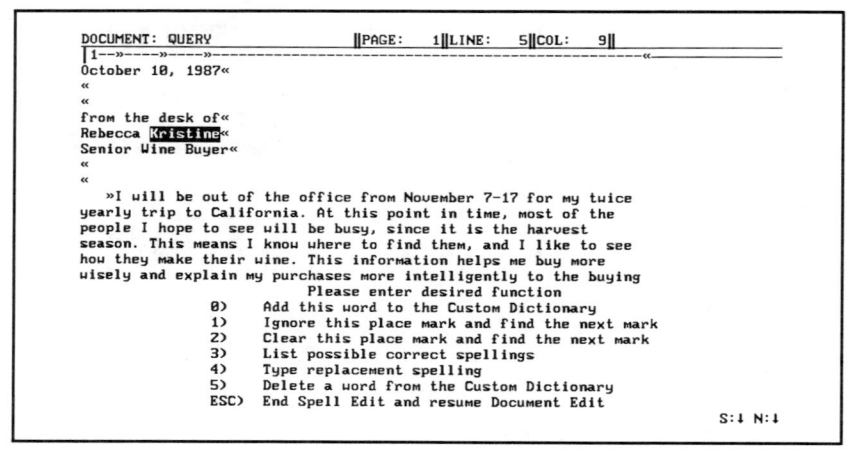

```
DOCUMENT: QUERY              ||PAGE:   1||LINE:   5||COL:   9||
|1--»----»----»--------------------------------------«-----
October 10, 1987«
«
«
from the desk of«
Rebecca Kristine«
Senior Wine Buyer«
«
«
    »I will be out of the office from November 7-17 for my twice
yearly trip to California. At this point in time, most of the
people I hope to see will be busy, since it is the harvest
season. This means I know where to find them, and I like to see
how they make their wine. This information helps me buy more
wisely and explain my purchases more intelligently to the buying
                    Please enter desired function
              0)   Add this word to the Custom Dictionary
              1)   Ignore this place mark and find the next mark
              2)   Clear this place mark and find the next mark
              3)   List possible correct spellings
              4)   Type replacement spelling
              5)   Delete a word from the Custom Dictionary
              ESC) End Spell Edit and resume Document Edit
                                                        S:1 N:1
```

Figure 4.3: The Spell Edit menu in the query memo

To find the correct spelling of a word you're unsure about, choose

3) List possible correct spellings

and you'll see a list of options.

As an example, in the query memo, the word *winemakers* was flagged during the spelling check. At this word, select option 3, and the prompt

Looking for correct spellings for:
winemakers

will appear in the lower half of your screen as Advantage II searches for possible alternative spellings.

When the search is complete, Advantage II will display a list of possible alternative spellings. These will appear in the lower half of the screen with each alternative numbered, as shown in Figure 4.4.

As you can see, Advantage II searches far and wide for possible alternatives to the flagged word. In every case where you select a list of possible correct spellings, Advantage II will come up with several choices. Before you select any of these, consult your dictionary to make sure you're using the word correctly and that its meaning is what you intend. Once you are satisfied with the meaning and use of the word, press the number next to the word you want to use, and

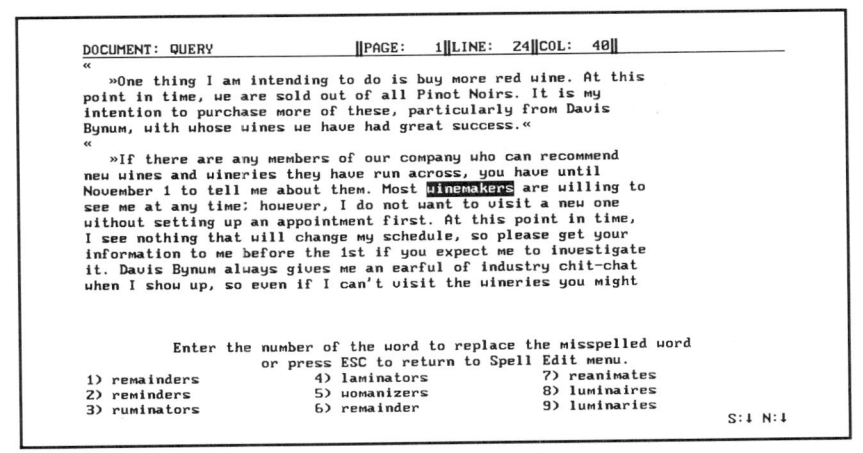

```
DOCUMENT: QUERY                    ||PAGE:   1||LINE:  24||COL:  40||
«
    »One thing I am intending to do is buy more red wine. At this
point in time, we are sold out of all Pinot Noirs. It is my
intention to purchase more of these, particularly from Davis
Bynum, with whose wines we have had great success.«
«
    »If there are any members of our company who can recommend
new wines and wineries they have run across, you have until
November 1 to tell me about them. Most winemakers are willing to
see me at any time; however, I do not want to visit a new one
without setting up an appointment first. At this point in time,
I see nothing that will change my schedule, so please get your
information to me before the 1st if you expect me to investigate
it. Davis Bynum always gives me an earful of industry chit-chat
when I show up, so even if I can't visit the wineries you might


              Enter the number of the word to replace the misspelled word
                    or press ESC to return to Spell Edit menu.
         1) remainders        4) laminators        7) reanimates
         2) reminders         5) womanizers        8) luminaires
         3) ruminators        6) remainder         9) luminaries
                                                                    S:↓ N:↓
```

Figure 4.4: List of possible spellings for *winemakers*

Advantage II will insert this selection automatically into your document, aligning the text correctly to adjust for a longer or shorter word. You will then return to the Spell Edit menu.

If none of the alternatives listed is acceptable to you, press Escape to return to the Spell Edit menu. You have the option at this point of accepting the flagged word or else typing in a new word or spelling of your choice. You do this by selecting on the Spell Edit menu

4) Type replacement spelling

This will cause the prompt

TYPE NEW SPELLING: Press F10 to continue

to appear on the bottom line of the screen. You are given 30 spaces in which to type an alternative spelling. When you have entered the correct word, press F10 to insert that word in place of the one that is flagged.

You'll know you've completed the spelling edit when the prompt

UNABLE TO FIND ANY MISSPELLING - PRESS ANY KEY

appears at the bottom of your screen. You should now remove the Speller/Dictionary Diskette and replace it with the System Diskette.

Removing Place Marks

You can choose to clear place marks as you proceed through the spelling edit—if a word is correct, for instance, but you don't want to add it to the Custom Dictionary—or you can choose to skip a place mark and come back to it later.

Flags will be cleared through the spelling edit whenever you select one of these settings:

> 0) Add this word to the custom dictionary
> 2) Clear this place mark and find the next mark

or if you select

> 3) List possible correct spellings

and you select one of the words listed. If you select on the Spell Edit menu

> 1) Ignore this place mark and find the next mark

the flag on that word will remain. If you select

> Esc) End spell edit and resume Document Edit

all flags in the text following the place where you select this option will remain.

You can leave the place marks in your document, since they will not affect printing. Or, if you want to clear all remaining flags, press Alt-Y. The prompt

> CLEARING PLACE MARKS

will appear on the right side of the status line and the prompt

> <<<PLEASE WAIT>>>

will appear at the bottom of the screen. When this prompt disappears, all place marks will have been removed. Now you can press F10 to save the document. Remember to replace the Speller/ Dictionary Diskette with the System Diskette when you return to other word-processing tasks.

CREATING A CUSTOM DICTIONARY

Advantage II refers to custom dictionaries as well as the main Webster dictionary each time it checks the spelling in a document. There is space on the Speller/Dictionary Diskette to create either one custom dictionary of approximately 5,000 entries, or several different custom dictionaries that collectively contain approximately 5,000 entries. The actual number depends upon the length of the words you enter. With technical words that are particularly long, you may run out of disk space before you reach the 5,000-word limit.

You can insert words into your custom dictionary when you edit a document that has been checked for spelling. After running several spelling checks, you will become familiar with words you use frequently that are not allowable according to the main dictionary. These are words you should enter into your custom dictionary. Once you do so, Advantage II will no longer flag these words. Several words you should be sure to enter are your name and address, the names of people you write to often, and the names and addresses of businesses you deal with.

BUILDING A CUSTOM DICTIONARY

Now, enter the MultiMate Advantage II word-processing program, and select on the main menu

> 7) System and Document Defaults

and on this menu select

> 3. Edit System Defaults

This will take you to the Edit System Defaults screen, which is shown in Figure 4.5. The last field on this screen, *Custom Dictionary?*, allows you to enter the name of the custom dictionary you want to build. As an example, type the name *Custom* in this field and press F10. Now, any words you instruct Advantage II to enter into your custom dictionary from the Spell Edit menu will be entered into your custom dictionary Custom. You can create additional custom dictionaries by repeating these steps and giving these dictionaries different names. For instance, you might want to use *Business* for business words, and *Medical* for medical words. You should be aware that Advantage II includes 30,000 legal terms in its main 110,000-word dictionary.

```
                          EDIT SYSTEM DEFAULTS

     Insert Mode [(P)ush / (D)rop Down]? P    Acceptable Decimal Tab [. or ,]?    .
     Allow Widows And Orphans?           Y    Number Of Lines Per Page?          55
     Automatic Page Breaks?              Y    Display Spaces As Dots [·]?         N
     Destructive Backspace?              Y    Speed Up Movement Between Pages?    Y
     Backup Before Editing Document?     N    Strikeout Character?                /
     Display Directory?                  Y    Display Document Startup Screens?   Y
     (D)ocument Mode or (P)age Mode ?    D
     (P)age Or (T)ext Associated Headers And Footers?                             P
     System Date Standard [(D)OS,(U)SA,(E)urope or (J)apan]?                      D
     Print Date Standard [(D)OS,(U)SA,(E)urope or (J)apan]?                       D
     Currency Symbol              $           (F)ootnotes Or (E)ndnotes?          F

     Section Numbering Style [(R)oman Or (N)umeric]?                              R

     Acceleration Rate [0-9]?            5    Acceleration Responsiveness [0-9]?  5
     Main Dictionary?              WEBSTER    Custom Dictionary?              CLAMFL



                    Press F10 when finished, ESC to exit              S:1 N:1
```

Figure 4.5: Adding a custom dictionary

DELETING WORDS FROM A CUSTOM DICTIONARY

The final choice on the Spell Edit menu allows you to delete a word you have entered into your custom dictionary. The principal reason for deleting words from a custom dictionary is to save space for more important words. Since space in your custom dictionaries is limited to approximately 5,000 entries, you may well find yourself bumping up against this limit while you still need to enter more special words.

You can begin deleting words from your custom dictionary by selecting

> 5) Delete a word from the Custom Dictionary

anytime the Spell Edit menu is displayed on the screen. When you press 5, the prompt

> TYPE WORD TO DELETE: Press F10 to continue

will appear on the bottom line of the screen. Again, you are allowed 30 spaces to type the word you want to delete. When you have entered the word you want to delete, press F10. The Spell Edit menu will disappear from the screen, the prompt

> PLEASE WAIT

will appear briefly at the bottom of the screen, and then the Spell Edit menu will reappear.

KEEPING A WRITTEN RECORD OF ENTRIES

There is no security prompt telling you if the word you have tried to delete is the correct spelling of the word in your custom dictionary. The sequence of events will be the same whether the word you tried to delete is in your custom dictionary or not. Therefore, you will have to be sure of the exact spelling of the word you want to delete. You might find it useful, therefore, to keep a separate list of the words you enter into your custom dictionaries. You can do this most conveniently by creating a document that lists your entries. Then, every time you update your custom dictionaries, you'll have to remember to also update this document.

USING ADVANCED UTILITIES TO MODIFY A CUSTOM DICTIONARY

You can also access and modify a custom dictionary through one of the utilities on the Advanced Utilities Diskette. Furthermore, the only way to view words in a custom dictionary is with the Custom Dictionary Utility. You'll learn more about using the advanced utilities in Chapter 8, for editing key procedure files. For now, you need only be concerned with accessing the appropriate utility.

To access the Custom Dictionary Utility, follow these steps.

1. If you are working with floppy disks, transfer the files WPSYSD.SYS from the System Diskette and WPHELP.TXT from the Boot Diskette to the Advanced Utilities Diskette. (With a hard disk, make sure these two files are on your hard disk.)

2. Exit from the word-processing function by selecting *Return to DOS* at the main menu. At the DOS prompt, type *mm* and press Return. (With floppies, make sure the Advanced Utilities Diskette is in drive A.)

3. At the MultiMate Advantage II Boot-up menu (refer to Figure 8.5), select *MultiMate Advantage II Utilities and Conversions* and press Return.

4. At the Advanced Utilities menu (refer to Figure 8.6), press the Space bar so that the light bar on the screen moves over the last option

   Custom Dictionary Utility

   and press F10. You'll see the Custom Dictionary Utility screen, which has three options:

   Edit an Old File
   Create a New File
   Delete a File

CREATE A NEW FILE

Press the Space bar to place the light bar over the second option

Create a New File

and press F10. The Create a New File screen (Figure 4.6) will then appear. The cursor will appear blinking in the file field. To create a new file using this screen, make sure the document drive designation is correct, and the pathway if you are using one, and then enter the name of the custom dictionary you want to create. For this example, enter the file name Business and press F10.

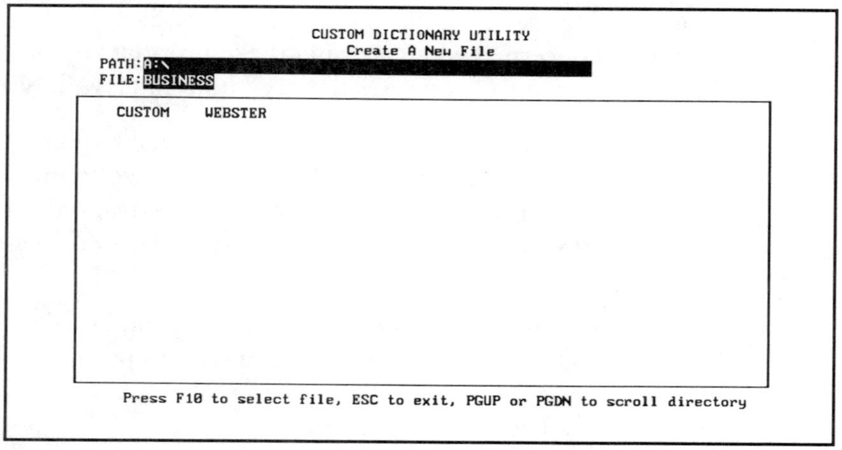

```
                    CUSTOM DICTIONARY UTILITY
                         Create A New File
           PATH: A:\
           FILE: BUSINESS
              CUSTOM     WEBSTER




           Press F10 to select file, ESC to exit, PGUP or PGDN to scroll directory
```

Figure 4.6: Create a New File screen for custom dictionary

Note that in this example, the Webster dictionary that comes with the Advantage II package appears on the screen, along with the Custom dictionary you created earlier in this chapter. The Business dictionary is where you can put all the special words you use for your business correspondence. When you want to place specific words into this dictionary, you will have to make sure that the name Business is entered into the Custom Dictionary field of the Edit Document Defaults screen.

To return to the Custom Dictionary Utility screen, press Escape. You can do this after you have created a new custom dictionary, or if you change your mind and decide that you do not want to create one after all.

DELETE A CUSTOM DICTIONARY

Once you are back in the Custom Dictionary Utility screen, you can delete the Business dictionary by pressing the Space bar to highlight

Delete a File

Then press F10 to go to the Delete File screen for custom dictionaries, which is similar to the Create a New File screen. You'll see all your custom dictionaries listed in this screen, and you need only use the cursor keys to highlight the file you want to delete, then press F10 to delete. A safety message will appear at the bottom of the screen

> ARE YOU SURE YOU WANT TO DELETE FILE?
> YES   NO

The Yes option is highlighted, and if you want to delete the highlighted file, just press F10. There is no security prompt to this procedure (Advantage II will not ask if you are sure about the deletion before erasing the file), so make sure that the highlighted file is the one that you want to delete. If you change your mind before you press F10, highlight NO by pressing the Space bar, and then press F10.

To return to the Custom Dictionary Utility, press Escape.

EDIT AN OLD FILE

You might want to edit a custom dictionary for four reasons:

- To add a new word
- To delete a word
- To view a word
- To reorganize a custom dictionary

To do any of these, you must select on the Custom Dictionary Utility screen

Edit an Old File

by pressing the Space bar. Then press F10 to go to the Edit an Old File screen (Figure 4.7).

First, you have to select the custom dictionary you want to work with by using the cursor keys. For this example, select the custom dictionary Custom and press F10. This will move you into the Edit Custom Dictionary screen, which offers two choices:

- *Modify Custom Dictionary* lets you add, delete, and view words in the custom dictionary you have selected.

- *Reorganize Custom Dictionary* lets you reorganize the custom dictionary you have selected.

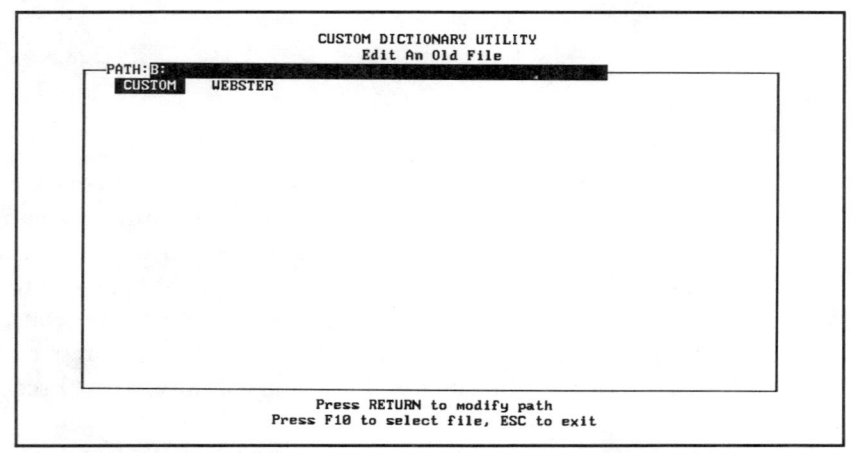

```
                    CUSTOM DICTIONARY UTILITY
                         Edit An Old File
┌─PATH:B:─────────────────────────────────────────────────┐
│  CUSTOM    WEBSTER                                      │
│                                                         │
│                                                         │
│                                                         │
│                                                         │
│                                                         │
│                                                         │
│                                                         │
│                                                         │
│                                                         │
│                                                         │
│                  Press RETURN to modify path            │
│              Press F10 to select file, ESC to exit      │
└─────────────────────────────────────────────────────────┘
```

Figure 4.7: Edit an Old File for a custom dictionary

Using the Space bar, select

Modify Custom Dictionary

and press F10. The Modify Custom Dictionary screen will appear, which also offers two choices:

Add Word
View/Delete Word

Let's discuss these options in turn.

Adding a New Word

If you use the Space bar to select

Add Word

and press F10, the Add Word to Custom Dictionary screen (Figure 4.8) will appear.

You can do three things in this screen:

1. You can enter a new word up to 49 characters long, then return to the Modify Custom Dictionary screen by pressing F10.

2. You can cancel the word you enter by pressing Escape.

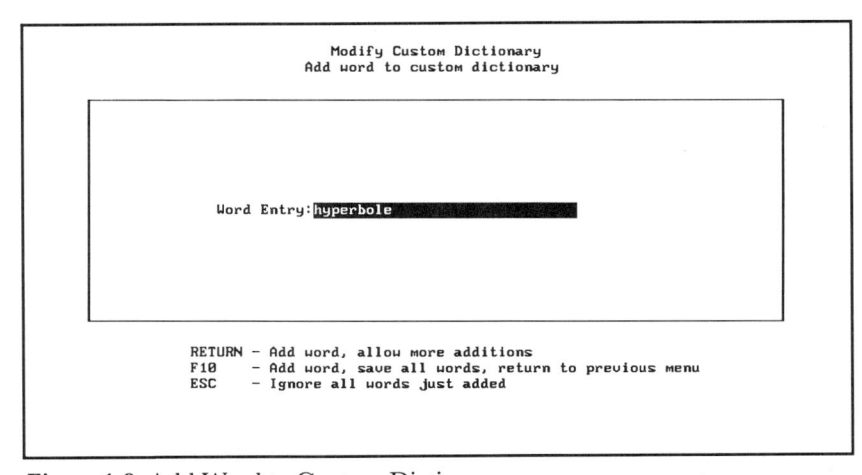

```
                     Modify Custom Dictionary
                    Add word to custom dictionary
┌─────────────────────────────────────────────────────────────────┐
│ ┌─────────────────────────────────────────────────────────────┐ │
│ │                                                             │ │
│ │                                                             │ │
│ │                                                             │ │
│ │            Word Entry: hyperbole                            │ │
│ │                                                             │ │
│ │                                                             │ │
│ │                                                             │ │
│ └─────────────────────────────────────────────────────────────┘ │
│       RETURN - Add word, allow more additions                   │
│       F10    - Add word, save all words, return to previous menu│
│       ESC    - Ignore all words just added                      │
│                                                                 │
└─────────────────────────────────────────────────────────────────┘
```

Figure 4.8: Add Word to Custom Dictionary screen

3. You can add several words in a row by pressing Return after each complete word.

As an example, enter the word *hyperbole* and then press F10 to enter it in the Custom dictionary.

Viewing a Word

To view or delete a word, start out from the Modify Custom Dictionary screen. Highlight *View/Delete Word* and press F10. The View/Delete Word in Custom Dictionary screen (Figure 4.9) will appear. The most recent word added to the dictionary, either through the advanced utility screens or from the Spell Edit menu, will appear on this screen. In this case, the word *hyperbole* is displayed. If there are more words in the custom dictionary you specified, they will also appear on this screen. If there are more words than can fit and you want to view them, you can scroll through the entire contents of the custom dictionary by moving the light bar with the cursor arrows, or press PgDn or PgUp, depending upon where you are in the list of words.

Note that this is the only way you can view the contents of your custom dictionaries. The words will be in the order in which you entered them, not in alphabetical order. Each screen can hold about 27 words—in three columns and nine rows. Wherever you deleted a word, you'll see a blank space (unless you've reorganized the dictionary, as you'll learn later in this chapter). To obtain a printed record of your cus-

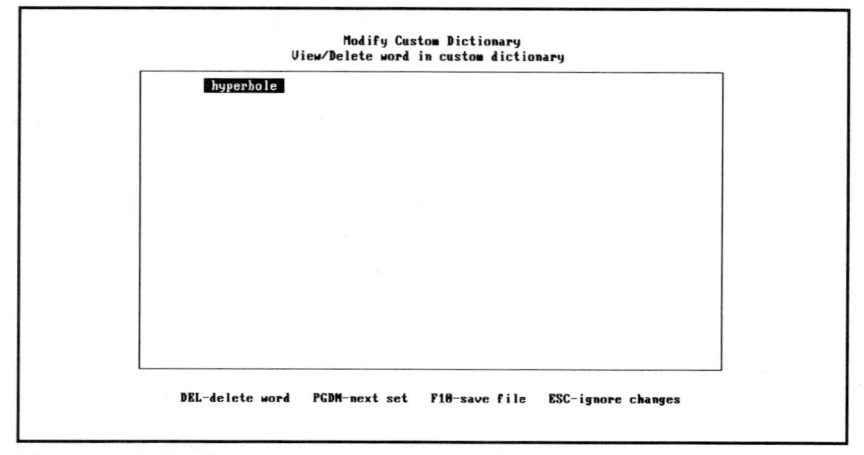

Figure 4.9: View/Delete Word in Custom Dictionary screen

tom dictionaries, you can use Quick Print (Ctrl-PrtSc) for each screenful of words.

Deleting Words

You delete words from the same screen where you view them (Figure 4.9). On the View/Delete Word in Custom Dictionary screen, place the light bar over the word you want to delete and press Delete. If, after deleting one or more words, you change your mind, press Escape. The prompt

Do you wish to escape without saving this page? (Y/N)

will appear at the bottom of the screen. Pressing Y for Yes will recover all words deleted so far in this session. If you delete a word by mistake, go back to the Add Word to Custom Dictionary screen. To return to the Modify Custom Dictionary screen, press Escape.

Reorganizing a Custom Dictionary

You should reorganize a custom dictionary whenever you delete more than a few words. Reorganizing a custom dictionary will clear out the blank spaces left in the custom dictionary where words were deleted. This provides more room for new words you might want to add, and reduces the amount of time it takes for the spelling check and spelling edit to search the dictionaries.

On the Edit Custom Dictionary screen, select

Reorganize Custom Dictionary

and press F10 to begin the reorganization. You'll see the prompt

PLEASE WAIT, REORGANIZING CUSTOM DICTIONARY . . .

It will remain on the screen until Advantage II has removed the blank spaces and moved the remaining words closer together.

USING THE THESAURUS

A thesaurus has also been included with Advantage II, and you will find it on your Thesaurus Diskette. All 360K on this floppy diskette are occupied with Webster's Thesaurus, but there is not enough room to accommodate all of Webster's entries. Only the more common words have been selected, amounting to about half the original number.

This thesaurus will assist you in selecting synonyms and definitions for words you have already placed in your text. Using the thesaurus is easier than checking your spelling.

As an example, check the word *pleased* in Letter1. Place the cursor anywhere on that word, and press Alt-T to activate thesaurus mode. The prompt

LOOK UP WHAT?

will appear on the right side of the status line. The word *pleased* should be highlighted. Now, press Alt-T to obtain a definition and synonyms for the highlighted word.

If you are using floppy disks, the prompt

INSERT THESAURUS DISKETTE IN DRIVE A - PRESS ANY KEY

will appear at the bottom of the screen. Insert that diskette and press any key to initiate the search. After a brief pause, Advantage II will find the citation for the word *pleased*. The entry will appear as shown in Figure 4.10.

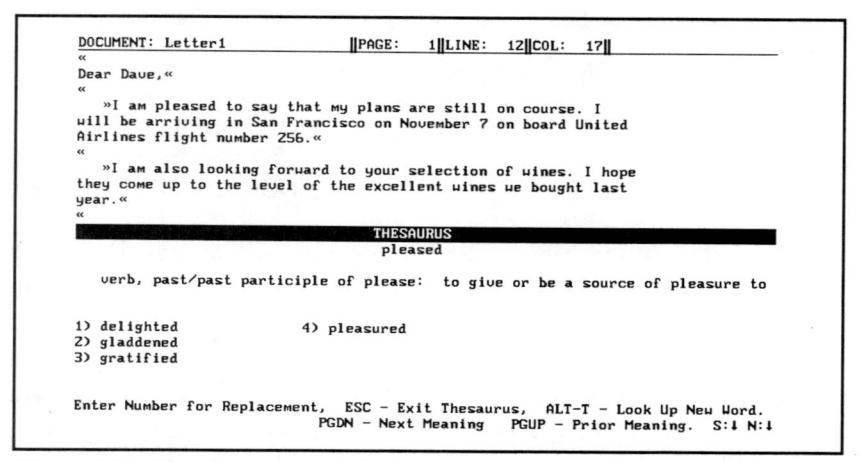

```
DOCUMENT: Letter1              ‖PAGE:    1‖LINE:   12‖COL:   17‖
«
Dear Dave,«
«
    »I am pleased to say that my plans are still on course. I
will be arriving in San Francisco on November 7 on board United
Airlines flight number 256.«
«
    »I am also looking forward to your selection of wines. I hope
they come up to the level of the excellent wines we bought last
year.«
«
                           THESAURUS
                            pleased
    verb, past/past participle of please:  to give or be a source of pleasure to


    1) delighted         4) pleasured
    2) gladdened
    3) gratified


    Enter Number for Replacement,  ESC - Exit Thesaurus,  ALT-T - Look Up New Word.
                      PGDN - Next Meaning   PGUP - Prior Meaning.   S:↓ N:↓
```

Figure 4.10: The thesaurus window

There is room in the window to display nine synonyms and definitions. Each one will have a number next to it. If there are more than nine choices, you can look at them by pressing the appropriate key: press PgDn to obtain the next list of meanings, and press PgUp to review the list of meanings you passed over.

Once you have glanced at all the options, you can select the one you prefer by entering its number. This will replace the original word with the new one. When you are finished with one selection, you can move to the next by pressing Alt-T.

You can check a phrase as well as a word, as long as the phrase is no more than 49 characters long. The same constraints that apply to highlighting a block of text apply to the thesaurus function. To search for the definition and synonyms of a phrase, you have to highlight the complete phrase. Then, follow the instructions as if you were checking a word.

As an example, move the cursor in Letter1 to the phrase *on course* in the first sentence. Make sure the cursor is on either letter of the word *on,* then press Alt-T. Move the cursor to the end of the word *course.* When the two words are highlighted, press Alt-T to begin the search for a synonym or definition. In a few moments, the prompt

No information found, press any key to continue

will appear in the window in the middle of your screen. This means that no information on the phrase was found in the thesaurus.

If you highlight too many characters, the prompt

TOO MANY CHARACTERS - PRESS ANY KEY TO CONTINUE

will appear on the bottom of your screen. You will have to reduce the number of characters in the block you have selected to 49 or less.

To exit the thesaurus, press Escape.

By now, you've learned how to create and revise a document so that it is letter-perfect. The next step is to learn how you can adjust such features as margins, add underlining or bold print, and create headers or footnotes. Chapter 5 covers these formatting features.

5

FORMATTING

THE APPEARANCE OF A DOCUMENT CAN BE ALMOST as important as its organization, spelling, and syntax. On a typewriter, you're restricted to minor adjustments such as line spacing, tab stops, and right margin. With Advantage II, you can alter the appearance of your text using such additional features as:

- Centering and indenting
- Draft, enhanced, bold, and shadow print
- Double underscore, strikeout, subscript and superscript
- Print pitch
- Underlining
- Footnotes
- Headers and footers
- Comments

You will learn how to use these features by employing format lines and screen symbols. Each one of these features can have a powerful effect on the appearance of your document.

MODIFY DOCUMENT DEFAULTS SCREEN

Before you learn how to specify different formats, it's useful to become familiar with the default settings you can change whenever you create a new document.

Beginning at the main menu, select

2) Create a Document

and press F10. The Document Summary screen shown in Figure 5.1 will appear, and this time you will enter more information on this

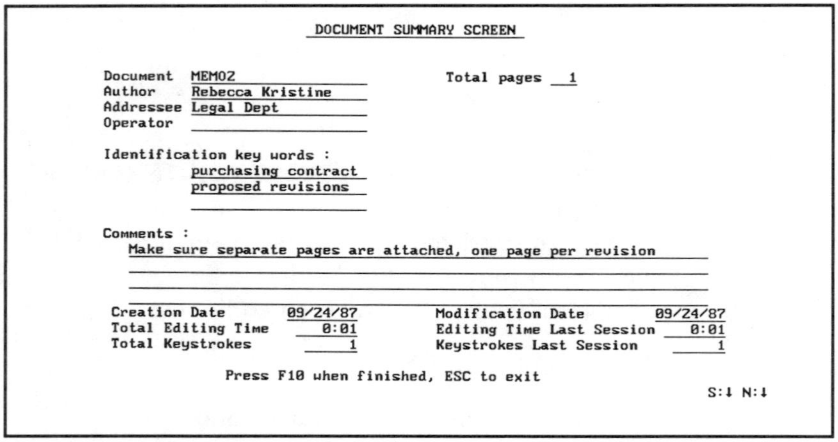

```
                    DOCUMENT SUMMARY SCREEN

     Document   MEMO2                    Total pages    1
     Author     Rebecca Kristine
     Addressee  Legal Dept
     Operator

     Identification key words :
                purchasing contract
                proposed revisions


     Comments :
                Make sure separate pages are attached, one page per revision



     Creation Date         09/24/87     Modification Date          09/24/87
     Total Editing Time       0:01      Editing Time Last Session     0:01
     Total Keystrokes            1      Keystrokes Last Session          1

             Press F10 when finished, ESC to exit
                                                            S:1 N:1
```

Figure 5.1: Document Summary screen for Memo2

screen. The additional information has been added to help you identify the contents of this document, called Memo2. When you have filled in your Document Summary screen as it appears in Figure 5.1, press F10. This will bring up the Modify Document Defaults screen, which you first saw in Chapter 1. Let's discuss each setting in turn.

Widows and Orphans

In printed material, widows and orphans are single lines of text that are separated from the rest of the paragraph, and appear at the top of the next page or the bottom of the preceding page, respectively. Such a single line, sometimes containing only a word or two, can degrade the appearance of a printed page. To avoid widows and orphans, you will want to change *Allow widows and orphans?* to N for no when you repaginate the document prior to printing.

When you write a document for the first time, however, whether it has widows and orphans is not important. If you answer N for no, Advantage II will shuffle your lines of text around to include at least two lines of a paragraph at the top or bottom of each page. This continual shuffling can make your editing more difficult. That is why the default setting is Y for yes, meaning that lines of text won't be rearranged.

Automatic Page Breaks

Advantage II will create automatic page breaks at the line number specified by the *Number of lines per page* field. The default setting is Y for yes. If you enter N for no, you can keep adding text to a page until the line count reaches 199, but you will have to press F2 to indicate the end of each page in your document.

Backup before Editing

The *Backup before edit document?* field allows you to instruct Advantage II to make an automatic backup of every document immediately before you edit it. This provides some security in case your original document file becomes damaged, or if you erase a portion of the document and then realize that was a mistake. Although the default is N for no, you should be aware that MultiMate Advantage II will record to disk all changes you make to a document each time you switch pages, in both document and page mode, regardless of your answer in this field.

The trade-off with backing up all your documents is that you can place only half as many documents on your document disk as you could without backup copies. Saving an original document as well as a backup means that every document is recorded twice. You might want to answer Y for yes in this field only for selected documents, those of crucial importance to you.

Acceptable Decimal Tab

The *Acceptable decimal tab* field is important when you create columns and use the Decimal Tab function (Shift-F4). You can select a period (American style: 5.21) or a comma (European style: 5,21) for a decimal point. (See Chapter 10.) The default decimal is the period.

Number of Lines per Page

The *Number of lines per page* field determines the length of each page. You can have up to 199 lines per page; the default value is 55 lines.

If you change this setting in the middle of a document, the pages that precede the change will remain set at the previous line length.

You will have to repaginate the entire document to set the new standard throughout your document. Refer to the section on Repagination, later in this chapter.

Document Startup Screens

Document startup screens are the screens you pass through when you want to work with a document, after you have named the document in the Edit a Document screen. When you create a document, the startup screens are the Document Summary screen and the Modify Document Defaults screen. When you edit a document, the only startup screen is the Document Summary screen.

The default entry in the Display Document Startup Screens field is Y for yes, which means that these screens will be shown before your document appears. You can speed up your entry into documents by changing this field to N for no, and your document will appear immediately. If you are going to use the same settings for most of your documents, and you frequently switch from one document to another, I recommend that you go ahead and change the default setting to N so that you can enter your documents more rapidly. However, you should be aware that if this field is set to N, you cannot create a library (see Chapter 7) or a data file (see Chapter 12).

Text-Associated or Page-Associated Headers and Footers

Headers and footers consist of text that appears at the top or bottom of a page. P, the default setting, stands for page-associated headers and footers. This means that you want headers and footers to appear on every page in the document. The other option is T, which stands for text-associated headers and footers. You can change the setting to T if you want your headers and footers to apppear on the same page as the text with which you created them. For more information, see the section on headers and footers later in this chapter.

Print Date Standard

There are four ways to print dates using six digits and separators. Month/day/year appears as MM/DD/YY, and is the American style (U). There are two international styles: the European style (E), or DD/MM/YY, and the Japanese style (J), or DD:MM:YY. A fourth style labeled D for DOS generally corresponds to the American style, but on some systems it might be different. The DOS style is the default setting.

Currency Symbol

The Currency Symbol field refers to the notation that you want to appear with figures aligned on a decimal tab and calculated by the program. You can enter any character in this field. The default symbol is the American dollar sign ($). When you enter this same character next to figures aligned on decimal tabs in your document, Advantage II will automatically place it next to the calculated total. (See Chapter 10 for more information.)

Footnotes and Endnotes

Footnotes contain additional information that appears at the bottom of a page and relates to the text above it. Endnotes are footnotes that appear at the end of a section, a chapter, or the entire document. The default setting in this field is F, for footnotes. The entry in this field overrides whatever footnote or endnote symbols you have placed in your document. For more information, see the section on footnotes and endnotes at the end of this chapter.

Section Number Style

The *Section number style* field applies to the advanced feature of creating outlines and tables of contents from longer documents (see Chapter 9). R stands for Roman style, which is numbered like this:

I.
   A.
      1.
         a.
            (1)
               (a)

N stands for Numeric style, most often used in technical documents, and is numbered like this:

1.
1.1.

1.1.1.
1.1.1.1.

Saving the Settings

Press F10 to set your choices in the Modify Document Defaults screen and go to the blank Document screen. Press Escape if you want to cancel any changes you made in the Modify Document Defaults Screen.

Calling Up the Modify Document Defaults Screen

If at any time you wish to look at or change the default setting for the document you are working on, press F10 to return to the main menu and select

7) System and Document Defaults

and press Return. You will see the screen shown in Figure 5.2.

Next, on the System and Document Defaults screen select

4. Edit Document Defaults

and you will see the screen shown in Figure 5.3. Advantage II will have already entered the title of the document you were working on

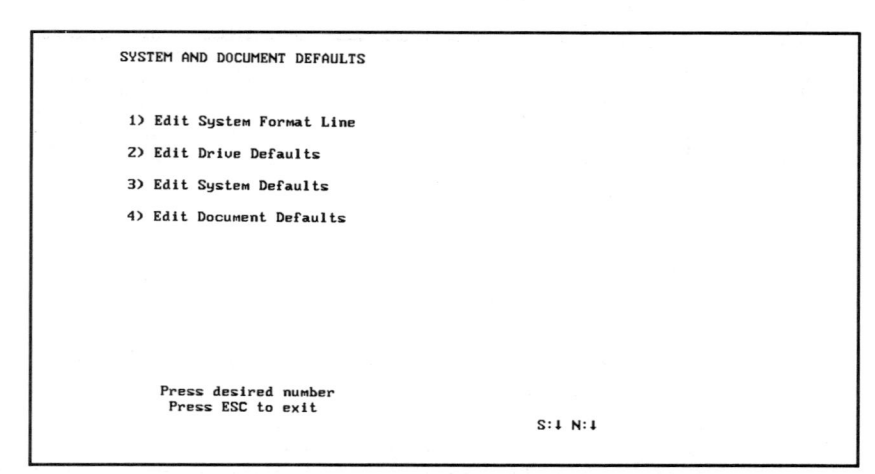

```
             SYSTEM AND DOCUMENT DEFAULTS


                1) Edit System Format Line
                2) Edit Drive Defaults
                3) Edit System Defaults
                4) Edit Document Defaults








                   Press desired number
                   Press ESC to exit
                                            S:1 N:1
```

Figure 5.2: System and Document Defaults screen

before you called up this screen. Press Return to bring up the Modify Document Defaults screen that is connected to the document you were just working on. You can modify the settings on this screen if you wish to. If you make changes to this screen and then decide you want to preserve the original settings, press Escape.

FORMAT LINES

Now go back to the Document screen for Memo1 and enter the memo shown in Figure 5.4. You can practice formatting features with this memo. The first formatting method is the format lines.

There are two general things to learn about format lines.

1. Format lines show up on your screen to help you to control the appearance of your document, but they will never appear on the printed page.
2. A format line affects only the text that follows it. You can insert a new format line at any place in your document, and thereby change the settings, but it will only have an effect on the text that comes after the new format line.

There are three format lines you can use while working with Advantage II. These are the system format line, the current format

```
                         EDIT DOCUMENT DEFAULTS
          Press F7 to Switch to the Edit Table of Contents Defaults Screen

              Drive:B              Document: _____
              Path: \
              Approximately 00304128 characters [00121 Page(s)] available on B:
    MEMO2







              Press F10 when finished, ESC to exit, PGDN to switch drives
              Press CTRL-HOME to select default path, CTRL-END for next path
                    Press F6 to display document directory         S:1 N:1
```

Figure 5.3: Edit Document Defaults screen

```
    To:      Legal Department
    From:    Rebecca Kristine
    Date:    September 24, 1987
    Subject: PROPOSED CHANGES TO WINE PURCHASING CONTRACT

         I would like to propose several changes to our wine
    purchasing contract. I have attached three pages to this memo
    showing these changes. Each page contains one clause that I would
    like to change, listing the changes I recommend.

         These recommendations are based upon a review of the current
    contracts now used by the major distributors. I have not simply
    copied our competitors' contracts. I am only presenting those
    that improve the quality of our contract. If you have any
    questions about these changes, please see me.

         I would like to point out that I will be taking a trip to
    California to negotiate our purchases of the 1986 vintage wines,
    during which time I plan to use this revised contract to make
    several purchases. Therefore, the sooner I receive your approval
    for these changes, the better.

                ADVANTAGES OF REVISING THE PURCHASING CONTRACT

         *    Make our terms more consistent with the competition.

         *    Show our suppliers that we care about what we ask them
              to sign.

         *    Afford us protection in case the contract ever goes to
              mediation or litigation.

                          CLAUSE 4: PAYMENTS

         This clause as it is presently written requires that we pay
    an amount equal to 50% of the stated list price of each case of
    wine we buy.

         Proposal:     Insert a blank space after "that we pay..." large
                       enough so that I can write a single lump sum. Some
                       of our purchases have been as high as $50,000, so
                       there should be sufficient space to include these
                       kinds of figures.
```

Figure 5.4: Text for Memo2

line, and the page format line. All format lines contain the same controls, but these controls can be changed at different points within the document—at the beginning of the document, at the beginning of a page, or in the middle of a page. The place where you change the format will determine the kind of format line you should use.

THE SYSTEM FORMAT LINE

You first saw a format line in Chapter 2, when you wrote Letter1. That format line, called the system format line, will appear at the top of page 1 of every document. Like all format lines, it will disappear when you move more than 23 lines, or a screenful of text, away from it. This line lets you set basic formatting features when you create a document. These settings will be used throughout your document unless you change them.

The three formatting features you can change in any format line are:

- Line spacing
- Tab stops
- Right margin

To change any of these three features, press F9, the Format Change key. Pressing F9 changes the appearance of the format line and moves the cursor onto it so that you can make your changes. Before you press this key, the format line appears as a series of dashes; after you press F9, the format line turns into dots along the baseline. This makes it easier for you to track the cursor position according to its column position.

If you press F9 now, the cursor will appear blinking in the format line, and the status line will show that it's in column 3.

FORMAT CHANGE

will appear on the right side of the status line. While this prompt is showing, you will be unable to edit any text in your document. To work with your document text, you must press F9 a second time to save all format changes and return your cursor to the text editing area of your document screen. If, before pressing F9, you decide that you want to cancel the changes you made to the format line, press Escape. This will take the cursor off the format line and restore the original settings.

Now let's discuss which features you can change.

Changing Line Spacing

Line spacing is the first feature you will encounter on your format line. The number to the left of your blinking cursor denotes the current line spacing. This number tells you how many lines down the text will appear each time your cursor reaches the right margin. Single spacing, denoted by 1, is the default setting. Press 2 for double spacing. All other types of line spacing are determined by entering a code, as shown in Table 5.1. To change line spacing, move your cursor over the existing code and overwrite it with the code for the kind of spacing you want. You won't see its effect until you print the document.

Changing Tab Stops

The tab stops are the second feature on the format line. These are denoted by an arrow pointing to the right in columns 5, 10, and 15. You can check these positions by moving your cursor down the format line with the → key.

To delete a tab stop, press the Space bar until the cursor moves over the tab stop and erases it. To create a tab stop, move the cursor to the position where you want a tab stop and press the Tab key. Immediately, a new tab mark will appear at the cursor position.

Right Margin

The right margin is the third formatting feature on the format line. The length of your text line is determined by the position of your right margin, and this position is marked on your format line with a <<. Move your cursor along the format line past the tab stops. You will find

SYMBOL	LINE SPACING
0	none
H	half space
1	single (default)
+	one and one half
2	double
=	two and one half
3	double

Table 5.1: Line spacing symbols on the format line

the default setting for line length is column 75 on the status line.

You can change the position of the right margin by moving your cursor with the ← and → keys. Since there is only one right margin, you do not need to erase the old mark before you create the new one. The maximum right-margin setting is 156. If you plan to use the default pitch of 10 characters per inch in the Document Print Options screen, you should change the right margin on the format line from column 75 to column 65 for a 1-inch right margin on a standard 8½-wide sheet of paper. You can change the default setting for the right margin of all new documents through the Edit System Format Line setting on the Document Management screen (see Appendix A).

Centering

With Advantage II, you can easily center a heading title. For example, in Memo1 you'd want to center

ADVANTAGES OF REVISING THE PURCHASING CONTRACT

You can either center the words as you enter them, or type the words first and center them afterwards.

To center text as you enter it, start with a blank line. Now press F3, the Centering key. This will create a short, double-pointed arrow midway between the right and left margins. The cursor will appear one space to the right of the arrow. Now type in the words to be centered. The words will spread out from the middle of the screen as you enter them. No matter how many characters you insert (up to the limit of the line length) or delete (down to the last character) this centered line will expand and contract from the center point. When you are finished entering the words to be centered, press Return. This will stop the centering function.

You can also center existing text. Place the cursor on the first character of the text to be centered. You can use either of the following procedures to center this text:

1. Press Plus (on the numeric keypad) and F3
2. Press Insert, F3, and Insert

Indenting

Indenting text is controlled by your tab stop settings. The column where indentation takes effect is determined by a tab mark. Also, the Tab key is used to indent text. The difference between tabs and indentations is that the indent function continues to operate on text for as many lines down the page as you wish it to, producing a *block indent*. Tabs only work on the one line where you press the Tab key.

To indent text, first make sure you have set tabs that correspond to any indents you may want to specify. Then move the cursor to one or more spaces before the tab position you want to use as the indent. Now press F4, the Indent key. This will place an arrow at the tab mark. Type your text. When you go to the end of the first line, word wrap will take your text to the next line down, but the text will all be indented.

When you come to the end of each item you want to indent, press Return. This will end the indentation function.

If you are typing a list of items, press Return a second time to create a blank line. Now press F4 to start the second indentation, type the text, and press Return to end the indent.

Inserting the System Format Line

The system format line normally appears only at the beginning of every document, but you can call it up at any place in the document. First, place your cursor where you want the system format line to appear, then press Ctrl-F9, and the prompt

FORMAT SYSTEM

will appear on the right edge of the status line. Press Escape if you want to cancel this operation. You can edit this line, if you wish, by pressing F9, the Format Change key. Then make the changes—line spacing, tab setting, or line length—and press F9 again. The changes you make will only affect text that follows this format line. If you call up the system format line again in the same document, the modified version will appear.

Although you can make changes to your system format line at any place in the document, I recommend that you leave the system format line the way it originally appears at the top of the first page. The current format line is the best one to use to change the format of text in the body of your document.

CURRENT FORMAT LINE

You use the current format line to look at or change any of the features controlled by the format line while you are working in the document. Position the cursor where you want this line to appear in your document, and press Shift-F9 to call up the current format line. The prompt

> **FORMAT CURRENT**

will appear on the right side of the status line. You can use the current format line to review the current settings and to change them. Press Escape if you want to cancel this operation. Like the system format line, the current format line will scroll off your screen when you move more than 23 lines away from it. You can continue to insert as many current format lines in your document as you wish to. If you make any changes, remember that only subsequent text will be affected.

PAGE FORMAT LINE

You should use the page format line for the most localized format changes in a document, such as entering numbers in multiple columns. If the first column begins on the left margin, and each column is 10 spaces wide, you can specify the appropriate tab stops for each column in the page format line. These settings most likely will not agree with your current or system format line.

You can insert a page format line by pressing Alt-F9. The prompt

> **FORMAT PAGE**

will appear on the right side of the status line. Press Escape to cancel this operation. If you inserted a current format line after the top of the current page and changed the settings, then the page format line would reflect not these changes but what exists at the top of the current page.

DELETING THE CURRENT OR PAGE FORMAT LINE

You can delete some format lines, but not the one that appears at the top of every page, that is, the format line composed of dashes. The ones you can get rid of are those that appear as dots on the baseline. To delete one of these, start by placing the cursor under the format line that you want to delete. Next press the Delete key, and the prompt

DELETE WHAT?

will appear on the right side of the format line. Next, press F9, the Format key, and the prompt

INCLUDING FORMAT LINE

will appear in the bottom left corner of your screen. Press F10 to complete the deletion or Escape to cancel it. If you press F10, all the text between the deleted format line and the next format line will be realigned according to the settings on whatever format line precedes it in the document.

SEARCHING FOR FORMAT LINES

You can search for format lines just as you searched for text, in order to review, replace, or delete them. You can search in either direction, but case sensitivity does not apply. After you place your cursor where you want the search to begin and specify the search direction, press F6, the Search key. The prompt

SEARCH MODE

will appear on the right side of the status line, and the prompt

SEARCH FOR:

will appear at the bottom of your screen. Press F9, the Format Change key, to search for a format line. Advantage II will start looking for the next format line, and it will place the cursor on the first character after the next format line. At this point, you can change this line, or you can continue to search for other format lines by pressing F6.

To change the line, press F9, make the changes, and press F9 again. Since changing a line ends the search, you need to begin the search anew if you want to find more format lines. To do this, press F6 and then F9.

REPLACING THE FORMAT LINE

Replacing format lines is handled in almost the same way as replacing text. The only difference is that, as with searching for format lines, case sensitivity does not apply. After you place the cursor in the position where you want the search to start, press Shift-F6, the Search and Replace key. Next decide whether you want to go backward or forward, if you want discretionary or global replacement, and whether you want to see replacements displayed on screen. I recommend that you use the discretionary option when replacing format lines—I'll explain why shortly. The prompt

REPLACE MODE

will show in the right corner of the status line.

At the prompt

REPLACE WHAT?

press F9 to instruct Advantage II to replace format lines. Immediately, the default system format line will be displayed at the bottom of your screen, along with the default settings for the line spacing and right margin, with the cursor blinking on it. Now you can change any of the format settings, including tab stops. When you've modified this format line to show all the values that you want to use for replacement, press F10 to begin the procedure.

During this procedure, the first line of the screen instructions say

Search and replace format lines.

indicating that Advantage II will search for all format lines in the specified text. If you have initiated a global replacement process, format lines will be replaced, regardless of whether they are standard ones that appear at the top of every page or special ones that you've set up within the document. I suggest that you select the discretionary option because this allows you to keep special formatting arrangements at selected positions within your document, as well as cancel the replacement operation at every pause (by pressing Escape). If you are executing a global replacement without displaying the replacements on the screen, all the changes will be made before you can save any of the existing formatting.

SPECIAL PRINTING CHARACTERISTICS

Printing variations include darker print, double underscore, and subscripts. These and other features are all created by inserting the control codes (shown in Table 5.2) into the text.

When you enter these symbols, they will show up on your screen, but they will not show up on your printed page. To create any of these special printing effects, you have to enter the appropriate screen symbol before and after the section of text you wish changed. Here are the steps to follow:

1. Position your cursor directly in front of the first character of the block you want to mark and press the Plus key (on the keypad).

2. Enter the appropriate screen symbol in this space.

3. Move to the place in your text where you wish the print mode to end, press the Plus key (on the keypad), and enter the screen symbol.

Note that the screen symbols take up space on your screen, but not on your printout. Thus, if you want columns or other text to line up correctly, take into account the space occupied by screen symbols. Neither the spaces nor the symbols will show up on the printed page (unless you use Quick Print). The symbols are intended only to denote that the text between these symbols will be changed when printed.

PRINT MODES

The *print modes* refer to the appearance of the print on the page. This should not be confused with *typefaces*, which refer to the specific design of the characters.

Function	Symbol
Bold Print	▊
Center	↔
Decimal Tab	▪
Double Underscore	⊥
Draft Print	δ
End Column Group	♦
Enhanced Print	∩
Footer	ƒ
Footnote	♫
Hard Column Break	◀
Hard Space	φ
Header	╫
Indent	→
Merge Code	├
Pause Printer	⌂
Print Pitch Font	P_t
Printer Control Code	μ
Required Page Break	⊥
Return	≪
Section Numbering	○
Shadow Print	╟
Soft Column Break	←
Soft Hyphen	≈
Space as Dot	·

Table 5.2: Control codes

The print modes affect the intensity of the print on the page. The four print modes available in Advantage II, in order of intensity, are draft, enhanced, bold, and shadow print. Figure 5.5 shows examples of these print modes.

The descriptions below are true for most printer but not necessarily for all of them. Printers are almost as complex as microcomputers, and each behaves in its own individual way. Certain terms such as *draft, bold,* and *shadow* print have been commonly understood for years, but new features such as *near letter quality* (NLQ) can change the effects of these older features. When you practice with print modes using Advantage II, start out by using all the default settings of your printer to see how they work with the print settings in the program.

Draft Print

Draft print is the printing mode most frequently used when writing documents. It is produced by a single pass of the print head over the paper. You request draft print with Alt-D, the Draft Print key.

FUNCTION	SYMBOL
Strikeout	+
Subscript	↓
Superscript	↑
Tab	≫

Table 5.2: Control codes (continued)

```
This is text printed in draft print.
This is text printed in enhanced print.
This is text printed in bold print.
This is text printed in shadow print.
```

Figure 5.5: Examples of text written in the four print modes

The system inserts the draft print symbol on the screen. All text subsequent to the symbol will be printed in draft mode. To end draft print, press Alt-N where you wish it to stop. This will cause enhanced print to start. Unless you specify another printing mode, Advantage II will toggle between draft and enhanced print.

Enhanced Print

The printer produces enhanced print with two consecutive passes of the print head on the paper. You specify enhanced print with Alt-N, the Enhanced Print key. The system will insert the enhanced print screen symbol. To end enhanced print, enter the draft print symbol by pressing Alt-D. You can press Alt-N again if you want to obtain enhanced print elsewhere in the document.

Bold Print

The printer produces bold print by printing each character twice before moving on to the next character. This slows the print head and therefore creates a stronger effect than enhanced print which prints the whole line before returning to print it again. To start bold print, use Alt-Z, the Bold Print key. The system will enter the bold print symbol in that space. You end bold print with Alt-Z.

Shadow Print

To produce shadow print, the printer prints each text line as usual with the first pass, and then prints the text line slightly to the right with the second pass. Shadow print is the darkest printing mode available in Advantage II. You initiate shadow print with Alt-X, the Shadow Print key. The system will insert the shadow print symbol. To end shadow print, use Alt-X.

OTHER SCREEN CODES

You can create different features on the printed page with other control codes. Figure 5.6 shows a screen with control codes.

Double Underscore

Double underscoring places a solid double line under everything between the two screen symbols that signify double underscore. As

```
┌─────────────────────────────────────────────────────────┐
│ DOCUMENT: codes         ‖PAGE:   1‖LINE:   9‖COL:   1‖  │
│ ↑1----------»--------------------------------------«    │
│ «                                                        │
│           »Double underscore        ≛«                  │
│     «                                                    │
│           »Strikeout character      ┼«                  │
│     «                                                    │
│           »Subscript                ↓«                  │
│     «                                                    │
│           »Superscript              ↑«                  │
│                                                          │
│                                                          │
│                                                          │
│                                                          │
│                                              S:↑ N:↓    │
└─────────────────────────────────────────────────────────┘
```

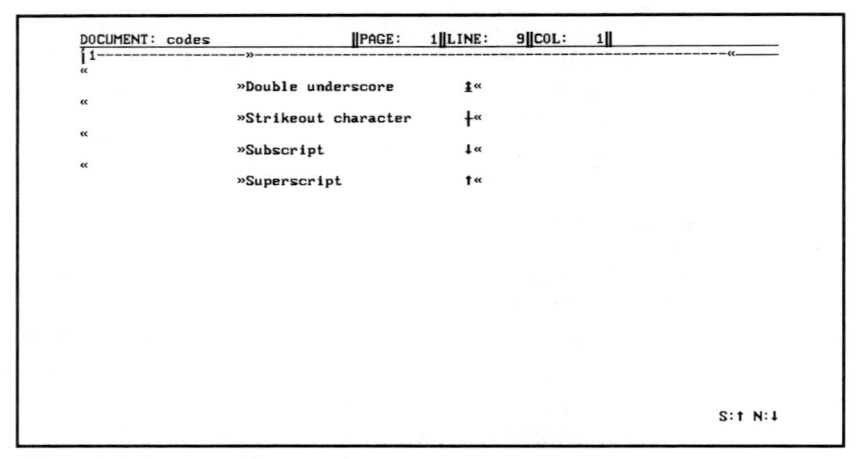

Figure 5.6: Screen with control codes

with all screen symbols, first create a space with the Plus key and then press Ctrl-Hyphen, the Double Underscore key. The system will insert the double underscore symbol. To stop double underscore, use Ctrl-Hyphen.

Strikeout Character

You use strikeout characters to show text to be deleted. This is particularly useful in amending contracts. During negotiations, words, sentences, and even entire clauses may be struck from the proposed contract. Both parties must agree to the changes, and one way to reach clear agreement is to display the parts that both parties have agreed to strike out.

To obtain strikeout characters, use Alt-O, the Strikeout Character key. The system will insert the strikeout character symbol. Strikeout characters can be stopped with Alt-O.

The most common type of strikeout character is the slash (/), but you can change this to any letter, mark, or number available on your keyboard. You change this character in the Modify System Defaults screen (see Appendix A).

Subscript and Superscript

Subscripts and superscripts are generally used with scientific and mathematical symbols, or to denote footnotes that appear at the bottom of a page or at the end of a chapter.

Subscripts fall half a line beneath the standard printing line, and superscripts rise half a line above. The screen symbol for a subscript is ↓, and the symbol for a superscript is ↑. You do not have to first create a space (with the Plus key) to enter the arrows.

To create a subscript, press Alt-W, the Subscript key. The system will insert the ↓ on your screen. Then enter the character or characters you want subscripted. To end the subscript, press Alt-Q, which will bring the ↑ onto your screen.

To create a superscript, press Alt-Q, the Superscript key. The system will insert the ↑. Then enter your superscript. Next, press Alt-W and you will see the ↓ on your screen.

Since subscripting and superscripting require your printer to roll the paper one-half line up and down the platen, make sure your system can handle these features. (If your printer does not support half-line spacing, it may print subscripts and superscripts a full line below or above the text line.)

Hard Spaces

Hard spaces are spaces that separate words but still keep the words on the same text line. Examples of text that benefit from the use of hard spaces are first initial and last name (M. Twain) and dates (May 1, 1985). You create a hard space by placing the cursor in the position where you wish a hard space to occur and pressing Alt-S, the Hard Space key. A hard space symbol will appear in the cursor position.

Revising and Canceling Screen Symbols

You can change any symbol you have entered by going back over it and entering a new symbol. You can also delete any symbol by placing your cursor over it and pressing the Minus key (on the keypad) once or Delete twice. Remember to delete symbols that are used in pairs, or else you will end up with text printed differently than what you expect.

HYPHENATION

After you create a document, you may want to go back and hyphenate certain words that are too long to fit at the end of a line. Advantage II lets you insert *soft hyphens* (ones that separate the syllables of a divided word) to create a more regular right margin. You can insert hyphens on a case-by-case basis, or you can work through the document reorganization window and have Advantage II either insert the hyphens automatically or wait for your decision. A soft hyphen symbol will appear as the hyphen on screen. If you change some of the text and the hyphenated word no longer falls on the right margin, the hyphen will disappear.

Case-by-Case Hyphenation

You create a soft hyphen from the keyboard by placing the cursor over the character in the word that will directly follow the hyphen and pressing Shift-F7, the Hyphen key. A soft hyphen symbol will appear at the cursor position, and the word will be divided at that point.

Hyphenating through Document Reorganization

You can instruct Advantage II how to handle hyphens by selecting the second option on the document reorganization window.

Let's try an example using Memo2. From that document, press Ctrl-2 to bring up the document reorganization window. You can also perform this task quickly using a pull-down menu. Press Alt-L, pull down the Layout menu, and select Document Reorganization. The document reorganization window will appear, as shown in Figure 5.7. Select Hyphenation, and you will be given three choices. The default setting is None, which means that Advantage II will not insert any hyphens in your document. Alt-2 toggles between the two other options: User Selected and Automatic.

When you select either type of hyphenation, you also have to consider the sixth field at the bottom of the screen, Hyphenation Zone Width. This tells Advantage II the largest number of empty spaces to allow between the end of the last word on the line and the right margin (as set on the current format line). The default setting is seven spaces, which means that Advantage II will look for lines that have eight or more spaces between the last character and the right margin. You can change the Hyphenation Zone Width setting by moving the cursor to that field and typing over the current entry.

The User Selected choice allows you to determine exactly where each hyphen should be placed. If you select the Automatic option, Advantage II will insert a hyphen after the last syllable it can squeeze in before the right margin.

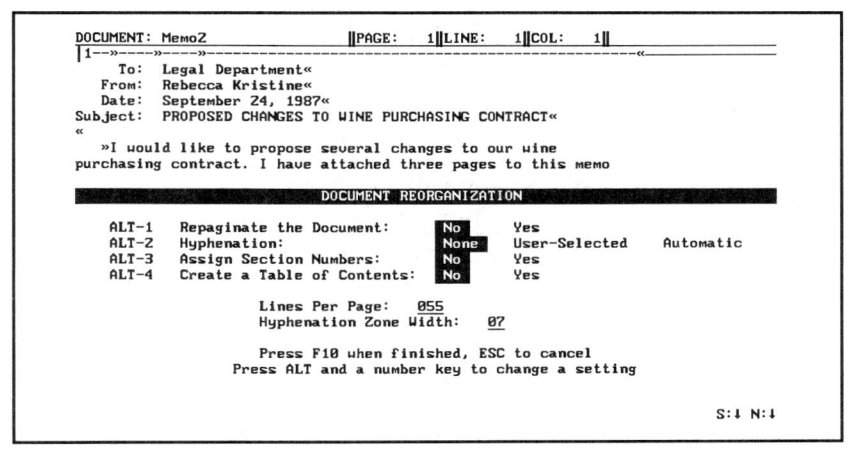

```
DOCUMENT: Memo2                    ||PAGE:   1||LINE:   1||COL:   1||
|1--»----»----»-----------------------------------------«----------
       To:   Legal Department«
     From:   Rebecca Kristine«
     Date:   September 24, 1987«
  Subject:   PROPOSED CHANGES TO WINE PURCHASING CONTRACT«
«
         »I would like to propose several changes to our wine
      purchasing contract. I have attached three pages to this memo
      ════════════════════ DOCUMENT REORGANIZATION ════════════════════
         ALT-1    Repaginate the Document:   No      Yes
         ALT-2    Hyphenation:              None     User-Selected   Automatic
         ALT-3    Assign Section Numbers:    No      Yes
         ALT-4    Create a Table of Contents: No     Yes

                         Lines Per Page:    055
                         Hyphenation Zone Width:   07

                       Press F10 when finished, ESC to cancel
                   Press ALT and a number key to change a setting

                                                                    S:↓ N:↓
```

Figure 5.7: Document reorganization window in Memo2.

User Selected

User-selected hyphenation is a precise procedure, and to perform it correctly can take a considerable amount of time. Begin by moving the light bar to User Selected and pressing F10. If you are using floppy disks, the prompt

INSERT DICTIONARY DISK WITH WEBSTER.HYD IN DRIVE A, PRESS ANY KEY

will appear at the bottom of the screen. Despite what it says about pressing any key to continue, you can still cancel the process by pressing Escape. Insert the proper disk and press a key. Next you will see the prompt

Reorganizing – please wait

at the bottom of the screen. When Advantage II finds the first place where the Hyphenation Zone Width value is exceeded, it will display the discretionary hyphenation window, as shown in Figure 5.8. This window presents seven selections for determining exactly where the hyphen will be placed. The cursor will appear under the first word that can be hyphenated, with the cursor blinking under the place where a hyphen will be inserted if you give Advantage II no more

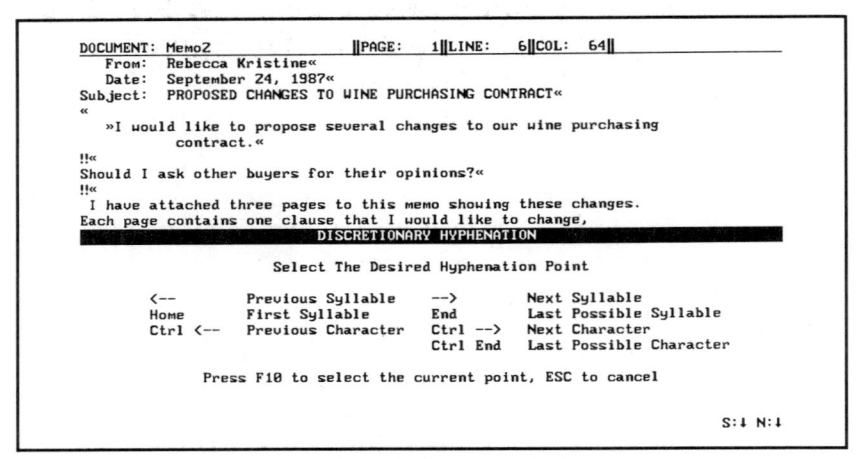

```
DOCUMENT: Memo2           ‖PAGE:    1‖LINE:    6‖COL:   64‖
    From:  Rebecca Kristine«
    Date:  September 24, 1987«
 Subject:  PROPOSED CHANGES TO WINE PURCHASING CONTRACT«
«
       »I would like to propose several changes to our wine purchasing
            contract.«
!!«
Should I ask other buyers for their opinions?«
!!«
 I have attached three pages to this memo showing these changes.
Each page contains one clause that I would like to change,
                        DISCRETIONARY HYPHENATION

                   Select The Desired Hyphenation Point

            <--         Previous Syllable    -->       Next Syllable
            Home        First Syllable       End       Last Possible Syllable
            Ctrl <--    Previous Character   Ctrl -->  Next Character
                                             Ctrl End  Last Possible Character

                 Press F10 to select the current point, ESC to cancel

                                                                    S:1 N:1
```

Figure 5.8: Discretionary hyphenation window in Memo2

instructions. By first word, I mean the first word after the current cursor position, or where you left the cursor when you began the document reorganization process. If you intend to hyphenate an entire document using this method, you will have to start at the beginning of the document.

Continuing with our Memo2 example, the first word to be hyphenated is purchasing, and the cursor appears blinking under the letter i. This is where Advantage II would automatically place a hyphen. You can press F10 to accept this hyphenation or use the keys or key combinations listed in the discretionary hyphenation window to move the cursor to another syllable or character. From the position automatically selected, you can choose to place the hyphen on the preceding or succeeding character, after the last character that will fit before the hyphen and right margin, or after any of the syllable breaks.

After you move the cursor where you want the word to be hyphenated, press F10 to insert the hyphen and move onto the next word that can be hyphenated. You can proceed this way to the end of the document, or you can cancel the procedure by pressing Escape.

Automatic

Selecting the Automatic option tells Advantage II to do all the work of hyphenation for you. Enter a Hyphenation Zone Width (or accept the default), place the light bar on Automatic, and press F10. Advantage II will place all hyphens automatically until it reaches the end of the document or you press Escape. If you press Escape to cancel the operation, all hyphens inserted up to that point will remain in your document unless you edit the document and delete them. You can delete soft hyphens by deleting their screen symbols, as with any other screen code.

PLACE MARKS

If you expect your page numbers to change, you can set place marks instead. As you learned in Chapter 4, place marks are used to mark certain words that should stand out from the rest of the text, such as misspelled words. You can also flag a character or a word if, for example, you want to return to a specific place in your document later, and don't want to spend extra time searching for this place. All you have to do is issue a command to go to the place mark—and be sparing in your use of place marks.

There are three things you can do with place marks:

- Set them in text
- Go to them directly
- Clear them from text

Setting Place Marks

To set a place mark, make sure the cursor is on the character you want to flag. Press Alt-F1, the Set Place Mark key, and a place mark will be set at that place in your document. No symbol will appear, but the character the cursor was on will begin to blink on and off. You can continue writing and editing your document after you set a place mark.

You can set as many place marks in a document as you want, but the more place marks you use, the less effective they become. A place mark is intended to mark a special location, perhaps a place where you hope to return to clear up a confused idea, or where you want to insert additional text. Place marks are useful when you can go to them more quickly than you can by flipping through the pages, and yet circumvent the more specific criteria for a text search. You'll want to postpone your spelling check until you've taken care of the special place marks you've set. Otherwise, you won't be able to distinguish between place marks, since they all look and act the same.

Go to a Place Mark

You can go directly to a place mark by pressing Ctrl-F1, the Go to Place Mark key. This function behaves the same as a discretionary search (see Chapter 3). It only searches in a forward direction, not backward, and it will only go to the next place mark. If you want to go to subsequent place marks, press Ctrl-F1 until you arrive at the one you are looking for.

Clearing Place Marks

You can clear place marks either individually or globally. To clear one place mark at a time, move the cursor to the place mark by pressing Ctrl-F1, and then press Alt-F1, the Set Place Mark key. This key acts as a toggle and will unflag a previously set place mark. You can press Alt-F1 again if you wish to reset the place mark.

To clear all place marks in a document, start anywhere in the document that contains the place marks you want to clear. Press Alt-Y, the Clear All Place Marks key, and the prompt

CLEARING ALL PLACE MARKS

will appear on the right side of the status line. In addition, another prompt

<<<PLEASE WAIT>>>

will appear at the bottom of the screen. The cursor will move to the beginning of the document and start clearing place marks. The document will disappear from the screen during the procedure. When all place marks are cleared, the prompt disappears, and the cursor will move to the beginning of the page where you started to clear the place marks.

If you want to halt the clearing process before it has finished, press Escape. The clearing process moves slowly enough so that you can follow it. All the place marks up to the point where you pressed Escape will be cleared, but all subsequent place marks will remain. If you exit from the document without clearing all place marks, they will remain in your document.

UNDERLINING

Underlining, while similar in appearance to double underscoring, is not created with a screen symbol. There are three different ways to underline text: character by character, alphanumerically, or textually. Regardless of the way you enter underlining, no symbols will appear on the screen. The underlined text will be highlighted on your display screen whether you have a color or a monochrome monitor.

Character by Character

Underlining character by character is the simplest method. Move your cursor to the first character you wish to underline and press Shift-Hyphen, just as you would on a standard typewriter. This will place a line under your chosen character. You can underline more quickly by holding down these keys and activating the autorepeat mode.

Alphanumeric

Alphanumeric underlining places a line under all letters and numbers, but not beneath spaces, punctuation marks, or other characters. To begin this underlining, press Alt-Plus (use the Plus key on the keypad). Press Alt-Plus again to stop alphanumeric underlining.

Text Underlining

Everything is underlined with text underlining, including spaces and punctuation. To begin this underlining, press Alt-Hyphen where you want it to start, and press Alt-Hyphen again to stop.

Revising and Canceling Underlining

All underlining can be revised at any time you want using standard editing keys. You can also erase any or all of your underlining by pressing Shift-Hyphen over the part of your text that has been underlined.

PAGE FORMATTING

The concept of a page is an important one in MultiMate Advantage II. The program saves a page at a time, controls some cursor movements a page at a time, and handles some formatting features a page at a time. Such formatting features are page length, page break, and page numbers, as well as techniques for combining pages, going to a specific page, and repaginating a document. Thus, it is important to pay attention to how you define a page. You learned how to specify the number of printed lines per page in the Edit Document Defaults screen, discussed earlier in this chapter. Now we'll discuss the other aspects of page formatting.

PAGE LENGTH

To set page length while you are editing a document, press Alt-F2. The prompt

LINES PER PAGE: [55]

will appear in the lower left corner of the screen. The default value for page length is 55 lines, which assumes 11-inch paper. You can change the page length by entering any number between 1 and 199. Just type over the existing number. You cannot create a page with more than 199 lines on it, which is a little less than three single-spaced pages. Once you have entered the new line count, press Return to set it.

You can specify automatic page breaks in the Document Print Options screen. Automatic page breaks always limit the page length to the number specified in the *Number of lines per page* field in the Modify Document Defaults screen. You can review the settings in this screen by exiting from the document, and on the main menu selecting

7) System and Document Defaults

(or pressing Alt-7 from the document). Press Return, and then select

4. Edit Document Defaults

to view the Modify Document Defaults screen.

You can also change the line length through the document reorganization window (Figure 5.7). The default setting in the fifth field is 55. Enter a new number if you want to change the line length in the current document. Pressing Return toggles between the fifth and sixth fields in the window.

PAGE BREAK

Advantage II will issue page breaks according to the default value for lines per page, or according to settings you have changed within the program. It is always possible to create a page break on any page in the document that is less than the specified line length by pressing F2, the Page Break key.

To see how page breaks work, practice this feature on the text in Memo2. When the document is displayed on your screen, press End to move the cursor to the first blank line after the text. The cursor position on the status line should show

> PAGE: 1 LINE: 33 COL: 1

Press F2, and the prompt

> <<PLEASE WAIT>>

will appear at the bottom of the screen. In a few moments, the text on your screen will disappear and nothing but the page format line will show on the screen. Take a close look at the page number. It has changed to 2. You are now on the second page of Memo2, and you have done this by breaking the page. Since no text was moved, page 1 will print out as you wrote it.

Breaking a Page in the Middle of Text

You can also break a page in the middle. Whenever you break a page in the middle, whether you are separating text or not, it is advisable to press Return at the point just ahead of where you want to break the page. This will guarantee that text intended for the current page will not spill over to the new page. Then, press F2 to create the page break.

COMBINING PAGES

You can combine two pages to make one page using either of two methods, depending upon whether the pages to be joined are adjacent or separated by one or more intervening pages.

Adjacent Pages

If you want to join adjacent pages, go to the first page you want to combine and move the cursor to the end of that page by pressing Ctrl-End. Then, press Shift-F2, the Page Combine key. This will erase the page break between the page you are on and the following page, and combine them into one long page. All format lines on both pages will be retained and their original settings kept intact. If the page format line at the top of the second page was different from that on the first page, the second page format line will also be displayed. (Generally, only one page format line is allowed on each page.) When you combine pages, you might want to scroll through the new combined page and review whatever format lines exist, to ascertain exactly what formatting features have changed in the new arrangement.

Nonadjacent Pages

If you wish to combine two or more pages that are not adjacent, you will have to resort to the move function, which was discussed in Chapter 3. Remember that there is a 199-line limit per page in MultiMate Advantage II.

GO TO PAGE

When you are working on very long documents, you may want to take a look at the text on a page that is far away from the one you are working on. You can move to any page by using the cursor-movement keys, but you will probably find the Go to Page function more helpful, provided you know the page number.

Press F1 to begin the Go to Page function. The prompt

    GO TO PAGE? [   ]

will appear in the lower left corner of the screen. The cursor will be blinking in the first of three positions inside the prompt box. You can enter a page number from 001 to 999. After you enter the page number, press Return. Advantage II will place the cursor on the first character of the page you requested.

Instead of entering a page number, you can press Home or End.

Home will take you to the first page of your document, and End will take you to the last page of your document.

If the prompt

- INVALID PAGE NUMBER -

appears at the bottom left corner of your screen, you have entered a page number that is greater than the last page of your document. Press Escape to start over again. In case you made changes to the current page, the prompt

Do you wish to escape without saving this page? (Y/N)

will appear at the bottom of the screen. Answer N if you want to save the changes and remain in the document.

PAGE NUMBERS

The correct page numbers of a document will always be maintained by Advantage II, and they will be displayed on the status line. It is your choice, however, whether you want these page numbers printed on paper or not. You can have page numbers printed on the page automatically, or you can enter them yourself.

Automatic Page Numbering

Page numbers are recorded to disk automatically. If you want these numbers to appear on the page, first you have to decide whether you want them to appear at the top of the page (as headers) or the bottom of the page (as footers).

The steps for creating page numbers are as follows:

1. Place the cursor on the page where you wish numbering to start. In most cases, this will be page 1.

2. Press Alt-H to create a header, or Alt-F to create a footer.

3. Press Return.

4. Enter the pound sign (#) as a place marker for the page numbers.

5. Press Alt-H to complete the header, or Alt-F to complete the footer.

See the section on headers and footers later in this chapter for instructions on how to further modify page numbering.

Arbitrary Page Numbering

You can enter page numbers that are different from the page numbers generated by Advantage II. You must first create a header or a footer, depending upon where you want the page numbers to be displayed. Then you enter the actual page number to be displayed. You create a header or a footer and specify a page number for each page.

REPAGINATION

When you add or subtract text from an existing page, the page length will change. This also happens when you combine pages, or create two pages where there was one before. In these cases, you should repaginate the document before you print it so that all its pages conform to the standard settings.

To repaginate, move the cursor to the beginning of the document, or to the beginning of the page where you want to start standardizing the line count. Now press Ctrl-F2. The document reorganization window will appear, as shown in Figure 5.7. Press Alt-1 to toggle the light bar from No to Yes for Repaginate the Document, the first option in the window.

If you wish to cancel the repaginate function at this point, press Escape. This will return you to your document as if nothing has happened. You can return to the window any time you wish by starting the process over again.

To repaginate, press F10. A prompt will appear in the middle of the bottom of the screen

Reorganizing - Please Wait

while repagination proceeds, deleting old page breaks and inserting new ones to accommodate the new line length.

Remember, you should always repaginate a document after you edit it and before you print it.

REQUIRED PAGE BREAK

If you repaginate, but you still want to maintain the original format of selected pages, you can insert a required page break. You will want to do this when text and a reference, such as a table or a list, must appear on the same page. To insert a required page break, place the cursor where you want the mandatory page break to occur. Then press Alt-B for break, which inserts a required page break symbol in the document and places a copy of the current format line beneath it, signifying the new page. The cursor will appear in the first position of this new page.

To delete a required page break, place the cursor over the symbol and press the Minus key on the numeric keypad. Then press Shift-F2, the Page Combine key, to rejoin the two pages and delete the format line of the page that was just created.

A required page break setting overrides the standard page-length setting. You should always repaginate a document after you edit it because some pages might contain more text lines than the default limit of 55, while other pages may contain less. Repagination will balance text so that all the pages are within the limits of the default setting, except where a required page break forces more text on a page or ends a page short of the 55 default lines.

FOOTNOTES AND ENDNOTES

A footnote appears at the bottom of a page and refers to text on that page. An endnote appears at the end of some text (such as at the end of a chapter, a section, or an entire document), and refers back to that text. The referenced text and the notes are associated by matching numbers, and the notes are numbered sequentially. Footnotes are handled by Advantage II as a special kind of paragraph on the page; endnotes are grouped together and placed on separate pages. Documents in Advantage II can contain either footnotes or endnotes, but not both.

CREATING FOOTNOTES

Footnotes and endnotes are created the same way. Their placement in the document as footnotes or endnotes is determined by a setting in the Modify Document Defaults screen (see details of this screen earlier in this chapter). The default setting is for footnotes. As an example, we will create a footnote, and then later change it to an endnote.

We'll begin by creating a footnote on the second page of Memo2. When the memo is displayed on the Document screen, press Ctrl-PgDn to move the cursor to the second page.

To create a footnote, first write the text that the footnote will refer to, then press Alt-V. For our example, press Alt-V in the sentence under CLAUSE 4: PAYMENTS (after *buy*). The text for Memo2 will disappear from the screen, and the footnote screen will appear in its place, as shown in Figure 5.9. This window is similar to the Document screen, except that the word FOOTNOTE has replaced the PAGE marker on the status line and you can see the footnote separator.

The separator is the graphic line that will appear in your printed document to separate text from the footnote references. You can view the separator when you are in the footnote window by pressing Alt-H, the Footnote Format Line/Separator key. The system format line for the current document will appear, along with another line in the body of the screen. This line of dashes is called the *footnote separator,* and the default setting is 25 dashes long. You can extend the length of the separator to column 80 for the maximum length, or you can erase it entirely. After you have changed the separator, press F10 to set it. You will next see the prompt

Do you want this separator to be the system default? (Y/N)

```
DOCUMENT: Memo2                    ||FOOTNOTE ||LINE:    1||COL:   22||
|1..»....»....».........................................................«
Act repealed in 1978.









                                                               S:↑ N:↓
```

Figure 5.9: Footnote window in memo2

at the bottom of your screen. Answering Y will set the separator as the standard for all other documents until you edit the separator again. Answering N will make the current separator valid only for the rest of the current document.

If you press Escape when the separator is showing, the prompt

Do you wish to escape without saving this separator? (Y/N)

will appear at the bottom of your screen. Answering Y will cause the separator to disappear, although you will remain within the footnote window. Answering N will save the currently displayed separator for the current footnote.

If you press Escape a second time, the prompt

Do you wish to escape without saving this footnote? (Y/N)

will appear at the bottom of your screen. Answering Y will return you to the place in your document where you were when you first pressed Alt-V to open the footnote window. Answering N will record the current footnote to disk, and the footnote window will remain on the screen.

When you create a footnote, you are actually creating a new, separate file on your document disk. This footnote file is given the special file name extension .FNT. When the document is printed, or when you want to view the text in the footnote, this file is accessed by Advantage II.

Notice that the footnote window has its own format line. You can set tab stops, line spacing, and right margins in your footnotes that are different from those in the body of your document. Footnotes and endnotes have the same symbol, a musical note. You can have up to three footnotes on a page.

Advantage II will number the footnotes automatically, and keep them in order whenever you repaginate the document. The footnote text will not appear on your screen except when you move the cursor over the footnote symbol and press Alt-V, the Footnote key. However, the footnote text will always appear on your printed page.

In the footnote window, the cursor will be blinking in the first space to the right of the footnote symbol. Type the text

Act repealed in 1978.

You can insert and delete footnote text as if it were normal document text. You cannot write a footnote that is longer than eight text lines, however. If your text spills past the end of the eighth line, it will disappear from the screen. You can modify the preceding text, deleting some of it, to bring the lost text back into the footnote window. In any case, only the text in the first eight lines will be printed.

When you have entered the footnote text as you want it to appear, press Alt-V a second time. The window will disappear and you will see the footnote symbol, a musical note, following its text reference. This symbol will not appear when you print the document. Instead, a number will designate the footnote, and this number will appear in the proper place. Advantage II will always begin by numbering the first footnote with the number 1, and each succeeding footnote with an incrementally higher number. You can begin numbering footnotes with another number by changing the setting Starting Footnote Numbers [001-749] in the Document Print Options screen. The maximum number of footnotes or endnotes allowed in a document is 250, however, you can still print footnote reference numbers up to 749.

To review, here are the steps for creating a footnote.

1. Place your cursor in the text where you want the footnote number to appear.
2. Press Alt-V.
3. Type the footnote (up to eight lines).
4. Press Alt-V a second time.

Another way to create footnotes is by using a pull-down menu. Here are the steps for that method:

1. Make sure that your cursor is in the position where you want the footnote reference number to appear, then press Alt-L to access the pull-down menu interface.
2. Move the light bar to the option marked SPECIAL.
3. Press F to move the light bar over Footnotes, or move the light bar down by pressing ↓ three times. The prompt

    Press F10 to select. Enter footnote text. Press F10 when finished

appears at the bottom of the screen.

4. Press F10 to display the footnote window.
5. Type the footnote text.
6. Press F10 again.

Footnote Format Line

The footnote format line can be changed in the same way other format lines are changed. Press F9 to move the cursor onto the footnote format line. Make your changes. Line spacing, tab marks, and right margin settings are identical to those in other format lines. Press F10 to save the changes and move the cursor back into the footnote text.

Editing Footnotes

The text of the footnote does not appear on your Document screen. To look at the footnote, move the cursor to the footnote symbol. Press Alt-V, which opens the footnote window and displays the footnote text you entered last time. You can change the text anytime you wish, using the same commands as for regular text. One exception is that you cannot copy text outside of the footnote window. When you've finished editing, press Alt-V.

Deleting Footnotes

A footnote is easy to delete. All you have to do is place the cursor directly under the footnote symbol that marks the footnote you wish to delete, and press the Minus key on the numeric keypad. When the symbol disappears, the footnote attached to it also disappears. If you have several footnotes in your document, you may want to check that you're deleting the footnote you intend to by pressing Alt-V, which will show you the footnote window. Then press Escape to return to your text, and proceed with the deletion.

CREATING ENDNOTES

Creating endnotes requires two additional steps: you must place note symbols on the last page of the document and change the

Footnotes/Endnotes field in the Modify Document Default screen from F to E. The last page of a document can be either the last page of the text, or a final page just for endnotes. When you have determined the last page in your document, place the cursor in the position where you want the first endnote to appear and press Ctrl-J, the Endnote key. A musical symbol will appear in that place, with a page break immediately following. The only thing different about an endnote symbol is its placement within the document. You should continue to place additional note symbols corresponding to the number of endnotes you want to display.

Changing between Footnotes and Endnotes

To change footnotes into endnotes, place note symbols using Ctrl-J, the Endnote key, at the end of your document and create endnote symbols at the places where you want the endnotes to appear. Make sure that the setting in the Modify Document Defaults screen has been changed to E for endnotes. This setting overrides all other instructions.

To change endnotes into footnotes, delete the note symbols that appear at the end of the document and make sure that the Footnote/Endnote setting in the Modify Document Defaults screen has been changed to F for footnotes.

HEADERS AND FOOTERS

Headers and footers are lines of text that appear at the top or bottom of every page or of several pages in your document. They are useful tools for keeping the reader's eye on book titles, chapter headings, or document section titles that carry over for several pages. You also need to use these tools for numbering your pages. You'll want to keep your headers and footers uncluttered as well as informative. The question of whether to put this information at the top of a page, in a header, or at the bottom of a page, in a footer, is up to you. You should consider the final page layout of your document before you make these decisions. You should consider such things as whether your document will be printed on both sides of the page, in which case you might want page numbers to appear on the outside margins of each facing page, and whether you are going to use footnotes, in which case you will probably want to place all other information at the top of the page. These are aesthetic considerations that can enhance your document or detract from it. Additionally, the kind of document you are writing can determine your page layout considerations. A memo designed for small circulation among colleagues will need less enhancement than a presentation intended to be read by anonymous stockholders.

Headers and footers, even though they remain distinct from the body of text in a document, are controlled by all the same settings as are the body of text. This means that the settings in the Modify Document Defaults screen and the Print Parameters for Document screen will determine where the text in headers and footers appears. As an example, when you print a document with a header in it, the header will begin on the first line as determined by the Top Margin setting on the Print Parameters for Document screen. If you leave this setting at the default of zero, the header will appear at the very top of the page. A setting of 6 will place the header six lines from the top. If you want blank lines between the header or footer and the text, enter them as part of the body of the header or footer.

Headers and footers are handled in two ways: associated with the text, or associated with the page. You can declare whether you want the headers or footers of a document to be text-associated or page-associated on the Modify Document Defaults screen, discussed at the beginning of this chapter. A *text-associated* header or footer is the same on every page of the document—a book title, for example. If you repaginate the document, the title will still appear on each page.

A *page-associated* header or footer must remain on a specific page or pages. For example, a chapter title or a section heading will be printed only on specific pages, and should not be reshuffled to other pages if you repaginate the entire document.

Creating Headers and Footers

Headers and footers are created in practically the same way, and they are as easy to create as footnotes. Here are the steps:

1. Move the cursor to the top (or bottom) of the page, wherever you want the header (or footer) to appear.

2. Press Alt-H for a header (or Alt-F for a footer).

3. Press Return.

4. Type the header (or footer) text (up to five lines).

5. Press Return.

6. Press Alt-H for a header (or Alt-F for a footer).

7. Press Return.

As an example, let's place a header in Memo2. Move the cursor to the top of the first page. Press Alt-H, the Header key. As soon as you do this, the header symbol will appear at the top left margin of the page. Press Return, and type the following text:

CONTRACT REVISIONS Page #

Press Return a second time. End the header function by pressing Alt-H a second time and then Return. This ensures that an empty line will appear between the bottom of the header and the first line of text on the page.

Now create a footer in Memo2. Move the cursor to the end of the first page, press Alt-F and Return, and enter the following text:

CONTRACT REVISIONS Page #

Press Return and Alt-F.

When you enter *Page #* in a header or footer, the program will enter sequential page numbers upon repagination. See the Page Numbers section, earlier in this chapter.

Placing Headers and Footers on Alternate Pages

You can make sure that a header or a footer will appear on only even- or odd-numbered pages by creating an *empty header* or *empty footer* on the first page of the sequence you wish to cancel. Thus, if you wish to cancel headers on even-numbered pages, create an empty header on the first even-numbered page where you want the header to stop. You create an empty header or footer just as you do a normal one, only you do not enter any text. A header will register in the program, but no text will be printed.

As an example, let's enter an empty header at the top of page 3 of Memo2. Move the cursor to the top of the page and press Alt-H, Return, Alt-H, and Return. Now enter an empty footer on the bottom of page 2. Move the cursor to the bottom of the page and press Alt-F, Return, Alt-F, and Return. Since the text in both your header and footer is identical, it can appear as a header on even-numbered pages and as a footer on odd-numbered pages.

Printing Date, Time, and Page Numbers Automatically

You can have the date and time when you printed the document appear in a header or a footer. Your computer will have to contain a clock and calendar to issue the date and time data. It is also possible to print the current page number, a slash, and the last page number of the document. This is a method of ensuring that no pages have been misplaced from the end of the document.

To print this data in your document, you have to place *system print* commands in the header or footer. You specify system print commands by typing them in capital letters surrounded by ampersands.

&DATE&
&TIME&
&PAGE&/&LPAGE&

They will appear wherever you place them in the header or footer.

Canceling Headers and Footers

To cancel a header or a footer, place the cursor on the header or footer symbol and press the Minus key.

COMMENTS

A new feature in Advantage II, called *Comments,* contains elements of both formatting and printing (the subject of our next chapter). Comments are text in a document that you can choose not to print. They provide a means to add elements without actually inserting new text into the document. For example, editors can use comments to record their ideas when reviewing a document

To add comments to a document in Advantage II is to truly benefit from electronic word processing. The comments will always appear on screen, both when you create the document and when you edit it. When it's time to print the document, however, you can choose either to print the comments along with the rest of the text, or else print the text alone without them.

CREATING COMMENTS

Comments are created in the insert mode. First place the cursor where you want the comments to begin. Next press the Insert key, and when the INSERT prompt appears on the status line, press Return to move the cursor to the first column on the next line. Now press Ctrl-[, the Comments key, and the Comments symbol, two exclamation points side by side (!!), will appear in the first space. Press Return again to begin the comment on a line of its own. Enter the text of the comment, then press Return and Ctrl-[a second time to place a second Comments symbol on the line beneath the comment text. Finally, press Return and Insert to exit insert mode and complete the procedure.

The Comments symbols inform Advantage II that the text contained between them is special, and that the comment text lines should not be counted in the document line count. This way, the actual text in the document is not distorted by the presence of the comments.

PRINTING COMMENTS

You determine whether or not to print comments by the Print Comments setting in the Document Print Options screen; it appears in the third group of settings on that screen. The default setting is N for no, which means that the comments will not be printed. Changing this to Y for Yes will cause all comments to be printed.

Because comment text lines are not counted as part of the document text lines, a page of text with more than a few lines of comments will spill over the page break and distort the page-break sequence. Do not expect perfect pages when you print comments.

As an example of using comments, let's enter a comment on the first page of Memo2. At the end of the first sentence of that memo, place the cursor after the period after the word *contract*. Press the Insert key and Return to move your cursor to the beginning of the next line. Press Ctrl-[to insert the side-by-side exclamation points. Now press Return again and enter the text

> **Should I ask other buyers for their opinions?**

Press Return after the question mark, and then press Ctrl-[a second time to mark the end of the Comments text. Now press Return for the last time, and press Insert to exit that mode.

This comment creates quite a gap in the document on the screen, as shown in Figure 5.10

To review, here's the procedure for entering comments:

1. Place your cursor in the position where you want the comments to begin appearing.

2. If you are going to insert comments into existing text, make sure that you are in insert mode.

3. Press Return to create a new blank line.

4. Press Ctrl-[, the Comments key, to enter a Comments screen symbol.

5. Press Return to create a second new blank line.

6. Enter the text of your comment.

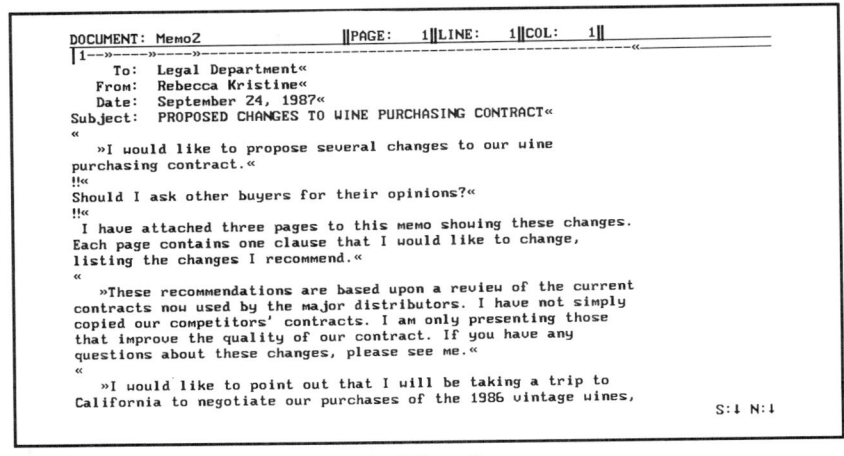

Figure 5.10: Viewing comments in Memo2 on screen

7. Press Return when you are finished entering comment text.

8. Press Ctrl-[a second time to enter a Comments screen symbol.

Now that you've learned how to format your documents, you'll find out what these formatting features look like when you print out the letter in the next chapter.

6

PRINTING

ONLY HALF YOUR WORK IS COMPLETE WHEN ALL you have done is created and edited a word-processed document. Although you can change the format on screen, and move blocks around to see where they look best, most people still prefer to see their words on paper before they can judge whether they wrote what they intended to. In any case, you must print a letter before you can send it.

This chapter will give you a good understanding of printing with MultiMate Advantage II. Do not be surprised if what you see on the printed page does not conform exactly to what you thought you put into a letter when you created it on the screen. After printing the letter, you will learn the details of the settings in the Print Parameters menu, how to change them, and what the changes will mean to your document.

PRINTERS

There are two broad groups of printers: impact printers and laser printers. Impact printers—dot-matrix, daisywheel, and ink-jet printers—comprise the largest number of printers in use today. In this chapter, I assume you are using an impact printer.

Laser printers can also reproduce documents from MultiMate Advantage II, but these printers require special instructions. I will discuss printing with these machines in Chapter 11.

To produce documents on a printer, you must first tell Advantage II which printer to use. This means you have to find the printer file that matches your printer and then instruct Advantage II to use this file. See Appendix B for instructions if you are using Advantage II for the first time.

CAUTION

Once you've installed your printer, pay extra attention to the features you have incorporated into the document you are printing. Notice which ones appear on the printed page, and which ones don't appear. This is the best way of checking which features your printer, or your print wheel, can print on paper. A wide variety of printing features exist, and not all print wheels or print heads carry the full complement of features. For example, a Courier print wheel uses the same character for the number *1* as it does for the lowercase *l*. If you are using Courier, make sure you do not need to distinguish between 1 and l. Check your printer manual for other guidelines.

PRINTING ONE SCREEN OR ONE PAGE AT A TIME

There are three ways to print in the Advantage II program: Quick Print, Hot Print, and through the Print menus.

You will usually use the Print menus to print, since that is the only way to print a document that is longer than one page. Quick Print and Hot Print enable you to print one screen or one page at a time, respectively.

QUICK PRINT

Quick Print provides only a rudimentary printout of what you see on your screen, without any formatting features, although the printout will contain whatever screen symbols were displayed on your screen that your printer can handle. All you need is to have your computer connected to your printer, and both machines plugged into an electrical connection. Quick Print does not require that you install a printer action table (PAT).

Even if your screen resolution is not very good, Quick Print is an excellent way to record screen images on paper. It is also a good way to make sure the electrical connection between your computer and your printer is solid and not subject to interference. All you do is locate the screen you wish to print and press Shift-PrtSc. If nothing happens, you should check several things: did you turn the printer on, and is it connected to your computer with a cable? If nothing happened when you pressed Shift-PrtSc, check your system thoroughly and then press Shift-PrtSc again. Figure 6.1 shows the first page of Letter1 printed with Quick Print.

```
DOCUMENT: Letter1              :PAGE:    1:LINE:    1:COL:    1:
31--/----/----/--------------------------------------------------.DDDDDDDDDDDDDDD
October 7, 1987.
.
.
.
Dave Bynum.
DAVIS BYNUM WINERY.
8875 Westside Road.
Healdsburg, CA  95448.
.
Dear Dave,.
.
    /I am pleased to say that my plans are still on course..I
will be arriving in San Francisco on November 7 on board United
Airlines flight number 256..
.
    /I am also looking forward to your selection of wines. I hope
they come up to the level of the excellent wines we bought last
year..
.
    /This is a busy time of year for you, I realize, because of
the harvest season. But I am looking forward to seeing you at
work. I understand that is a rare sight..
                                                          S:  N:
```

Figure 6.1: Quick Print example

HOT PRINT

Hot Print operates in a similar manner to Quick Print. You can obtain a printout of the page displayed on your screen, with formatting features, without having to go through the Print menus. You determine which page will be printed by placing the cursor anywhere on the page. Whether the cursor is at the beginning or end of the page, the entire page will be printed. To obtain a Hot Print, press Ctrl-PrtSc. You will see the prompt

HOTPRINTING

on the right side of the status line.

There are five differences between Quick Print and Hot Print.

1. When you print a page using Hot Print, you obtain a full document page instead of just a screenful. Note that a screen shows only 23 lines, but a page can have up to 199 lines (the default page length is 55 lines).

2. All formatting features of the document page are printed with Hot Print. The program uses the printer default settings or, if there is a Printer Parameters for Document screen attached to the document, it uses those settings.

3. No screen symbols are printed.

4. To print with Hot Print, you must place the appropriate PAT file on the disk.

5. You can only print documents with Hot Print, but Quick Print will print whatever appears on your screen. A document page printed with Hot Print will look just like a document printed through the Print menus.

PREVIEW PRINTING

Preview mode for printing is a truly remarkable feature introduced with Multimate Advantage II. This printing mode allows you to view an enhanced version of the text of the current document. In preview mode, the text appears on the screen almost as it will when you print it. This is not true WYSIWYG (what you see is what you get), but it is close. No screen symbols show, and the line spacing is correct. By eliminating the screen codes, which can be very distracting, and showing the actual line spacing, which can have a dramatic effect on the appearance of a document, preview mode helps you visualize the printed version. You can preview the current page of the document, another page, a selection of pages, or an entire document.

You can use Quick Print or Hot Print to print out 25 lines of previewed text at a time. It will look very similar to text printed in the normal way, except the left margin will be flush with the left edge of the paper, and the page will have only 25 lines instead of the standard 55 lines (or whatever page length you've set).

Previewing the Current Page

To preview the current page, press Alt-I, the Preview Current Page key. The screen will go blank, and then the beginning 25 lines of the current page will scroll into view and freeze. You see the text on a "clean screen," without any status or format lines or prompts. You can preview the next 25 lines of the same page by pressing any key but Escape to continue. Press Escape to stop previewing the page.

Previewing Multiple Pages or Another Page

To preview multiple pages of a document, press Alt-3, the Preview Multiple Page key, from anywhere within the document that you want to see. The Print Document Options screen for the current document will appear. In the first field on this screen, Start Print at Page Number, enter the number of the first page you want to preview. Enter the number of the last page in the series that you want to see in the second field, Stop Print at Page Number. Next move the cursor to the tenth field, Use:, and enter C for console. This tells Advantage II that you want to use the display screen as the printing device. Finally, press F10 to begin the process. You'll soon see the prompt

> PLEASE WAIT − Searching for Page *xxx* − *Page xxx*

on an otherwise blank screen. This prompt informs you how far along Advantage II is in locating your range of pages to preview. The first *xxx* is the beginning page number to preview, and the second *xxx* is the number of the page currently being processed.

It will take a few moments for the program to work through a long document if you want to preview just the last few pages. After Advantage II finds the pages, the first 25 lines of your selected range will appear on the screen in preview mode. Press any key to continue previewing the text, 25 lines at a time.

To preview a single page that is not the current one, follow the procedure outlined above for multiple pages, and enter that page number in both the Start and Stop Print at Page Number fields on the Print Document Options screen. Advantage II will search for that page, then display its first 25 lines. Again, press a key to preview the next 25 lines.

PRINTING A LETTER

To print a document using the Print menus, begin at the main menu and select

> 3) Print a Document

and you will see the Print a Document screen, shown in Figure 6.2. This screen asks you for the name of the document you wish to print. The screen also shows which drive your document disk is in. The default setting is B, and the letter B should be displayed after the word DRIVE: if you are using floppy disks. If the document you want printed is on another drive, enter that drive designation, then press

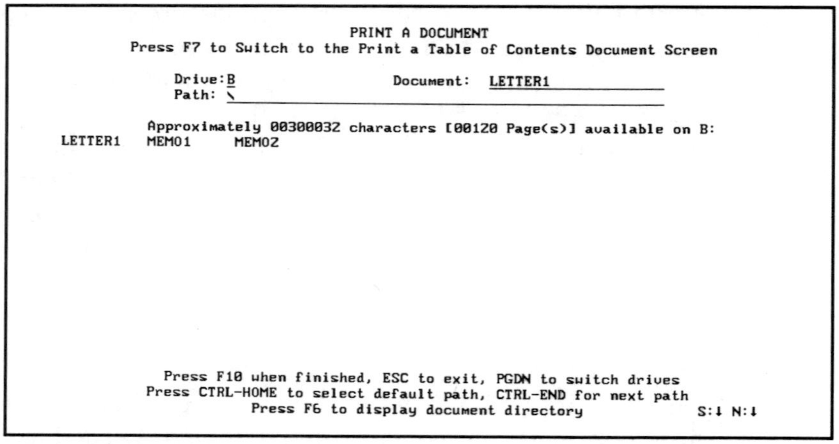

```
                        PRINT A DOCUMENT
         Press F7 to Switch to the Print a Table of Contents Document Screen
              Drive: B                Document:  LETTER1
              Path: \

              Approximately 00300032 characters [00120 Page(s)] available on B:
    LETTER1    MEMO1      MEMO2




              Press F10 when finished, ESC to exit, PGDN to switch drives
              Press CTRL-HOME to select default path, CTRL-END for next path
                    Press F6 to display document directory        S:1 N:1
```

Figure 6.2: Print a Document screen

Return. If appropriate, enter the pathnames in the Path field.

The Print a Document screen also displays the first eight letters of all document titles on the designated drive in the document directory in the middle section of the screen. You should be able to see the three documents you have created so far—Letter1, Memo1, and Memo2—listed in that directory. If there are more files, you can scroll through them. The number of files on a floppy disk is limited to 128 files (MS-DOS's limit) or less, depending on the capacity of the disk.

The first document you will print is Letter1, so enter it in the document name field. Then press Return, which will take you to the next print screen.

The Document Print Options screen, shown in Figure 6.3, displays 29 fields that can change features in any document before you print it. Advantage II provides default settings for most of these fields, but you can change the defaults and enter special information to customize the print settings for each document you print. All the settings are discussed in detail later in this chapter.

Your document name Letter1 should appear in the upper right corner of the Document Print Options screen, along with its drive letter. For the moment, press F10 to accept the default settings on the screen and initiate printing Letter1. After a momentary delay, the printer will start printing your document on paper. When the printing is complete, the main menu will appear on the screen. Once you have the

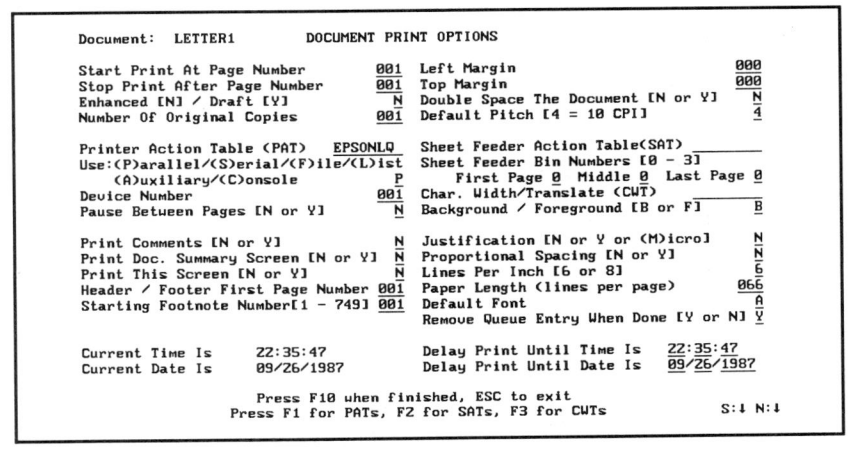

```
Document:  LETTER1          DOCUMENT PRINT OPTIONS

Start Print At Page Number      001   Left Margin                        000
Stop Print After Page Number    001   Top Margin                         000
Enhanced [N] / Draft [Y]          N   Double Space The Document [N or Y]   N
Number Of Original Copies       001   Default Pitch [4 = 10 CPI]           4

Printer Action Table (PAT)   EPSONLQ  Sheet Feeder Action Table(SAT) _____
Use:(P)arallel/(S)erial/(F)ile/(L)ist Sheet Feeder Bin Numbers [0 - 3]
    (A)uxiliary/(C)onsole         P       First Page 0  Middle 0  Last Page 0
Device Number                   001   Char. Width/Translate (CWT)
Pause Between Pages [N or Y]      N   Background / Foreground [B or F]     B

Print Comments [N or Y]           N   Justification [N or Y or (M)icro]    N
Print Doc. Summary Screen [N or Y] N  Proportional Spacing [N or Y]        N
Print This Screen [N or Y]        N   Lines Per Inch [6 or 8]              6
Header / Footer First Page Number 001 Paper Length (lines per page)      066
Starting Footnote Number[1 - 749] 001 Default Font                         A
                                      Remove Queue Entry When Done [Y or N] Y

Current Time Is      22:35:47         Delay Print Until Time Is   22:35:47
Current Date Is      09/26/1987       Delay Print Until Date Is   09/26/1987

              Press F10 when finished, ESC to exit
         Press F1 for PATs, F2 for SATs, F3 for CWTs          S:1 N:1
```

Figure 6.3: Document Print Options screen

finished copy in hand, check it for errors and correct them. Figure 6.4 shows a printout of Letter1.

To summarize, here are the steps for printing a document:

1. Select

   3) Print a Document

   from the main menu and press Return.

2. On the Print a Document screen, enter the drive and pathname (if necessary) and document name to be printed, and press Return to go to the Document Print Options screen.

3. On the Document Print Options screen you can change the print settings, or accept the defaults and start printing by pressing F10.

4. If necessary, press Escape to escape or press Alt-P to have printing pause.

HOW TO STOP THE PRINTER

Before you go any farther, you should know how to stop the printer. You can stop it in two ways: completely, or just get it to

```
September 24, 1987

Dave Bynum
DAVIS BYNUM WINERY
8875 Westside Road
Healdsburg, CA  95448

Dear Dave,

     I am pleased to say that my plans are still on course. I
will be arriving in San Francisco on November 7 on board United
Airlines flight number 256.

     I am also looking forward to your selection of wines. I hope
they come up to the level of the excellent wines we bought last
year.

     This is a busy time of year for you, I realize, because of
the harvest season. But I am looking forward to seeing you at
work. I understand that is a rare sight.

Regards,


Rebecca Kristine
Senior Wine Buyer
```

Figure 6.4: Letter1 printed from Print menus

pause. (These methods do not work with Quick Print or Hot Print; you cannot stop either of these processes until the full screen or page has been printed.)

To stop the printer completely, press Ctrl-Break. The printer might run for a few moments, depending upon the capacity of the printer *buffer* or memory. Then the Printer Queue Control screen will appear. You'll learn more about this screen in Chapter 11. For now, we are concerned with the File Status messages in the lower half of the screen. The Hold field will appear in reverse video, and the cursor will be in the left side of the document directory, blinking beneath the first letter of the title of the document that you stopped printing. Actually, the printing is just on hold. Press 1 to stop printing completely by removing the document from the print cycle, or press 5 to resume printing where you left off. Then press Escape to return to the main menu.

If you turn off the printer, or deactivate it by pressing its Pause or Off Line button, the prompt

PRINTER NEEDS ATTENTION. PRESS ESC TO CONTINUE.

will appear blinking in reverse video in the lower right corner of the screen. You can continue printing if you turn the printer on and press Escape. You can stop the printing process entirely by turning your printer on and off, emptying the printer buffer as Advantage II continues to fill it up, but this is not a recommended procedure.

If you just want the printer to pause for a minute or two, press Alt-P. The printer might run for a few moments while it empties its buffer, but this command will cause the computer and the printer to pause. When you wish to resume printing , press Alt-P again. You might find this procedure helpful if you have to take a phone call in the same room where you are printing.

Advantage II allows you to continue on with other word-processing activities while it prints a document. However, you cannot work on the document that is currently printing. If you try to return to this document, the message

SORRY ... DOCUMENT IS CURRENTLY PRINTING.
UNABLE TO EDIT THE DOCUMENT AT THIS TIME.

will appear in the middle of a screen, along with the prompt

Press any key to return to the Main Menu

SELECTING PRINT PITCH AND FONTS FROM WITHIN A DOCUMENT

Multimate Advantage II allows you to change the pitch and font of the text in your document. *Pitch* refers to the number of text characters per inch. *Font* refers to the form and appearance of the characters.

CHANGING THE PRINT PITCH

The default setting for pitch is pica, or 10 characters per inch. To change the pitch in a document while you are working with it, place your cursor in the exact position where you want the different pitch, and then press Alt-C, the Print Pitch/Font key. When the Pitch/Font symbol (see Table 5.2) appears in the cursor position, press a number from 1 to 9 to change the pitch. Pica pitch is number 4. Entering a lower number will place characters further apart, and entering a higher number will place characters closer together. The following are the print pitch codes:

CODE	CHARACTERS PER INCH
1	5
2	6
3	8.5
4	10
5	12
6	13.2
7	15
8	16.5
9	17.6

Note that if you specify proportional spacing, the program will ignore the print pitch setting.

CHANGING THE PRINT FONT

Examples of different fonts are italics and colors. The number of fonts available to you depends on the capabilities of your printer and the font options provided in the PAT file that communicates with your printer. (Note that even when an option is shown in that file, your printer may not be able to produce it.)

To view a list of the fonts available in the default PAT of your system, press Alt-C, and after the Print Pitch/Font symbol appears, press Shift-?. The fonts and their letter codes will appear in the font directory window in the lower half of your screen. The font directory for the PAT designed for Epson FX printers is shown in Figure 6.5.

To change the font in a document, place the cursor exactly where you want the new font to begin, and press Alt-C. You will see the Pitch/Font symbol at that position. Next enter the letter of the font you want to select (as listed in the PAT for your printer), and then press F10. Press Escape if you want to exit the procedure without making any font changes. You can select more than one font at the same time. For example, the EXPSONFX.PAT, as shown in Figure 6.5, indicates that you can change the font to italics and also print the text in red.

If you are going to be using a different printer for a specific document and want to change the font to a selection on the PAT for that printer, press Return to view the PAT directory. The PAT directory covering a range of Epson printers is shown in Figure 6.6. Enter the PAT file name in the field at the bottom of the screen.

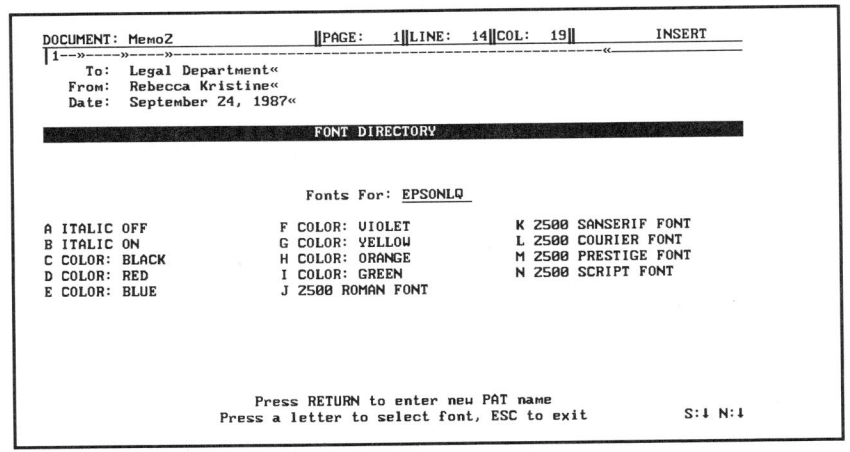

```
DOCUMENT: Memo2              ||PAGE:  1||LINE:  14||COL:  19||         INSERT
|1--»----»----»---------------------------------------------«--
    To:   Legal Department«
    From: Rebecca Kristine«
    Date: September 24, 1987«
                              FONT DIRECTORY


                           Fonts For: EPSONLQ

        A ITALIC OFF         F COLOR: VIOLET      K 2500 SANSERIF FONT
        B ITALIC ON          G COLOR: YELLOW      L 2500 COURIER FONT
        C COLOR: BLACK       H COLOR: ORANGE      M 2500 PRESTIGE FONT
        D COLOR: RED         I COLOR: GREEN       N 2500 SCRIPT FONT
        E COLOR: BLUE        J 2500 ROMAN FONT




                      Press RETURN to enter new PAT name
                   Press a letter to select font, ESC to exit       S:↓ N:↓
```

Figure 6.5: The font directory window for the EXPSONFX.PAT

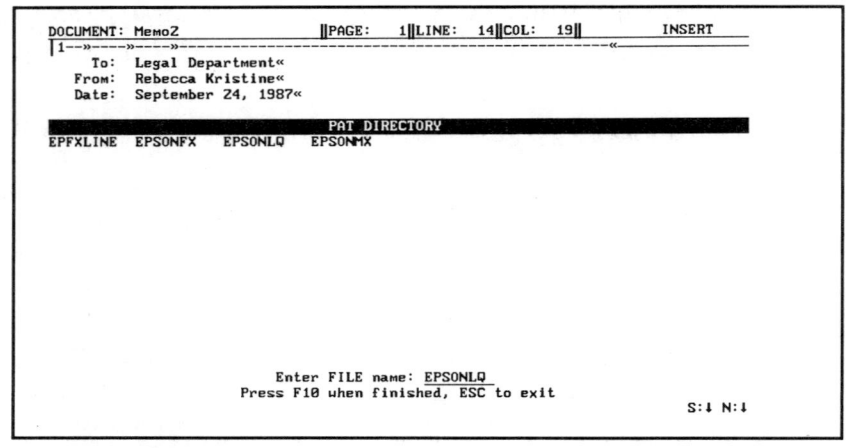

```
DOCUMENT: Memo2              ||PAGE:  1||LINE:  14||COL:  19||        INSERT
|1--»-----»-----»-----------------------------------------«-
     To:  Legal Department«
   From:  Rebecca Kristine«
   Date:  September 24, 1987«
                              PAT DIRECTORY
  EPFXLINE   EPSONFX    EPSONLQ    EPSONMX




                      Enter FILE name: EPSONLQ
                     Press F10 when finished, ESC to exit
                                                              S:1 N:1
```

Figure 6.6: PAT directory with several Epson PATs

If you enter the name of a PAT file that is not on your System Diskette, a beep will sound, and the prompt

PAT not found

will appear at the bottom of the screen. You can only view the fonts of a PAT already copied onto your System Diskette. Pressing Escape will return you to the most recent font directory.

CUSTOMIZING DOCUMENT PRINT OPTIONS

Now that you can see what a document printed with the default settings in the Document Print Options screen looks like, take a closer look at the settings so you can become familiar with them. Note that you can access this screen directly from the Document screen by pressing Alt-3. (Remember to press 3 from the main keyboard, not the numeric keypad.) Thus, you can check print settings while you are working on a document.

Page Numbers

You can specify the beginning and ending page numbers of a document you want to print with the Print at Page Number and the Stop Print at Page Number fields.

In the Start Print at Page Number field, enter the number of the page where you want the printer to start printing. The default setting is 1, since in most cases you will want to start at page 1. To print less than the full document, specify the page number on which the text you want to print begins.

In some cases, you might want the number printed on the page to be different than the number Advantage II gives the page. The maximum number of pages you can have in a single document is 254, but you can specify any page number up to 999. For example, you might want to break a book-length document into several documents, or chapters. If you want the pages numbered sequentially throughout, then you will need to assign new page numbers to each successive chapter. (If you want page numbers above 1000, you will have to create headers or footers with those numbers; see Chapter 5.)

The default setting for the Stop Print at Page Number field is the last page number of your document. You need only change this setting if you want the printer to stop before it gets to the last page. If you want to print only a single page of your document, enter the same number in this field that you entered in the Start Print at Page Number field.

Enhanced/Draft Print

The Enhanced/Draft Print Setting allows you to toggle between the default enhanced printing and the draft printing option. You have explored draft print in Chapter 5. You can also obtain *draft print* from this screen by answering Y; N will result in enhanced print. If you have put any control codes in your document that contradict these answers, the symbols will take precedence over this menu setting.

Number of Original Copies

The Number of Original Copies field allows you to request more than one copy of your document. If you request multiple copies, the printer will finish the first copy completely before it starts on the second. The maximum number is 999.

Margins

You will usually want to change the Left Margin field, which controls the distance from the left margin to the left edge of the paper. The default and minimum setting is 0, which puts the margin at the leftmost edge of a standard 8½-inch wide piece of paper. Changing this setting to 010 moves the left margin of text 10 columns to the right of the paper edge. With the default print pitch of 10 characters per inch, this setting will give you a 1-inch left margin.

You will probably also want to change the default Top Margin setting of 0 lines, which has printing begin at the top edge of the paper. To obtain a standard 1-inch, or 6-line, top margin, enter 006 in this field.

Double Space the Document

The Double Space the Document field allows you to change between the two most common types of line spacing, single and double spacing, without having to change the line spacing in every format line of the document. The default for this setting is N, meaning all spacing instructions contained within the document will be followed. Changing the field entry to Y overrides the document codes and prints all text double-spaced.

Using this option to double space a document tells Advantage II to spread an original single page onto two pages. This means that certain elements of the original single page will appear only once over the two pages. For example, a format line and any headers or footers will appear only on every other page (this also applies to page numbers created as headers or footers).

Default Pitch

You can specify the size of the typeface by entering a number from 1 to 9 in the Default Pitch setting. The most common pitch is pica, or 10 characters per inch, which you obtain by accepting the default, 4. This number is the print pitch code discussed earlier. This feature depends on your printer's capabilities.

Printer Action Table

The Printer Action Table field allows you to specify the printer you will be using to print your documents. You have to load the PAT file for your printer onto your System Diskette or your hard disk, as discussed in Appendix B.

Once the correct PAT file is installed, enter the code name for the table in the Printer Action Table field. You can view the list of available PATs by pressing F1, which will bring up the PAT window. Most printers can use the TTYCRLF PAT that comes installed on the System Diskette. Up to 16 codes for the PATs installed on your System Diskette or hard disk are displayed at the bottom of the Print Parameters screen. If you have loaded more than 16, you can scroll through the list using the Space bar.

If you work in an office where various printers are available, make sure you have installed the PAT files for every machine you might use. This will enable you to go to the first available printer or to use a printer that allows you to print special features. Refer to Appendix B for more information about PATs.

Parallel, Serial, List, Auxiliary, File

You need to specify the method your computer will use to send information to your printer by entering the first letter of Parallel, Serial, List, Auxiliary, or File. Parallel is the standard connection for most printers. Check your printer documentation to find out which method your printer uses.

Device Number

The Device Number field allows you to select one of up to three printers on which you can print your Advantage II documents. You must have the appropriate PAT files transferred to the proper disk for each printer you want to use.

Pause between Pages

The Pause between Pages setting can only be on (Y) or off (N). If you answer Y, the printer will pause after each printed page. One reason to have the printer pause after each page is if you want to feed single sheets of paper into your printer. Pressing F10 will bring up the main menu, and when the program is ready to print the first page, it will sound and display the flashing prompt

> **PRINTER PAUSE BETWEEN PAGES. PRESS ESC TO CONTINUE.**

This pause gives you time to make sure that your printer is ready. Press Escape to print the first page. About halfway through printing the first page, the beep will sound again and the prompt will reappear. Press Escape again to continue printing with the second page. Otherwise, the printer will stop after the first page and not continue until you press Escape. You cannot create or edit a document while you are using printer pause mode.

Sheet Feeder Parameters

In addition to telling the program which kind of printer you are using, you also need to specify if you are going to use a single-sheet feeder machine, and which one it is, in the Sheet Feeder Action Table field.

Some sheet feeders pull pages from a series of paper bins. The First Page field allows you to instruct which bin—1, 2, or 3—the sheet feeder should pull from when it starts. Similarly, Middle and Last Page are the second bin and third bin the sheet feeder will pull from.

Specialized Fields

The Character Translate/Width Table field requests a command that needs to be custom-written and placed within your PAT file. Writing such programs is a task for experienced programmers, but basic instructions are given in Appendix B.

The Header/Footer First Page Number function relates to advanced features of headers, footers, and automatic page numbering. For more details, see the section on headers and footers in Chapter 5.

The Starting Footnote Number field lets you tell the program how to start numbering your footnotes. In some scientific documents, each section would begin a new sequence of numbered footnotes.

Background/Foreground

Printing in the foreground is the default printing method. This means that when you are printing, you cannot use the computer for anything else. Foreground printing is the best method to use when you have instructed the printer to perform particularly complicated procedures; you can obtain Foreground by entering F.

Background printing allows you to edit a document, or do other work on your computer, while a document is being printed. Enter B for background printing.

Print Comments

The Print Comments field allows you to print comments you have inserted in the document (see the section about comments at the end of Chapter 5). The default setting is N, for no. Change it to Y to have the comments print with the document.

Print Document Summary Screen and Print This Screen

Answer Y to Print Doc. Summary screen if you want a copy of the Document Summary screen printed on the page before the document begins printing. Answer Y to Print This Screen if you want a copy of the Document Print Options screen printed before the document. N, for no, is the default setting for both these fields.

Justification and Spacing

Justification refers to the alignment of the text along the right margin. Most typed pages are ragged right, which means text doesn't align on the right edge, and line lengths vary. Enter N if you want your text to be ragged right.

Enter Y if you want right-justified text, in which the right margin is even and the program inserts extra spaces between words to obtain a constant line length. Depending on the line length, right justification can make your text more difficult to read because the spaces can vary widely.

Your third choice for justification is M for micro, which produces right-justified text but places the extra spaces within words. This gives a more balanced appearance to each text line and makes for easier reading. Some printers do not support this feature.

The two choices you have for Lines per Inch are 6 (the standard value) and 8. Experiment with these settings to see how they affect the page length and appearance.

Proportional spacing determines whether each character will have an equivalent amount of space (N for no) as on a typewriter, or will have space proportional to the width of the character (Y for yes). Most typeset material (this book, for instance) uses proportional spacing: i takes up less space than W. This choice is a question of taste, and it also depends upon your printer's capabilities.

Document Page Length

The Document Page Length field is used by the printer to determine the length of each page—that is, the paper size—of your document. The default value is 66 lines for standard 11-inch paper printed at 6 lines per inch.

Default Font

To change the primary font used in your document, change the letter in the Default Font field. Enter the letter that corresponds to the font's code in the PAT that appears in the PAT field on this screen. Single-font printers will use the default setting A. Refer to the section on changing print fonts earlier in this chapter, or to Appendix B, Printer Installation, for more information about fonts.

Remove Queue Entry When Done

A *queue* is a waiting list of documents to be printed. You can leave documents in the printing queue (N for no) in case you want to print them again, or remove them from the queue and make room for more documents (Y for yes).

Time and Date and Delay Print

The computer fills in the Current Time Is field if you have a clock operating in your computer. The time is displayed as HH:MM:SS, which denotes hours, minutes, and seconds.

The Delay Print Until Time Is field allows you to enter a specific time, in the HH:MM:SS format, which will initiate printing if you leave your printer and computer turned on. This function requires a clock connected to the DOS system in your computer.

The Current Date Is field is filled in by your computer, as long as you entered a date when you started your system.

The Delay Print Until Date Is field allows you to enter a specific date in the MM/DD/YY format (American style), to initiate printing if you leave your printer and your computer turned on. This function requires that you enter a date when you start your system, and that your computer has a clock and calendar connected to the DOS system.

PART II

ADVANCED FEATURES

7

Working with Libraries

A LIBRARY IN MULTIMATE ADVANTAGE II CONSISTS OF paragraphs that you use frequently when you write your documents. Such text is also called *boilerplate*. You can create a library for each category of documents you handle. You can use a library to save short passages that you use all the time, such as letterheads and letter closings, as well as names and addresses of people and companies you write to often. You can also save longer items you might not use as often, but that are time consuming to type even the first time, such as product descriptions and contract clauses. The variety of your library entries is determined by what you write and how often you write it. Placing these sections of text in a library for ready use can save you a great deal of time. Employing a library saves you not only the time of recreating text; it also ensures that the text you insert is correct, since you need only check your text for accuracy the first time you use it.

The three basic procedures for working in a library are creating the library file, attaching it to a document, and inserting entries.

CREATING A LIBRARY

To create a library, you begin the same way you do when you create any other kind of document. At the main menu, select

   2) Create a Document

When the Create a Document screen appears, enter the name you want to use to identify the library you are creating. You should put some thought into this name before you enter it. Since you can build as many libraries as you want, you should try to gather as many entries with a similar purpose in the same library as you can. You will probably use some entries more often than others, but the name you give each library should be comprehensive enough to describe all the entries in the library. After you have built several libraries, you will find that a distinctive name for each one helps you find the library you want to use.

For example, say you wish to build a library of phrases and text that you frequently use in your business letters. Enter the name *Buslets,* signifying business letters, for this library. When you are creating a library, you must pass through the Document Summary screen. If you have set up your system to bypass this screen (by changing the setting for Display Document Startup Screens on the Edit System Defaults screen from Y to N), you will have to reset it to create libraries. Even though you have to pass through the Document Summary screen to create a library, do not enter any information on that screen.

When the Document Summary screen for Buslets appears, you'll see the prompt

> When finished, press F10 for document, ESC to exit
> F5 for library (leave screen blank) or SHIFT-F10 for
> Info-Handler

at the bottom of the screen. (Info-Handler refers to data files that serve as a database in Advantage II.) Press F5 without entering anything on this screen. Because you only see the Document Summary screen before you create a library, and not when you enter an existing one, it is pointless to put any information on this screen—you will never see it again.

Creating an Entry

When you press F5, you will see a screen that is blank except for a question at the bottom asking

> Library Entry Name? [   ]—Press F6 for a list of entries

To identify each entry in a library, you are limited to three spaces in which you can enter only letters and numbers. Advantage II distinguishes between uppercase and lowercase letters in library entry names. If you try to enter any character other than letters or numbers, such as a punctuation mark or other symbol, you will hear a beep, and the cursor will still be waiting for you to enter an acceptable character.

When you create these entries, you will be placing them on separate, consecutive pages of your library. Each library can hold up to 254 entries, which is the page limit of any Advantage II document.

WORKING WITH LIBRARIES *159*

Although a library entry can be only one page long, each entry can contain up to 150 lines of text.

After you have entered the name, press Return. The entry name will appear in the status line at the top of your screen, taking the place of what used to be the the page number on the Document screen. There are two other changes between the library entry document screen and the Document screen. In place of the word *DOCUMENT,* you will now see the word *LIBRARY,* and instead of the word *PAGE,* you will see the word *ENTRY.* Figure 7.1 shows the library entry status line.

Before you start typing the text of the entry, make sure that the format line conforms to the standard format line of your business letters. This entry will be copied to the document exactly as it appears on the library entry document screen, but if the format lines differ, the library entry will be reformatted to conform to the document's settings. For example, if you prefer the closings of your letters to be flush with the right margin, you will have to create them that way.

When you have finished creating the entry, you have two choices.

1. You can continue creating more entries: press F2, the Page Break key, to create a new page for the next entry.

2. You can save this new entry and exit from the current library; press F10, the Save/Exit key.

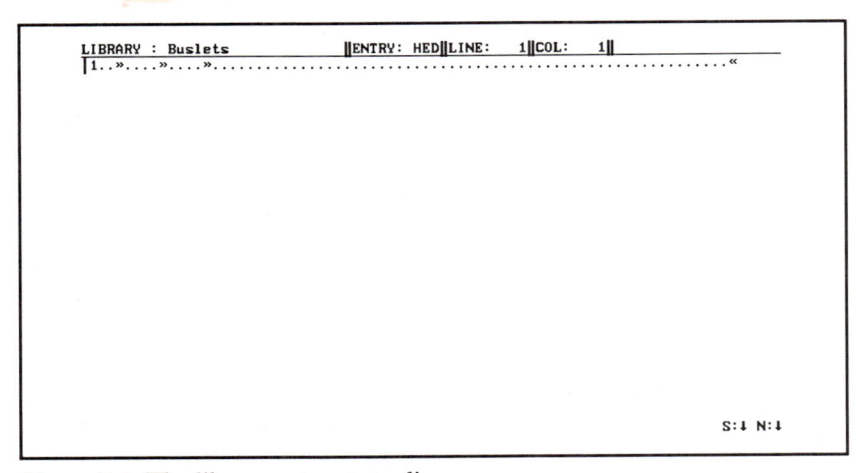

```
LIBRARY : Buslets           ||ENTRY: HED||LINE:    1||COL:    1||
|1..»....».....................................................«
                                                          S:↓ N:↓
```

Figure 7.1: The library entry status line

Examples

Suppose you want to create three entries for the library called Buslets:

- A letterhead
- A memo reference
- A letter closing

For the letterhead, follow the steps for creating a library.

1. At the main menu, select

   2) Create a Document
2. Enter the library name *Buslets* and press Return.
3. Press F5, the Library key.
4. At the prompt

   Library Entry Name? [   ]—Press Shift-F6 for a list of entries

   enter the name of the first library entry, HED (which stands for letterhead), and press Return.

You will then see the entry name HED in the middle of the status line on your library entry document screen. This name is a good example of a mnemonic name to select either for a library or for an entry in that library. The library is Buslets, so all entries should be about business letters. HED doesn't make much sense by itself, but when you remember that it is a part of the Buslets library, *heading* is the first word that comes to mind.

If you want to add a second letterhead later, you can use the name *Hed,* since entry names are case-sensitive. This means you could enter nine letterheads with the name *HED* in the nine possible combinations of uppercase and lowercase letters—though it might be more reasonable to use LH1, LH2, or LHa, LHb, for instance.

At the library entry document screen, enter the following lines of text and center both of them so that they look like this:

WINES EN MASSE
1234 Boston Post Road   Mamaroneck, NY 10543   914-456-7890

WORKING WITH LIBRARIES   *161*

This is the entire entry for HED. Center each line in this entry by pressing F3 before typing the first character. Make sure you press Return after the second line. You need not always press Return after entering the last line of text, but it is advisable. The hard carriage-return symbols of an entry will always show on the screen. These become part of the document into which the entry is inserted, and they are symbols you always want to keep track of. In most cases, a library entry will be a self-contained section of text, such as HED, and a hard carriage return will be required to maintain the proper sequence of text lines that follow the heading.

HED is now your first library entry. To move to the next entry, you move to the next page by pressing F2, the Page Break key. The prompt

    <<<PLEASE WAIT>>>

will appear at the bottom of the screen while Advantage II creates a second page, and then Advantage II will ask you to enter the name of the new entry. If you try to enter HED as the name of the second entry, you will hear a beep, indicating that Advantage II will not allow you to use this name. Each entry name in a particular library must be unique. Enter the name *Mem* for memo for the second entry, and type the following words:

    from the desk of
    Rebecca Kristine

Press Return. This entry need not be centered. Since all entries will be transferred exactly as you create them, you must have a clear idea of what the entry will look like in relation to the complete document.

Now press F2 to create the third entry. Call this entry END, for the closing of a business letter. Type

    Sincerely,

and press Return four times, then type

    Rebecca Kristine
    Senior Wine Buyer

and press Return. The three entries HED, Mem, and END now comprise the library Buslets.

To save these entries and exit from the library, press F10. If you change your mind while creating a library entry, press Escape, and then enter Y at the prompt to cancel the entry.

ATTACHING A LIBRARY

Creating a library is only half the job of working in the library. You haven't accomplished anything useful until you create a working document in which to use the library entries repeatedly. There is no point in creating a library unless you use it often enough to justify the extra effort of creating it.

To use the library, you must first attach the library to the document that will receive one or more entries from the library. Go to the document that will receive the library entries, and place your cursor in the position where the library text will appear. Next, attach the library to the document by pressing Shift-F5, the Library Attachment key. The prompt

```
Drive:   Library Document:
Path:\
```

will appear at the bottom of the screen. Specify the library you want by entering the library name, which can have up to eight characters. Advantage II will look for this library on the drive shown in the prompt. (If the library is in another drive, you can change to that drive by pressing the ← key, which will move the cursor to the drive field. After you have entered the correct drive, press Return.)

If you enter the name of a library that doesn't exist on the specified drive, or a drive that doesn't contain the library name you entered, the prompt

--UNABLE TO FIND LIBRARY--Press any key to continue

will appear at the bottom of your screen.

If you press F5 (the Library key) instead of Shift-F5 (the Library Attachment key) to attach a library, the prompt

--NO LIBRARY CURRENTLY ATTACHED--

will appear in the bottom left corner of the screen.

If you have entered the correct information, after a few moments the prompt

LIBRARY ATTACHMENT SUCCESSFUL

will appear at the bottom of your screen. The library you want to use is attached to the document, and you are ready to select entries and insert them into your document.

Only one library at a time may be attached to a document. It is easy to attach other libraries by following the steps described above. You do not need to do anything to "disattach" the previous library, because attaching a new library does this automatically. You can keep on attaching libraries, one at a time, as often as you want.

Now let's try an example. Suppose you want to attach your Buslets library to a new document called Letter2. Create that document now.

Before you begin to write this letter, you will first enter the letterhead. To do this, leave the cursor at the top of the page when the Document screen for Letter2 is first displayed. Press Shift-F5, and the prompt

Drive: Library Document:
Path:\
Press F10 when finished, ESC to cancel, F6 for directory

will appear at the bottom of the screen. Enter the library name Buslets. Remember to change the drive designation if your library is not on the B drive. When the drive and document fields are correctly filled, press Return. If the prompt

LIBRARY ATTACHMENT SUCCESSFUL

appears, you are ready to start inserting entries.

INSERTING LIBRARY ENTRIES

Inserting library entries is similar to attaching a library to a document. Make sure the cursor is located where you want the first entry to appear, then press F5, the Library Entry key. The prompt

Library Entry Name? [   ]--Press F6 for a list of entries

will appear at the bottom of the screen. Type the three-character name of the entry you wish to insert.

If you are not sure which entry you want, or the exact way to spell it, press F6 and a list of all the entries in the library will be displayed on the screen. Unfortunately, the way this list screen is arranged, you cannot tell if a two-character entry name begins or ends with a space. This is important, because to insert the correct entry, you must enter its exact name using all characters and spaces. I recommend, therefore, that you always use the full three characters you are allowed when you create entry names.

For this example, type the entry name HED and press Return. The entry should appear at the top of the document, on the first line, where you placed the cursor. Your screen should now look like Figure 7.2.

Enter the rest of the letter:

September 24, 1987

Ken Pickerall
WEATHERFORD CORKS
345 Fourth Street
San Francisco, CA 94111

Dear Ken,
    Just a quick note to say I'll be in your area for ten days beginning October 20. I haven't arranged my schedule yet, and there are some people I must see. But I would like to spend some time with you, so I'll call when I get into town.

Now place your cursor at the beginning of the second line beneath the last text line of the letter and press F5, the Library Entry key. At the prompt requesting the entry name to insert, type *END* and press Return. Letter2 should now look like Figure 7.3.

EDITING ENTRIES IN A LIBRARY

Editing an entry in a library is no more difficult than creating one. There are several reasons for changing or editing entries in a library. You may want to do one of the following:

- Alter text in an existing entry
- Change the name of an existing entry

- Add more entries to a library
- Delete entries from a library

A library can expand or contract, depending upon the entries you need to use regularly. You are limited to 254 entries per library, which is a large number of entries to remember. I recommend that before you approach this limit, you separate your entries into several smaller and more coherent libraries. You can begin your edit just as

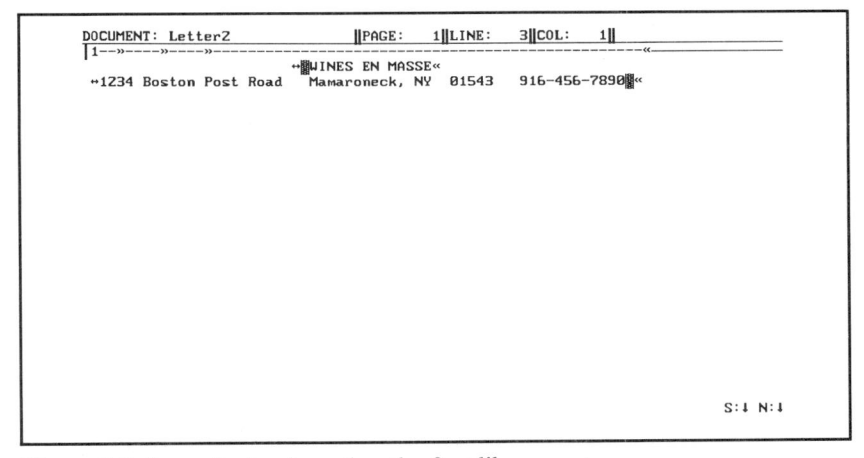

Figure 7.2: Letter2 after inserting the first library entry

Figure 7.3: Letter2 after inserting the second library entry

you do with any other document, by selecting at the main menu

1) Edit a Document

Type the name of the library that contains the entry you want to edit in the document field. The first entry of the library will appear on the screen. You will not see a Document Summary screen because there is none attached to a library.

If the first entry on your screen is the one you want to edit, you can start that edit now. All the editing controls of a normal Document screen are at your disposal.

If this first entry is not the one you want to edit, press F1, the Go To key. The prompt

Library Entry Name? [   ]—Press F6 for a list of entries

will appear at the bottom of the screen. You can enter the name of the entry you want to edit, if you know the name, or you can search the list of entries by pressing F6. You can flip through entries by pressing PgDn for the next entry, and PgUp for the previous entry. This allows you to check each entry in the order it was created. You can also go directly to the last page by pressing F1 and the End key. You can also return to the first entry at any point within the library by pressing F1 and the Home key. Although you can't go to a specific page number, you can move through the entries of a library just as you move through the pages of a standard document.

For example, let's edit the entry Mem. Press F2 and enter the name *Mem*. When that entry appears on your screen, place your cursor on the second line and delete *Kristine*. You have decided you prefer using a casual note for colleagues around the office, and there is only one Rebecca in the company. The memo note should now look like this:

from the desk of
Rebecca

If you think that this note looks better if both lines are centered, place the cursor on the letter *f* and press Insert. Then press F3, the Center key, and press Insert a second time to center the line. Repeat the procedure for the name Rebecca. The memo note should now look like this:

>from the desk of
>Rebecca

When you are finished editing this entry, press F10 to save it and return to the main menu. If you want to edit another entry, press Shift-F10. This will save the edits made up to this point, but you will remain in the library. To go to the next entry, press F1.

Editing the Library Entry Format Line

When you copy a library entry into a document, the format line of that entry is not copied to the document along with the text. The text of the library entry will conform to the format set in the document, and in some cases this could cause a problem. With the three examples you created and edited in the previous sections of this chapter, no problems of format arose. Text centered in the library entry document screen will be recentered in the Document screen.

There are cases where a difference in format can be troublesome. In most cases, this change will occur with the tab stops. If your entry includes spaces in the text line created by tab stops, when copied to a document the entry will assume the document's tab stop positions. As an example, take a look at Figure 7.4, which has text aligned

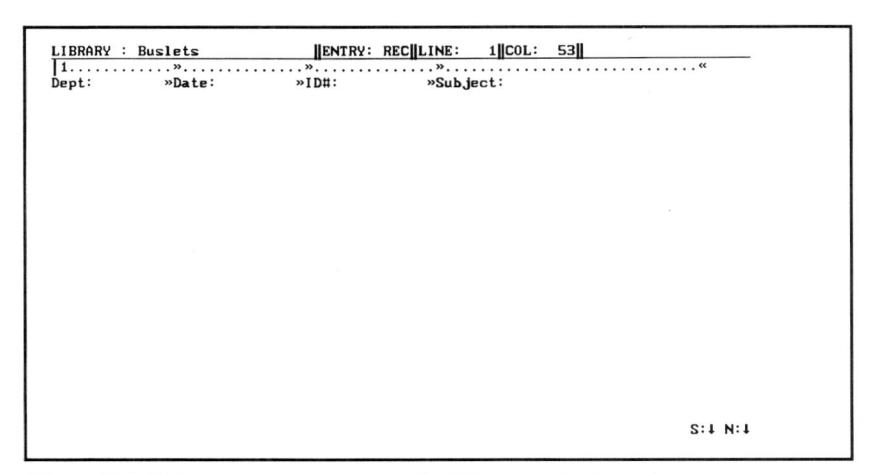

```
LIBRARY : Buslets       ||ENTRY: REC||LINE:    1||COL:   53||
|1...........»..............»...............»........................«
Dept:         »Date:        »ID#:         »Subject:




                                                              S:↓ N:↓
```

Figure 7.4: Library entry text created with normal tab settings

according to tab settings in columns 15, 30, and 45. If you copy this entry to a document where the tab settings have been changed to columns 5, 10, and 15, the text would revert to the format shown in Figure 7.5.

To copy text and retain its preset format, you have to create a second format line on the first text line of the entry. You can create the additional format line either when you create the entry or when you edit it. Place your cursor on the first text line of the entry, and press the key combination that inserts the format line you wish to use.

  Ctrl-F9 System Format Line
  Alt-F9   Page Format Line
  Shift-F9 Current Format Line

Remember that a format line, even when inserted in a library entry, will continue to control the format of all the text that follows it, until you change the format line again. You can reinsert the standard format line at any point by pressing the keys shown above. (Refer to Chapter 5 for more details on format lines.)

Changing the Name of an Entry

You can change entry names in a library as easily as you can change text within an entry. The most frequent reason for changing

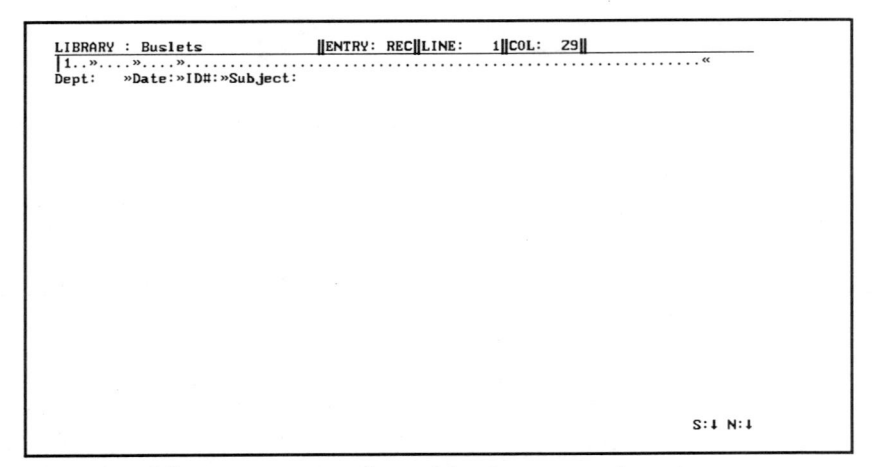

```
LIBRARY : Buslets            ||ENTRY: REC||LINE:    1||COL:  29||
[1..»....»....»...................................................«
Dept:   »Date:»ID#:»Subject:




















                                                          S:↓ N:↓
```

Figure 7.5: Library entry reconfigured for document tab settings

an entry name is that the library has grown to the point where many similar entries have exhausted the range of three-character names you can give them and still recall what each one contains.

To change an entry name, enter the library name on the Edit a Document screen. This will take you directly into the first entry of the library. Then press F1, the Go To key, and type the name of the entry you want to change. When that entry appears on the screen, press F5, the Library Entry key. The prompt

Library Entry Name? [   ]--Press F6 for a list of entries

will appear at the bottom of the screen. The entry whose name you want to change should remain on the screen. Type the new three-character name for that entry and press Return to set it.

For example, let's change the name of the entry *END* to *CLO,* for closing. END is too broad a term for something as specific as letter closings. You should always keep the tactics of naming entries foremost in your mind when you are naming them or renaming them. Select 1 on the main menu and enter the name Buslets in the document field of the Edit a Document screen. This will take you directly to the first entry, HED. Press F1 here and type the name *END*. When the END entry appears, press F5 and type the new name, *CLO*. Then press Return. The old entry END has now become the new entry CLO.

To review, here are the steps for editing a library entry or changing its name.

1. Select Edit a Document on the main menu.

2. Type the name of the library that contains the entry to be edited or renamed, and press Return.

3. Press F1, the Go To key, and type the name of the entry you want to edit or rename.

4. To edit the entry, use the regular editing procedures. To rename an entry, press F5, the Library key, and then type in the new name for the entry.

5. Press Shift-F10, the Save key, if there are other entries you want to rename or edit. Press F10, the Save/Exit key, to save and return to the main menu.

To keep track of your entry names and what they refer to, you can print out copies of each library on paper, and keep the file of these entries in handy reach.

PRINTING COPIES OF LIBRARY ENTRIES

Each time you edit an entry or change a name, you should print out a new copy of the library that has been changed. You can print a library and all the entries in it just as you print any other document. Each entry will appear on its own printed page. One limitation to keep in mind is that there is no way to change the printed format of the library entries. They will all be printed according to the default settings in the Document Print Options screen. Follow the printing procedure in Chapter 6, giving the library name as the name of the document you want printed.

You should print a library when you create it, and whenever you have added, edited, renamed, or deleted any entries. Note that in a long library file, you can use Hot Print (Ctrl-PrtSc) to obtain printouts of selected entries.

ADDING NEW ENTRIES TO A LIBRARY

As you write business letters, you will find plenty of opportunities to use boilerplate text. For example, suppose you have a friend on the West Coast, Suzanne Taddich, who designs labels for many of the better wineries. You don't get out to the West Coast very often, and you find her a valuable source of information on wineries, because she visits them regularly to talk with marketing managers and sketch views of the vineyards for possible label pictures. You'd like to make sure you keep in touch with her, but you don't want to bother her with telephone calls; you just want to send a note about the kinds of wines you are looking for. With this purpose in mind, it would be helpful to include a heading for letters to Suzanne as an entry in your Buslets library.

The procedure for adding a new entry to a library is similar to the editing procedure.

1. Select *Edit a Document* on the main menu.
2. Enter the name of the library you wish to add to *Buslets,* and press Return.
3. Press F1, the Go To key, and then press End to go to the last entry.
4. Press Ctrl-End, the End of Page key, and then F2, the Page Break key, to create a new page. You will see the prompt

    Library Entry Name? [   ]—Press F6 for a list of entries

5. Enter the name of the new entry, Suz, and press Return.
6. Type the text of the new entry:

    Suzanne Taddich
    BACCHUS PRINTS
    5565 White Cottage Lane
    Rutherford, CA 94573

7. When you are finished and the heading is correct, press F10, the Save/Exit key, and the new entry Suz will become the last entry in your library Buslets.

COPYING ENTRIES FROM A DOCUMENT

You can also copy text from a document into a library. This is a handy way of adding an entry to a library. To copy the section of text directly from the document into the library, you must start from the document that contains the text you wish to add to the library. Let's use the letter from Figure 7.3. If you are going to keep in touch with Suzanne on a regular basis, you should also keep in touch with Ken. Bring the letter you wrote to Ken, Letter2, to your document screen. Next, attach the library Buslets to this letter. Place the cursor on the first letter of the text you wish to appear as an entry in the library. In this case, it is the letter K in the first occurrence of the word Ken. This is in Letter2. When the cursor is in the correct position, press Alt-J, the Library Copy key, and the prompt

> **LIBRARY COPY WHAT?**

will appear on the right side of the status line.

If you have not attached a library yet, the prompt

> **- NO LIBRARY CURRENTLY ATTACHED -**

will show on the bottom line instead. In this case, press Escape, press Shift-F5 to attach the appropriate library, and proceed with the copy operation.

Now move the cursor to the last character of the text you wish to copy. This should be the comma after the second occurrence of the name Ken. This text will be highlighted. When all the text you want to appear as an entry has been highlighted, press Alt-J a second time. The prompt

> **Library Entry Name? [   ] — Press F6 for a list of entries**

will appear at the bottom of the screen. Type the three-character entry name here: *Ken*. If an entry with the name Ken already existed in the Buslets library, the prompt

> **Entry exists. Press ESC to cancel, any key to replace contents.**

would appear at the bottom of the screen. When this occurs, press Escape, and Advantage II will give you another chance to pick a unique entry name. You shouldn't have this problem with Ken.

Once you have entered the name Ken, press Return. The prompt

> **- Copy to library complete -**

will appear at the bottom of the screen. This informs you that the heading Ken for letters to Ken Pickerall is now an entry in the library Buslets.

COPYING ENTRIES FROM ONE LIBRARY TO ANOTHER

A good library handling technique is to place as many related entries as you can into a single library, but there will be times when you want to save time by using the same entry in two different situations. As an example, you might want to use the letterhead HED both on business letters and on contract forms. If you have created a separate library for contracts called Contlib, for contract library, you might want to include the *HED* entry in it. Since that entry has already been created in the Buslets library, you can simply copy it into Contlib.

Unfortunately, you cannot use the external copy command to do this. You have to pass the HED entry from Buslets to Contlib by way of a document. Create this document and call it *Bus*. Once you are in the Document screen, attach Buslets by pressing Shift-F5, type the library name *Buslets,* and press Return. Next, press F5, type *HED,* and press Return. HED should now appear in the empty Document screen of Bus. This completes the first half of the procedure.

To copy HED into Contlib, first create Contlib and make sure it has at least one other entry in it. Attach Contlib to Bus and press Alt-J to highlight the text of Bus. Next, press End to move the cursor to the end of the text, and press Alt-J a second time to set the highlighted block. Type the name you want to give this entry in Contlib (you can use HED if you want to) and press Return. In a few moments, the prompt

- Copy to library complete -

will appear at the bottom of the screen. Press F10 to exit from Bus.

Now you can delete the document called Bus or keep it as a tool for moving other library entries.

DELETING ENTRIES FROM A LIBRARY

Some of your entries will become obsolete after a while, and you will find that you no longer use them. It is a good practice to keep your libraries as up to date as possible. This not only frees space in the library, but it also alleviates the problem of trying to keep track of useless information. The solution to this problem is to delete entries you no longer use.

Deleting library entries is easy. All you have to do is edit an entry and erase all the text, which creates a blank page.

1. Select *Edit a Document* on the main menu.

2. Type the name of the library that has the entry you want to delete, and press Return.

3. Press F1, the Go To key, and type the name of the entry you want to delete.

4. Delete all the text in the entry, and Advantage II will delete the entry name from the library.

If there are only a few characters in the entry, you can use the Minus key (on the numeric keypad). If there is a considerable amount of text, but no more than a screenful, press the Delete key and then the End key. Pressing Delete a second time will delete all text on the screen. To delete more than a screenful of text, press Delete, then go to the end of the entry by pressing Ctrl-End, and press Delete again.

5. If the deleted entry is not the last entry, press Shift-F2, the Page Combine keys. The entry with text deleted will disappear completely, and all subsequent entries will move up to fill in the missing page.

Using libraries is one way you can magnify the power of your keystrokes beyond the commands of the function keys. In the next chapter, you will discover ways to employ even more powerful functions that will combine library entries with other commands.

8

KEY PROCEDURES

A *KEY PROCEDURE,* OR *MACRO,* IS A SEQUENCE OF keystrokes that can be stored on disk and then recalled by pressing a few keys. The principal advantages of using key procedures are speed and reliability. Executing a key procedure by entering a short file name enables you to perform a complex procedure quickly and correctly, and it saves you from having to recreate the procedure each time you want to use it.

In this chapter, you will first learn how to create key procedures and use them in specific applications. Then you will learn how to edit and change them. There are seven basic tasks you can perform while working with key procedures:

- Build key procedures
- Execute key procedures
- Pause in the middle of executing a key procedure
- Prompt in the middle of executing a key procedure
- Replay key procedures
- Rename key procedures
- Edit key procedures

You will develop your skills with key procedures by advancing through this list in the order these tasks are shown. The building blocks for all key procedures are the commands provided in MultiMate Advantage II, see Appendix C to review those commands.

WHAT IS A KEY PROCEDURE?

The function keys in MultiMate Advantage II are essentially predefined key procedures. For instance, pressing F10, the Save/Exit key, instructs Advantage II to perform three steps:

1. Record the document to disk
2. Exit from the document

3. Return to the main menu

If you wanted to perform these steps without using F10, you would have to press three key combinations:

1. Shift-F10 to record the document to disk
2. Escape-Y (for yes) to exit from the document
3. Escape-Y to return to the main menu

Key procedures are designed to speed up your work and make it more accurate. In that respect, a key procedure resembles a library entry: both consist of a sequence of keystrokes stored for repeated use. But a library entry can store only text, not commands. A key procedure can store text as well as commands and any other function obtained from keyboard input, including creating columns, checking spelling, accessing DOS directly, and full-function math. Another difference is that a library entry is executed all at once, but a key procedure is executed keystroke by keystroke. Each keystroke command is completed before the next keystroke is begun. When you create a key procedure, keep these processing steps in mind. The real power and flexibility of key procedures comes when you create key procedures to automate the functions you use most often.

BUILDING A KEY PROCEDURE

You can build a key procedure file from anyplace within MultiMate Advantage II. If you build a key procedure while you are in a Document screen, the keystrokes you enter will show up on the screen as you enter them. You should think through the sequence of keystrokes before you begin. Although you can correct errors you make when building a key procedure, all your keystrokes will be played back; thus, the mistakes will appear and then be corrected as part of the key procedure when you execute it. In any case, you should replay the key procedure immediately after it is built and check it for errors, and create it anew if necessary.

You begin building a key procedure by pressing Ctrl-F5, the Build Key Procedure File key. The prompt

Ctrl

will appear momentarily in the lower right corner. Next the prompt

Drive: Key Procedure:
Path:
Press F10 when finished, ESC to cancel, F6 for directory

will appear at the bottom of the screen. This prompt has the same fields as the opening prompt for creating a library, except that there is a field for the name of the key procedure instead of one for the name of the library. As usual, the file name can have up to eight characters. You cannot use spaces or punctuation, and these document names are not case-sensitive, as are the three-letter library entry names.

Once you've entered the file name, press F10. The prompt

B

for *build* appears in reverse video in the bottom right corner of the screen, between the Caps Lock arrow and the N for Num Lock. Now you can enter the keystrokes you want to save as the key procedure. Every key that you press after this point, until you end the building stage, is saved as part of the key procedure, and it is saved in the order you enter it. You can use any key on the keyboard: all letters, punctuation, and spaces, as well as the formatting keys, such as the Return and Tab keys, and all function keys. You can even include keystroke combinations, such as Alt-Z for bold print. You can also insert the full range of screen symbols.

You won't see the keystrokes reflected on the screen as you enter the key procedure. If you are in a Document screen, though, whatever text you type will appear on the screen. (To see a record of your keystrokes, you can use the Advanced Utilities method discussed later in this chapter.)

When you finish entering the keystrokes, press Ctrl-F5 to end the building stage, and the *B* on the bottom right of the screen will disappear.

Key Procedure Example

Now let's try an example, using key procedures to create a letterhead for a business letter. This is the same thing you accomplished with a library entry.

You can start creating a key procedure anywhere in MultiMate Advantage II, but if you begin this example in a blank Document screen, you can replay the key procedure as soon as you have finished building it and check it for errors. You can create all the examples in this chapter on this same Document screen.

1. Prepare your "work slate" by selecting on the main menu

   2) Create a Document

2. On the Create a Document screen, type the file name, *KeyProcs*.

3. Begin building the key procedure by pressing Ctrl-F5, the Build Key Procedure File key. Wait for the letter *B* to appear in the lower right corner of your screen before you start entering keystrokes.

4. At the prompt

   Drive: Key Procedure:
   Path:\
   Press F10 when finished, ESC to cancel, F6 for directory

   type KP1, for key procedure one, and press F10 to continue.

5. Type the series of keystrokes shown in Figure 8.1. It's important to enter the keystrokes exactly as they are shown.

6. Press Ctrl-F5 to complete the building of a key procedure and record it to disk.

7. Press F10 to save and exit the procedure.

Remember *not* to press Return after each keystroke. The keystrokes are placed on individual lines in the figure to distinguish them from each other. Each time you press the Return key while you are building a key procedure, you place another entry into the key procedure. A hard carriage return will be executed for each Return you enter into the key procedure.

```
F3
Caps Lock
Alt-Z
WINES EN MASSE
Alt-Z
Caps Lock
Return
F3
1234 Boston Post Road    Mamaroneck, NY 10543    916-456-7890
Return
```

Figure 8.1: Keystroke listing for KP1

The key procedure KP1 will create a letterhead identical to the one you inserted in the library Buslets, for the entry HED.

You cannot cancel a key procedure entry by pressing Escape. Because the operation of all keys (except key combinations using Ctrl) is suspended while you are building a key procedure, pressing Escape will simply insert the Escape key function into the key procedure.

The work-slate document serves as a record of the key procedure file. The key procedure text is recorded and saved as a page of a document. This means that you can add text, such as a name for the key procedure, to the document. However, this is not where you edit key procedures (the keystrokes that don't display characters or text on the screen won't appear in the document). Editing is performed on the Key Procedure File Edit Utility screen, which is discussed in detail later in this chapter.

Error Messages

When you are building a key procedure, you may see two error messages on your screen if you run out of disk space on the document disk. The message

FILE CREATION ERROR. TOO MANY FILES ON THE DISK. PRESS ANY KEY TO CONTINUE

means there is not enough room on the document disk to begin building a key procedure file. The other message

FILE BUILDING ABORTED. NO ROOM ON DISK. PRESS ANY KEY TO CONTINUE

means you ran out of disk space while entering keystrokes in a key procedure file.

If you get either one of these error messages, you will have to create the key procedure on a document disk that has more space available on it. You can either take some files off the current document disk, or you can insert a new document disk that has more room on it. Note that a key procedure file can be executed within a document only when the document and the key procedure file are on the same document disk.

You'll learn another way to create key procedures near the end of this chapter, after you've learned about the Advanced Utilities menus.

EXECUTING A KEY PROCEDURE

It is a good practice to execute a key procedure immediately after you build it, to make sure that you have built it correctly. Since every keystroke is recorded when you build a key procedure, you might find that what the key procedure does is not what you intended.

To check the performance of KP1, the letterhead key procedure you just built, you can remain in the same document. Place the cursor where you want the result of the key procedure to appear. Press Ctrl-F8, the Key Procedure Execute key, and the prompt

```
Drive:   Key Procedure:
Path:\
Press F10 when finished, ESC to cancel, F6 for directory
```

will appear on the bottom of the screen. Type the name KP1, press F10, and the letterhead will start to appear on the screen.

Advantage II will replay the sequence of keystrokes just as you entered them in the KP1 file. There are two things you should notice right away. First, the key procedure will begin at your cursor position where you pressed Ctrl-F8. Second, the letter *E* (for execute) appears in reverse video where the *B* appeared earlier.

As the key procedure is executed, you should be able to follow the keystrokes. The text of the letterhead will appear just about as quickly as an excellent typist could enter the keystrokes from the keyboard. If a mistake appears, you will probably recognize right away what you did wrong. This short example also illustrates the speed and reliability of key procedures. You could probably not match the speed of the execution if you were typing the entry from the keyboard character-by-character, nor could you be 100 percent accurate, as you can with a correctly built key procedure.

The key procedure is finished when all the keystrokes have been played, and there are no further prompts.

Error Messages

When you try to execute a key procedure, you may see either of two error messages. If you enter the name of a key procedure file that does not exist, the message

FILE NOT FOUND. PRESS ANY KEY TO CONTINUE.

indicates that you either entered an incorrect file name, or you designated the wrong drive as the document drive. With floppy disks, a key procedure file can only be executed from a disk in the designated document drive (usually drive B). If you get this error message, check both the file name and document drive. Press any key to clear the message, then refer to either the Document Summary screen or the Edit Document Defaults screen to see the exact file name and the document drive.

If Advantage II runs across an error in the key procedure file while the file is executing, the message

EXECUTION ABORTED DUE TO READ ERROR. PRESS ANY KEY TO CONTINUE.

will appear. This is most likely the result of the computer incorrectly reading the instructions in your key procedure file. You can interrupt the rest of the execution by pressing Ctrl-Num Lock. You can then restart the execution of the key procedure by pressing Return.

PAUSE DURING EXECUTION

A special method for building a key procedure allows you to enter customized text in the middle of a key procedure. The letterhead macro KP1 allows you to enter a specific section of prerecorded text into a document, but you can also provide for different text that you want to insert with the same procedure. All you need do is insert a pause in the key procedure where you want to insert the section of customized text.

You enter the pause when you are building a key procedure file just as you enter any other command. Press Ctrl-F6 wherever you want the key procedure to pause, and the prompt

PAUSE

will appear in the lower left corner of the screen for a few moments and then disappear. You cannot enter additional keystrokes while this prompt is on the screen. Once it disappears, you can either continue building the key procedure or end it. There is no limit to the number of pauses you can enter into a key procedure file. Be aware, though, that the more pauses you enter, the longer the execution of the file will take.

When you execute a key procedure file with a pause in it, the key procedure will execute keystrokes until it encounters the pause. At the pause, execution will stop, and the prompt

PRESS (C) TO CONTINUE. PLEASE ENTER DATA, THEN CTRL-F6 TO RESUME.

will appear at the bottom of your screen. You have two choices:

1. You can press C, enter text, and then continue with the execution by pressing Ctrl-F6, the Pause key.

2. You can decline to enter text and proceed with execution by pressing Ctrl-F6.

Note that if you begin entering text without first pressing C, the program will nonetheless assume the first letter of your text was the letter prompt. Thus, the first letter of your customized text entry will not appear on the screen or in the document. Always enter C before you enter customized text at the first prompt.

If you have more than one pause in the key procedure file, subsequent pauses will cause the prompt

PLEASE ENTER DATA, THEN CTRL-F6 TO RESUME.

to appear at the bottom of the screen. Only the first prompt requires that you enter C to continue.

Now let's try an example. Suppose you want to expand upon the letterhead by inserting a pause. Begin by pressing Ctrl-F5, the Build

Key Procedure File key, and type the file name KP1. This is the same one you used last time, so you'll see the prompt

CONTENTS OF FILE ALREADY EXISTS. DO YOU WISH TO REPLACE? (Y/N)

appear at the bottom of the screen. Press N. (If you press Y, you will delete the original KP1. You can thus delete a key procedure file easily and create a new one in its place.) Since you do not want to delete KP1 now, type KP2 at the file name prompt. Now build KP2, using the keystrokes in Figure 8.2.

KP2 differs from KP1 in several ways. At the first pause (Ctrl-F6), you can insert the current date. At the second pause, after the word *Dear*, you can insert the name of the person you are writing to. The third pause allows you to decide whether you want to insert your standard business closing or type in a customized one.

Executing a Key Procedure Using a Pause

You can execute KP2 by pressing Ctrl-F8 in the same screen where you created it. After entering the name KP2, press F10. The

```
F3
Caps Lock
Alt-Z
WINES EN MASSE
Alt-Z
Caps Lock
Return
F3
1234 Boston Post Road    Mamaroneck, NY 10543    916-456-7890
Return
Return
Return
Ctrl-F6
1986
Return
Return
Return
Return
Return
Dear
Ctrl-F6
Return
Return
Ctrl-F6
Sincerely,
Return
Return
Return
Return
Return
Rebecca Kristine
Return
Senior Wine Buyer
Return
```

Figure 8.2: Keystroke listing for KP2

text in KP2 will begin to unfold the same way it did in KP1, however, where KP1 stopped after completing the letterhead, KP2 pauses and issues the first pause prompt instead. At this point, press the letter C and then type the date

September 24,

Make sure to place a space after the comma. You can go back and change this text if you enter it incorrectly before you resume the key procedure. You can even go back and edit text that was already entered by the key procedure. If you do edit the text, you must return the cursor to the position it would normally be in when the key procedure resumes before you press Ctrl-F6 to instruct it to continue execution. The key procedure simply picks up where it left off, and it will pick up wherever the cursor is positioned.

Press Ctrl-F6 to continue. Advantage II will complete the date by adding the year, and then the cursor will drop down four lines. The first word of the greeting, *Dear,* will appear, and again, a pause halts the key procedure. This is where you can enter the name of the person you are writing to, and then type the body of your letter. For example, you could type in the following note:

Mike,
   Just a note to let you know I'll be in your area the week of November 10-17. Don't be surprised when I give you a call at the last minute.

When you have entered the final period, press Return twice, then stop. This is where you press Ctrl-F6 to continue. You want to include as many keystrokes in a key procedure as you can, to save time and ensure better accuracy. In this case, the last hard carriage return after all the text has been entered is a part of the key procedure. Pressing Ctrl-F6 will add the symbol and enter an extra line before the third and final pause appears.

This last pause gives you the choice of inserting your standard closing beginning with *Sincerely,* or typing in a customized closing. If you press Ctrl-F6, the standard closing will be inserted. If you type a different version, press Ctrl-F8 immediately afterward to end the key procedure.

PROMPT DURING EXECUTION

A second type of pause does not allow you to enter any text in the middle of a key procedure. This kind of pause is called a prompt, and it is designed to allow you either to continue with the key procedure or else to cancel its execution at a specific point. This allows you to build a key procedure in sections—or *modules*—and then enter the sections as applicable. You cannot leap around and select only the modules you want to include in the key procedure; you can only select them in order.

To enter a prompt in a key procedure file, press Ctrl-F7, the Prompt key. The word

PROMPT

will appear at the bottom of the screen. It will disappear a few moments later. A prompt has now been inserted at that place in the key procedure.

When you execute this procedure, it will pause at the place where you have instructed it to, and the prompt

DO YOU WISH TO CONTINUE OR STOP? (C/S)

will appear at the bottom of the screen. This is the only prompt you get. You have two choices:

1. You can press C to continue executing the key procedure up to the next prompt or pause.

2. You can press S to stop and exit from the key procedure. You will remain in the document regardless of when and where you stopped.

To illustrate the use of a prompt, let's build a key procedure called KP3 that provides you with a separate closing for a letter. Press Ctrl-F5 to create the new file KP3, then type the keystrokes given in Figure 8.3.

When you execute KP3 at the end of your letters, it will provide you with a standard closing, but it will also allow you to add additional text if this text is necessary to the letter.

The first prompt occurs two lines below your title. You can press S for stop at this point, and this closing will look identical to your usual

```
        Sincerely,
        Return
        Return
        Return
        Return
        Return
        Rebecca Kristine
        Return
        Senior Wine Buyer
        Return
        Ctrl-F7
        Return
        cc: file
        Return
        Ctrl-F7
        Return
        Enclosure
        Return
```

Figure 8.3: Keystroke listing for KP3

closing. If you press C for continue, the additional text *cc: file* will appear. A second prompt will occur two lines below that, if you want the text *Enclosure* to appear.

There is a final prompt at the end of the file. If you enter a prompt anywhere within a key procedure, you must enter a second prompt at the end of the file listing. A key procedure file will continue to replay itself until it comes to the next prompt, so you must provide a place to answer S for stop. If you did not include the final prompt in the listings for KP3, and you answered C to the previous prompt to include the text *Enclosure,* then the word *Sincerely* would begin on the next line, and KP3 would replay to the next prompt, ad infinitum.

BUILDING A KEY PROCEDURE WITHOUT TEXT

Some key procedures don't include any text, but serve only to execute commands. For example, you can create a key procedure file that takes you from the main menu into the editing mode for your business letters. To do this, first create a document called Business. Set the right margin on the format line to 65 and then exit from the Document screen by pressing F10.

Now, to begin building the file, at the main menu press Ctrl-F5, the Build Key Procedure key. The cursor, which on the main menu is normally blinking in the prompt field, will appear in the key procedure file name field at the bottom of the screen. Type in the name *ED* and press F10 to set this name. The cursor will return to the prompt field, and you can record the usual keystrokes for editing a document. Press 1, for Edit a Document. Next type the file name *Business*. Press Return to enter the Document Summary screen, and then press F10 to go to the Document screen. Now press Ctrl-F5 to signal the end of the ED key procedure file. Again, here are the commands to build ED.

>   1

>   Return

>   *Business*

>   Return

>   F10

To execute this key procedure and check it for errors, you will have to exit from the Document screen and return to the main menu. Since you built the file as you went through the actual steps of accessing the Document screen for Business, there is little chance you made an error. But you can execute this key procedure only from the main menu. If you try to execute it from any other part of the program, Advantage II may crash, or disappear from your screen.

This example emphasizes the importance of knowing what you want to do when you build a key procedure. Although a key procedure can automate much of your keyboard input, it is not always wise to use a key procedure.

REPLAYING A KEY PROCEDURE

If you want to replay one key procedure before you've created another one, you can do so without going through the usual procedure. Simply press Alt-R, the Replay Key Procedure key. You might use this shortcut to execute the same macro in a different part of the document. Or, if Advantage II ran into an error and failed to execute the key procedure on its first attempt, press Alt-R to try again. Remember that Advantage II will replay only the key procedure whose name was last entered at the name prompt.

NAMING AND RENAMING KEY PROCEDURES

Selecting names for key procedure files is as important as selecting the proper names for libraries and their entries. Try to use names you can readily identify. You can keep a written record of the text in each key procedure by printing it, using Hot Print (Ctrl-PrtSc) or Quick Print (Shift-PrtSc) (see Chapter 6). With more complex key procedures, you could keep a handwritten list of the keystrokes.

A helpful method for keeping track of key procedures is to use the Comments section on the Document Summary screen, as shown in Figure 8.4. You can see the key procedures you have created in this chapter in the Comments field, along with a brief description of what each key procedure will do. You can obtain a Hot Print (Ctrl-PrtSc) or a Quick Print (Shift-PrtSc) of the screen.

Renaming a Key Procedure File

If you need to rename a key procedure file, you will have to use the DOS command RENAME. You can only use the Document Management utility screens, including the Rename a Document screen, for file names with the extension .DOC. (A file name extension is the last three letters following the period in a file name, as seen on the DOS prompt.) Key procedure files are always given the file name extension .KEY.

```
                    DOCUMENT SUMMARY SCREEN

        Document   BUSINESS              Total pages   1
        Author     Rebecca Kristine
        Addressee  _____
        Operator   _____

        Identification key words :
                   Generic business
                   letter

        Comments :
            KP1 - letterhead
            KP2 - structure of letter including optional closing
            KP3 - closing variation, with cc: file and Enclosure before pauses

        Creation Date       09/26/87    Modification Date        09/26/87
        Total Editing Time    0:04      Editing Time Last Session   0:01
        Total Keystrokes       118      Keystrokes Last Session       42

                    Press F10 when finished, ESC to exit
                                                              S:↓ N:↓
```

Figure 8.4: Key procedures identified in Document Summary Comments field

To use the DOS command RENAME, return to the main menu and select

9) Exit Word Processor

You now have to go to the drive containing the document disk where the key procedure file is recorded. To do this, enter that drive letter and a colon. To make sure you have found the correct drive, type

DIR

and press Return, and a list of the files on that drive will be displayed. (You can enter any DOS command in uppercase or lowercase letters, but when you issue a DIR command, all file names will appear on the screen in uppercase.)

Now type the DOS command

RENAME [OLD FILE NAME].KEY [NEW FILE NAME].KEY

substituting the old and new file names, and press Return. Be sure to put one space after RENAME and another space before the new file name. If you insert additional spaces, you may get an error message, and you will have to retype the command.

The file has been renamed once the drive prompt reappears on the screen. To check the success of the renaming procedure, enter the DIR command and check the list of files.

For example, let's change KP1 to KEYPROC1.

1. Exit from MultiMate Advantage II by returning to the main menu and selecting

    9) Exit Word Processor

2. As soon as you are in DOS, you'll see the drive prompt on the screen. If you are using floppy disks, the prompt will probably be :A>. If you are working with a hard disk, the prompt will probably be :C>. Now go to the document disk drive. If you are using floppy disks, the document drive is usually B; for a hard disk, C.

3. Check the contents of the drive with the DIR command, and make sure the file KP1.KEY is on it.

4. Rename the file by typing the command

   RENAME KP1.KEY KEYPROC1.KEY

   and pressing Return.

5. Issue another DIR command to check the contents of the drive. The new name should now show up.

ACCESSING DOS DIRECTLY

A new feature of Multimate Advantage II, called DOS Access, can take you to DOS directly from the program and return you to Advantage II just as quickly. To use this shortcut, press Ctrl-2, the DOS Access key, from anywhere within the Advantage II word-processing program. You will hear a beep, the screen will go blank momentarily, and then you will see the prompt message

   DOS Access requires returning to MultiMate when done
   Type EXIT when ready to return

in the top left corner of the screen. Next your system prompt will appear on the screen; an A: for floppy-disk users, a C: for hard-disk users. You can now work freely with MS-DOS operating system commands.

If you are using floppy disks, you will not be able to access DOS this way until you copy the COMMAND.COM file from your DOS disk to your MultiMate Advantage II System Diskette. If you try to access DOS directly without copying COMMAND.COM to the System Diskette, the prompt shown above will appear, but it will be followed immediately by an error message

   Can not find COMMAND.COM

at the bottom of your screen. You will be returned to wherever you were in Advantage II when you first pressed Ctrl-2. More detailed instructions about copying COMMAND.COM are given in Appendix A.

After you have completed your DOS functions and want to return to Advantage II, type EXIT at the DOS prompt. Any combination of uppercase or lowercase letters for EXIT will work. You will be returned to wherever you left the program.

There are a few provisos to remember when you access DOS directly. First of all, you should not try to start up or delete any memory-resident programs (such as SideKick and SuperKey) from memory. Second, you should not rename or delete the document you had on the screen when you accessed DOS. The best use of this feature is for short-term "housekeeping" (or maintenance) of disk files, such as copying a batch of files from one disk to another for backup purposes, and printing out a list of files on a disk or in a subdirectory. After accessing DOS directly from MultiMate Advantage II, you can remain in DOS as long as you want to. But if you are going to spend a lot of time working with DOS, I recommend that you exit MultiMate Advantage II first.

EDITING KEY PROCEDURE FILES

Editing a key procedure file requires a few more steps than editing any other kind of document in MultiMate Advantage II. Because you can't view the keystrokes from a screen available through the main menu, you must access the file through menu selections on the Advanced Utilities Diskette.

If you are using a hard disk, load the files from the Advanced Utilities Diskette into the same file directory as the other Advantage II files (see Appendix A).

If you are using a two-floppy system, you will have to switch disks during the editing operation. You can avoid some of this inconvenience by copying several files from three disks onto the Advanced Utilities Diskette:

- WPSYSD.SYS from the System Diskette
- WPHELP.TXT from the Boot Diskette
- The key procedure files you want to edit from the document disk; in this case, copy KEYPROC1.KEY, KP2.KEY, and KP3.KEY.

Now, exit from MultiMate Advantage II by selecting

9) Exit Word Processor

at the main menu.

If you are working with a hard disk, and all the proper files are loaded on it, type *mm* and press Return at the C> prompt.

The *mm* command will cause the MultiMate Advantage II Boot-up menu to appear on the screen, as shown in Figure 8.5.

Once the Boot-up menu appears, select

3) Utilities and Conversions

If you are working with a two-floppy system, remove the Boot Diskette from drive A and replace it with the System Diskette. Now press Return to bring the Advanced Utilities menu, shown in Figure 8.6, onto the screen.

On this menu, use the Space bar to highlight

Key Procedure Files Utility

and press F10 to accept this selection. The Key Procedure Files Utility menu, shown in Figure 8.7, will then appear on the screen. With this menu, you can choose to edit an old—or existing—key procedure file, create a new file, or delete a key procedure file. Before you make a selection, you have to determine whether you need to switch disks again. If you are working with a two-floppy system, replace the Advanced Utilities Diskette in drive A with the document disk that holds the key procedure file you want to edit. If you have already

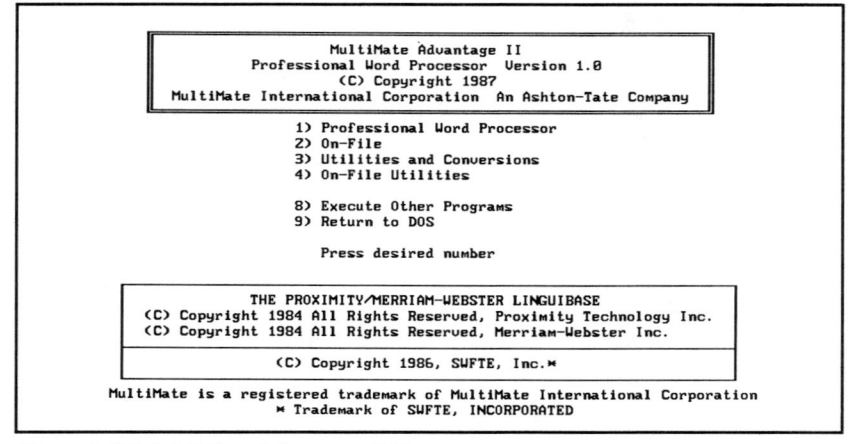

```
                    MultiMate Advantage II
            Professional Word Processor  Version 1.0
                       (C) Copyright 1987
         MultiMate International Corporation  An Ashton-Tate Company

                1) Professional Word Processor
                2) On-File
                3) Utilities and Conversions
                4) On-File Utilities

                8) Execute Other Programs
                9) Return to DOS

                      Press desired number

              THE PROXIMITY/MERRIAM-WEBSTER LINGUIBASE
       (C) Copyright 1984 All Rights Reserved, Proximity Technology Inc.
       (C) Copyright 1984 All Rights Reserved, Merriam-Webster Inc.

                  (C) Copyright 1986, SWFTE, Inc.*

       MultiMate is a registered trademark of MultiMate International Corporation
                    * Trademark of SWFTE, INCORPORATED
```

Figure 8.5: MultiMate Advantage II Boot-up menu

transferred this file to the Advanced Utilities Diskette, then you can continue without switching disks.

Press the Space bar so that

Edit a File

is highlighted, and press F10 to accept this solution. Advantage II will

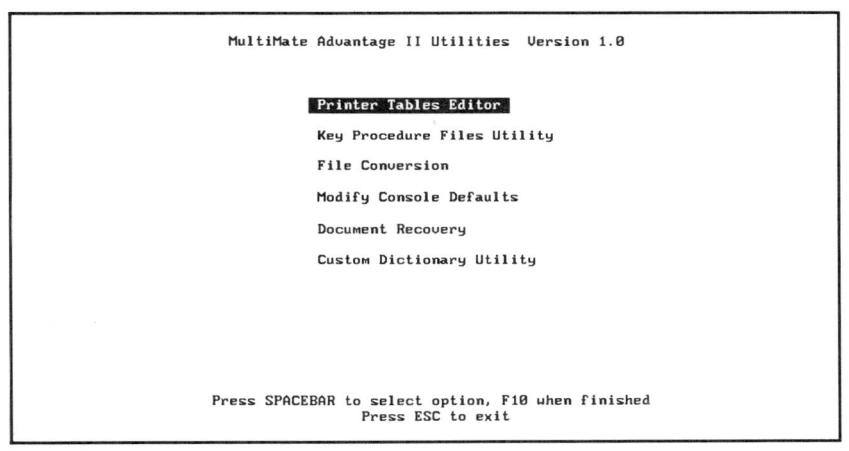

```
            MultiMate Advantage II Utilities  Version 1.0

                        Printer Tables Editor
                        Key Procedure Files Utility
                        File Conversion
                        Modify Console Defaults
                        Document Recovery
                        Custom Dictionary Utility




              Press SPACEBAR to select option, F10 when finished
                              Press ESC to exit
```

Figure 8.6: Advanced Utilities menu

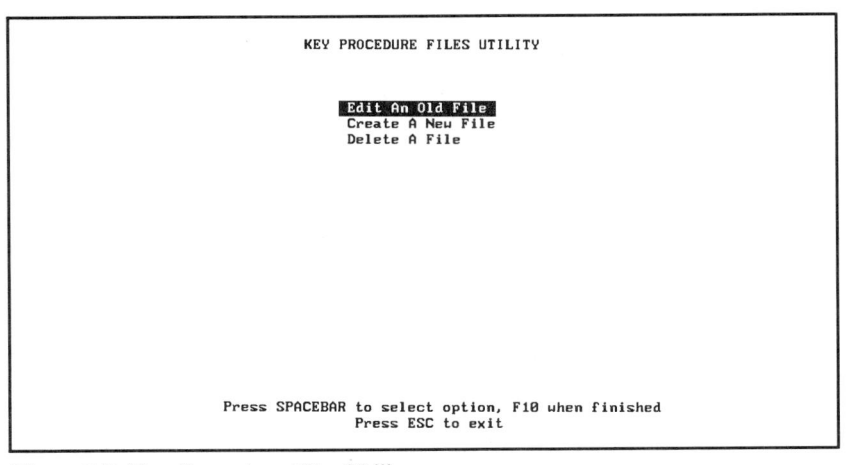

```
                        KEY PROCEDURE FILES UTILITY

                              Edit An Old File
                              Create A New File
                              Delete A File







              Press SPACEBAR to select option, F10 when finished
                              Press ESC to exit
```

Figure 8.7: Key Procedure Files Utility

then read the files on the disk in drive A and display a list of all the key procedure files located on this disk, as in Figure 8.8.

Select the file you want to edit by moving the cursor with the arrow keys and highlighting the name of the file. When the proper file is highlighted, press F10 to accept this selection. If you press Return while you are in this screen, you will toggle in and out of the highlighting mode. When you are not in highlighting mode, the cursor will appear on the letter just after the prompt

PATH: A:

This allows you to switch to another pathway on your hard disk so that you can access files from it. You can alternate between file highlighting and path selection by pressing Return.

Now you are ready to enter the screen where you will edit a key procedure file. This might seem like a lot of trouble. In many cases, particularly if the key procedure file is a small one, you are wiser to delete it and create it anew. But it's often worthwhile to edit a larger key procedure, particularly one that contains several pauses or a series of screen changes. The editing procedure has been specifically designed for this purpose.

Now let's see an example. To review, here's how to access the screen

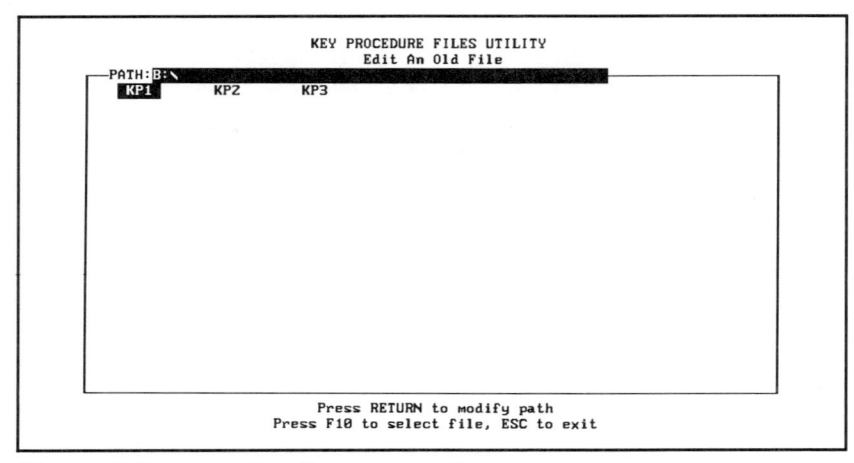

Figure 8.8: Key procedure files you can edit

where you want to edit a key procedure:

1. Exit from MultiMate Advantage II by accessing DOS from within the program (by pressing Ctrl-2), or by selecting Exit Word Processor on the main menu.

2. At the DOS prompt, type *mm* and press Return. If you are using a two-floppy system, remove the System Diskette and replace it with the Boot Diskette. Make sure that UTIL.EXE has been copied to the Boot Diskette.

3. Select *Utilities and Conversions* on the Boot-up menu and press Return.

4. Highlight *Key Procedure Files Utility* on the Advanced Utilities menu and press F10.

5. Highlight *Edit a File* on the Key Procedure Files Utility screen and press F10.

6. Highlight the key procedure file name to be edited, *KP2,* and press F10. When this file appears on the screen, every keystroke that makes up KP2 should be displayed in the order in which you entered the keystrokes, as in Figure 8.9. This is the only screen on which you can see all the keystrokes you've entered.

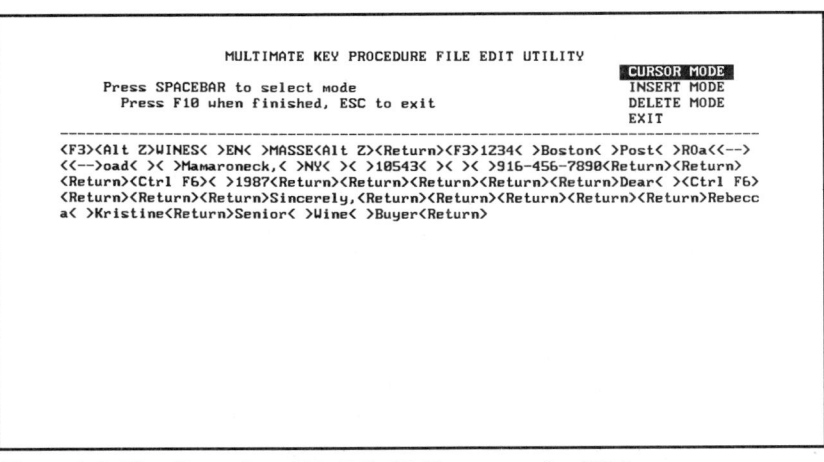

```
                    MULTIMATE KEY PROCEDURE FILE EDIT UTILITY
                                                              CURSOR MODE
              Press SPACEBAR to select mode                   INSERT MODE
              Press F10 when finished, ESC to exit            DELETE MODE
                                                              EXIT
---------------------------------------------------------------------------
<F3><Alt Z>WINES< >EN< >MASSE<Alt Z><Return><F3>1234< >Boston< >Post< >R0a<<-->
<<-->oad< >< >Mamaroneck,< >NY< >< >10543< >< >< >916-456-7890<Return><Return>
<Return><Ctrl F6>< >1987<Return><Return><Return><Return><Return>Dear< ><Ctrl F6>
<Return><Return><Return>Sincerely,<Return><Return><Return><Return>Rebecc
a< >Kristine<Return>Senior< >Wine< >Buyer<Return>
```

Figure 8.9: Key Procedure File Edit Utility screen for KP2

The File Edit Utility screen is divided into two sections: the top half is called the *Mode Control,* and the bottom half is called the *Key Procedure Display.* Let's discuss these sections before continuing with the example.

MODE CONTROL

Mode Control displays instructions for moving between the four modes. Two modes, Insert and Delete, are for actual editing. The Cursor mode allows for cursor movement. The Exit mode lets you exit from the key procedure file displayed and either edit another one or else quit the file edit utility. These four mode selections are listed on the right side of the Mode Control section. Table 8.1 shows which keys to use in each mode, and what happens when you use them.

KEY PROCEDURE DISPLAY

Key Procedure Display is the area where all the keystrokes in the file are displayed, and where you will edit the actual keystrokes. The file is displayed as a continuous string of keystrokes in the order in which you entered them. Each keystroke, including spaces, is surrounded by a pair of angle brackets, and text appears between other keystrokes. Spaces appear like this

< >< >

Mode	Purpose	Keys
Cursor	Move cursor to position in display area where you want to edit the file	All cursor keys
Delete	Delete keystrokes from a file	Delete key only
Insert	Add keystrokes to a file	Any key
Exit	Save all changes made during edit and return to Key Procedures File Edit main menu	Return

Table 8.1: Editing modes in Mode Control

with one space between each pair of brackets. Note that the ← and → keys are presented as

<←> and <→>

so that the arrowheads are identical to angle brackets, and may seem misleading.

The Key Procedure Display looks and works differently than any other screen you have worked with in MultiMate Advantage II. Your range of editorial control is limited to inserting keystrokes, deleting them, and moving the cursor around the screen to select keystrokes to insert or delete.

Editing KP2

Now let's return to the example. Take a closer look at Figure 8.9. At the end of the first line of keystrokes, notice the word

ROa

This reflects an error made when KP2 was first created. Recall that if you make a mistake while entering keystrokes, every keystroke will be recorded. You can, however, use the ← key to back up over your error, then enter the correct text.

<<–><<–>oad

Whenever KP2 is executed, the mistake will be recreated and then corrected as part of the execution.

You can correct this mistake using the key procedure file edit utility. First place the cursor at the place you want to insert or delete. In the Mode Control section of the screen, press the Space bar to highlight *Cursor Mode*. The prompt

Use Cursor Keys to Move Cursor
Press CTRL-M to Change Mode

will appear on the left side of the Mode Control section. The only thing you can do in the Cursor mode is move the cursor. You cannot insert or delete any keystrokes. When you see this prompt, press F10. This will place the cursor in the Key Procedure Display section of the screen, at the first keystroke. Move the cursor to the end of the first row of keystrokes, to the letter *O*. Now press Ctrl-M to change modes. This will return you to the top half of the screen.

Deleting Keystrokes

Press the Space bar so that *Delete Mode* is highlighted, and then press F10. This will return the cursor to the place you left it, under the capital *O*. The prompt

```
Press DEL to Delete Key at Cursor
Press CTRL-M to Change Mode
```

will appear on the left side of the Mode Control section. The only thing you can do when you are in this mode is delete keystrokes. You cannot move the cursor or insert keystrokes. You can delete keystrokes only by pressing the Delete key. (You cannot delete keystrokes by pressing the Minus key.)

Pressing Delete four times will delete the capital *O* as well as the *a* and the two ← immediately following. Notice that the keystrokes to the right of the cursor will move to the left as you delete each keystroke. This is why you should begin deleting a series of adjacent keystrokes by placing the cursor on the first keystroke of the series. When you are finished deleting, press Ctrl-M to return to the top section of the screen.

Inserting Keystrokes

The first mistake was corrected by simply deleting keystrokes. There is still another mistake in the key procedure file KP2. Again, it is a mistake that is displayed briefly during execution, but subsequent keystrokes correct it. This second mistake occurs in the last text word of the key procedure:

```
BUy<<−><<−>uyer
```

To correct the mistake, highlight *Cursor Mode* and move the cursor over the capital *U*. Press Ctrl-M and highlight *Insert Mode*. The only thing you can do in the Insert mode is insert keystrokes. You cannot move the cursor or delete keystrokes. The prompt

```
Insert at Current Location
Press CTRL-M to Change Mode
```

will appear on the left of the Mode Control section. Press F10 and then press *u*. This will insert the lowercase *u* and move the cursor one position to the right of that letter. Now enter the letters *yer* and you will see them appear in the proper sequence on the screen. The capital *U* and all keystrokes after it will move to the right as you insert new keystrokes.

After making these insertions, press Ctrl-M and highlight *Delete Mode*. Your cursor is already in the proper position, so press F10 and then press Delete eight times. This will complete the second correction and now KP2 should be perfect.

If at any time while you are making changes to a key procedure file you press Escape, the prompt

DO YOU WISH TO EXIT WITHOUT UPDATING THE KEY PROCEDURE FILE?
YES NO
Use SPACEBAR to Select, F10 to Continue, ESCAPE to Cancel

will appear at the top of the Mode Control section. If you select YES, the key procedure file will disappear from the screen, and any changes you have made so far will not be recorded. If you select NO, the prompt

<<<PLEASE WAIT>>>

will appear for a few moments at the bottom of the screen. When it disappears, you will be able to continue with your edit where you were when you pressed Escape.

CREATING KEY PROCEDURES IN ADVANCED UTILITIES

Although the standard way to build a key procedure file is to press Ctrl-F5 while you are in the Advantage II word-processing program, you can also build key procedure files within Advanced Utilities. You might even find the method easier in Advanced Utilities, if you have the appropriate files copied onto a single floppy disk, or located on the same pathway on your hard disk.

To build a file, access the Key Procedure Files Utility menu (Figure 8.7). Highlight

   Create a New File

on that screen, and press F10. The Create a New File screen, shown in Figure 8.10, will then appear. Enter the name of the key procedure file you are going to create—KP4—in the file name field, and press F10. The Key Procedure File Edit Utility screen (Figure 8.9) will then appear.

Highlight *Insert Mode,* press F10, and enter the keystrokes in Figure 8.11. You can see what the sequence of these keystrokes should look like on the screen in Figure 8.12. After the last keystroke, press Ctrl-M and highlight *Exit.*

This key procedure is quite handy if you are using the drop down insertion mode. In this mode, all text after the cursor position disappears from the screen, except for a few words at the bottom of the

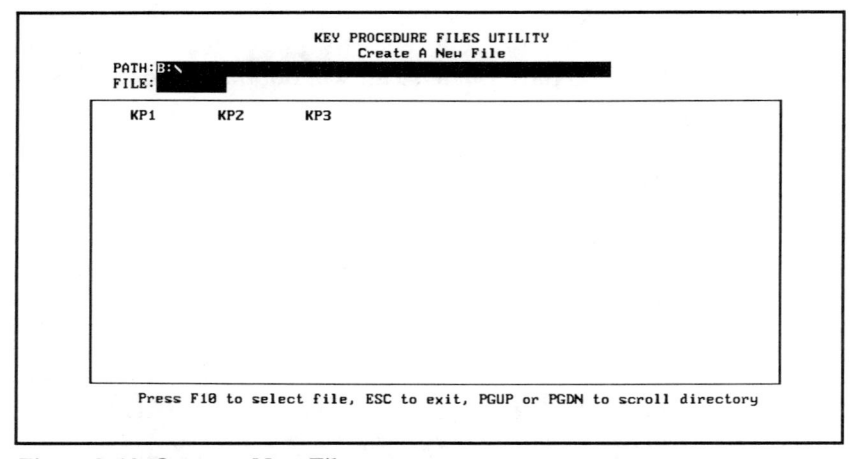

```
                         KEY PROCEDURE FILES UTILITY
                              Create A New File
              PATH: B:\
              FILE:

                 KP1       KP2       KP3




              Press F10 to select file, ESC to exit, PGUP or PGDN to scroll directory
```

Figure 8.10: Create a New File screen

```
         Insert
         . [space] . [space]: [3 lines of alternating dots and spaces]
         Return
         Home
         Insert
```

Figure 8.11: Keystroke listing for KP4

screen. KP4 allows you to insert text in a document in the midst of other text, so that you can see what comes both before and after the insertion.

When you execute KP4, all the text preceding the point where you begin execution will move up three lines. These are the three lines of spaces and dots that you inserted into the key procedure file. Several lines of text should remain on your screen so that you can keep the context of what follows in mind. You can type over the dots and not affect the preceding text. If your insertion exceeds three lines, you can execute KP4 as many times as you want. When you are done, press Delete, Return, and Delete again. This will erase the remaining dots and join the preceding text with what you have inserted.

DELETING A FILE

To delete a file using Advanced Utilities, go to the Key Procedure Files Utility screen (Figure 8.7) and highlight *Delete a File*. Then press F10, and the Delete File screen, shown in Figure 8.13, will appear. Use the Space bar to highlight the file listed on this screen that you want to delete, and press F10. There is a safety feature built into this delete function. After you select the file and press F10, the prompt

ARE YOU SURE YOU WANT TO DELETE FILE?
YES NO

```
                    MULTIMATE KEY PROCEDURE FILE EDIT UTILITY
                                                              CURSOR MODE
          Press SPACEBAR to select mode                       INSERT MODE
          Press F10 when finished, ESC to exit                DELETE MODE
                                                              EXIT
    ----------------------------------------------------------------------
    <Ins><  >.<  >.<  >.<  >.<  >.<  >.<  >.<  >.<  >.<  >.<  >.<  >.<  >.<  >
    .<  >.<  >.<  >.<  >.<  >.<  >.<  >.<  >.<  >.<  >.<  >.<  >.<  >.<  >.<  >
    .<  >.<  >.<  >.<  >.<  >.<  >.<  >.<  >.<  >.<  >.<  >.<  >.<  >.<  >.<  >
    .<  >.<  >.<  >.<  >.<  >.<  >.<  >.<  ><  >.<  >.<  >.<  ><Return><Ins>
```

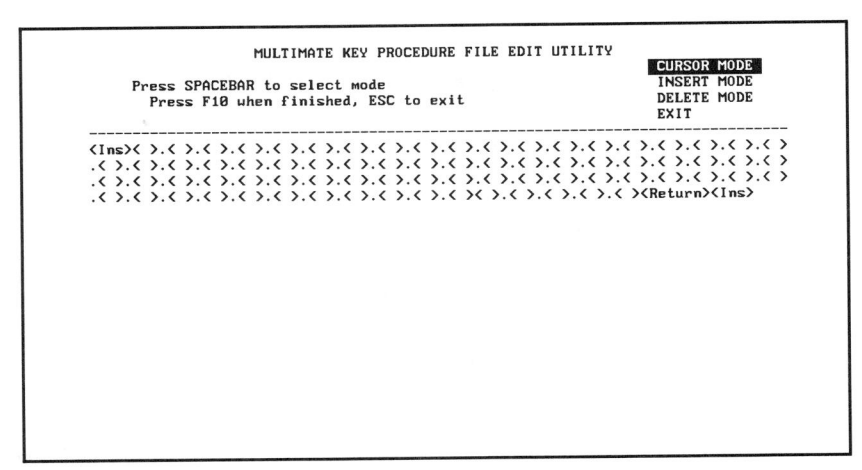

Figure 8.12: KP4 entered in File Edit Utility screen

will appear at the bottom of the screen. This is your only chance to reconsider; you can't undo the deletion later. Since YES is the default setting, pressing F10 again will delete the file you have designated.

EXITING FROM THE KEY PROCEDURE FILE EDIT UTILITY

Anytime you are satisfied with the changes you made to a key procedure by editing an old file or creating a new one, highlight *Exit* in the Mode Control section of the File Edit Utility screen. This will return you to the Key Procedure Files Utility screen. This is also the screen that you go to after deleting a key procedure file. Pressing Escape here will take you to the Advanced Utilities screen. You can go directly into the Advantage II word-processing program by selecting

1) Professional Word Processor

If you enter the word-processing program from the Boot-up menu, this menu will reappear when you exit the word processing program from the main menu.

If you wish to return to DOS, select

9) Exit Word Processor

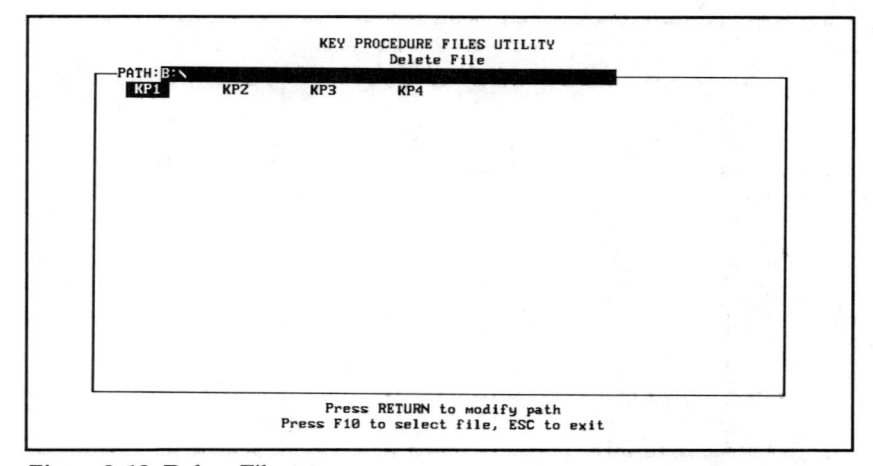

Figure 8.13: Delete File screen

If you are using the DOS Access feature, type EXIT at the DOS prompt.

Key procedures are powerful tools. They require close attention when you create them, but they will provide excellent performance when created correctly and used often. The key is to design key procedures that will save you time. Pay attention to what you do when you work with Multimate Advantage II. Chances are you can speed up your performance and make your work easier by coming up with key procedures that work for you.

In the next chapter, you'll learn how to make long documents more comprehensible with section numbering, and you'll learn how to create a table of contents.

Numbering Sections and Creating Tables of Contents

LONG DOCUMENTS OFTEN BECOME MORE CLEARLY focused when they are divided into sections, which are then marked with subheads. The reader can scan the entire document before tackling the details. In addition, the reader can go back and quickly review specific sections.

Dividing a document into these sections is called *section numbering* in MultiMate Advantage II. After you determine which sections of text you want numbered, Advantage II will go through the document and number them for you in sequential order. This section numbering can be an end in itself, for very long reports, or else you can use it as a precursor to creating a table of contents for the document.

Quite often, documents are preceded by a table of contents. Advantage II will create a table of contents for you, as long as the document has been section-numbered first. In effect, the table of contents is produced by deleting the text within each section, and listing only the section titles. Advantage II will update both the section numbers and a table of contents derived from them whenever you change the text within a document. You will learn all of these procedures in this chapter.

SECTION NUMBERING

You can number sections in two different ways. You can take an existing document, divide the text into various sections, and number and title these sections. Or you can create a document for the first time, and assign section numbers and titles as you add text. In either case, before you begin, you should be familiar with the contents of the document. Advantage II will indent, number, and format the sections for you, but it is up to you to determine the importance and order of each section. You will have to number sections before you can create a table of contents, because the table of contents is derived from the numbered sections. The table of contents can be included with the report, or it can serve as a handy outline. Although you can create an outline first and then add text between the headings, I do not recommend this procedure.

Before you assign section numbers to either a new or an existing document, you have to decide two things:

- Section numbering style: Roman or Numeric
- Format of section numbers and titles

Let's first discuss section numbering style.

Section Numbering Style

You specify the section numbering style for a specific document on the Modify Document Defaults screen (see Chapter 5). If you want the style to be the same for all documents, you set this on the Edit System Defaults screen. Roman style, used in traditional outlines, labels the heading levels with I, A, 1, a, (1), and (a). Numeric style, used in technical outlines, labels the heading levels with 1, 1.1, 1.1.1, and so on. There is a limit of six levels in both the Roman and Numeric styles, and you won't be using all six except in extraordinary circumstances.

If you want to add section numbers to a new document, pay attention to the Modify Document Defaults screen before you create the document. The last setting on that screen is

Section Numbering: [(R)oman Or (N)umeric]

and the default setting is *R* for Roman. You can change this setting to *N*.

If you want to add section numbers to an existing document, on the main menu, select

7) System and Document Defaults

This will cause the System and Document Defaults menu (Figure 5.2) to appear on your screen. On this menu, select

4) Edit Document Defaults

This will move you into the Edit Document Defaults screen (Figure 5.3), where you can type the name of the document whose formatting defaults you want to change. Type the name of the document you wish to modify, and the Modify Document Defaults screen

NUMBERING SECTIONS AND CREATING TABLES OF CONTENTS 209

appear. It is on this screen that you can set the section numbering for a specific document.

you want to change the default section numbering style for all ments, on the System and Document Defaults screen, select

3) Edit System Defaults

the Edit System Defaults menu (Figure 4.3) will appear. Change entry in the Section Numbering Style field near the bottom of screen.

Section Numbering Format

Once you have set the numbering style, you have to decide how you want the section numbers to line up in relation to the left margin of the page. If you use the Numeric style of sectioning, you will probably want to have the numbers lined up on the left margin.

The Roman style allows for more flexibility in format. The two most common formats for Roman style are to have the numbers and letters lined up along the left margin

    I.

    A.

    1.

    a.

    b.

    B.

or else indented for each section and subsection

    I.

      A.

        1.

          a.

          b.

      B.

Now let's look at an example. You'll be working with the report shown in Figure 9.1. Create a new document with the name Report, and type the text just as you see it in Figure 9.1. You are going to divide this text into sections in three ways, and then you will extract a table of contents from it.

```
                REPORT ON WINE BUYING TRIP TO CALIFORNIA

                            by Rebecca Kristine

         This report will describe my observations and purchases made
    during my recent wine buying trip to California. As you may
    already know, I purchased a record number of wines during this
    trip. I think these purchases are wise, and I will use this
    report to explain why.

         I arrived in San Francisco November 7. I spent the first day
    preparing my schedule for the following week by calling around
    and confirming several appointments. Even though the weekend was
    coming up, this time of year is the harvest season in the wine
    business, and everyone I wanted to meet was working in their
    cellars.

         Saturday afternoon I drove up to the Napa Valley, an hour's
    drive north of San Francisco. I was afraid I would miss a good
    part of the fall season on the East Coast, but the leaves on the
    grape vines were turning vivid fall colors. I arrived at the town
    of St. Helena before dinner, and managed to stroll its two blocks
    before the shops closed. I was curious to see what wines the
    locals were drinking themselves. Red and white wines share an
    equal amount of shelf space. The white wine boom might be
    continuing in the rest of the country, but California, which sets
    the pace, seems to be switching back again.

         John Nicciloni's son, Nick, had invited me to dinner at his
    house about twelve miles outside of town, but I was afraid of
    getting lost on the country road at night, so Nick met me in town
    for dinner. No one from WINES EN MASSE had seen anyone else in
    the family since John died. I still think their wines are the
    best Italian-style domestic reds for casual drinking.

         Nick is willing to continue the current contract his father
    signed. It isn't due to expire until the end of the year, but I
    left him a copy of the new contract so he could review it. If we
    stay in touch with Nick, we should be able to continue with the
    exclusive rights to distribute his wine outside of California.

         Fortunately, Nick was eager to display not only his own
    wines, but those of other smaller wineries as well. He was
    particularly enamored of a 1982 Pinot Noir from a winery called
    Bay Cellars. I would have been willing to stop there. Nick,
    however, insisted that I try them all. I'm afraid I got a late
    start the next morning. I will have more to say about Bay Cellars
    farther along in this report.

         I had a luncheon appointment at Burgess Cellars, about five
    miles out of town. To keep the morning frost off the vines, the
    smudge pots were out, and the dew machines were roaring away when
    I woke up. The fog lifted by the time I arrived at Burgess
    Cellars. This winery used to be known as Souverain Cellars, whose
    wine we bought twenty years ago. In particular, I am recommending
```

Figure 9.1: First two pages of the report

Because you'll be trying several different formats, you'll first want to make copies of the original report. To make a copy, select

6) Document Management

> Burgess' Pink Zinfandel. I am not a fan of Zinfandel wine, but I have been encouraged to locate several Zinfandels for our line. I am keen on finding out the committee's reaction to this wine.
>
> Rob Pecceta was my host for dinner. His winery is near the town of Calistoga. Rob runs a clean winery. He's an MBA graduate and runs his business by the books. That doesn't seem to prevent him from making excellent wines. He also beats the bush for public recognition. This is important in a market which is crowded with oversupply. Rob volunteered to come back east for a week or so of visiting important distributors and retail customers. I mentioned the conference of distributors we are planning to host in Washington, and Rob said he would block out that week unless he heard otherwise from us. I think Rob would make a dynamic speaker.
>
> Next morning I was able to visit Hans Kologne Champagne Cellars. This wasn't on my itinerary as planned, but I rose at 6 AM to make up for the previous day, and was lucky enough to find Hans at work in his riddling room. I couldn't take much of his time, and he says he has no problem selling every ounce of champagne he produces. Nevertheless, he said he would like to see some of his product in the major markets on the East Coast. I managed to select four cases of old and new champagnes, which have already arrived at the office, and which I am guarding closely.
>
> I made it in time for lunch with Dave Bynum at his winery. Dave and Doris had the picnic tables spread with food and wine when I arrived, and I partook of an excellent lunch with the winery crew. Surprising what one learns when one talks with the workers. One of the hands had worked at Bay Cellars a few weeks before, and he recommended that I go out of my way if I have to to visit that winery. Dave seconded that recommendation.
>
> No other winemaker puts more of his personality into his product than Dave. As has been the case since he first started making wine, Dave's Pinot Noirs are his best. He has vintages in quantity going all the way back to 1980, but nothing in quantity farther back than 1983. We have options on this wine, as well as his 1984s, and Dave would like us to exercise them. I recommend that we exercise these options at the next meeting. We are completely sold out of Dave's Pinot Noirs, and have been taking back orders for the last six weeks.
>
> Dave has produced no Merlot the last two years. He preferred to sell the grapes to Budrick Cellars. I realize several committee members will be disappointed to hear this, since Dave's Merlot is a favorite. I have called Jerzy Budrick and he promised to send us samples as soon as he has the time.

Figure 9.1: First two pages of the report (continued)

on the main menu, and then select

1) Copy a Document

on the Document Management screen (Figure 3.5). Make four copies, and name the documents Flush, Tab, Numeric, and Numtab.

FLUSH-LEFT NUMBERING

We'll begin the exercise with flush-left numbering. First, you'll specify Roman style for the document called Flush. Then you will number the sections flush along the left margin and type in section titles, as shown in Figure 9.2. A new paragraph has been created by moving the last sentence in the third paragraph into a paragraph of its own. Whenever you number sections of a casually written report, you might want to check to make sure that each important point will stand out in its own section.

Here are the steps to follow to create flush-left numbering.

1. To identify a section, place the cursor on the indent symbol (≫) in the first paragraph of the document Flush.
2. Press Alt-U, the Section Number key. The section number symbol

    ☼

    will appear on the screen, and the cursor will move over one space. Press the Insert key to enter insert mode. Press the Space bar to enter a blank space, and then type the section title, which can be as long as the line length.

For this example, type

Introduction

and press Return to put a hard carriage return symbol after the section title. Now press the Insert key a second time to exit insert mode. If you made a mistake when entering the title, you can go back to edit the title, just as you can edit any other text on a Document screen. Be careful not to type over the section number symbol, or you will erase

```
                    REPORT ON WINE BUYING TRIP TO CALIFORNIA
                              by Rebecca Kristine

        I. Introduction
              This report will describe my observations and purchases made
        during my recent wine buying trip to California. As you may
        already know, I purchased a record number of wines during this
        trip. I think these purchases are wise, and I will use this
        report to explain why.

        A. Prepare for my visits
              I arrived in San Francisco November 7. I spent the first day
        preparing my schedule for the following week by calling around
        and confirming several appointments. Even though the weekend was
        coming up, this time of year is the harvest season in the wine
        business, and everyone I wanted to meet was working in their
        cellars.

        B. Impressions of local market
              Saturday afternoon I drove up to the Napa Valley, an hour's
        drive north of San Francisco. I was afraid I would miss a good
        part of the fall season on the East Coast, but the leaves on the
        grape vines were turning vivid fall colors. I arrived at the town
        of St. Helena before dinner, and managed to stroll its two blocks
        before the shops closed. I was curious to see what wines the
        locals were drinking themselves. Red and white wines share an
        equal amount of shelf space.

        1. red wines rising
              The white wine boom might be continuing in the rest of the
        country, but California, which sets the pace, seems to be
        switching back again.

        II. Nicciloni update
              John Nicciloni's son, Nick, had invited me to dinner at his
        house about twelve miles outside of town, but I was afraid of
        getting lost on the country road at night, so Nick met me in town
        for dinner. No one from WINES EN MASSE had seen anyone else in
        the family since John died. I still think their wines are the
        best Italian-style domestic reds for casual drinking.

        A. Nick is willing to continue with current contract
              Nick is willing to continue the current contract his father
        signed. It isn't due to expire until the end of the year, but I
        left him a copy of the new contract so he could review it. If we
        stay in touch with Nick, we should be able to continue with the
        exclusive rights to distribute his wine outside of California.

        B. Nick introduces me to new wineries - esp Bay Cellars
              Fortunately, Nick was eager to display not only his own
        wines, but those of other smaller wineries as well. He was
        particularly enamored of a 1982 Pinot Noir from a winery called
        Bay Cellars. I would have been willing to stop there.
```

Figure 9.2: Section numbers flush along left margin

it. If you do inadvertently delete the symbol, you can reenter it. Place the cursor in the correct position, make sure the prompt

    INSERT

is showing on the right side of the status line, and then press Alt-U.

3. To create the next section, move to the beginning of the second paragraph and press Alt-U to insert a section number symbol at the left margin, and then type in the title. Remember to enter a hard carriage return by pressing Return after each title and subtitle. Note that for the highest level of heading (I), or level 1, you need only press Alt-U once. To indicate each successive level, you need to press Alt-U the number of times corresponding to the heading level: twice for level 2 (A), thrice for Level 3 (1), and so on.

Continue entering section number symbols on the first line of each paragraph on the first page of Flush, then enter the appropriate section title, and finally press Return. When you come to the third paragraph, separate its last sentence into a new paragraph, and number and title it as shown in Figure 9.2.

4. Next, instruct Advantage II to assign section numbers. Press Ctrl-Home twice to return to the top of the first page, and then press Ctrl-F2, the Document Reorganization key.

The document reorganization window will appear in the lower half of your screen, as shown in Figure 9.3. The third choice on this screen

ALT-3 Assign Section Numbers:

is set No, for no section numbering.

5. Press Alt-3 to move the light bar from No to Yes (Alt-3 toggles between the two choices).

You need to make one more change in the document reorganization window (you can change as many settings as you like at the same time). Because you added new text to the document, you should repaginate it.

6. Press Alt-1 to change the setting for the Repagination the Document option from No to Yes.

Repagination takes extra time, so you should not have Advantage II perform this task unless you've made changes that may affect the length of one or more pages.

```
DOCUMENT: Flush              ‖PAGE:   1‖LINE:  13‖COL:   1‖
[1--»----»----»-------------------------------------«--
                 ··REPORT ON WINE BUYING TRIP TO CALIFORNIA«
  «
                        ··By Rebecca Kristine«
  «
I. Introduction«
      »This report will describe my observations and purchases made
during my recent wine buying trip to California. As you may
                    ▓▓▓▓▓▓▓▓▓▓▓ DOCUMENT REORGANIZATION ▓▓▓▓▓▓▓▓▓▓▓
       ALT-1     Repaginate the Document:    No    Yes
       ALT-2     Hyphenation:                None  User-Selected  Automatic
       ALT-3     Assign Section Numbers:     No    Yes
       ALT-4     Create a Table of Contents: No    Yes

                      Lines Per Page:      055
                      Hyphenation Zone Width:   07

                    Press F10 when finished, ESC to cancel
                  Press ALT and a number key to change a setting
                                                              S:1 N:1
```

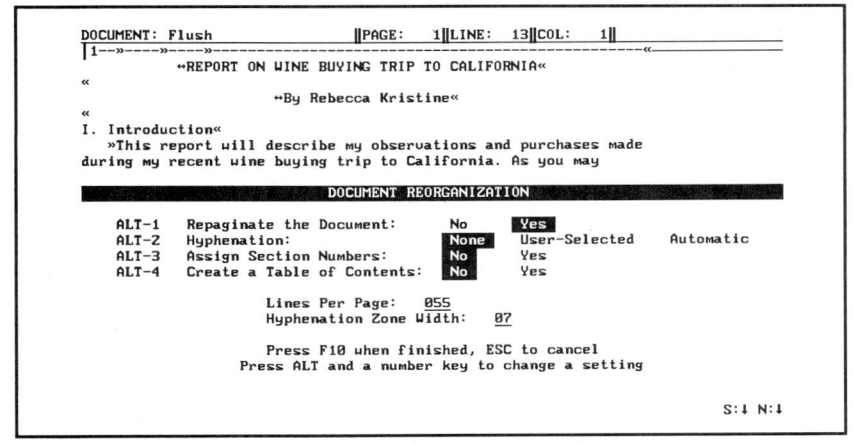

Figure 9.3: Assigning section numbers and repaginating the flush document

7. Press F10 to replace the section number symbols with Roman style sequential numbering.

While Advantage II is doing this, the prompt

Reorganizing – Please wait

will appear at the bottom of the document reorganization window. When the section numbers have all been assigned, the document reorganization window will disappear from the screen. Your document should now look like Figure 9.2.

NUMBERING WITH TAB INDENTS

The second format in which section numbers can appear is arranged according to tab stop positions. Each level can then be indented the same amount, so you can see the relative importance of each topic at a glance. Figure 9.4 shows the first page of the report with section numbers indented.

To arrange the section numbers in this format, begin with the document called Tab.

1. From the Document screen of Tab, set the appropriate tab stops in the system format line. Press F9, the Format Change

```
                    REPORT ON WINE BUYING TRIP TO CALIFORNIA
                              by Rebecca Kristine
           I. Introduction
                 This report will describe my observations and purchases made
           during my recent wine buying trip to California. As you may
           already know, I purchased a record number of wines during this
           trip. I think these purchases are wise, and I will use this
           report to explain why.

              A. Prepare for my visits
                 I arrived in San Francisco November 7. I spent the first day
           preparing my schedule for the following week by calling around
           and confirming several appointments. Even though the weekend was
           coming up, this time of year is the harvest season in the wine
           business, and everyone I wanted to meet was working in their
           cellars.

              B. Impressions of local market
                 Saturday afternoon I drove up to the Napa Valley, an hour's
           drive north of San Francisco. I was afraid I would miss a good
           part of the fall season on the East Coast, but the leaves on the
           grape vines were turning vivid fall colors. I arrived at the town
           before the shops closed. I was curious to see what wines the
           locals were drinking themselves. Red and white wines share an
           equal amount of shelf space.

                 1. red wines rising
                 The white wine boom might be continuing in the rest of the
           country, but California, which sets the pace, seems to be
           switching back again.

           II. Nicciloni update
                 John Nicciloni's son, Nick, had invited me to dinner at his
           house about twelve miles outside of town, but I was afraid of
           getting lost on the country road at night, so Nick met me in town
           for dinner. No one from WINES EN MASSE had seen anyone else in
           the family since John died. I still think their wines are the
           best Italian-style domestic reds for casual drinking.

              A. Nick is willing to continue with current contract
                 Nick is willing to continue the current contract his father
           signed. It isn't due to expire until the end of the year, but I
           left him a copy of the new contract so he could review it. If we
           stay in touch with Nick, we should be able to continue with the
           exclusive rights to distribute his wine outside of California.

              B. Nick introduces me to new wineries - esp Bay Cellars
                 Fortunately, Nick was eager to display not only his own
           wines, but those of other smaller wineries as well. He was
           particularly enamored of a 1982 Pinot Noir from a winery called
           Bay Cellars. I would have been willing to stop there.
```

Figure 9.4: Report with indented Roman-style section numbers

key, and erase existing tab stops as you press the Tab key to place new ones in columns 3, 6, and 9.

You should always have a clear idea when you start of exactly how many levels of sections you are going to use, and how many spaces you need to contain the numbering, including periods and spaces.

For instance, the document Tab uses three levels:

   I. Introduction
      A. Prepare for my visits
      B. Impressions of the local market
         1. red wines rising

Tab stops three spaces apart allow one space each for the section number, the period, and a space before the title. (Of course, if you had many major headings, you would need to allow more spaces for higher Roman numerals, such as III and VIII.)

2. To create indented section numbers, first place the cursor on the first line of the first paragraph. Now press Alt-U to insert a section number symbol, press the Space bar to insert a space, and type the title.

You don't need to insert tab stops for a level 1 head because it is not indented, but is flush against the left margin. So you will begin to make use of the tab stops in the second paragraph.

3. Press Tab or Indent to move the cursor to the first tab stop. Now press Alt-U two times to insert two section number symbols, denoting level 2. Then, as usual, press the Space bar and type the title. Follow the same steps for the third paragraph.

4. The fourth paragraph is the single sentence that became a paragraph. Since *red wines rising* is a level 3 head, press Tab or Indent twice and then press Alt-U three times to insert three section number symbols. Then type the section title.

Now when you assign section numbers to this example by working through the document reorganization window, your example should be identical to Figure 9.5. Notice that only the section titles, not the associated text beneath them, are indented. Even so, the tab settings are too close together to make the levels obvious between text paragraphs. If the indents are too large, however, the section titles will appear to be centered on the page.

When you use tab stops to line up section numbers, you will have to use the same tab stops throughout the document. This is accomplished most easily if you use the system format line throughout. If you must use several different format lines in a document with section numbers, make sure that the first several tab positions correspond to your section numbers.

Advantage II is flexible enough that you can try one set of tab stops, and if they don't work out you can change them. The document will be realigned as soon as you press F9 to change the format and move the cursor to the format line. Still, the more time you spend thinking about your format beforehand, the more time you will save later.

EDITING SECTION NUMBERS

You can change the level of section numbers by deleting or adding section number symbols, just as you would delete or add text. When you delete the symbols, if you have already generated section numbers, you should delete the numbers as well. If you change the levels or arrangement of section numbers and want to see the document displayed correctly, press Ctrl-F2 to bring up the document reorganization window. Press Alt-3 to change the Assign Section Numbers setting from N to Y. Then press F10, and when the window disappears, the section numbers will be adjusted according to your revisions.

NUMERIC SECTION NUMBERING

When you use the numeric style of section numbering, you are limited to the flush-left format. The text in Figure 9.5 shows the sections on the first page of the report numbered in the Numeric style.

To create this style of numbering, begin with the document called Numeric.

1. Place the cursor on the tab symbol in the first paragraph.

2. Press Alt-U to enter a section number symbol, then enter a space and the title, and press Return.

3. Press Alt-U twice to enter two screen symbols each for the second and third paragraphs (1.2 and 2.1), and press Alt-U three times to enter three symbols for the fourth paragraph (1.2.1). As usual, add a space and the title, and press Return, for each section head.

```
               REPORT ON WINE BUYING TRIP TO CALIFORNIA
                          by Rebecca Kristine

     1. Introduction
            This report will describe my observations and purchases made
     during my recent wine buying trip to California. As you may
     already know, I purchased a record number of wines during this
     trip. I think these purchases are wise, and I will use this
     report to explain why.

     1.1. Prepare for my visits
            I arrived in San Francisco November 7. I spent the first day
     preparing my schedule for the following week by calling around
     and confirming several appointments. Even though the weekend was
     coming up, this time of year is the harvest season in the wine
     business, and everyone I wanted to meet was working in their
     cellars.

     1.2. Impressions of local market
               Saturday afternoon I drove up to the Napa Valley, an hour's
     drive north of San Francisco. I was afraid I would miss a good
     part of the fall season on the East Coast, but the leaves on the
     grape vines were turning vivid fall colors. I arrived at the town
     of St. Helena before dinner, and managed to stroll its two blocks
     before the shops closed. I was curious to see what wines the
     locals were drinking themselves. Red and white wines share an
     equal amount of shelf space.

     1.2.1. red wines rising
            The white wine boom might be continuing in the rest of the
     country, but California, which sets the pace, seems to be
     switching back again.

     2. Nicciloni update
            John Nicciloni's son, Nick, had invited me to dinner at his
     house about twelve miles outside of town, but I was afraid of
     getting lost on the country road at night, so Nick met me in town
     for dinner. No one from WINES EN MASSE had seen anyone else in
     the family since John died. I still think their wines are the
     best Italian-style domestic reds for casual drinking.

     2.1. Nick is willing to continue with current contract
            Nick is willing to continue the current contract his father
     signed. It isn't due to expire until the end of the year, but I
     left him a copy of the new contract so he could review it. If we
     stay in touch with Nick, we should be able to continue with the
     exclusive rights to distribute his wine outside of California.

     2.2. Nick intrdoucts me to new wineries - esp. Bay Cellars
              Fortunately, Nick was eager to display not only his own
     wines, but those of other smaller wineries as well. He was
     particularly enamored of a 1982 Pinot Noir from a winery called
     Bay Cellars. I would have been willing to stop there.
```

Figure 9.5: First page of report in Numeric style

Note that the procedure is the same as for other numbering styles: press Alt-U *n* times for a level *n* heading.

4. When you are finished entering all the section titles for Numeric, press F10 to exit from the document, and go to the

Modify Document Defaults screen for the Numeric document (as described at the beginning of this chapter). Then, change the Section Number Style setting from R for Roman to N for Numeric.

5. Return to the Document screen and press Ctrl-F2 to access the document reorganization window. Change the Repaginate the Document setting to N and Assign Section Numbers to Y.

6. Press F10 to commence section numbering. In a few moments, Numeric should have section numbers arranged by level in Numeric style.

ALIGNING NUMERIC-STYLE NUMBERING WITH DECIMAL TABS

You can also align Numeric-style numbers with tabs, but you would only want to do this with a single tab stop. Such an arrangement is shown in Figure 9.6.

Normally, Numeric section numbers line up along the left margin. For the first nine level-1 heads, only a single digit will appear between the decimal and the left margin. But when there are ten or more levels, the numbers will no longer line up at the decimal point:

9.5.1

9.5.2

10.1

10.1.1

10.1.2

To restore alignment of the level-1 numbers, you can specify a decimal tab. Usually, the decimals will align at the first tab setting. In any case, you should maintain the same tab setting throughout the document. Note that you can easily delete excess decimal tabs.

Now go to the document called Numtab.

1. Place the cursor on the tab symbol in the first paragraph, and press Insert to enter insert mode.

```
                REPORT ON WINE BUYING TRIP TO CALIFORNIA
                           by Rebecca Kristine

     1. Introduction
          This report will describe my observations and purchases made
     during my recent wine buying trip to California. As you may
     already know, I purchased a record number of wines during this
     trip. I think these purchases are wise, and I will use this
     report to explain why.

          1.1. Prepare for my visits
               I arrived in San Francisco November 7. I spent the first day
          preparing my schedule for the following week by calling around
          and confirming several appointments. Even though the weekend was
          coming up, this time of year is the harvest season in the wine
          business, and everyone I wanted to meet was working in their
          cellars.

          1.2. Impressions of local market
               Saturday afternoon I drove up to the Napa Valley, an hour's
          drive north of San Francisco. I was afraid I would miss a good
          part of the fall season on the East Coast, but the leaves on the
          grape vines were turning vivid fall colors. I arrived at the town
          before the shops closed. I was curious to see what wines the
          locals were drinking themselves. Red and white wines share an
          equal amount of shelf space.

               1.2.1. red wines rising
                    The white wine boom might be continuing in the rest of the
               country, but California, which sets the pace, seems to be
               switching back again.

     2. Nicciloni update
          John Nicciloni's son, Nick, had invited me to dinner at his
     house about twelve miles outside of town, but I was afraid of
     getting lost on the country road at night, so Nick met me in town
     for dinner. No one from WINES EN MASSE had seen anyone else in
     the family since John died. I still think their wines are the
     best Italian-style domestic reds for casual drinking.

          2.1. Nick is willing to continue with current contract
               Nick is willing to continue the current contract his father
          signed. It isn't due to expire until the end of the year, but I
          left him a copy of the new contract so he could review it. If we
          stay in touch with Nick, we should be able to continue with the
          exclusive rights to distribute his wine outside of California.

          2.2. Nick introduces me to new wineries - esp Bay Cellars
               Fortunately, Nick was eager to display not only his own
          wines, but those of other smaller wineries as well. He was
          particularly enamored of a 1982 Pinot Noir from a winery called
          Bay Cellars. I would have been willing to stop there.
```

Figure 9.6: Numeric-style section numbering aligned with a decimal tab

> 2. Then press Shift-F4, the Decimal Tab key. This will place a solid box, denoting a decimal tab, at the first tab stop.

You could continue to enter decimal tab stops on the text line, at each tab stop, but you only need to use the first one for section numbering in the Numeric style. If the first tab stop is in column 3, you can have three digits between the decimal and the left margin. This gives you enough space to have up to 999 level-1 sections; if you need more, move the decimal tab setting to the right.

3. Now press Alt-U to insert a section number symbol for the first level-1 head.

4. Continue to add the rest of the subheadings in the usual manner: a single decimal tab and two section number symbols each for the second and third paragraphs (both level 2), and a single decimal tab and three section number symbols for the fourth paragraph (level 3), and so on.

5. When you've finished adding section numbers to the document, bring up the document reorganization window (Ctrl-F2) and assign section numbers to Numtab.

Your Numtab document should look like Figure 9.6.

CREATING A TABLE OF CONTENTS

You can create a table of contents from any document that has had section numbering assigned with Alt-U. In effect, Advantage II deletes the text between section numbers and extracts the section headings to create the table of contents.

To create a table of contents, begin with a document that has section numbering. Let's use the document called Tab as an example. Begin at the Document screen.

1. Press Ctrl-F2 to display the document reorganization window.

2. Press Alt-4 to change the fourth setting

    ALT-4 Create a Table of Contents

from N to Y.

3. Press F10 and wait until the document reorganization window disappears from the screen. That's it—the table of contents has been created.

Unlike section numbering, the table of contents is not displayed on the screen when Advantage II has finished creating it. The table of contents you have just created is attached to the document much as the Document Summary screen is attached.

You have to follow several steps to view the table of contents.

1. Exit from the document Tab by pressing F10.

2. At the main menu, select

    1) Edit a Document

3. When the Edit a Document screen appears, the name Tab should remain in the document field. Press F7, the Table of Contents key, and the Edit a Table of Contents Document screen, shown in Figure 9.7, will appear.

4. Press F10 to bring up the Document Summary screen for Tab.

5. Press Return, and the table of contents you just created should appear on the Document screen.

The table of contents for Tab should look like the beginning of Figure 9.8.

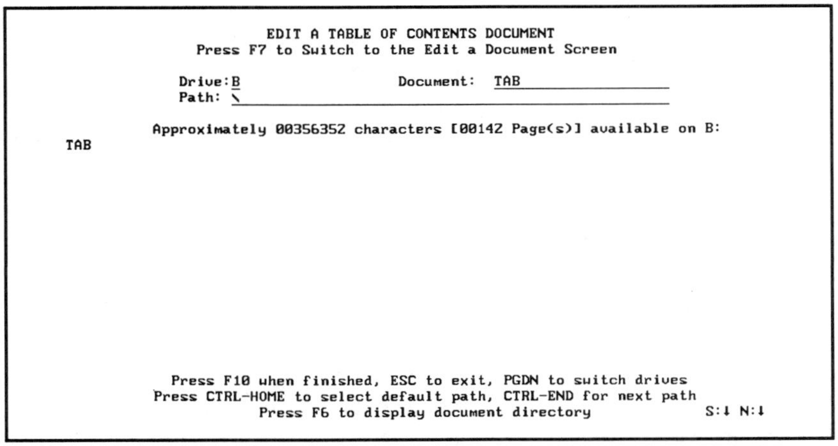

```
                    EDIT A TABLE OF CONTENTS DOCUMENT
                Press F7 to Switch to the Edit a Document Screen

            Drive:B              Document:   TAB
            Path: \

            Approximately 00356352 characters [00142 Page(s)] available on B:
   TAB




                Press F10 when finished, ESC to exit, PGDN to switch drives
             Press CTRL-HOME to select default path, CTRL-END for next path
                      Press F6 to display document directory         S:1 N:1
```

Figure 9.7: Edit a Table of Contents Document screen

```
       I. Introduction.....................................1
          A. Prepare for my visits........................1
          B. Impressions of local market..................1
             1. red wines rising..........................1
      II. Nicciloni update................................1
          A. Nick is willing to continue with current contract..1
          B. Nick introduces me to new wineries - esp Bay Cellars..1
     III. Burgess Cellars update..........................2
          A. Formerly Souverain Winery....................2
             1. watch out for their Pink Zinfandel........2
      IV. Pecceta Vineyards...............................2
          A. Rob is willing to do PR......................2
       V. Hans Kologne Champagne Cellars..................2
          A. Hans interested in east coast market.........2
      VI. Bynum Winery update.............................2
          A. Dave mentions Bay Cellars Winery.............3
          B. Dave's Pinot Noirs still excellent...........3
             1. quantities on hand........................3
             2. need to exercise our options on Dave's Pinot Noirs..3
                a. we are out of stock with Dave's Pinots.3
          C. No Merot this year...........................3
             1. Dave mentions Budrick Cellars Merlot......3
```

Figure 9.8: Table of contents for Tab

Advantage II will create a table of contents using only the settings of the *system* format line; all other format lines in the document are ignored. In more complicated documents, the format lines may change in several places, and you will have to incorporate all the important tab stops into the system format line. When you check the settings on the system format line, make sure you refer to the format line that appears at the top of the first page of the document.

EDITING THE TABLE OF CONTENTS

You can edit a table of contents just like any other document. For example, in the table of contents for Tab, say you want to remove the three-letter abbreviation *esp* from II.B. First, move the cursor over the *e* in *esp*. Press the Minus key (on the keypad) three times (or the Delete key six times) to delete these three characters. Notice that the page reference for II.B. has moved left three spaces. To restore the page reference to its proper position, place the cursor anywhere on the dotted line. Now enter three more dots by pressing Insert once and then entering three periods.

Note: Changing a table of contents doesn't change the heading in the document. If you want the headings in the document to match those in the table of contents exactly, the best way to ensure that they do is to change the document heads first.

Whenever you add text to a document that has section numbering and that has a table of contents attached to it, you should generate a new table of contents. This new table of contents will automatically replace the old one.

If you want to delete a table of contents, you will have to use the DOS DELETE command. A table of contents is created in a separate file from the document and recorded that way on the disk, with the file extension .TOC.

You can exit from the table of contents by pressing F10, and you can always reenter the table of contents by following these steps:

1. Select *Edit a Document* on the main menu and press Return.

2. Press F7 on the Document Summary screen to bring up the Edit a Table of Contents Document screen.

3. Type the name of the document whose table of contents you want to see, and press Return.

In addition, you can print a copy of the table of contents by using Hot Print. Simply press Ctrl-PrtSc for each page you want printed.

Section numbering is a useful tool when you are working with very long documents. Naturally, you won't want to divide a short document into sections or create a table of contents for it. With documents that run to a great length, such as scientific treatises and management consulting reports, dividing them into sections is crucial to help readers to tackle them. So too is a table of contents necessary for those readers who wish to scan the contents as they prepare to digest a lot of information.

Section numbering is only one way to divide a document into specific parts. There is a more specific way of containing text and numbers within the bounds of a column, and even drawing borders around these sections to highlight them. This is what you will learn in the next chapter.

10

COLUMN APPLICATIONS

COLUMNS ALLOW YOU TO PRESENT TEXT IN SPECIAL formats that dramatically change the appearance of your documents. You can use three kinds of columns in MultiMate Advantage II: tab, bound, and snake. After you have created these column boundaries, the text remains within them. Tab columns are ideal for arranging rows of figures or text in a list. However, tab columns are simply text lined up at tab stops, as discussed in Chapter 5. In this chapter, you'll learn about snake and bound columns, which are created in column mode. A bound column behaves like a footnote, where text that doesn't fit into the limits of the column disappears. Certain documents such as expense statements are enhanced by bound column format, and you can use mathematical operations with such columns.

For other documents, such as newspaper or magazine articles, snake columns are the solution. *Snake columns* are more flexible than bound columns. A snake column is bound only on the right and left margins. Text flows from the top of one column to the bottom, and then moves to the top of the next column. When you use snake columns, you can insert or delete text in the middle of the column, and the text will still snake continuously to the next column.

Columns, because of their boundaries, provide an excellent form for performing other functions, such as sorting information in a certain order, calculating rows or columns of numbers, and drawing lines and boxes around specific information to emphasize it.

CREATING COLUMNS

Snake and bound columns are created in a similar way: You design the limits of the columns on a format line, and then you use tab stops and bracket signs, as detailed in this chapter, to specify which kind of column you are creating.

Column format lines are different from standard document format lines, and bound and snake columns have different format lines. In the format line, you specify the width of each column and the space between columns. Furthermore, with bound columns, you need to set the location of each column, since bound columns can vary in size. Figure 10.1 shows a format line for bound columns, and Figure 10.2 shows a format line for snake columns.

Now let's discuss how to create each column type.

CREATING BOUND COLUMNS

Before you create the column format, you must decide three things.

1. How many bound columns do you want to use?
2. How wide will the columns be?
3. How wide will the space between columns be?

Once you have answered these questions, you can proceed to create the number and size of columns you want to appear on your page.

Note that cursor movement within columns differs from regular cursor movement (see Table 10.1).

You can create up to eight columns per page. When you create bound columns, you can vary the size of each column on the page as well as the space between each column. Note, however, that each bound column cannot exceed one page (the number of lines per page can be up to 199, if you've set it in the Modify Document Defaults screen).

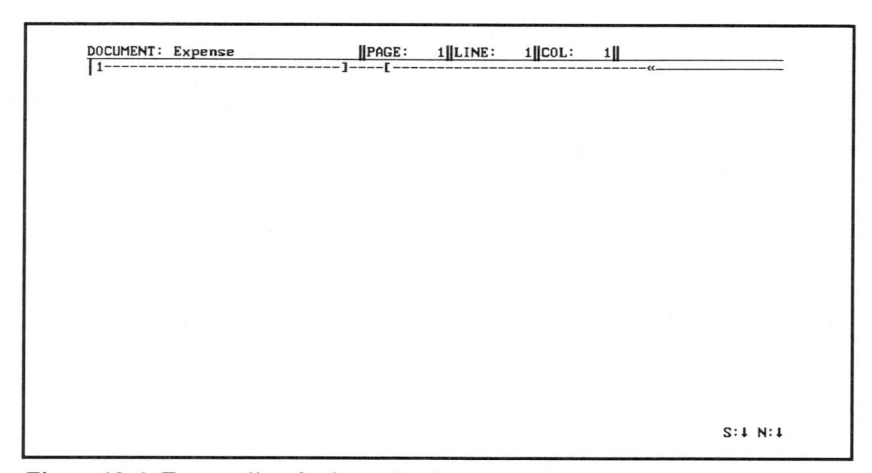

Figure 10.1: Format line for bound columns

```
DOCUMENT: Article          ‖PAGE:   1‖LINE:   1‖COL:   1‖
 1--»---------]4«
```

                                                                    S:↑ N:↓

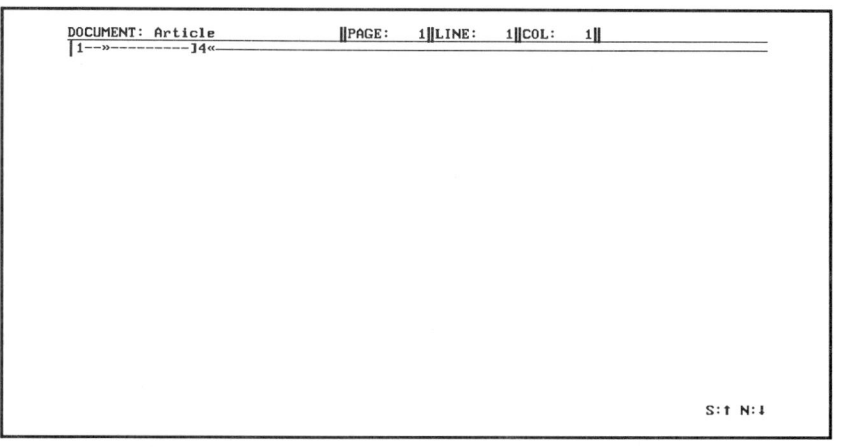

Figure 10.2: Format line for snake columns

COLUMN CURSOR MOVEMENTS	
Key	*Action*
Shift-→	Moves cursor to first character in same row of next column*
Shift-←	Moves cursor to last character in same row of preceding column*
	Within column mode (Shift-F3)
↓	Moves cursor to next column group
↑	Moves cursor to preceding column group
Home	Moves cursor to top of current column*
End	Moves cursor to bottom of current column*
Alt-F3	Moves cursor to first position of the line*
Alt-F4	Moves cursor to last position of the line*
	*Within the same column group

Table 10.1: Cursor movement for columns

For the examples in this chapter, create a new document called Expense.

Begin by pressing F9, the Format Change key, to set the right and left boundaries for your bound columns. You'll see the prompt

FORMAT CHANGE

on the right side of the status line. You need to clear the format line of all unnecessary tab stops, and you can do this by holding down the Space bar until all the tab stops disappear. The left-hand and right-hand limits of each column are determined by where you place the opening and closing brackets ([,]), on the format line. Use the [and] keys on the keyboard.

To set the left-hand limit of the first column, you can either accept the default (column 1), or you can place the opening bracket in the column where you want the left side of the first column to be. You cannot start a column in column 2, which contains the line-spacing code, because overwriting that code would eliminate line spacing. To set the first column, move the cursor on the format line to the desired column and press the [key. The opening bracket should appear in the proper column. (If you press the wrong key, simply press the Space bar to delete it.) Insert the closing bracket for the right-hand limit of the first column, and proceed similarly for the rest of the columns. If the right-hand limit of the last column is identical to the right margin, you do not need to insert the final closing bracket. Advantage II will insert a default setting of 2 spaces between each column unless you instruct it otherwise.

If you later decide to change the settings on the format line, follow the same procedure: press F9, then insert the opening and closing brackets. If you are planning to change the size of columns, you should do so only one column at a time, and then check the new arrangement before you change anything else. Press F9 to set the new limits. The text in the column whose width you changed will reformat to the new width. (If you erased one bracket and accidentally forgot to create a new one, the text in that column will disappear. Don't worry; you haven't lost the text. Press F9 again and enter the bracket you forgot. Press F9 a second time to view the change, and the old text will reappear on the screen.)

Example of Bound Columns

For an example, you will create a memo showing expenses. To work with this memo, enter the document called Expense and type the text as it appears in Figure 10.3.

```
November 28, 1986


from the desk of
Rebecca


        I have returned from a highly successful buying trip to
California. Samples of the wine I bought will arrive shortly,
and they can be passed around for sampling. The shipping costs
for this wine should probably be included in the costs of my
trip, if you want to calculate the entire cost of this trip. I
will not know those costs until all the shipments arrive, and
they will probably arrive after the 15 day limit allowed for
filing a reimbursement request.
        The information that follows is a listing of the expenses of
my trip to California.
```

Figure 10.3: First part of Expense memo

When you reach the last line of text, press Return three times to insert two blank lines. Now press Shift-F9 to insert a current format line. The prompt

FORMAT CURRENT

should appear on the right side of the status line. You will use this format line to set the limits for the columns. You need to use two columns to list the expenses. With a line length of 65 columns, you can have 30 spaces per column and 5 spaces between columns.

Accept the default setting (column 1) for the first left-hand column limit. Now press the Space bar to remove all the tab stops in the current format line. (This is not necessary, but you will find it more convenient to work with an empty format line.) Now place tab stops in columns 8 and 18. Move the cursor to column 30 and enter a left-facing, or closing, bracket. Place a right-facing, or opening, bracket in column 35 to begin the second column, and then place tab stops in columns 45 and 56. You can enter a closing bracket in column 65 or press Return to accept the right margin setting as the second column's right margin. Now move the cursor to column 30 and insert the closing bracket. Insert the opening bracket in column 35, and either insert the closing bracket in column 65 or press Return in column 65 to set the right margin.

Now press F9 to set this format line. The prompt

FORMAT CHANGE

should disappear from the status line.

Once you have set the side limits of the bound columns, the next step is to determine the top limit of the two columns. To do this, place the cursor on the line where you want the columns to begin. Then press Shift-F3, the Column Mode key. The prompt *COLUMN MODE* will appear on the status line. Enter the first column of the text in Figure 10.4 to the Expense memo. Notice that you can center text within a bound column and also use tab stops.

When you have finished entering the text in the first column, press Shift-F3, the Column Mode key, and press Return. This will place a hard column break symbol below the last line of text and move the cursor to the top of the second column. Now save the Expense document by pressing F10.

```
            One-time expenses                    Daily expenses

      plane ticket      $374.34         11/11      hotel      $110.96
      car rental        $310.55         at Miyako

                                        11/11      meals      $   9.75
             Entertainment                         misc       $   2.35

      11/11     dinner  $  70.00        11/12      meals      $  12.55
      with K. Pickerall
                                        11/13      meals      $   6.87
      11/13     lunch   $  28.00                   misc       $   7.60
      w/S. Taddich
                                        11/14      hotel      $  75.50
      11/14     lunch   $  17.00        at Mountain Home
      w/D. Bynum                                   meals      $  26.00
                                                   misc       $   6.54
      11/15     dinner  $  55.00
      w/R. Fallen &
      B. Gleason

      11/16     lunch   $  12.50
      w/D. Troll
```

Figure 10.4: Column text in Expense memo

CREATING SNAKE COLUMNS

Since snake columns are continuous, each snake column will have the same width and space between columns. Thus, you need specify only two things: the column width and the number of columns.

As with bound columns, you can change these features on the format line for a snake column by pressing F9, erasing the old settings by pressing the Space bar, and inserting the brackets to specify the column width. (In this case, if you forget one of the brackets and then press F9, all the text will disappear from the screen, not just one column. Return the cursor to the format line by pressing F9, and add the missing bracket to bring the lost text back to view.)

The next step is to enter the number of snake columns you want on the page. You do this by typing the number of columns on the format line directly after the closing bracket. Next, press Return to set the number of columns, and then press F9 to set the changes to the format line.

Example of Snake Columns

As an example, create a new document called Article. This will be a report on your trip to California for your company's in-house newspaper. This in-house newspaper is printed with MultiMate Advantage II, so the editor needs the document on disk.

When the Document screen for Article appears, press F9 to change the format line. Make sure the *FORMAT CHANGE* prompt appears on the status line. Retain the tab stop in column 5, for paragraph indents, but erase the second and third tab stops. In column 15, enter

]4

since the editor prefers that articles be submitted in four columns. With four columns, each 15 spaces, the standard 65-column line has 5 spaces to distribute between all columns. Press Return and then F9 to set the column features.

Now type the text that appears in Figure 10.5. Press Tab once to begin each paragraph. On your screen, you will see the text running down the left side of your screen in one narrow column 15 spaces wide. Press Return after you enter the name Kristine. At this point, you need to end this single long column with an end column group symbol. To do this, press Ctrl-Shift, the End Column Group key.

When you instruct Advantage II to repaginate the long column, it will become four columns. First, press Shift-F3, the Column Mode key. The prompt

COLUMN MODE

will appear on the right side of the status line. Now press Ctrl-F2, the Repagination key. In a moment, the single long column of text will appear as four equivalent columns, as shown in Figure 10.6.

Note: You may not see the bottom lines of the columns; you can see them by scrolling down. Each bottom line ends with →.

```
          ACQUISITIONS-  I have been asked to tell you all about my recent
     trip to California. I'd rather talk about the wines I tasted,
     but I realize some of you like to travel for other reasons.  It
     is true what they say about California cuisine - you sure don't
     get much on your plate. But the prices don't reflect that.
     Often, the cheapest item on the menu was the wine. Perhaps that
     will be good for our business.
          The Napa Valley has changed since I was last there three
     years ago. What used to be the sleepy working town of St. Helena
     has blossomed into a burg of some renown. I could have spent my
     entire time in that town, eating my meals in a different
     delightful restaurant each day, tasting almost as many wines as
     I found by traveling 1,000 miles.
          But I promised not to talk about wines. OK. The weather. It
     was foggy most of the time. I keep on hearing about sunny
     Calif., but I must end up in the wrong place each time I go.
          Well, that's it. Come by my office and I'll tell you in
     person.
          Kristine
```

Figure 10.5: Text for Article

EDITING TEXT WITHIN COLUMNS

Editing text within columns is similar for bound and snake columns. Indeed, such editing is practically identical to editing text within any standard document: you can insert, copy, move, and delete text. But editing text within columns calls for some special considerations. There are three differences you should watch out for.

1. Highlighting to copy, move, or delete text within columns behaves differently from highlighting in standard documents. Thus, you'll usually need to use a protected mode.

2. Pay attention to special column symbols within columns, such as the soft column break symbol and the end column group symbol. If you erase them, the text in the columns will be readjusted, sometimes to your surprise. You can inadvertently erase these symbols either by typing over them or by skating over them by pressing the Space bar.

3. Before you repaginate text in snake columns with the intention of distributing text better, you need to change a default setting in the Modify Document Defaults screen.

HIGHLIGHTING

Highlighting text for both snake and bound columns is identical to the method of highlighting text in a standard document. With

```
ACQUISITIONS-     much on your     of St. Helena     to talk about
     I have      plate. But the   has blossomed    wines. OK. The
been asked to    prices don't     into a burg of   weather. It
tell you all     reflect that.    some renown. I   was foggy most
about my         Often, the       could have       of the time. I
recent trip to   cheapest item    spent my         keep on
California.      on the menu      entire time in   hearing about
I'd rather       was the wine.    that town,       sunny Calif.,
talk about the   Perhaps that     eating my        but I must end
wines I          will be good     meals in a       up in the
tasted, but I    for our          different        wrong place
realize some     business.        delightful       each time I
of you like to        The Napa    restaurant       go.
travel for       Valley has       each day,             Well,
other reasons.   changed since    tasting almost   that's it.
     It is true  I was last       as many wines    Come by my
what they say    there three      as I found by    office and
about            years ago.       traveling        I'll tell you
California       What used to     1,000 miles.     in person.
cuisine - you    be the sleepy         But I            Kristine
sure don't get   working town     promised not
```

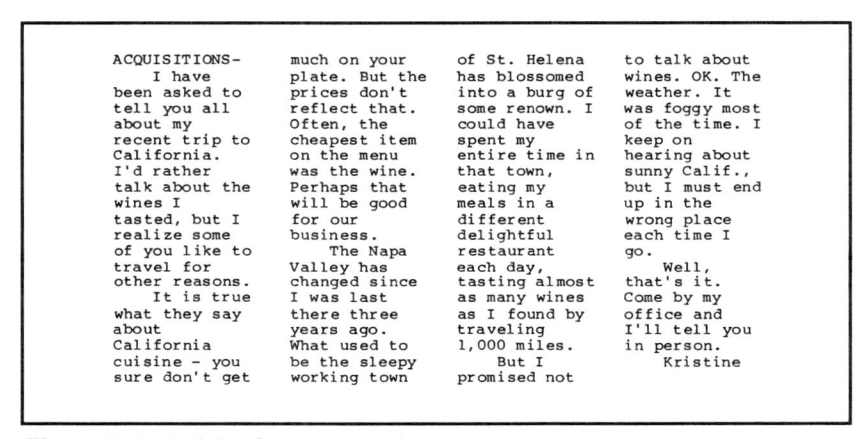

Figure 10.6: Article after repagination

columns, you can use highlighting to move, delete, and copy text both internally and externally, as well as to make or insert library entries and check spelling. You can begin to highlight text that precedes columns, and end the highlighting either within a column or after the end of a column. Highlighting is unaffected by column boundaries.

Whenever you move text that includes columns, you will have to move the column format lines with the columnar text, or else that text will readjust itself to the format of the section to which the columnar text was moved. You can highlight format lines the same way as text.

COPYING COLUMNAR TEXT

Text within columns can be copied using the procedures for copying text in standard documents (see Chapter 3). Quite often when you do this, however, the text will reposition itself according to the format of its new position. Thus, you also need to copy the column format line. If you want to copy columnar text to another place on the same page, use the column mode copy procedure. (Note that column mode copy cannot cross pages.)

To begin column mode copy, move the cursor to the first character of the text you want to copy and press Shift-F3. The prompt *COLUMN MODE* will appear on the status line. Next, press F8, the Move key, and the prompt *COLUMN COPY* will replace the previous prompt. Also, another prompt

<←> and <→> to Define Width THEN <↓> to Define Length.

will appear at the bottom of the screen. These instructions allow you to tell Advantage II exactly what section of the column you want to copy.

As an example, let's say you want to copy the category *One-Time Expenses* on the Expense memo (refer to Figure 10.3) to a position below the existing columns. Place the cursor on the center symbol, which precedes the word *One.* Press Shift-F3, the Column Mode key, and then F8, the Copy key. (Don't press all three keys at once, or you'll see the external copy prompt. If this happens, press Escape and try again.) The prompt

COLUMN COPY

will appear on the right side of the status line. In response, press the ← key six times. (If you make a mistake with the arrow keys, you can press Escape and try again.) This will move the cursor to the left side of the column, and it will highlight the six spaces. Next, press the → key 29 times to move to the right side of the column. You'll see the highlight expand as you move the cursor. Then press the ↓ key five times so that six lines are highlighted, and press F8 again. The prompt

TO WHERE?

will appear on the status line. Press the End key or PgDn (as many times as necessary to reach the end of the document) to place the cursor after the existing columns. You cannot move the cursor beyond one line after the last line of text while you are in column mode copy, so press F8. The One-time expenses category should appear in this new position, and the prompts will disappear from the screen.

As a finishing touch, add an explanation to the copied text. Press End to make sure the cursor is at the bottom of this new column, then type the words

These expenses were covered by the company credit card.

Inserting Columnar Text

You can add text to columns that have already been created in two ways:

1. By typing over existing columnar text
2. By using the column mode insert procedure

Typing over existing text is recommended only for minor changes, such as transposed letters. In such cases, you do not have to insert extra characters. If you used the Insert key to add extra characters in the column, the text would be pushed past the bottom limit of the column, whether it was a snake or bound column.

The column mode insert procedure has been designed to place the Insert key in a *protected* mode for columns. Before beginning, make sure the format line of the column you are going to work with has been set correctly, with left and right boundaries and tab stops. The length of the column will change after the column insert, however.

When the format line is correct, move the cursor to the position where you want to insert text. Press Shift-F3, the Column Mode key. The prompt *COLUMN MODE* will appear on the right side of the status line. As soon as this prompt appears, press the Insert key. The previous prompt will be replaced by the prompt *COLUMN INSERT* on the right side of the status line. In addition, the prompt

> INSERT # of Columns 00 # of Lines 00 Press F10 to Continue

will appear at the bottom of the screen. Unfortunately, the use of the word *columns* here may be confusing. In this context, *columns* refers to cursor columns—as on the status line—not to the number of snake or bound columns. For example, go to the document Article; you must first exit from column insert mode by pressing Escape. Then place the cursor on the column format line, and press F9. Now move the cursor to the first closing bracket, and you'll see that it's in column 15. Since the first opening bracket was in column 1, the *# of Columns* is 15. Now return to column insert mode by pressing Shift-F3 and Insert.

The maximum number of columns you can enter is 99, even though a standard MultiMate Advantage II document can have up to 156 characters per line. Make sure you enter two digits—07 for seven columns, for instance—then press Return, and the cursor will move to the next item.

For the number of lines, you can enter any number from 01 to 99. If you press Return after filling in this field, the cursor will return to *# of Columns*. You can go back and forth between the two entries and change the figures until they are exactly as you want them.

With column mode insert, you cannot add so much space that the existing text is forced onto the next page. This feature will not cross pages.

If you decide not to insert any new space in the column after all, press Escape; to proceed with the column mode insert function, check that the column and line entries are correct and press F10 to set them. Immediately, at the cursor position, you'll see the number of blank text lines you instructed Advantage II to insert in the column. All text following the insertion will be moved down the same number of lines.

SORTING

You can sort columnar text and numbers in either ascending or descending order. As an example, we'll sort the text in the Daily expenses column of the Expense1 memo to group together the expenses in each category: hotel, meals, and misc. Follow this procedure:

1. Align the text you want to sort on a margin. In this case, delete the dates already on the left margin, as well as the tab stops that position the labels hotel, meals, and misc in the middle of the column to bring them flush with the left margin of that column. You will also have to delete several hard carriage returns so that these labels appear on successive lines, without any intervening blank lines.

2. Place the cursor at the top left of the column. This is an important step. The text or numbers you want to sort will be defined through highlighting, and the higlighting will begin at the cursor position.

3. Press Shift-F3 and then F5, the Sort key. This will bring up the prompt

    <←> and <→> to Define Width THEN <↓> to Define Length.

4. Highlight the section of text that you want to sort. Move the cursor over to the right side of the column, and then down to the bottom of the column.

5. Press F5 a second time to bring up the sort window, as shown in Figure 10.7.

6. For this example, accept the default answers and press F10 to begin the sorting procedure. (We'll discuss the sorting options shortly.) In a few moments, the information in the Daily expenses column should appear, as shown in Figure 10.8.

Notice that the dollar amounts were also sorted within each expense category. This occurred because the default setting for the third option in the sort window, Rearrange, is Entire Line, which means that all the elements of the column line will be sorted together. If you changed the setting to Defined Text Only, just the highlighted text would have been sorted. The default setting for the first option in the sort window, Sort Using, is First Word, which has Advantage II sort on the first character of the first word in the column. The alternative, Last Word, results in a sort on the first character in the last word in the column. (Our example has only one word in the column, so this setting does not apply.) The second option, Order, allows you to sort in either ascending (the default) or descending order.

```
DOCUMENT: EXPENSE              ||PAGE:   1||LINE:  12||COL:  49||          COLUMN SORT
      ↔One time expenses«                 ↔Daily expenses«
«                                  «
plane ticket  ■$274.34«            hotel■$110.96«
car rental    ■$310.55«            meals■$  9.75«
        »total■$584.89«            misc ■$  2.35«
«                                  meals■$ 12.55«
        ↔Entertainment«            meals■$  6.87«
11/11   »dinner■$ 70.00«           misc ■$  7.60«
with K. Pickerall«                 hotel■$ 75.50 «
«                                  meals■$ 26.00 «
11/13   lunch  $ 28.00«            misc ■$  6.54 «
                                     SORT


       ALT-1   Sort Using:   First Word              Last Word
       ALT-2   Order:        Ascending (0-9, A-Z)    Descending (Z-A, 9-0)
       ALT-3   Rearrange:    Entire Line             Defined Text Only



                        Press F10 when finished, ESC to cancel
                      Press ALT and a number key to change a setting
                                                                     S:↓ N:↓
```

Figure 10.7: Sort window in Expense1 memo.

```
DOCUMENT: EXPENSE              ||PAGE:   1||LINE:   3||COL:  35||
|1-------»---------»---------]----[---------»---------»---------«-----------
      ↔One time expenses«                 ↔Daily expenses«
«                                  «
plane ticket  ■$274.34«            hotel■$ 75.50 «
car rental    ■$310.55«            hotel■$110.96«
        »total■$584.89«            lunch■$ 12.50 «
«                                  meals■$  6.87«
        ↔Entertainment«            meals■$  9.75«
11/11   »dinner■$ 70.00«           meals■$ 12.55«
with K. Pickerall«                 meals■$ 26.00 «
«                                  misc ■$  2.35«
11/13   lunch  $ 28.00«            misc ■$  6.54 «
w/ S. Taddich               «      misc ■$  7.60«
                       «                 total $1352.28 «
11/14   lunch  $ 17.00 «           «
w/D. Bynum             «           ◄
                       «
11/15   dinner $55.00  «
w/R. Fallen            «
                       «
11/16   lunch  $ 12.50 «
w/D. Troll             «
                       «
                                                                     S:↓ N:↓
```

Figure 10.8: The Daily expenses column of the Expense1 memo sorted by category

Sorting Using a Pull-Down Menu

You can also sort columns by making a selection from a pull-down menu. To do this, follow these steps:

1. Place the cursor at the top or bottom of the text you want to sort.
2. Press Alt-L to access the pull-down menu interface.
3. Press the → key to highlight the Special option.
4. Make sure that the light bar is on the Sort selection, then press F10 to begin sorting.
5. Highlight the width and length of the column to be sorted.
6. Press F10 a second time.
7. Make your selections in the sort window.
8. Press F10 a third time to execute the sort.

That's all you need to do to sort using the pull-down menu interface. You can press Escape to cancel the sort at any time before you reach step 8, or after you press F10 the third time to execute the sort.

MOVING COLUMNAR TEXT

There are three ways you can move columnar text:

1. Move within a column
2. Move part of a column outside the column
3. Move complete columns to another part of a document

You can perform all three of these moves using F7, the Move key, as usual—that is, in an unprotected mode. If you do, however, you will probably distort the limits of those columns. To protect against these possible distortions, you should use F7 in a protected mode. To do this, first press Shift-F3, the Column Mode key. Before you move any columnar text, check the settings in the column format line and change them, if necessary.

Moving Text within a Bound Column

To move text within a bound column, you can safely use the unprotected mode, since the column end limit will usually remain the same. If you move text that begins or ends in the middle of a line, you might end up with more lines in the column than when you started out. In this case, the limit of the bound column will adjust for the new column size, as long as the column does not have to spill over to the next page. Bound columns cannot travel beyond the page they are created on.

To move text, place the cursor on the first character of text to be moved and press F7, the Move key. Next, move the cursor to the last character of text to be moved and press F7 a second time. Finally, staying within the bounds of the column, move the cursor to the place where you want to move the highlighted text and press F7 a third time.

Balancing Snake Columns

When you move text within a snake column, follow the same procedure as for bound columns, but you must add an extra step to balance the text within the column. Text in a snake column runs continuously, so one column will grow smaller when you move text out of it, and another will grow larger when you move text into it. Balancing text in a snake column distributes the text more evenly throughout the several columns that comprise the single snake column.

To balance a snake column, first enter a protected mode by pressing Shift-F3, the Column Mode key. Then press in succession:

1. Ctrl-F2, the Document Reorganization key
2. Alt-1, the Repagination key
3. F10 to begin snake column balance

As an example, in the document Article, move the first paragraph after the second paragraph.

1. Place the cursor on the first letter, *I,* and press F7.
2. Next, move the cursor to the period at the end of the first paragraph and press F7.
3. Finally, move the cursor to the beginning of the third paragraph, which is in the second column, by placing the cursor on

the letter *T* (in *The*), and press F7. Immediately, the first paragraph will move from the first column to the second column. But if you press PgDn, you will see that the first column is now much shorter than the second column.

4. To balance these columns, press Shift-F3 to obtain the prompt *COLUMN MODE* on the status line, and then press Ctrl-F2, AH-1, and F10. Almost immediately, the four columns that comprise Article will be balanced to similar lengths. Then press Shift-F3 again or Escape to leave column mode.

Moving Text between Columns

You can move text between columns the same way as in a standard document.

Moving Part of a Column outside the Column

You can move part of a column outside the column the same way text is moved within and between documents. You must realize, however, that the columnar text will be reformatted to the settings of the document's format line. Thus, you may first want to copy the column section rather than move it, so you can see the results of the reformatting and be able to change your mind easily.

Moving Columnar Text with Column Mode Move

If you want to copy text from a column to another place on the same page, and you want to keep all formatted features of the column intact, you can use a procedure called column mode move. Place the cursor at the beginning of the text you want to move. Press Shift-F3, the Column Mode key, and the prompt *COLUMN MODE* will appear on the status line. Next, press F7, the Move key, and the prompt *COLUMN MOVE* will replace the previous prompt. In addition, the prompt

<←> and <→> to Define Width THEN <↓> to Define Length.

will appear at the bottom of the screen. This allows you to prescribe the exact limits of the block you want to move.

As an example, let's say you want to take the One-time expenses out of the first column and put them in a column of their own. To do this, begin by placing the cursor on the center symbol preceding *One-time expenses*. Press Shift-F3, and when the prompt COLUMN MODE appears on the status line, press F7. Now, the prompt COLUMN MOVE will replace the previous prompt, and you can begin to highlight the text you want to move. The prompt at the bottom of the screen

<←> and <→> to Define Width THEN <↓> to Define Length.

will help you do this. Press the ← key six times to move the cursor to the left margin. You should notice that the highlight will expand with the cursor movement. Now press the → key 29 times, highlighting one line within the column.

Now that you have marked the width of the column, you can begin to mark the length. To do this, press the ↓ key three times, highlighting the next four lines. Then press F7 to fix the length of text to be moved. Immediately, the text you want to move will disappear from the screen, though it remains in the computer memory. (In fact, if you wanted to cancel the column mode move procedure at this point, you could press Escape and the text would reappear in its original position. This is your last chance to cancel the column mode move procedure.)

Now move the cursor to the place on your page where you want to move the columnar text. To do this, press the End key, which will put the cursor at the end of the text on the page, or beneath the columns already created. Press F7, and the text to be moved will reappear in the new position, and in the correct format.

You can only use column mode move for moving text on the same page. To move columnar text to a different page, copy the entire column, including the format line, to another page, and then insert or delete text as you see fit.

Whenever you remove text from a snake column, remember to balance the text that remains inside the snake column by pressing Shift-F3, Ctrl-F2, Alt-1, and F10.

Deleting Columnar Text

To delete small sections of text within a column, you can use the Minus or Delete key just as you would to delete text in a standard document. To delete larger sections of columnar text, you should use column mode delete. This behaves like other protected column modes.

As an example, say you wanted to delete the last paragraph in Article. To do this, place the cursor on the tab symbol before the word *Well* and press Shift-F3. The prompt *COLUMN MODE* will appear on the right side of the status line. Next, press the Delete key, and the prompt *COLUMN DELETE* will replace the first prompt. Another prompt

<←> and <→> to Define Width THEN <↓> to Define Length.

will appear at the bottom of the screen. This allows you to instruct Advantage II, as you did with the column mode move procedure, exactly what section of the column you want to delete.

For this example, press the ← key three times to reach the left border of the column. You probably won't remember the column numbers of the left and right sides of a snake column, since they were created by Advantage II. Highlighting the text line is your most accurate method for setting the side limits. At the left edge, press the → key 13 times. Now press the ↓ key five times to highlight the next five lines of text. At the end of the last paragraph, but before you get to the name *Kristine,* press Delete again. All the text highlighted in column mode delete will then disappear from the screen, and the prompt *COLUMN DELETE* will disappear from the status line.

Since this is a snake column whose dimensions you have changed, you should balance the text as described in the previous section.

DECIMAL TAB

You first learned about the decimal tab in Chapter 9, when you learned to create section numbers using the Numeric method. The decimal tab can also prove useful in column mode when you want to arrange groups of figures in aligned rows or columns. If you align the numbers on a decimal tab, you can have Advantage II calculate totals.

When you specify decimal tabs, decimal points will occur at the tab stops. There are two things to decide before you can begin creating decimal stops.

1. Make sure that the tab stops on the format line correspond to the positions where you want your decimals to line up.

2. Decide which kind of decimal you want to display in the document: a period (American style) or a comma (European style).

If necessary, change the setting from period (the default) to comma in the Acceptable Decimal Tab field on your Modify Document Defaults screen.

Once you have set the proper tab stops and selected the type of decimal, you can create your first decimal tab stop by pressing Shift-F4, the Decimal Tab key. This will create a decimal tab symbol at the first tab stop. Next, type the number you want to appear in that position. The decimal tab symbol and all figures you enter at this point will move to the left each time you enter another figure, until you enter the decimal. (If you are using a period for a decimal, enter a period; if you are using a comma, enter a comma.) As soon as you enter the decimal point, the figure will automatically line up with its decimal in the tab position.

If you wish to create more columns of aligned decimals, you can press Shift-F4 as many times as you like to create more decimal tabs. If you change the decimal tab stop on the format line, the figures aligned on their decimal points will change to the new tab position. You can experiment with various alignments to find the arrangement that best suits your document.

As an example, let's learn how to alter the Expense memo so that the expense figures line up on decimal tabs. First, make a copy of Expense and call it Expense1. Accept the default setting for marking a decimal with a period. Then change several tab stops on the column format line in Expense1. Begin by erasing the tab stop in column 25 and creating a tab in column 30 by pressing the Tab key. Next, erase the tab stop in column 55 and create a new one in column 60. These new tab stops will be the ones along which you will align the columns of expense figures.

Press F3, the Center key, to center the category title, and type *One-time expenses,* press Return twice, and type *plane ticket.* Now you are ready to enter the decimal tab. Press Shift-F4, the Decimal Tab key. A decimal point should appear at the tab stop in column 25. As you type *$374.34,* the decimal tab symbol, the dollar sign, and the first three figures will all move to the left. As soon as you enter the period, the following numbers will appear where you typed them.

Figure 10.9 shows you what the Expense1 memo should look like with decimal tab symbols in the proper positions. Type the remainder of the text and numbers into Expense1, using Shift-F4 to insert decimal tab stops in the second column.

```
DOCUMENT: Expense                ||PAGE:   1||LINE:  22||COL:  16||
|1-------»----------»----------]----[----------»----------»----------«----------
              ↔One time expenses«                ↔Daily expenses«
«                                       «
plane ticket  ■$274.34«            11/11    »hotel■$110.96«
car rental    ■$310.55«            at Miyako«
              »total■$584.89«      «
«                                  11/11    »meals■$  9.75«
              ↔Entertainment«               »misc ■$  2.35«
11/11  »dinner■$ 70.00«            «
with K. Pickerall«                 11/12    »meals■$ 12.55«
«                                  «
11/13  »lunch ■$ 28.00«            11/13    »meals■$  6.87«
w/ S. Taddich«                              »misc ■$  7.60«
«                                  «
11/14  »lunch ■$ 17.00«            11/14    »hotel■$ 75.50«
w/D. Bynum«                        at Mountain Home«
«                                           »meals■$ 26.00«
11/15  »dinner■$55.00«                      »misc ■$  6.54«
w/R. Fallen«                                »total    ■«
«                                       ♦
11/16  »lunch ■$ 12.50«
w/D. Troll«
       »total■◄
                                                              S:1 N:1
```

Figure 10.9: Figures aligned on decimal tabs

You can realign numbers on decimal tab stops if the figures were originally created using standard tab stops. As an example, return to the original *Expense* memo and move the cursor to the first standard tab stop in a column, before $310.55. All you have to do is press Shift-F4, the Decimal Tab key, and the decimal tab symbol will replace the standard tab symbol. You can change all the standard tab symbols this way. If you want the format of the columns in Expense to match that of Expense1, press F9 and change the tab stops from 20 to 25, and from 55 to 60. When you press F9 to set these new tab stops, the figures with decimal tabs will line up according to the new settings.

DECIMAL TABS IN ROWS

You can also line up figures horizontally with decimal tab stops. This arrangement gives you less room for figures than columns because the text labels take up space. The length of the row is determined by the length of the format line. When you create decimal tabs in rows, you will usually have to pay closer attention to the position of additional tab stops compared to columns.

As an example, let's rearrange the category of One-time expenses that you copied to the bottom of the Expense1 memo. If you inserted decimal tab stops in Expense as well as Expense1, the two documents should be identical, and you can continue to make further changes on either one.

1. Begin by inserting the system format line at the bottom of the two columns. To do this, press Alt-F9, and when the system format line appears, erase all existing tab stops by holding down the Space bar until you reach the end of the format line in column 65.
2. Now press the ← key to return the cursor to column 21 on the format line. Press the Tab key and create a tab stop.
3. Create five more tab stops in columns 30, 38, 48, and 54.
4. To convert the text and figures from columns into rows, erase the hard carriage return symbols.
5. To rearrange the text and figures under this new format line, delete the center symbol before the word *One*. Place a colon after the word *Expenses,* and place the words *plane ticket* on the first tab stop. Delete the word *ticket* to make more room in the row. Create a decimal tab for the *plane* expense figure by pressing Shift-F4, and then bring up the figure $374.34. Complete this rearrangement so that the rows look like Figure 10.10.

Using decimal tab stops by themselves doesn't change the appearance of Expense1 from the original Expense memo very much. The utility of decimal tabs only becomes apparent when you perform column calculations using decimal tabs.

COLUMN CALCULATIONS

You can perform six kinds of mathematical calculations on a column of two or more figures:

- Addition
- Subtraction
- Multiplication
- Division

- Exponents
- Percentages

To do any kind of calculation, you must first align the figures along decimal tabs, and then create a final empty decimal tab where you want the calculated total to be displayed. You can place the tabs anywhere on the line; the characters in the equation can be typed together (as in 6*2) or spread out (as in 6 * 2).

Advantage II will perform the calculation when you put the cursor on the final decimal tab and press the Column Calculation key (Ctrl-F4 for columns, Ctrl-F3 for rows). There are several limitations to this calculating ability:

- Calculations can be performed only on a single row or column.
- Calculations can be performed only on a single page.
- Subtotals cannot be calculated, unless you reach one total in a row and then add that total to figures arranged in a column.

Addition

As an example of both column and row calculation, you can use the Expense1 memo.

Column Addition Move the cursor to the end of the first column and place it on the last hard carriage-return symbol, after the last name *Troll,* just before the hard column break symbol. Press Insert, Return, Return, and Tab, and type *total.* Press Insert to complete the insert mode. Press Shift-F4, the Decimal Tab key, but do not enter a number this time. This creates a blank decimal tab symbol for the total in the Entertainment expense column.

```
          One-time expenses:  plane  $374.34    car    $310.55   total  -$684.89
          These expenses were covered by the company credit card.
          Entertainment                                                  $1352.28
          Daily expenses                                                  $258.12
          Less cash advanced                                             -$500.00
                                            Total due                    $425.51
```

Figure 10.10: One-Time expenses arranged in a row

To perform the calculation, move the cursor to the decimal tab symbol, press Ctrl-F4, the Vertical Addition key, and the calculation will begin. A message will flash on the bottom of your screen

PLEASE WAIT

while Advantage II performs the calculation. The length of time it remains on your screen will depend upon the complexity of the calculation. In this case, it shouldn't last for more than a second. The figure $1352.28 will appear, aligned along the last decimal tab symbol, as the total for Entertainment expenses. Note that the dollar sign was automatically placed before the total amount. The program will place both dollar signs and commas in the total if these signs appear in the numbers in the calculation.

You can perform a similar calculation for the second column, Daily expenses. Place your cursor on the last hard carriage-return symbol for this column, after the figure $6.54 for misc. expenses. Press Insert, Return, Return, and Tab, and type *total*. Press Shift-F4 to create the blank decimal tab symbol where Advantage II will place the calculated total. Press Insert a second time to complete the insert mode. Now move the cursor to the blank decimal tab symbol and press Ctrl-F4, the Vertical Addition key. The Daily expenses total $258.12 will appear at the decimal tab symbol.

Row Addition Horizontal, or row, addition is similar to vertical calculation. For the bottom row of figures in Expense, you must first expand the final format line. Move the cursor to that format line, press F9, and move the cursor to the end of the line with the → key. Expand the format line to column 70. Then move the cursor back by pressing the ← key and press Tab to create a new tab in column 65. This is where the row total will appear. Press F9 to set the new format line settings.

Move the cursor past the figure $310.55 and press Shift-F4, the Decimal Tab key. This will create the blank decimal tab symbol for the row total. Move the cursor so it is over that symbol and press Ctrl-F3, the Horizontal Calculation key. The total for One-time expenses, $684.89, will appear.

Subtraction

You can subtract numbers during the calculations. The procedure is identical for both column and row calculations, although there are three ways to indicate numbers to be subtracted.

- −$500.00
- $500.00−
- ($500.00)

Use the Minus key on the main keyboard. If Advantage II has to display a negative total, it will follow these rules:

- If the −$500.00 form has been used at all, then the total will have the same form.
- If the $500.00− form has been used and the −$500.00 has not, the total will follow the former form.
- If the ($500.00) form has been used, then that form will be used in a negative total.

As an example of subtraction, you can sum the Expense report after the horizontal calculation.

1. Place the cursor directly after the $684.89 and press Return. Type *Entertainment* and press Tab five times. Next, press Shift-F4, the Decimal Tab key, and enter the total for Entertainment, $1352.28, from the bottom of the first column.

2. Press Return and type *Daily expenses,* press Tab five times, and then press Shift-F4 for another decimal tab. Now enter the figure $258.12 from the bottom of the second column.

3. Press Return and type *Less cash advanced,* press Tab five times and then press Shift-F4 for another decimal tab. Enter the figure *−$500.00* (you can use any of the three choices for indicating subtraction).

4. Press Return, Tab, Tab. Type *Total due,* press Tab twice, and press Shift-F4 to create a final decimal tab. On this decimal tab, you will calculate the total due for your expenses.

Move the cursor back so it is on this decimal tab and press Ctrl-F4, the Vertical Calculation key. The figure $1795.29 should appear in the *Total due* row.

But wait a minute. The One-time expenses were charged to a company credit card. This is not money due to you. To make this report accurate, move the cursor so it is on the *6* of the One-time expense total of $684.89. Press Insert and enter a minus sign. Press Insert again to complete the insert procedure. Now move the cursor to the final decimal tab for column calculation, indicating the total due to you. Press Ctrl-F4 to recalculate the total, and Advantage II should give you the revised figure of $425.51. The final version of Expense1 should look like Figure 10.11.

Multiplication

To multiply two numbers, you place a multiplier symbol between the two numbers. This symbol can be either an asterisk obtained by pressing Shift-8, or an at sign obtained by pressing Shift-2.

Row Multiplication   As an example, if you want to multiply 6 times 2 in a row, you would enter one of the following equations:

   6*2=

or

   6@2=

Then you would move the cursor back under the last decimal tab and press Ctrl-3 to begin the calculation.

The following are the steps for the row multiplication example above:

1. Press Shift-F4 to place the first decimal tab.

2. Type *6* and then press Shift-8 to enter an asterisk (or Shift-2 for an at sign).

```
November 28, 1986

from the desk of
Rebecca

    I have returned from a highly successful buying trip to
California. Samples of the wine I bought will arrive shortly,
and they can be passed around for sampling. The shipping costs
for this wine should probably be included in the costs of my
trip, if you want to calculate the entire cost of this trip. I
will not know those costs until all the shipments arrive, and
they will probably arrive after the 15 day limit allowed for
filing a reimbursement request.
    The information that follows is a listing of the expenses
of my trip to California.
         One-time expenses                Daily expenses

plane ticket        $374.34       11/11      hotel      $110.96
car rental          $310.55       at Miyako
        total       $684.89       11/11      meals      $  9.75
          Entertainment                      misc.      $  2.35
                                  11/12      meals      $ 12.55
11/11     dinner    $ 70.00
with K. Pickerall                 11/13      meals      $  6.87
                                             misc.      $  7.60
11/13     lunch     $ 28.00
w/S. Taddich                      11/14      hotel      $ 75.50
                                  at Mountain Home
11/14     lunch     $ 17.00                  meals      $ 26.00
w/D. Bynum                                   misc.      $  6.54

11/15     dinner    $ 55.00                  total      $258.12
w/R. Fallen &
B. Gleason

11/16     lunch     $ 12.50
w/D. Troll

        total       $1352.28
One-time expenses:  plane  $374.34   car   $310.55   total -$684.89
These expenses were covered by the company credit card.
Entertainment                                              $1352.28
Daily expenses                                              $258.12
Less cash advanced                                         -$500.00
                        Total due                           $425.51
```

Figure 10.11: Expense1 memo with calculations completed

3. Press Shift-F4 to place the second decimal tab.

4. Type *2* and then the equal sign.

5. Press Shift-F4 to place the final decimal tab.

6. Move the cursor to the space beneath the final decimal tab, and press Ctrl-F3 to begin the calculation.

Column Multiplication   You can multiply columns of numbers by aligning the figures along the same vertical decimal tab position. Multiplying 6 times 2 in a column would look like this:

```
6
*2
```

or

```
6
@2
```

You must align the numbers along vertical decimal tabs and create a third decimal tab on the line beneath them.

To begin the calculation, place the cursor on the empty decimal tab and press Ctrl-F4 (Ctrl-F3 is for *row* calculations).

Division

To divide one number by another, place a division symbol between the two numbers. This symbol can be either the slash mark (/) on the main keyboard or the division symbol (÷) on the MultiMate Advantage II Math keyboard (special keyboards are discussed in Chapter 11). For this second symbol, press Alt-K three times and then Ctrl-S.

Row Division   As an example, if you want to divide 6 by 2 in a row, you would enter one of the following equations:

6/2 =

or

6 ÷ 2 =

To complete the calculation, follow the steps for multiplication.

Column Division   You can divide numbers in columns by following the same steps for column multiplication, but use the division symbol instead of an asterisk or at sign. For example, use the equation:

```
   6
  /2
```

or

```
   6
 ÷ 2
```

Exponents

To calculate exponents, you use the superscript and subscript signs, obtained by pressing Alt-Q and Alt-W, respectively. As an example, if you want to find the square root of 6, you would enter the equation:

6↑2↓ =

Here are the steps for calculating this example:

1. Type *6*.
2. Press Alt-Q for a superscript.
3. Type *2*.
4. Press Alt-W to bring the cursor back down to the text baseline.
5. Place the cursor under the final decimal tab.
6. Press Ctrl-F3 to begin the calculation.

Be sure to place the decimal tab for the number 2 after the superscript sign.

Percentages

Percentages are calculated using the multiplication and percent signs. Place the percent sign (%) after the second figure. As an example, if you want to calculate 50 percent of 6, you would enter the following equation:

6*50% =

Place the cursor under the final decimal tab and press Ctrl-F3 to begin calculation.

LINE AND BOX DRAWING

MultiMate Advantage II gives you a limited graphics ability with the word-processing program. You can draw various kinds of lines in and around the text in your documents. Drawing lines and boxes is easy. You need only decide what kind of line you want to draw and where you want to draw it. You are limited to six different lines, and you have to draw them on strictly horizontal and vertical axes. These limitations, however, enable you to draw boxes and other confined shapes anywhere on your Document screen, as well as enhance your text with shading and borders.

To insert lines of varying widths in your document, you must print your document on a dot-matrix or laser printer that can print the full range of graphics features. A daisywheel printer will either not print the lines at all, or else substitute selected text characters for the lines you created on your screen. Experiment with your printer. Note that Advantage II provides special PAT files that will enable some printers to produce higher resolution or better lines and boxes. (Appendix B gives instructions for installing PAT files.) Even with these special PAT files, some printers won't print the lines you see on the screen, but will substitute letters or numbers for the line graphics. If this occurs, contact MultiMate International, which will provide the correct PAT file for your printer, as long as you are a registered user.

In any case, you can begin drawing lines without exiting from the Advantage II word-processing program. In fact, you can draw lines and boxes anywhere in Advantage II documents. You will probably find this procedure most useful when you are working with columns of figures. It is often just as useful to draw lines and boxes in documents for other reasons: separating numbered sections from each other, boxing footnotes, and separating headers and footers from the main text on a document page. You will find the techniques for drawing lines and boxes easy to learn, and once you learn them in conjunction with columns, can use them with other text, too.

To toggle the line and box drawing function on and off, press Alt-E, the Line Draw key. As soon as you do this, the prompt *LINE*

DRAW MODE will appear on the right side of the status line. At the same time, the prompt shown in Figure 10.12 will appear along the bottom of the screen. This shows you the six types of lines you can use, along with two control modes that allow you to move around the screen to position your lines and modify lines already drawn. You "draw" the actual lines with the cursor keys.

As an example, let's draw lines around three sections of text in Expense1: the two bound columns and the final section of text that follows the columns. Figure 10.13 shows what Expense1 looks like with lines and boxes drawn around the three sections.

To create the lines shown in the figure, first prepare the space the line will occupy. A drawn line occupies a complete cursor column or text line, depending upon whether the line is vertical or horizontal, so you must make sure that there is sufficient room to draw a line so that it does not erase existing text.

In the case of the first bound column in Expense1, you will have to create a blank line between the format line and the first One-time expenses title. This blank line will contain the drawn line. You create the blank line by first pressing Escape to exit from line drawing mode. Then place the cursor on the center symbol before the word *One* and press Insert. Now press Return and Insert again, and the blank line will appear. Press Alt-E to reenter line drawing mode. To accommodate the drawn line, clear a second line down the left margin of the first column. Press the ↓ key twice and place the cursor on

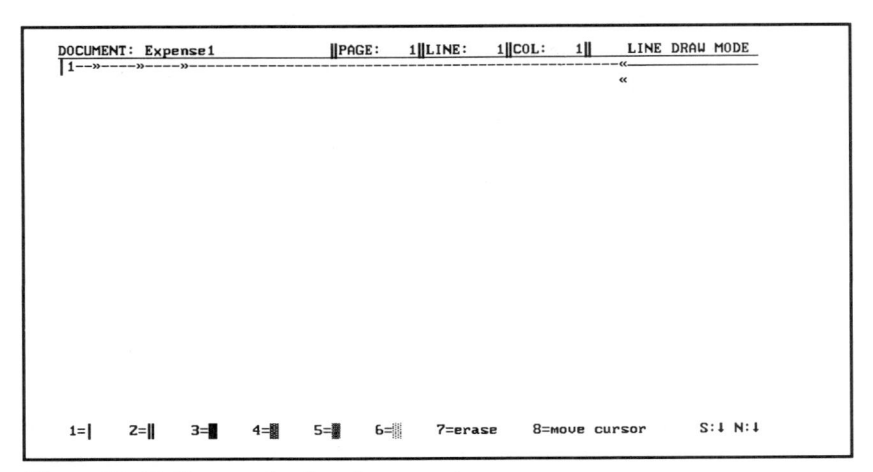

Figure 10.12: Prompt for line draw mode

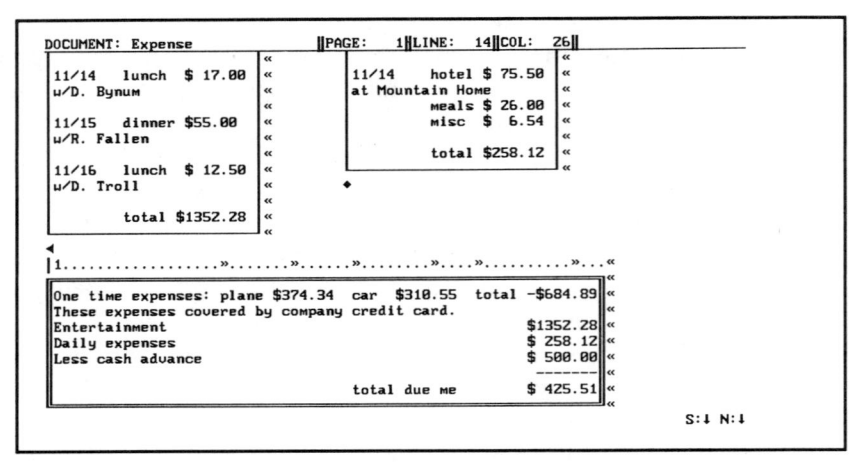

```
DOCUMENT: Expense                    ||PAGE:    1||LINE:   14||COL:   26||
                                «
11/14   lunch   $ 17.00    «    11/14     hotel $ 75.50  «
w/D. Bynum                 «    at Mountain Home         «
                           «                meals $ 26.00 «
11/15   dinner $55.00      «                 misc $  6.54 «
w/R. Fallen                «                              «
                           «                total $258.12 «
11/16   lunch   $ 12.50    «                              «
w/D. Troll                 «
                           «            ◆
        total $1352.28     «
                           «
◂
|1..................».......».......».........»....».............»...«
                                                                      «
One time expenses: plane $374.34  car  $310.55  total -$684.89 «
These expenses covered by company credit card.                 «
Entertainment                                        $1352.28  «
Daily expenses                                       $ 258.12  «
Less cash advance                                    $ 500.00  «
                                                     --------
                                  total due me       $ 425.51  «
                                                               «
                                                         S:1 N:1
```

Figure 10.13: Line and box drawings in Expense1

the first letter in *plane*. Now press Insert, the Space bar, and Insert again to restore the text. Do this for each instance where a character is flush with the left margin. There are 13 such instances. As you readjust this text, note that the characters move over one space, but the numbers corresponding to them do not. This is because the decimal tab keeps them in their original alignment. This is a good thing to remember when you create columns that you plan to put in boxes.

You must also create a blank line between the end of the text in the first column and the hard column break symbol that occurs on the line after the total. You will want to draw a line under this total, and it is impossible to draw a line through a hard column break. Normal text-editing symbols, such as tab symbols and return codes, will readjust for any lines drawn over them, and the arrangement of the text will remain unaffected. To make space between the end of the text and the hard column break symbol, place the cursor on the return code directly after the number *8* in *$1352.28*. Press Insert, Return, and Insert again to restore the text.

The column has been designed so that no text lies flush with the right margin of the column. If this were the case, tab stops within the column would have to be readjusted, or else the right-hand limits of the column would have to be expanded.

To begin drawing your first line, return the cursor to the first position beneath the column format line. Press Alt-E, the Line Draw key, and press 1, which selects the narrowest line width. Next press the ↓

key 27 times. This should result in a line down the left side of the first column. If you arranged the blank spaces correctly, you should be unable to move the line more than 27 spaces down. The hard column break symbol will prevent this.

Now press the → key 29 times. This will draw a line of the same thickness along the bottom of the column. You will be unable to extend the line beyond the right side of a column, because it is impossible to draw lines beyond column margins. Now press the ↑ key to continue drawing the line up the right side to the top of the column, and then press the ← key to draw the line back to the beginning point.

Since you have completed your first box, press Alt-E to exit line draw mode. You need not exit from line draw mode to move the cursor, however. Just press 8 while in the line draw mode to move the cursor without drawing a line.

Before you can draw a border around the text in the second column, you must first change the arrangement of text in the column as you did in the first, to accommodate a line without erasing text. You do this the same way you rearranged text in the first column. Remember to move the hard column break symbol down one more line.

For the third line and box drawing, move the cursor to the first position beneath the system format line that controls the layout of the third group of expense figures. Create a blank line between the format line and the text. Create room along the left margin for the line you are going to draw. Now press Alt-E, the Line Draw key, and select the double line by pressing 2. Now press the ↓ key seven times to draw the left line. Next, press the → key 64 times. To move quickly, you can hold the → key down while it autorepeats, and the complete bottom line will be drawn much more rapidly. Press the ↑ key seven times, and then hold down the ← key until you've completed the box. Notice how the inside line of the double line joins at a corner to give a clear double-line effect around the bend.

To employ the full features of line draw mode, you can add lines above the totals. You can print a document with more than 55 lines per page, but it won't look as nice. Go back to the top of the memo Expense1 and delete a blank line separating the date from the memo heading, and delete a second line between the heading and the memo.

Now return to the bottom of the memo and insert a blank line between the figure −$500.00 and the line *Total due*. You do this by placing the cursor on the return code directly after the figure −$500.00 and pressing Insert, Return, and Insert. This will create an extra line, and it will even move the bottom drawn line down to accommodate the extra space. But two gaps will appear at the right and left margins in the drawn line. You can fill in the gaps by moving the cursor and then entering the line draw mode (Alt-E), or else entering the line draw mode (Alt-E) first and then moving the cursor (press 8). In either case, once the cursor is positioned, press the line code (2) to fill in the gap.

Creating columns in your documents opens up your ability to create much more sophisticated documents. You can use bound columns to separate and highlight specific kinds of text, such as numbers. And you can use snake columns to rearrange the flow of your text so that it can be scanned more conveniently, as with newspaper text.

Your ability to use columns is enhanced in Advantage II by your ability to line up columns of figures along a decimal tab and calculate sums either in columns or rows. You can enhance the appearance of these figures by creating lines and boxes. You can also use these lines to enhance text in any kind of document you can produce with MultiMate Advantage II.

In the next chapter, you'll learn about advanced printing techniques, including merge printing.

11

ADVANCED PRINTING

PRINTING IS AN EASY PROCEDURE WHEN ALL YOU need to do is print a simple document. You learned how to do this in Chapter 6. Various other documents, however, require special handling when the time comes to print them. You will learn what kinds of documents these are and how to print them in this chapter.

Advanced printing comprises three major areas:

- Merge printing
- Queue printing
- Special keyboards and characters

With merge printing, you can combine standard text, such as a letter, with varying information, such as different names and addresses. Queue printing allows you to organize a series of unrelated documents for printing in a designated order. Finally, you can use several specialty keyboards that allow you to print characters that aren't available in most word-processing programs. You can write text in German, French, or Spanish, using the correct accents, and you can also include scientific notation.

MERGE PRINTING

Merge printing refers to the repetitive printing of a single document that will be sent to many people and must reflect these differences. Usually, merge printing is used to prepare letters in which the text remains substantially the same, but the name, address, and other specific information change with each letter. Careful preparation ensures a successful merge operation.

For a merge printing, you need to create three kinds of documents: the Merge document, the List documents, and the Result documents.

You create the Merge document first. It contains the foundation text, as well as several *merge item names,* which contain the variable information that will change from letter to letter.

Next, you need to create the List documents, which contain the specific information for the merge item names that will appear in each Result document.

The Result documents are the actual printed copies you obtain when you combine the text in the Merge document and the variable information in the List documents. The accuracy, appearance, and effectiveness of the Result documents depend upon your care and attention in creating the Merge and List documents.

CREATING A MERGE DOCUMENT

The Merge document must contain two things: the text that you want to appear in every letter, and the merge item names that contain the variable, personalized data. This data is what distinguishes one merge-printed letter from the next. A Merge document can at times contain a third item: special commands that instruct Advantage II to print the information in selected merge item names in special ways.

You can enter and edit text in a Merge document just as you do with any other document.

Entering Merge Item Names

Special conditions apply when you begin to enter a merge item name, however. Before you enter any names, you should plan the item names you are going to use and how you want to spell them. These item names will be re-created in the List document, which feeds information to the Merge document. The item names in both documents must be identical, including spaces and capitalization.

A merge item name should be one discrete unit of information. A merge item name can be a person's name, a title, the company name, the address, the city, the state, or the zip code. Each of these can be a merge item name, and it is inadvisable to combine two or more into one merge item name. As an example, you might want to refer to *Dave Bynum* by name several times in a letter, but only to his title of *Owner* once in the heading. If you combined the name and title in the same merge item name, the combination would always be presented in full.

A better question is whether you want to divide the name *Dave*

Bynum into two merge item names: first name and last name. This allows you to use his full name in the heading, but to begin the salutation with just the first name, *Dave*. These are the sorts of considerations you must give to merge item names before you enter them.

Let's go over the procedure before trying an example. To insert a merge item name in a Merge document, move the cursor to the position in the document where you want the item name to appear in print. When the cursor is in position, press Alt-M, the Merge Code key, and a merge code symbol will appear. The cursor will be to the right of the symbol. Directly following the merge code symbol, type the label for the merge item (that is, *firstname* rather than *Dave*). You can use from 1 to 12 characters for this label, which gives you some flexibility. You can use complete English words for your merge items, and you do not have to resort to abbreviations and code words, as you do with library entries and key procedure file names.

When you have finished entering the merge item name, press Alt-M a second time, creating a second merge code symbol at the end of the item name. This now becomes the place where information from the List document will appear in the Merge document. Be careful to place merge code symbols (Alt-M) directly before and after the characters in the merge item name. Avoid placing spaces and extraneous characters in merge item names. These names will not be printed in the Result document, but they could affect the results of the merge printing.

As an example, let's say you want to write a thank-you letter to the winemakers you visited when you traveled to California. Begin by creating a new document and call it Thanks. Then proceed to enter the text as it appears in Figure 11.1, following these steps:

1. Enter the date, and press Return four times.

2. Now, prepare to enter the merge item names in the return address. Make sure the cursor is at the left margin, and press Alt-M. Type *firstname,* and press Alt-M to end the merge item. Press the Space bar—since you want a space between first and last names—then press Alt-M, type *lastname,* and press Alt-M.

3. Press Return. For the next three lines, the procedure is the same: press Alt-M, enter the merge item name, and press Alt-M. Remember not to insert extra spaces between the merge symbols, and double-check the spelling.

4. Press Return. Then press Alt-M, type *city,* and press Alt-M. Next, enter the comma and a space. Proceed to press Alt-M, type *state,* and press Alt-M. Now enter two spaces—the standard spacing between the state and zip code. Press Alt-M, type *zip,* and press Alt-M.
5. Press Return twice, and enter the salutation: type *Dear* (no comma), enter a space, press Alt-M, type *firstname,* press Alt-M, and enter a comma.
6. Finally, press Return twice and Tab once, and enter the two paragraphs of the letter as usual.

The merge item names in the Merge document Thanks now need their counterparts in a List document.

CREATING A LIST DOCUMENT

Since the List documents contain the specific information for the merge item names of the Merge document, you use the same merge item names as in the Merge document. Otherwise, there would be no transfer of information from one document to the other. The merge item names for each printed letter constitute a *record,* and each record occupies one page of the List document.

Let's go over the procedure before trying an example. You begin creating a List document just as you do a standard document. When

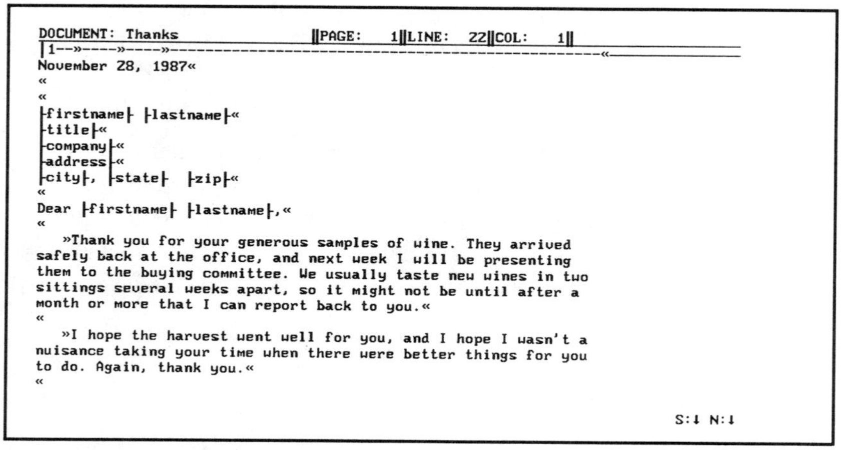

```
DOCUMENT: Thanks                 ||PAGE:    1||LINE:  22||COL:    1||
|1--»----»----»-----------------------------------------------«
November 28, 1987«
«
«
├firstname├ ├lastname├«
├title├«
├company├«
├address├«
├city├, ├state├  ├zip├«
«
Dear ├firstname├ ├lastname├,«
«
   »Thank you for your generous samples of wine. They arrived
safely back at the office, and next week I will be presenting
them to the buying committee. We usually taste new wines in two
sittings several weeks apart, so it might not be until after a
month or more that I can report back to you.«
«
   »I hope the harvest went well for you, and I hope I wasn't a
nuisance taking your time when there were better things for you
to do. Again, thank you.«
«

                                                        S:↓ N:↓
```

Figure 11.1: Merge document

the blank Document screen appears, press Alt-M to place a merge code symbol in the first position on the screen. Next, type the first merge item name that you are using in the Merge document and press Alt-M directly after the last character. Press Return, and then type the specific information for that item. Do not begin this variable field with a merge code symbol, but do end the field with Alt-M. Continue until you have entered all the merge item names in the Merge document, along with specific information for the first merge letter.

All the merge item names in the Merge document must also be in the List document if you want specific information to appear in the right places on the Result document. If you ignore a field, that merge item name will remain blank when printed. Be careful: if you misspell a merge item name in the List document, the information will not be transferred to the Result document. You can enter the merge item names in any order you wish.

To create the List document that will provide information for your Thanks letter, begin by creating a standard document (which will serve as your data file), and call it Thanklst (for the list of people who will be getting the Thanks letter).

1. Press Alt-M to create a merge code symbol in line 1, column 1, and then type the merge item name *firstname*. Press Alt-M, press Return, and type the name *Dave*. Press Alt-M at the end of this variable information.

2. Press Return and Alt-M, type the merge item name *lastname,* press Alt-M, and press Return.

3. Continue to enter all the merge item names that appear in the Thanks letter, following the example shown in Figure 11.2. Whenever you create a record in a List document, double-check all merge item names and the placement of merge code symbols. A single mistake with any of them can cause a letter to print incorrectly.

When you are creating a series of records in the List document, each record must be placed on a page of its own. You do this by pressing F2, the Page Break key, after finishing each record. Then, for each record, you could enter the merge code symbols with Alt-M, the merge item names, and the variable information.

A quicker method is to copy the first record onto the second page,

```
DOCUMENT: Thanklst            |PAGE:    1|LINE:   17|COL:    1|
|1--»----»----»--------------------------------------------«
|firstname|«
Dave|«
|lastname|«
Bynum|«
|title|«
Winemaker|«
|company|«
DAVIS BYNUM WINERY|«
|address|«
8075 Westside Road|«
|city|«
Healdsburg|«
|state|«
CA|«
|zip|«
95448|«


                                                      S:1 N:1
```

Figure 11.2: First record in *Thanklst* List document

so that you don't have to retype the merge item names. You can do this by bringing the record for Dave Bynum onto your screen and pressing F2, the Page Break key. When page 2 appears, leave it blank and return to page 1, which contains the record for Dave Bynum. Now press Home to make sure the cursor is in the first position of this record. Next, press F8, End, and F8 to begin the copy function, move the cursor to the end of the first record and highlight it, and end the highlight. Press PgDn to go to page 2, and press F8 to insert the first record on page 2. You will still have to enter the new specific information, overwriting the old, but the field names and Alt-M codes will be correct—as long as you have created the first record correctly.

An even quicker alternative—but only if you are creating quite a few records—is to build a key procedure file that will insert merge code symbols and merge item names on each page. All you have to do is press Ctrl-F5, the Key Procedure Build key, before you create your first record. Proceed until you come to the specific information for the first merge item name, and press Ctrl-F6 in place of the specific information. This will cause the key procedure to pause so you can enter the specific information. At the end of the record, press Ctrl-F7 (for a prompt, so you can quickly create one record after another) and then Ctrl-F5 (to end), and press F2 to begin a new page. Then, to enter the specific information, call up this key procedure file and press Ctrl-F8 to execute it for each record. At each pause, enter the specific information. (To review key procedures, see Chapter 8.)

Now try either the copy function or a key procedure to insert the entries shown in Figure 11.3.

PRINTING RESULT DOCUMENTS

All the work up to this point has been to load two documents, the Merge document and the List document, with information that will be combined and printed. To start printing the Result documents, select on the main menu

5) Merge Print a Document

This causes the Merge Print a Document screen (Figure 11.4) to appear. Enter *Thanks* in the Merge Document Name field, and press Return. (Note that if Thanklst was the last document you worked with, then *Thanklst* will appear in the Merge document field. Just replace *Thanklst* with *Thanks.*) Make sure your documents are in the drives specified in the Drive fields; if not, change the drive specifications.

The Merge Data File field requires some explanation. There are three kinds of merge data files you might want to use:

1. A List document created in MultiMate Advantage II.

2. A data file from Advantage II's On-File database (discussed in Chapter 13).

3. Information from another database not connected to Advantage II. You can import information from most popular database programs (see Chapter 12 for details).

```
              2nd EXAMPLE          3rd EXAMPLE          4th EXAMPLE
   firstname  Jerzy                Darcy                Toby
   lastname   Budrick              Kolodney             Friar
   title      Winemaker            President            Oenologist
   company    BUDRICK CELLARS      THE RED & WHITE      FRIAR'S
   address    810 Cragmont         PO Box 1917          220 Whitehall
   city       Fiddletown           Berkeley             St. Helena
   state      CA                   CA                   CA
   zip        95629                94703                94574
```

Figure 11.3: Three more entries for the List document Thanklst

For this example, type *Thanklst* in the Merge Data File field and press F10. The prompt

Record(s) [00001] to [99999]

will appear on the Merge Print a Document screen, allowing you to select the range of record numbers from which you want information printed. Record numbers are the same as page numbers in your List document. When you use a List document for the merge data file, you are limited to the maximum page count for a document: 255 records.

If you want to print information from all the records in the merge data file, you can accept the default value for the lower limit by pressing Return, and then enter the number of records for the upper limit. If you overestimate the number of records, Advantage II will print the specified number of Result documents, but the last few will simply have blanks in the merge item name fields. If you accept the 99,999 default by mistake, you can halt printing by pressing Escape. Press F10 to set the upper limit and move you into the Document Print Options screen connected to the Merge document Thanks.

When the settings in the Print Options Document screen are correct (refer to Chapter 6), press F10 to begin the merge print. The prompt

PLEASE WAIT...PRINTING A DOCUMENT

will appear at the bottom of the screen.

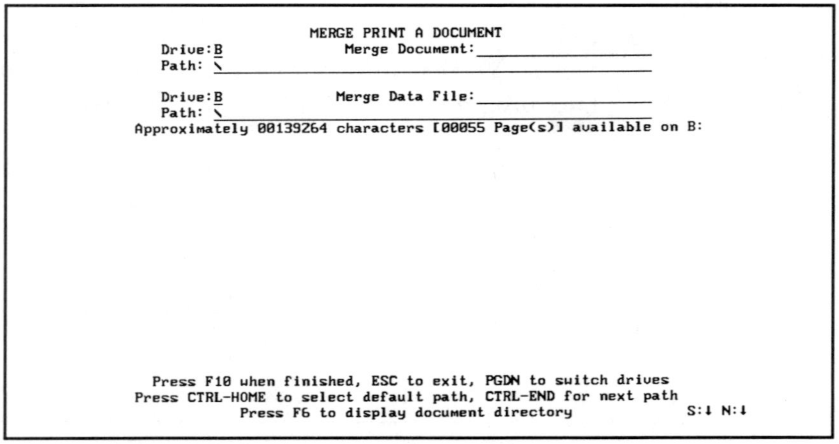

```
                        MERGE PRINT A DOCUMENT
           Drive:B           Merge Document:_____
           Path: \

           Drive:B           Merge Data File:_____
           Path: \
           Approximately 00139264 characters [00055 Page(s)] available on B:










                Press F10 when finished, ESC to exit, PGDN to switch drives
                Press CTRL-HOME to select default path, CTRL-END for next path
                       Press F6 to display document directory      S:1 N:1
```

Figure 11.4: Merge Print a Document screen

Canceling Merge Print

You can cancel a merge print any time during the print cycle by pressing Escape. If you changed the pause setting on the Document Print Options screen, the message

> PRINTER PAUSE BETWEEN PAGES, PRESS ESCAPE TO CONTINUE

will appear at the bottom of the screen after each Result document has been printed. To escape without continuing to the next page, quickly press Escape twice.

Whether you selected Foreground or Background printing on the Document Print Options screen, merge printing always takes place in the foreground mode.

MERGE PRINTING FROM THE KEYBOARD

It is possible to enter information into a Result document directly from the keyboard during merge printing. You can have the printer pause at every merge item name, and fill in all the information for each record.

If you wish to enter all the information in a series of merge-printed letters, all you have to do is enter the name of the Merge document you want printed in the Merge Print a Document screen (Figure 11.4). Do not enter a List document or merge data file name. Note that the number of records you accept is immaterial; you just get the one letter for which you are making manual entries. Press F10, leaving the Merge Data File field blank, and Advantage II will begin to print the text of the Merge document. The prompt

> PLEASE WAIT...PRINTING A DOCUMENT

will appear in the middle of the screen. When Advantage II starts to process the first merge item name, the program will not find a corresponding field in a List document because there is no List document. The prompt

> REPLACE:<merge item name>
> WITH :_____

will appear at the bottom of the screen. Type the information as you want it to appear in the Result document by filling in the field after *WITH*. You can insert up to 20 characters. Press Return when you are finished, and Advantage II will move to the next merge item name. When you have added information for all the merge item names in the first Result document, Advantage II will start printing the text for the next Result document. If you want several copies of each document for which you are entering information, make sure to change the Number of Original Copies field in the Document Print Options screen attached to the Merge document you are printing.

SPECIAL COMMANDS

You can insert four special commands (see Table 11.1) in a Merge document that will affect the appearance of the Result document. You enter these commands in a Merge document where you want them to take effect. You must bracket them with merge code symbols (Alt-M), or else Advantage II will not read the commands correctly. Let's see how each command works.

Omit If Blank

Use the Omit if Blank command when your Merge document

COMMAND	CODE	INSTRUCTIONS
Omit if Blank	OB	Omit blank spaces or lines in Result document when there is no variable information in the merge data file
Repeat	REPEAT##	Repeat information from a single record a specified number of times
Next	NEXT	Repeat information from several records a specified number of times
End Repeat	END REPEAT	End the repeat function

Table 11.1: Special commands for merge printing

contains a merge item name that has no counterpart in the List document. As an example, say you have just started merge printing letters to various winemakers. You will be doing this often in the future, but the purpose of subsequent printings will probably vary. For the moment, you are only beginning to explore the uses of a List document, and you don't want to put too much into it before you know what you need in it. In such a case, you will find a *reference field* helpful. This is a field where you can cite specific information that you explain further along in the body of the letter. You could cite a wine type and vintage, and then discuss its price and release date in the letter, or you could cite an invoice number in the reference field and then address the problem of shipping or damage in the text of the letter.

To accommodate a reference field, insert a new merge item name called *ref* in the Merge document Thanks. Type the code *OB* directly after it, because at this point you have nothing specific to enter in this field. The *ref* and the *OB* must each be bracketed by merge code symbols (Alt-M), and the OB code must follow immediately after the merge item name *ref* to nullify it. Figure 11.5 shows you what your Merge document Thanks looks like after you have inserted a reference field and then nullified it with OB.

When you add the *ref* field to the List document, and you want variable information in that field to be printed in your letters, all you have to do is erase the OB code with its two merge code symbols in the Merge document.

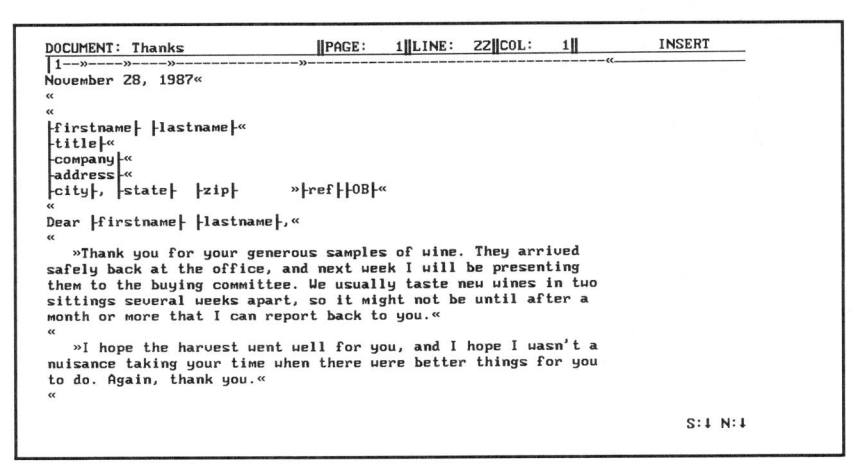

```
DOCUMENT: Thanks              ||PAGE:   1||LINE:  22||COL:   1||        INSERT
|1--»----»----------------»-----------------------------«-
November 28, 1987«
«
«
|firstname|  |lastname|«
|title|«
|company|«
|address|«
|city|, |state|  |zip|       »|ref||OB|«
«
Dear |firstname|  |lastname|,«
«
    »Thank you for your generous samples of wine. They arrived
safely back at the office, and next week I will be presenting
them to the buying committee. We usually taste new wines in two
sittings several weeks apart, so it might not be until after a
month or more that I can report back to you.«
«
    »I hope the harvest went well for you, and I hope I wasn't a
nuisance taking your time when there were better things for you
to do. Again, thank you.«
«
                                                              S:1 N:1
```

Figure 11.5: Merge document Thanks with new field *ref* nullified

Repeat and End Repeat

The Repeat and End Repeat commands control the repetition of information in a single record. These two commands always appear together. You will use these commands most often to print duplicate labels. The Repeat command occurs directly before the batch of fields to be repeated, and includes a two-digit number that instructs Advantage II how many times to repeat printing the batch. The End Repeat command is placed directly after the batch and marks the end of the batch of fields.

As an example, say you want to create postal labels for the thank-you letters you are going to generate, and you also want to create two more labels so that you can mark the sample bottles of wine you brought back with you from each winery.

To prepare to print these labels, create a separate document called Labels. You can use external copy (Shift-F8) to transfer the heading from your Merge document Thanks into Labels. Standard labels hold six lines of printed text, but the heading only holds four lines of text. You must enter two blank lines by pressing Return three times after the *zip* field. These lines will contain no text in the label, but they instruct Advantage II to move ahead to the correct position on the next label.

Before you print the labels, you need to enter the Repeat and End Repeat commands in the right place. Figure 11.6 shows you where to do this. You can use insert mode to enter the commands. You must enter two digits in the number field after REPEAT.

Next

The Next command must be used in conjunction with the Repeat and End Repeat commands, when there is text to be repeated during the printing. Using the Next command changes the purpose of the two-digit number that follows the REPEAT code. Instead of using that number to calculate how many times it should reprint records, Advantage II will use it to calculate how many records it should print before the section of text is repeated.

As an example, say you wanted to prepare a list of all the winemakers in your List document. You can use this list to show the committee which wineries will be represented with wines during the next tasting. Using a label format and printing the list on standard paper will allow the committee members to make notes next to each winery name. Yet you don't want this list to circulate outside the committee room. You can use text repeated by the Next command to ensure that both of these purposes are met, as shown in the Merge document in Figure 11.7. You can center the two lines of text that appear before and after the special commands, since the listings will be printed on standard-size paper.

```
DOCUMENT: Labels              ||PAGE:   1||LINE:   8||COL:   1||
 1--»----»-----»-------------------------------------------«
├REPEAT:03┤«
├firstname┤ ├lastname┤«
├title┤«
├company┤«
├address┤«
├city┤, ├state┤ ├zip┤«
├END REPEAT┤«



                                                          S:1 N:1
```

Figure 11.6: Merge document Labels with Repeat and End Repeat commands

```
DOCUMENT: Labels              ||PAGE:   1||LINE:  16||COL:   1||        INSERT
 1--»----»-----»-------------------------------------------«
            »List of wineries supplying samples for tasting«
«
«
├REPEAT:8┤«
├NEXT┤«
├firstname┤ ├lastname┤«
├title┤«
├company┤«
├address┤«
├city┤, ├state┤ ├zip┤«
«
«
«
├END REPEAT┤«
            »This list is the property of WINES EN MASSE«



                                                          S:1 N:1
```

Figure 11.7: Merge document Labels with Next command

Notice that the number after the REPEAT code has been changed to 08, because you want eight listings printed on each page. With 6 lines per listing, including the blank line, eight listings will use 48 text lines, leaving 2 lines for the one-liners at top and bottom and 5 blank lines to be distributed after the first text line and before the last text line. Once you add the extra lines—or adjust the lines per page setting—the two text lines will fall at the top and bottom of each page.

The Result document printed from this Merge document will contain eight listings per page, with the line of text that comes before the REPEAT code printed at the top of the page, and the line of text that comes after the END REPEAT code printed at the bottom of the page, as shown in Figure 11.8. Subsequent pages will contain eight more listings, with the same one-liners at the top and bottom of each page.

QUEUE PRINTING

Queue printing allows you to arrange the order in which documents will be printed. To specify a queue, first select on the main menu

   3) Print a Document

Enter the name of the document you want to print on the Print a Document screen. Next the Document Print Options screen will appear for the document you want to print. Make sure that all the settings on this screen are correct, and then press F10 to begin printing. Now select the subsequent documents to print. As soon as more than one is ready to print, you have created a *queue*, or waiting line, of documents to be printed. They will print in the order you loaded them.

You can make changes to this queue by accessing the Additional Print Functions screen. To do this, first select on the main menu

   4) Additional Print Functions

The Additional Print Functions menu (Figure 11.9) will appear. On this menu, select

   1. Printer Queue Control

```
          List of wineries supplying samples for tasting

          Dave Bynum
          Winemaker
          DAVIS BYNUM WINERY
          8075 Westside Road
          Healdsburg, CA  95488


          Jerzy Budrick
          Winemaker
          BUDRICK CELLARS
          810 Cragmont
          Fiddletown, CA  95629


          Darcy Kolodney
          President
          THE RED & WHITE
          PO Box 1917
          Berkeley, CA  94703


          Toby Friar
          Oenologist
          FRIAR'S
          220 Whitehall
          St. Helena, CA  94574


          John McCorn
          Cellarmaster
          ANGWIN HILLS WINES
          Black Mountain Road
          Angwin, CA  94508


          Bill Easter
          Owner
          CORKING CELLARS
          1205 Solano Court
          Albany, CA  94706


          Richard Hasslepuss
          Proprietor
          CHABLIS CHATEAU
          45 Morley Hill
          Piedmont, CA  94611


          Richard Redding
          BAY WINE CELLARS
          213 Paseo Del Tulare
          Emeryville, CA  94614


               This list is the property of WINES EN MASSE
```

Figure 11.8: First page of Result document Labels

The Printer Queue Control screen (Figure 11.10) will appear next. The five options on this screen allow you to control all the documents that you want to send to the printer for printing. The names of these documents will appear below the five options. You can designate which option you want to apply to any of the documents not yet

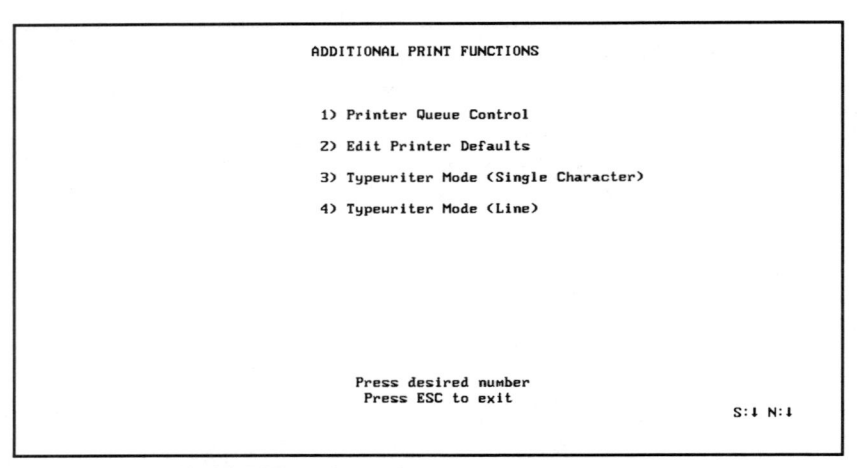

```
                    ADDITIONAL PRINT FUNCTIONS


                    1) Printer Queue Control

                    2) Edit Printer Defaults

                    3) Typewriter Mode (Single Character)

                    4) Typewriter Mode (Line)




                           Press desired number
                           Press ESC to exit
                                                              S:1 N:1
```

Figure 11.9: Additional Print Functions menu

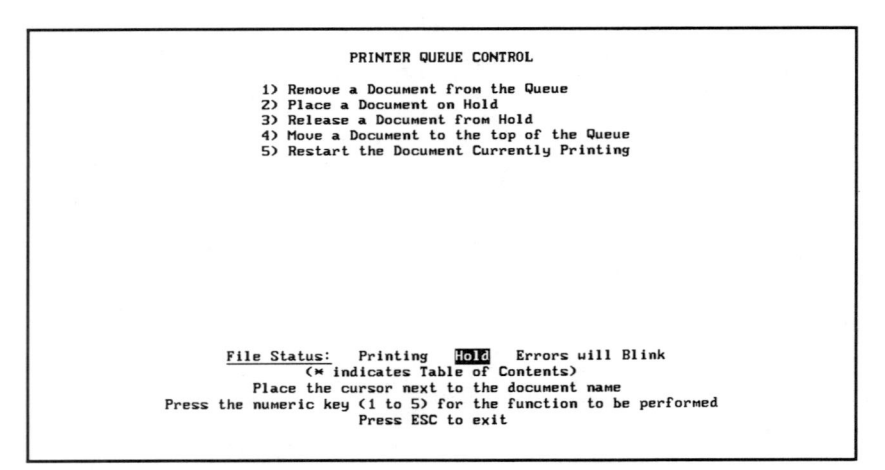

```
                         PRINTER QUEUE CONTROL
                    1) Remove a Document from the Queue
                    2) Place a Document on Hold
                    3) Release a Document from Hold
                    4) Move a Document to the top of the Queue
                    5) Restart the Document Currently Printing




              File Status:  Printing   Hold   Errors will Blink
                          (* indicates Table of Contents)
                  Place the cursor next to the document name
            Press the numeric key (1 to 5) for the function to be performed
                              Press ESC to exit
```

Figure 11.10: Printer Queue Control screen

printed, by using the arrow keys to place the cursor on the first character in the document name. Then press the appropriate number key (1 to 5) corresponding to that option.

BYPASSING THE MAIN MENU

There might be times when you want to print a series of short documents, perhaps some of them having similar titles, and you want to make sure you print the right ones. You can print one document and then move quickly into another document to view it and see if it is the one you want to print, and then move quickly into the Merge Print a Document screen to change the queue. You can bypass the main menu by pressing the Alt-number key combination for the function you want to perform.

As an example, if you are starting to print Letter1 in a queue that is stacked with Letter1 through Letter10, but you forgot to whom some of these letters are addressed, you can edit, say, Letter3 by selecting on the main menu

   1) Edit a Document

then typing *Letter3*. At this point, you need to press F10 once or twice, depending on whether you pass through startup screens. After you have taken a look at the contents of Letter3 and realize you do not want to print this letter, you can enter the Additional Print Functions screen directly by pressing Alt-4. You can now access the Printer Queue Control screen and cancel the printing of Letter3 before it starts to print. You can move directly back into the Edit a Document screen by pressing Alt-1. Such speed is not generally an important factor except when time is short, and you might find this the case when you stack up documents to print in a queue.

You can access all the functions listed on the main menu directly from some other place in the program by pressing the Alt-number key corresponding to the number of the function on the main menu.

TYPEWRITER MODES

You can use the printer to enter text on paper in the same way you use a typewriter by employing either of the typewriter modes in the Additional Print Functions screen (Figure 11.8). The first mode allows you to type text directly onto paper, and the second mode allows you to create up to six lines of text on the screen first and then print them.

Helpful Hints When Using Typewriter Modes

You can use only a limited number of nonalphanumeric keys in the typewriter modes. The keys you can use and their effects are displayed in both typewriter mode screens. You can use all the special characters of the alternate keyboards (see the next section) with either typewriter mode, and you can build and execute key procedure files.

If you are printing a document and try to access either of the typewriter modes, the prompt

Cannot use typewriter mode while printing

will appear on the bottom of your screen. You must wait until the complete document has been printed before you can enter typewriter mode.

Here are some rules to remember when typing in either typewriter mode:

1. You can enter up to 80 characters in a single line. There is no way to extend or shorten this limit, since there is no format line in either typewriter mode screen.

2. Word wrap does not operate in typewriter mode.

3. The characters printed through either typewriter mode screen will always print in the default pitch setting of 10 characters per inch.

4. If you are printing documents stacked up in a print queue, you must wait until the printer finishes printing a document. Then you can enter typewriter mode, and the printer will halt printing of the queued documents until you exit from the typewriter mode.

In addition, if you want to underline text while using typewriter mode, you must follow this sequence:

1. First, enter the text. Make sure you write down the column numbers where you want underlining to start and stop, because you have to reposition the cursor to enter the underlining with the _ key. (You can guess, but you might be wrong.)

2. Now use the Backspace or ← key to move the cursor where you want underlining to begin. As soon as you move the cursor to the left, the line of text entered up to that point will be printed.

3. Add the underlining, and press Return when you're done. If

you are careful where you start and stop the underlining, it should be printed directly beneath the proper text after you press Return.

Single Characters

The simplest method for typing directly onto paper is Typewriter Mode (Single Character). You can type a single character if you want to, but in fact no text will be printed until you press one of the output keys shown on the screen (see Figure 11.11). This means you can enter a full line of text on the screen before the first character is printed. To use this method, select option 3 on the Additional Print Functions screen.

On the Typewriter Mode (Single Character) screen, the cursor will appear just above the LINE and COLUMN position indicators at the bottom of the screen. These indicators mark the position on the paper where the character in the current cursor position will print. You will probably use this screen primarily to type names and addresses on envelopes or fill in preprinted forms. To do so, you will have to become adept at positioning the paper beneath the print head, and following strictly the LINE and COLUMN indicators at the bottom of the screen.

```
                TYPEWRITER MODE (SINGLE CHARACTER)
                Characters typed are sent to the printer.
    Press:                         To output:
        BACKSPACE (or ←)              Backspace
        SPACEBAR (or →)               Space
        RETURN                        Carriage Return & Line Feed
        HOME (or F7)                  Carriage Return
        ↓ (or F8)                     Line Feed
        F9                            Form Feed
        F10 (or ESC)                  Exit




    LINE:    1 COLUMN:   1                                      S:1 N:1
```

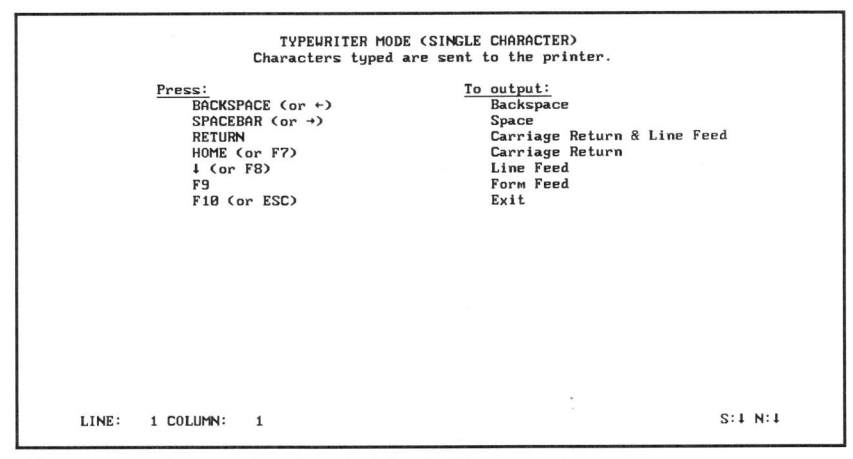

Figure 11.11: Typewriter Mode (Single Character) screen

Lines of Text

Option 4 on the Additional Print Functions menu, Typewriter Mode (Line), allows you to handle single lines of text with greater freedom than the single character screen does. You can see the line mode screen in Figure 11.12.

Text will begin to appear in the same position on this screen as it did on the single-character screen, but you can enter only one line of text at a time. After you enter this line, you can choose either to print it immediately or else insert it into the next position on the screen above the line where you entered it. The screen allows you to enter and store up to six different lines of text, one line at a time. You can then print any of the lines by following the instructions on the screen.

Repeatedly printing a single line of text like this is useful for printing return addresses on letters. The text lines of a return address stay the same from one printing to the next, although each line is different.

SPECIAL KEYBOARDS

Six alternate character sets (or keyboards) are available in MultiMate Advantage II:

- Normal
- Romance
- Germanic
- Math
- Graphic1
- Graphic2

These special character sets are shown in Figure 11.13. To use one of the alternate keyboards, press Alt-K, the Alternate Keyboard key. The name of the keyboard in use will be displayed on the right side of the status line for a few moments, and then disappear. Once you have selected an alternate keyboard, you can access the special characters you want to use by pressing the Ctrl key and the letter key that corresponds to the special character you want.

```
                    TYPEWRITER MODE (LINE)
              Up to 80 characters may be entered per line
Press:              To:
    RETURN              Print Current Line ending with Carriage Return & Line Feed
    F6                  Print Current Line
    F7                  Print Current Line ending with Carriage Return
    F8 (or ↓)           Print Current Line ending with Line Feed
    F9                  Print Current Line ending with Form Feed
    F10 (or ESC)        Exit

F1 sends the following line to the printer:

F2 sends the following line to the printer:

F3 sends the following line to the printer:

F4 sends the following line to the printer:

F5 sends the following line to the printer:

Current Line:
LINE:    1 COLUMN:    1                                              S:↓ N:↓
```

Figure 11.12: Typewriter Mode (Line) screen

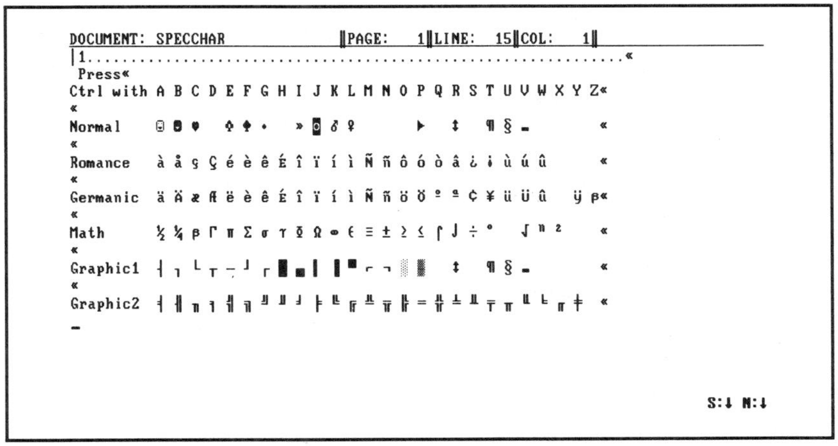

Figure 11.13: Special characters on the alternate keyboards

You can continue to access special characters on the keyboard you selected until you press Alt-K again, at which time the next keyboard in the series will be displayed. The keyboards will continue to cycle in the order listed in Figure 11.13, and you can select Normal to return to the normal keyboard.

If you have selected an alternate keyboard, but you don't want to use the special character set, the normal keyboard will remain in effect until you press the Ctrl key. Your printer might not be able to print some or all of these special characters. If you anticipate using any of these alternate keyboards, create a test document and experiment with using and printing the special characters you are interested in, or check your printer documentation to find out which characters are supported by your printer.

Pound Symbol

The British pound symbol is a special character that is available from the normal keyboard. To enter this character into text, press Ctrl-L, the Pound Symbol key. Again, whether this special character will print or not depends upon your printer.

PRINTING DOCUMENT SUMMARY SCREENS

A special print command that you might want to use from time to time enables you to print a series of Document Summary screens for all the files on your document disk. This is a handy way to keep track of your files, although it requires that you enter sufficient information in your Document Summary screens so that a printed record can help you determine what is in the file attached to each summary.

To print Document Summary screens, on the main menu select

   6) Document Management

The Document Management menu, which you first saw in Chapter 3, will appear. Two choices on this screen apply to Document Summary screens:

   5) Print Document Summary Screens
   6) Search Document Summary Screens

PRINT DOCUMENT SUMMARY SCREENS

If you want to view or print a particular Document Summary screen, select 5 on the Document Management screen. The screen for Print Document Summary Screens (Figure 11.14) will appear.

There are two ways to view a Document Summary screen: on the screen or printed on paper. You select which way you want to view

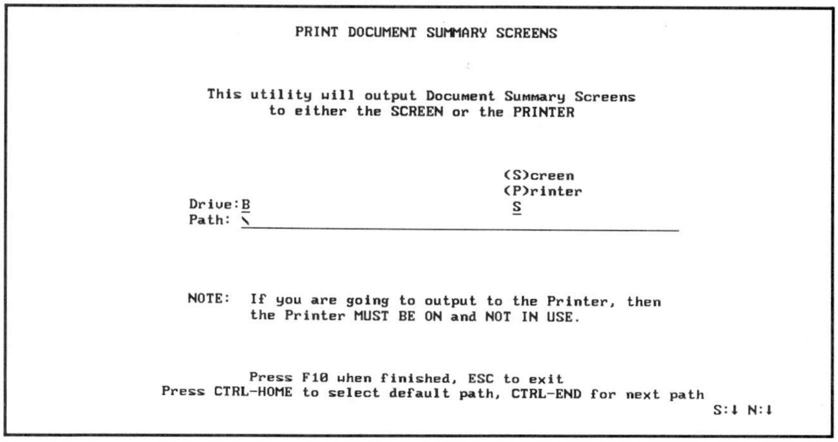

```
                    PRINT DOCUMENT SUMMARY SCREENS


              This utility will output Document Summary Screens
                     to either the SCREEN or the PRINTER


                                              (S)creen
                                              (P)rinter
          Drive:B                                S
          Path: \


          NOTE:  If you are going to output to the Printer, then
                 the Printer MUST BE ON and NOT IN USE.


                      Press F10 when finished, ESC to exit
              Press CTRL-HOME to select default path, CTRL-END for next path
                                                            S:1 N:1
```

Figure 11.14: Print Document Summary Screens screen

the Document Summary screen by accepting the default setting S for screen in the third field, or else changing it to P for printer. You can also change the document drive designation in the first field, as well as enter a directory designation in the second field.

When you press F10 to accept the settings, an empty Document Summary screen will be displayed. The only difference between this Document Summary screen and all others is that an additional line of text at the top shows that you are accessing it through the Print Document Summary Screens option. You can then view the Document Summary screens for all the documents on your document disk by pressing any key except Escape. If you press Escape, a blank screen will appear for a moment, then the prompt

PRESS ANY KEY TO EXIT

will appear at the bottom of the screen. When you exit, you return to the Document Management menu.

If you want to locate a particular Document Summary screen, press any key except Escape, and a succession of Document Summary screens will appear on the display. These screens will appear in the same order as the documents to which they are attached appear on the Edit a Document screen. For example, Figure 11.15 shows what the Document Summary screen for the List document Thanklst looks like.

Printing a Document Summary Along with a Document

If you change the Print Doc. Summary Screen option on the Document Print Options screen to Yes, the Document Summary attached to the document will be printed on the first page when you print the document. The text of the document will begin on the second page, although it will be numbered page 1 if you are using page numbers.

SEARCH DOCUMENT SUMMARY SCREENS

If the list of documents is very long, and you are not sure of the name of the document you are looking for, you can speed up the search for a particular Document Summary screen by selecting on the Document Management screen

6) Search Document Summary Screens

The Search Document Summary Screens screen (Figure 11.16) will appear. This screen resembles the screen for Print Document Summary Screens, and it offers you the same three settings. Pressing F10 causes an empty Document Summary screen to appear. It is up to you to fill in the name of the Document Summary screen you are searching for. This allows you to do two things. You can go directly to the Document Summary screen of your choice, and print or view

```
                        DOCUMENT SUMMARY SCREEN

            Document   Thanklst              Total pages  25
            Author     Rebecca Kristine
            Addressee
            Operator

            Identification key words :
                       List Document
                       attached to Thanks
                       letter
            Comments :
                       Contains records of 25 winemakers I visited during my fall 1987
                       trip to California.


            Creation Date         11/25/87    Modification Date       11/25/87
            Total Editing Time       0:11     Editing Time Last Session   0:04
            Total Keystrokes         1139     Keystrokes Last Session       99
                       Press F10 when finished, ESC to exit
                                                                   S:1 N:1
```

Figure 11.15: Document Summary screen for Thanklst

it, or you can collect a list of related Document Summary screens with similar file names for viewing or printing.

For example, if you entered *Thanks* in the title field and pressed F10, a momentary delay would ensue and then the Document Summary screen for the thank-you letter Thanks would appear. If, however, you entered only the name *Thank* in the first empty screen, another screen would appear with the two file names Thanks and Thanklst on it, as shown in Figure 11.17. Advantage II has searched for every file name that begins with the five letters *Thank*. If there is a

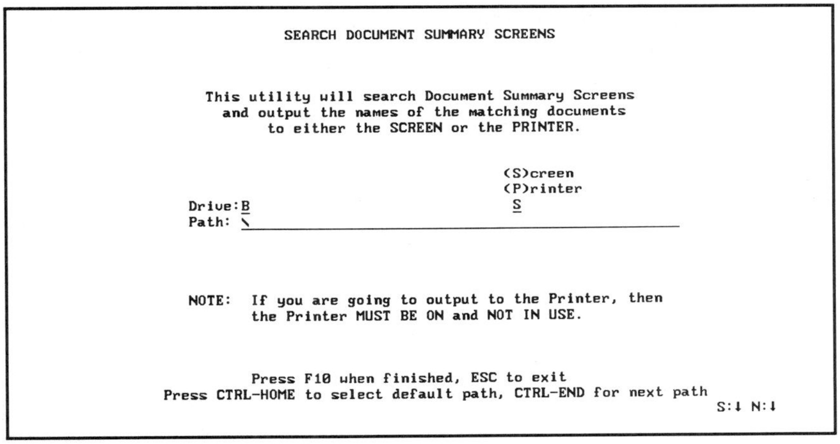

```
                    SEARCH DOCUMENT SUMMARY SCREENS


              This utility will search Document Summary Screens
                 and output the names of the matching documents
                       to either the SCREEN or the PRINTER.

                                          (S)creen
                                          (P)rinter
                 Drive:B                      S
                 Path: \


                 NOTE:  If you are going to output to the Printer, then
                        the Printer MUST BE ON and NOT IN USE.


                          Press F10 when finished, ESC to exit
                Press CTRL-HOME to select default path, CTRL-END for next path
                                                                      S:1 N:1
```

Figure 11.16: Search Document Summary Screens screen

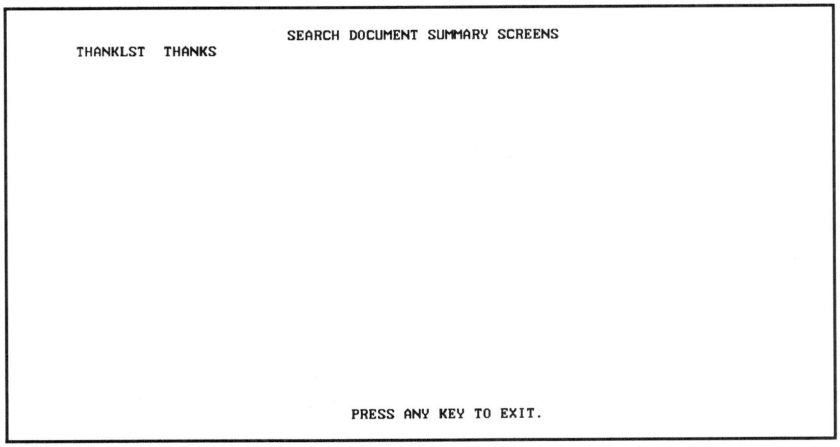

```
                              SEARCH DOCUMENT SUMMARY SCREENS
          THANKLST   THANKS












                                  PRESS ANY KEY TO EXIT.
```

Figure 11.17: Search list for *Thank*

perfect match—as there was for Thanks—then the Document Summary screen for that one file will appear. If there is no perfect match, but there are several files with the same first letters you have entered, all those files will be displayed. You can then select which ones you want to view or print. Thus, when you select new names for your files, remember that you can easily search for related files if the first few letters of their file names are the same.

Advanced printing techniques are really only extensions of the simple print command. Merge printing allows you to repeat text with variable information in the text, and queue printing allows you to stack up documents to print in a certain order. These procedures can get complicated, but the menu selections in Advantage II will lead you through the choices.

In the next chapter, you'll learn about handling information with merge data files.

12

Advanced Merging

INFORMATION HANDLING IS CRUCIAL TO ALL COMpanies, from managing inventories to keeping track of personal contacts. You can use MultiMate Advantage II to manage and organize information in various ways. You can use List documents (described in Chapter 11) for simple merge printing if you only want to keep track of a dozen or so names and addresses. This is a useful tool but not very powerful.

There are two other ways to handle data with Advantage II documents: merge data files and the On-File database. Merge data files will be discussed in this chapter, and the On-File database will be the subject of the next chapter. A merge data file is created as a document in the Advantage II word-processing program, and it multiplies the power of a List document. If you want to sort and print more than a dozen names and addresses, you will find merge data files very handy.

MERGE DATA FILES

A *merge data file* is a database that consists of a series of data file records. The information in these records is displayed according to a format determined by a template designed specifically for the merge data file. You can create and change merge data files like standard documents, although there are more restrictions with a merge data file, as you'll learn.

DESIGNING A TEMPLATE

The first step in creating a merge data file is to design a *template,* which sets the form in which all information for each record will be entered. Before you can begin designing this template, you must first create a new document. Select on the main menu

2) Create a Document

Enter a merge data file title just as you would any standard document title, and press F10. On the bottom of the Document Summary screen that appears next, you should see the prompt

> To create:LIBRARY-Leave screen empty, Press F5, DATA FILE-Press Shift-F10

You can add any information to this screen that you want, but once you are ready to continue, press Shift-F10 (instead of F10). This instructs Advantage II that the document you are about to create will be handled as a merge data file instead of as a normal document.

When you exit from the Document Summary screen, you will go directly into the Document screen. There is no Modify Document Defaults screen attached to a merge data file. On the Document screen, you change nothing on the format line except the tab stop settings, assuming the default tab stops do not match those you want to use when you design a template. Leave the line-spacing code at the default value of 1. You should notice that the right margin is in column 80, 5 more spaces than the default setting for a standard Document screen. Never change this setting when you are working with a merge data file. You must always create a merge data file with a right margin of 80 and maintain that setting.

As an example, let's begin creating a merge data file that will supersede the List document called *Thanklst* that you created in Chapter 11. You have decided that such a document is too limiting for your purposes. You want to maintain information on more than 255 entries. You want to handle these entries and edit them with greater freedom than is allowed in a List document. And there might be times when you want someone other than yourself to do this editing and updating, so the records must be accessible and easy to understand. These are all reasons for using a merge data file rather than the more limited List document.

First, you must create a template—the form that contains all the categories of information you'll want to use. On the Create a Document screen, type the name *Wineries* and press Return. Now press Shift-F10 to create the merge data file. Nothing in the Document screen where you create the template will indicate that you are working with a merge data file instead of a standard document. (Even when you were creating a library, the word *Library* appeared on the Document screen. Not so with a merge data file.)

When the Document screen for Wineries appears, press F9 to change the tab stops. Erase the three default settings and place five new tab stops in positions 3, 14, 38, 48, 58, and 64. (Figure 12.1 shows you what the Wineries template will look like.) When these tab stops are in place, press F9 to keep them.

You can use six features within merge data file records. These are:

- Text
- Labels
- Label separators
- Data fields
- Default data
- Prompts

Each of these will be explained in further detail as you create the Wineries template.

Text Entries

After you have created the new tab stops and the cursor is in the first position in the screen, press Return to place one blank line at the top of

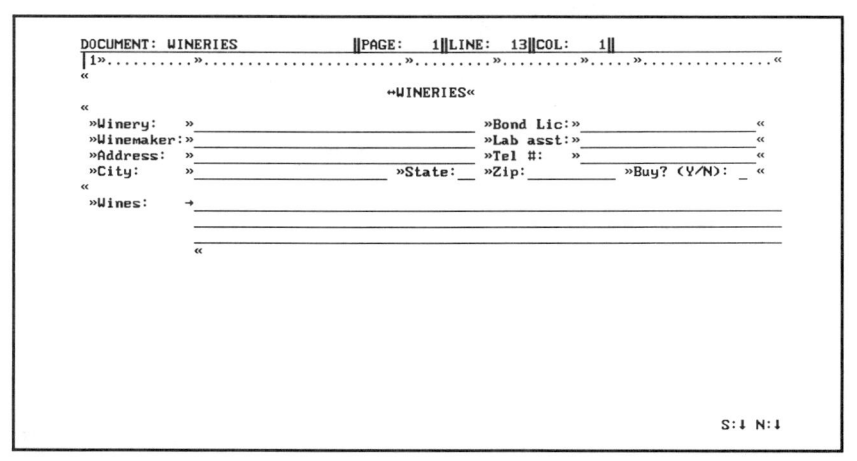

```
DOCUMENT: WINERIES              ||PAGE:   1||LINE:  13||COL:   1||
|1»..........».....................»........».........».....»..............«
«
                              ↔WINERIES«
    «
   »Winery:    »_____  »Bond Lic:»_____ «
   »Winemaker:»_____   »Lab asst:»_____ «
   »Address:  »_____   »Tel #:   »_____ «
   »City:     »_____   »State:__ »Zip:_____ »Buy? (Y/N): _ «
«
   »Wines:    →_____
              _____
              _____
          «
                                                                S:↓ N:↓
```

Figure 12.1: Template for merge data file Wineries

the template. Now press F3, the Center key, and type

WINERIES

Press Return twice to place a blank line between this title and the body of the template. The title will appear at the top of each record in the file, and this is an example of a *text* entry.

Labels

A *label* is a word or phrase that identifies a category of information. In the List document, the category name (called merge item name) had to be placed directly above the corresponding variable information. In a merge data file, the category name (called a label) appears *next to* the corresponding variable information. You can use up to 79 characters in a label, which is the width of a single text line with one space to spare for a separator. (You'll learn what a separator is in the following section.)

To create your first label, press Tab to begin the label three spaces from the left margin. The space between the left margin and the first letter of the label will be used for graphic features. Type the label *Winery*.

Label Separators

Immediately after the label, type a colon. This colon is called a *label separator,* and it separates the label from the data field. (You can use only a colon.) This separation distinguishes the characters in the label from those in the data field, and ensures that only those characters in the data field are merged into Result documents upon printing.

Data Fields

A label and its label separator are always followed by a *data field,* which contains the variable information corresponding to the label, and which varies from record to record. The variable information in a merge data file can remain blank, or it can fill up as much space as is available in the data field of the template.

After you have typed the label and the colon, press Tab. This is where you begin to create the data field corresponding to the label *Winery*. This does not mean you begin typing the name of the first winery. You are still only creating a master template, not creating individual records. You must first mark the limits of each data field, and you do this by underlining the length of the text line you want to contain variable information.

For this example, begin at the second tab stop position (column 14). Hold down Shift while you press the Underline key from column 14 to column 45. This marks the limits of the data field for the label Winery, and it will hold up to 32 characters.

Press Tab to move to the third tab position and type *Bond Lic* followed immediately by a colon. This is the second label, designating the winery's bonded license number. Press Tab to move to the fourth tab position and create an underline extending to column 75. This marks a data field corresponding to *Bond Lic* that can hold up to 17 characters. Continue to create the labels and data fields on the next two lines as they are illustrated in Figure 12.1. Remember to press Return at the end of each line.

On the fourth line, create the label and data field for *City* as you have created the others so far. Shorten the length of this data field so that it ends in column 36. Press Tab and type *State,* followed by a colon.

Note that if you make your data field too wide, you can use the Delete key to shorten it. Similarly, you can widen a data field by pressing Insert and typing additional underlines.

Default Data Fields

Now you will create a default data field. A *default data field* contains information that will appear in all or most of the records in the merge data file. You use default data whenever you accept the settings in any of the screens in the Advantage II word-processing program. Using default information saves time when filling in data file records.

To create a default data field, you do not simply underline the limits of the data field; you also enter the text that remains constant in all records. You do this by entering the text while in auto-underline text mode. Press Alt-Underline and then type the letters *CA,* for California. Most of the wineries your company buys wine from are in California, and accepting the default in this field will save you time when you fill out each record in this file. On those occasions when you purchase wine from a state other than California, you can enter that state abbreviation in this field. Enter the Zip field normally.

Prompts

The next field is where you create a prompt. A *prompt* is information you type in a label that gives you a choice of answers for the corresponding data field. Press Tab after creating the Zip field, and type *Buy?(Y/N)* followed by a colon. Underline one space for the single-letter answer (Y or N) you will place in this field. The label for this field is *Buy?*, which means, "Has the company bought from this winery before?" This label is followed by the prompt that serves as a reminder that you should answer yes or no to this question. Usually, a prompt will provide an either/or choice—such as yes/no, male/female—although not always. In this case, you could extend the prompt to *(Y/N/?)*, the third option noting that you don't know whether *Wines En Masse* has bought from this winery before.

Press Return twice after this one-space data field to begin the last label. This creates a blank line before the last field. Type *Wines:*, and then press F4, the Indent key. This label corresponds to the largest data field in a record, which lists the wines purchased from the winery shown. In some cases, this list could be long, and if you ever want to print out the contents of each record, you will want this list of wines to remain contiguous. To ensure that this will occur, press Shift-Underline, and hold them down so they autorepeat. If you make sure to begin this label and data field on line 8, you can extend this data field to the end of line 11, which gives you three lines in the data field. Word wrap will make sure the underlining remains continuous and yet extends to the next line down at the right margin.

When you arrive at the right margin on the last line, make sure the cursor is in column 80, and press Return. This will set the hard carriage-return symbol just beneath the last line. This marks the end of the last data field, and your template for the merge data file Wineries is complete.

Line and Box Drawing

A template can be made more attractive as well as easier to handle if you use line and box drawings to frame the entire template, or if you divide information into boxes. As an example, look at Figure 12.2. The label and data field for *Wines* is separated from the rest of the template because the list of wines will change more often than will the data on the winery.

To duplicate this example, begin by creating a blank line between the field *Wines* and all the other fields above it. You can do this by placing the cursor on the tab symbol in front of *Wines,* and press Insert, Return, and Insert. Now move the cursor to the first position in the blank line just created and press Alt-E, the Line and Box Drawing key. (To review the instructions for line and box drawing, refer to Chapter 10.) Select option 2, the thin double line, on the prompt at the bottom of the screen. Using the cursor keys, create a box by moving the line along the left margin to the top of the screen, then across the top to the right margin, and down the right margin to the blank line where you started. Finish the first box by moving the line to the left until you reach the starting position. Exit from line draw mode by pressing Alt-E again.

You should notice how the line you draw moves all screen symbols outside the limits of the box. This makes the template more attractive, but it turns off the effect of the screen symbols. This is why you will not box in the lower half of the screen. If you do, you will cancel the indent symbol, and your first record will display only a single line for the Wines data field.

Reminders for Creating Templates

Templates are similar but not identical to standard Advantage II documents. A template has a few restrictions placed on it that a

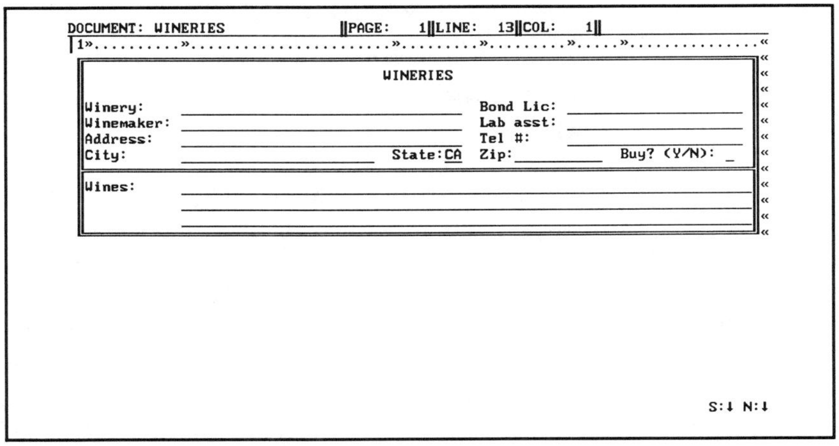

Figure 12.2: Template for Wineries enhanced with line and box drawing

standard document does not. When creating templates, you must do the following:

1. Press Shift-F10—not F10 alone—to exit from the Document Summary screen and enter the Document screen when first creating a template.

2. On the Document screen, leave the line spacing at 1. A template cannot be longer than 66 lines. Working with double line spacing will allow only half that capacity.

3. On the Document screen, leave the right margin at the default setting of 80 columns. A template always contains 80 columns—no more and no less.

4. Many editing functions will work with templates. Column mode will not. All cursor keys work the same. When a key or a command does not apply, the prompt

    INVALID KEY

    will appear on the right side of the status line.

CREATING RECORDS

After you have designed the template you want to use for all the records in your merge data file Wineries, make sure the cursor is at the very bottom of the template. Then press F2, the Page Break key, to begin entering data into your first record. The prompt

ARE YOU SURE YOU WANT TO LEAVE THE TEMPLATE PAGE?(Y/N)

will appear. Press Y to create the first record.

When the template for this first record appears on the screen, it will look exactly as you designed it. There is a difference in the format line of a record, however, as you'll notice in Figure 12.3. *REC#*—or record number—replaces the page number; *TOT#*—or total number of records in file—replaces the line number; and *SELECTED* replaces the column number, allowing you to select or unselect records for printing, as you'll learn later in this chapter. All records remain selected until you unselect them.

Figure 12.3 shows the contents of the first record. To enter this information, your cursor should appear in the first position of the data field for *Winery*. Type *Dave Bynum* and press Return. Notice that the cursor jumps to the first position of the next data field to the right of the one you were in. You do not have to wade through the blank spaces and label characters to enter the next data field. This demonstrates the ease of use provided by your template. When you create each record, you can move around the data fields quickly and accurately. You are limited to entering and changing only variable data, not the labels. The cursor movements for creating and editing merge data file records are presented in Table 12.1.

You can continue creating records by pressing F2, the Page Break key, and entering the data in each record.

EDITING A TEMPLATE

You edit a template the same way you edit a standard document. On the main menu, select

1) Edit a Document

Enter the name of the merge data file that contains the template you want to change and press Return. Change the Document Summary screen if you wish, and then press F10 to enter the Document screen

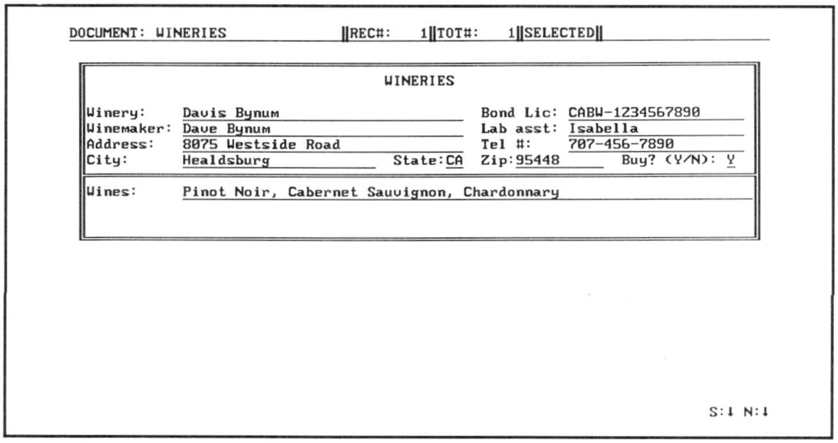

```
DOCUMENT: WINERIES            ‖REC#:    1‖TOT#:    1‖SELECTED‖

                              WINERIES
Winery:    Davis Bynum                    Bond Lic: CABW-1234567890
Winemaker: Dave Bynum                     Lab asst: Isabella
Address:   8075 Westside Road             Tel #:    707-456-7890
City:      Healdsburg          State:CA   Zip:95448    Buy? (Y/N): Y

Wines:     Pinot Noir, Cabernet Sauvignon, Chardonnary


                                                             S:1 N:1
```

Figure 12.3: First record in Wineries merge data file

CURSOR MOVEMENTS WITHIN A RECORD	
KEY	ACTION
←	Previous character or field
→	Next character or field
Back Tab	Previous data field
↑	Previous data field line above
Return or Tab	Next data field
↓	Next data field line below
Home	First data field in record
PgUp	First data field in record, when cursor is not in first position of first data field
End	Last data field in record
PgDn	Last data field in record, when cursor is not in last position of last data field

CURSOR MOVEMENT BETWEEN RECORDS	
KEY	ACTION
PgUp	Previous record, when cursor is in first data field
Ctrl-PgDn	Previous record, same data field
PgDn	Next record, when cursor is in last data field
Ctrl-PgDn	Next record, same data field
F1-Page #, Return	Any record in file
F1-Home	First record in a file
F1-End	Last record in a file

Table 12.1: Cursor movements with merge data file records

that contains the template you want to edit.

If you edit a template before you create any records using the template, you can use the same editing functions as you did to create a template. If you want to edit a template after you have created one or more records, you will have to take special care that the changes will not affect the records already created. Any changes made to a template will also be made in all records in the file attached to the template you are changing. If you shorten the length of a data field, you could lose data in records where this field is filled up, and if you delete a label, you could lose the contents of the data field entirely.

To prevent this inadvertent loss of data, prompts have been built into the system to remind you of possible complications, and safety prompts will point out which changes might result in the loss of information.

Changing the Size of Data Fields

Expanding the size of a data field should cause no problems, as long as the expansion does not push the line length of the template beyond the 66-line limit. If you want to shorten a field, you might lose data. When you have changed one or more data fields in a template, the message

> **SHORTENED FIELD LENGTH MAY CUT OFF DATA. DO YOU WISH TO CONTINUE? (Y/N)**

Press Y to continue. Press N if you realize that shortening a field might result in data loss.

As an example, you might find that four lines are too much for the label *Wines*. You can shorten this data field on the template using the Delete or Minus key, or by placing the cursor at the end of the new and shorter limit, and pressing the Space bar to erase the remainder of the underline. As long as this new shortened length does not fall short of the space needed to list wines for all the existing records in Wineries, then you can answer Y when the reminder prompt appears.

Renaming Labels

Labels can be renamed without fear of losing data, as long as you substitute a new label name for each old one. When you try to leave the template after changing one or more label names, you'll see the prompt

> **(label name) MISSING. HAS IT BEEN RENAMED? (Y/N)**

The original label name will appear in the first position of this prompt. If you have renamed this label, you can answer Y to this prompt. For backup security, another prompt will appear at the bottom of the screen. You should enter the new label name, up to 12 characters long, in the prompt

> WHAT IS THE NEW LABEL NAME?_____ PRESS F10 TO CONTINUE

and press F10. There is a chance that Advantage II will not recognize this label name. If it does not, you will see the prompt

> LABEL(label name)SPECIFIED IN RENAME DOESN'T EXIST. PRESS F10 TO RETRY

Enter the name of the label a second time and press F10.

Adding Labels and Data Fields

You can add new labels and corresponding data fields to a template by using the Insert key. Records that already exist will reflect these additions.

Deleting Labels and Data Fields

You can delete labels and data fields with the Delete key. Make sure you delete the entire label and its corresponding data field. When you leave the template, the prompt

> (label name)MISSING, HAS IT BEEN RENAMED(Y/N)?

will appear. Press N to continue with the deletion of the label and data field. To protect from inadvertent deletions, a second prompt

> ARE YOU SURE YOU WANT THE LABEL DELETED?(Y/N)

will appear. You should take this as a reminder that when the label and data field are deleted, all the information in every record contained within the data field will also be deleted. Press Y to complete the deletion. If you press N, you will return to the template, where you can figure out what you want to do next.

Moving Labels and Data Fields

You can move labels and corresponding data fields within a template by using the move function (F7).

Adding Default Data

You can change a data field to include default data by placing the cursor at the beginning of the field you want to change and pressing Alt-Underline, the Auto Underline Text key. Next type the data that will serve as the default data, and complete the change by pressing Alt-Underline again.

Leaving the Template

When you want to leave the template, you have three choices:

- Go to a record by pressing F1 and a record number, then either Ctrl-PgDn or PgDn.
- Create a new record by pressing F2, the Page Break key.
- Exit from the merge data file by pressing F10.

Additional Error Messages

When you leave a template, Advantage II checks the template for any inadmissable changes. In addition to the prompts described for each appropriate editing function, there are seven other error prompts you may encounter, listed in Table 12.2.

EDITING MERGE DATA FILES

Once you have settled on the most useful template, you can edit the merge data file in three ways:

- Add new records
- Edit existing records
- Delete records

Error Message	Meaning/Action to Take
PAGE TOO LARGE, EXCEED 66 LINES	Template must be no longer than 66 lines/Shorten record length
FORMAT LINES MUST BE 80 COLUMNS	Template format line must be 80 columns long/Change format line to this length
TEMPLATE HAS NO DATA FIELDS	Template must contain at least one data field/Create a label and corresponding data field, or else press Escape to cancel template creation
NUMBER OF FIELDS EXCEEDS 255 FIELDS	Template cannot exceed 255 fields/Delete labels and corresponding data fields until this maximum is reached
FIELD SIZE EXCEEDS 255 CHARACTERS	Data fields cannot exceed 255 characters/Shorten oversize data fields
(label name) IS DUPLICATE	First 12 characters of all label names must be unique/Change at least one character in duplicate labels
SHORTENED FIELD LENGTH MAY CUT OFF DATA. DO YOU WISH TO CONTINUE?(Y/N)	Data may be lost because you shortened a data field/Press Y if it's okay to proceed

Table 12.2: Additional error prompts for editing templates

Adding New Records

You can add records at any position in a merge data file. You designate the position while you are in the Document screen that displays the template for that merge data file. Begin at the main menu by selecting

    1) Edit a Document

Enter the name of the merge data file to which you want to add records, and press Return. The Document Summary screen will appear. Press F10, and the template will appear on the screen. Press F1, the Go To key, and at the prompt

   GO TO [ ]

enter the number of the record that should precede the record you are adding. Press Return to enter this number, and at the prompt

   ARE YOU SURE YOU WANT TO LEAVE THE TEMPLATE
   PAGE?(Y/N)

press Y. When the requested record appears, press F2, the Page Break key, to create a new record with the next record number. This record will contain empty data fields that you can now fill with information. The numbers for all records subsequent to this new record will be increased by one digit.

If you want to create a new record before the first record, you can press F2, the Page Break key, in the template. At the prompt

   ARE YOU SURE YOU WANT TO LEAVE THE TEMPLATE
   PAGE?(Y/N)

press Y. A new record 1 appears with blank data fields. All subsequent record numbers will be increased by 1.

If you want to add a record to the end of the file, press F1 at the template screen, and then press End. When the last record in the file appears, press F2, and a new blank record will appear as the last record in the file.

Editing Existing Records

You can edit a record in four ways. Table 12.3 shows the editing functions you can perform and the keys you use to perform them. Always make sure that the cursor is in the data field you wish to edit before you press the appropriate keys.

Function	Procedure
Insert characters	Press Insert, then press the keys for the characters you wish to insert, then press Insert again to set the additions.
Delete characters	Press Delete to delete characters.
Search	Press F6, enter the text you wish to locate, and press F6. Search will proceed through all subsequent records but only in the data field where the cursor was positioned at the start of the search. (For example, you can search for all wineries in Napa if you enter *Napa* with the cursor in the City field.)
Replace	Press Shift-F6, enter the text to replace, press Shift-F6, enter replacement text, press Shift-F6. Replacement will proceed through all subsequent records, but only in the data field where the cursor was positioned at the start of the replacement.

Table 12.3: Editing functions for merge data file records

Deleting Records

You can delete a record from any place within the merge data file. Press F1, the Go To key, and at the prompt

    GO TO [ ]

enter the number of the record you want to delete. Press Return, and if the prompt

    ARE YOU SURE YOU WANT TO LEAVE THE TEMPLATE
    PAGE?(Y/N)

appears, press Y. Now press Shift-F2, the Page Combine key, and when the prompt

> ARE YOU SURE YOU WANT TO DELETE THIS RECORD? (Y/N)

appears, press Y to complete the deletion. The record numbers for all records subsequent to this deleted record will be decreased by 1.

SORTING RECORDS

You can sort all the records in a merge data file according to a single data field. This sort can be organized numerically or alphabetically, and in ascending or descending order. You begin this function by placing the cursor on the data field by which you wish to sort. This data field can be in any record of the merge data file you want to sort. Whether the sort will be alphabetical or numerical will depend upon the first character in the data field you are sorting. Press F5, and the merge data file sort window will appear at the bottom of your screen, as shown in Figure 12.4. Press Alt-1 to toggle between the two choices of sorting the data field in ascending or descending order. Whether the sort will be alphabetical or numerical will be determined by the contents of the data field you are sorting.

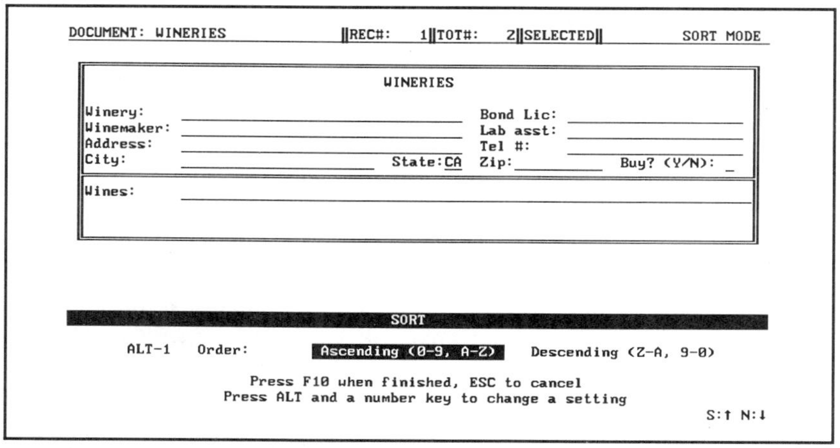

Figure 12.4: Merge data file sort window

All sorts are arranged according to the sequence of characters in the designated data field. MultiMate Advantage II has three kinds of characters. When you sort in ascending order, blanks take first place, text and numbers come second, and extended characters are placed last. Extended characters are anything other than blanks, text, and numbers. When you sort in descending order, the hierarchy is reversed, and extended characters are placed first. It is impossible to select only a portion of the records in one file to sort. A sort will organize all records in the merge data file you've specified.

SELECTING AND UNSELECTING RECORDS

You can mark individual records in a merge data file for printing by *selecting* them. You can then print these selected records by themselves, or else combine them with a Merge document to produce a series of Result documents. You can *select* and *unselect* records in two ways: individually or as a group. In both cases, you have to start from within the merge data file. If you want to select records individually, go to the first record you want to select or unselect by pressing F1, the Go To key. Enter the number of the record you want to select and press Return. When that record appears on the screen, press Alt-F1, the Select key. The prompt

SELECTED

will appear on the format line. You can toggle back and forth between the selected and unselected modes by pressing Alt-F1, the Select key.

To select a group of records, you will have to pick a continuous batch of records that runs from any record within the file all the way to the end of the file. There is no way to select files in a batch that does not end at the end of the file. (You can limit the files to be printed within the selected group by designating a range of records on the Print a Document screen, or on the Merge Print a Document screen.) Go to the first record of the batch by pressing F1, the Go To key, enter the number of the first record of the batch, and press Return. When the first record appears on the screen, press Alt-Y, the Group

Select key. On the bottom of your screen, you will see the record selection window:

> **RECORD SELECTION**
> ALT-1 All remaining records will be Selected Unselected
> Press F10 When finished, ESC to cancel
> Press ALT and a number key to change a setting

Press Alt-1 to toggle between selecting and unselecting all remaining records. You can press Escape to cancel the selection.

MERGE PRINTING WITH MERGE DATA FILES

If you want to combine information on records that have been selected within a single merge data file, proceed with the directions for merge printing as described in Chapter 11. When the Merge Print a Document screen appears, enter the name of the merge data file that contains the selected records. This is where you can also select a narrower range of selected records to be printed. To do this, change the settings in the prompt

Records [00001] to [99999]

to cover the limits of the records you want to print. Do not change these numbers if you want all the selected records to print. After you have entered the name of a Merge document, you can press F10, and the Document Print Options screen attached to the Merge document will appear. You can change the settings on this screen as you see fit. Pressing F10 will begin the merge print.

PRINTING RECORDS AND TEMPLATES

You can print individual records as they appear on the screen. I recommend that you do this each time you create a merge data file as well as when you change any records. You can print the entire file when you first create it, and then at a later date print only those records that you add or change. You begin this printing at the main menu by selecting

5) Merge Print a Document

The Merge Print a Document screen (Figure 11.4) will appear. Enter the name of the merge data file that contains the records you want to print in the field for Merge Document. Do not enter the merge data file name in the Merge Data File field; leave this field blank. Press F10 to accept the entry, and at the prompt

Records [00001] to [99999]

enter the range of records you want to print. Do not change these numbers if you want all the records in the merge data file printed. Press F10, and the Document Print Options screen attached to the merge data file will appear. Change the settings as you see fit. Press F10 to begin the printing. Each record will print out on its own page, and everything in the record will appear on the page, including labels, separators, blank fields, and default values.

You can also print the blank template for the merge data document by first selecting on the main menu

3) Print a Document

Then enter the name of the merge data file that contains the template you want to print, and press Return. The Document Print Options screen attached to the merge data file will appear, where you can change the settings as you see fit. Pressing F10 will begin the printing of the template. All items on the template will appear in print, including label names, separators, default data, and blank fields, if there are any.

To review, the steps for creating a template and maintaining the records are:

1. Design the template.
2. Enter the data for each record using this template.
3. Edit the data to keep records up-to-date.

4. Select records for printing.
5. Print selected records by themselves, or insert the information into a Merge document to create a series of record documents.

DIRECT dBASE MERGE

A new feature in Advantage II is the ability to merge the information from a dBASE II, III, or III PLUS data file directly into a MultiMate document. The only requirement is that the field names in the document must match those in the dBASE file.

To use a dBASE data file, enter its name and any pathnames you are using in the Merge Print a Document screen.

The one dBASE item that cannot be merged into a MultiMate document is a memo field. Also, you must be careful when merging numbers and dates. Document fields for numbers must be aligned along decimal tabs in order for them to line up correctly after a merge printing. With dates, you must make sure that their format in the dBASE file corresponds exactly to the format set in the Print Date Standard Field in the Edit System Defaults screen (Figure 4.5).

MERGING WITH INFORMATION FROM ANOTHER DATABASE

Importing information from foreign databases is easier than converting other kinds of documents because databases are made up of discrete records and nothing else. The boundaries of each record are clear, as are the boundaries of each field within the record. There are two ways to import information from foreign databases, and your choice is determined by the size of your record fields. These two ways are called sequential data file merge and random data file merge.

SEQUENTIAL DATA FILE MERGE

Sequential data file merge places record separators between each record, field separators between each field, and field delimiters at the beginning and end of each field. This marks the records and the fields within each record as separate units. Once the records and fields are so marked, you can import and export them to a wide variety of different databases.

As an example of the delimited layout, two records you placed in the List document Thanklst would, when delimited, run on two lines, as shown in Figure 12.5.

The record separator is designated by the new line where each subsequent record begins. An invisible code is inserted between each record in the sequentially delimited file that instructs the program reading the file that a carriage return and a line feed are indicated at this point. The field separator is the comma appearing between fields. And the field delimiter is the double quote that appears before and after the characters in each field.

Record and field separators are always the same. You can choose the character that will serve as the field delimiter, and this choice deserves some thought. You cannot use the character you use as a field delimiter in any of the fields as data, or else the field will be broken at that point. When you use quotes, all quotes will be interpreted as field delimiters.

Creating a Sequential File

A sequential data file must be generated by a special program contained within the database program. Most popular databases contain such a program, but if the one you want to import information from does not contain such a program, then you will have to generate a random data file merge, which is explained later in this chapter.

You can create a sequential data file using dBASE II, dBASE III, and dBASE III PLUS with the following command:

```
USE <file name>
COPY TO <new file name> DELIMITED WITH "
```

The character you place at the end of this command will be used as the field delimiter.

```
"Dave","Bynum","Winemaker","DAVE BYNUM WINERY","8075 Westside Road","Healdsburg","CA","95448"

"Jerzy","Budrick","Winemaker","BUDRICK CELLARS","810 Cragmont","Fiddletown","CA","95629"
```

Figure 12.5: Delimited version of Thanklst

Using a Sequential Data File

You can now use this sequential data file to provide information during a merge print by reconstructing the Merge document Thanks that you created in Chapter 11. You must insert a merge block at the top of the letter. This merge block consists of the word *define* surrounded by two merge code symbols: type Alt-M, *define,* Alt-M. All text in this define block can be uppercase or lowercase letters. The next line is

    file type sequential

which instructs Advantage II that the program is about to encounter fields delimited sequentially. If all subsequent records are separated by a carriage return and line feed, all files are separated by a comma, and quotes delimit each record, then you can proceed entering all record information on the following lines. The define block is ended by typing Alt-M, *end define,* Alt-M, after all field names have been entered. Figure 12.6 illustrates this layout.

You must enter the field names of all the fields used in the sequentially delimited file, even if you do not use information from all the fields in the merge item names of the Merge document. As an example, the merge item name title was removed from the letter, so no titles will be printed. The field name title must still appear within the define block.

```
DOCUMENT: thanks              ‖PAGE:   1‖LINE:  22‖COL:   1‖
|1..»....»....».........................................................«
├define├«
file type sequential«
field name firstname«
field name lastname«
field name title«
field name company«
field name address«
field name city«
field name state«
field name zip«
├end define├«
«
November 28, 1986«
«
«
├firstname├ ├lastname├«
├company├«
├address├«
├city├, ├state├  ├zip├«
«
Dear ├firstname├,«
_
                                                              S:↑ M:↓
```

Figure 12.6: Define block for a sequentially delimited data file

Some databases allow you to create sequential files using different separators and delimiters. If you create a sequentially delimited file using a record separator other than a carriage return and line feed, or a field separator other than a comma, or a field delimiter other than quotes, you will have to inform Advantage II of these changes. Each change will require a separate instruction, and all instructions will have to be inserted between the command *file type sequential* and the first field name. In addition, the new separator character must be typed between single quote marks. If you used a comma for the field delimiter, quotes for the record delimiter, and a colon for the record separator, then you would type these instructions:

```
field delimiter ','
field separator '"'
record separator ':'
```

None of the text within a define block will appear on the printed page of a Result document.

RANDOM DATA FILE MERGE

Most major database programs place their information in records and fields that are designed by the person using the program. You name and give a length to all fields, then proceed to enter information in the fields. The field lengths set the record length, and from the first to the last record, these field and record lengths remain the same, even if they are not filled with information.

Unlike a sequential data file, a random file contains records and fields all of the same length. Yet a random file is more powerful than a sequential file. A computer can process the information in a random file more quickly than that in a sequential file, and it is more likely that the program will ignore information in a sequential file than in a random file.

For example, a database could list information for wineries with the following field sizes:

```
firstname: 10 characters
lastname: 10 characters
title: 10 characters
company: 25 characters
```

address: 25 characters
city: 22 characters
state: 2 characters
zip: 5 characters

Then, the information listed in the random file would look like this:

Dave......Bynum.....Winemaker.DAVE BYNUM WINERY........8075 Westside Road.......Healdsburg............CA95448

The dots represent the blank spaces of the field size selected. You will have to ascertain the number of spaces in each field of the random file from which you want to import information.

Using a Random Data File

To use a random data file, you must set up a define block as you did for the sequential data file, only you must insert another instruction for each field name. Type Alt-M, *define,* Alt-M, at the top of the Merge document, and on the next line type *field type random.* On the following line, you have to tell Advantage II the size of each field in the random database. Type *field name* and the name of each field, as before, only add the word *size* and the size of each field before you go on to the next field. The field name does not have to correspond to the field name in the original random data file, but it does have to match the field names shown in the Merge document. Figure 12.7 illustrates what the Merge document Thanks should look like if it is to correctly receive information from a random data file with fields identical to the other data files you have been creating.

As with the previous Merge document, the information in the define block will not print in the Result documents.

MERGE PRINTING WITH MERGED DATA FILES

To run a merge printing with a sequentially delimited data file or a random data file, select on the main menu

5) Merge Print a Document

```
┌─────────────────────────────────────────────────────────────┐
│ DOCUMENT: THANKS           ║PAGE:    1║LINE:  22║COL:   1║  │
│ 1--»----»----»-------------------------------------«_____  │
│ ┤define├«                                                    │
│ field type random«                                           │
│ field name firstname 10«                                     │
│ field name lastname 10«                                      │
│ field name title 10«                                         │
│ field name company 25«                                       │
│ field name address 25«                                       │
│ field name city 22«                                          │
│ field name state 2«                                          │
│ field name zip 5«                                            │
│ ┤end define├«                                                │
│ «                                                            │
│ November 28, 1987«                                           │
│ «                                                            │
│ «                                                            │
│ ┤firstname├ ┤lastname├«                                      │
│ ┤company├«                                                   │
│ ┤address├«                                                   │
│ ┤city├, ┤state├ ┤zip├«                                       │
│ «                                                            │
│ Dear ┤firstname├,«                                           │
│                                                  S:1 N:1    │
└─────────────────────────────────────────────────────────────┘
```

Figure 12.7: Define block for a random data file

You can now enter the name of the redesigned Merge document in the Merge Document field, and the name of the data file you want to use in the Merge Data File field. Enter the appropriate drive and subdirectory designations, and press F10. The Document Print Options screen attached to the Merge document you want to print will appear, and you can change the settings and accept defaults as you wish. Pressing F10 in this screen will begin the merge print.

ON-FILE

IF YOU WANT TO DO MORE WITH YOUR RECORDS than you can with merge data files, but you don't want to work with a complex database program, On-File is the database for you. On-File is designed to handle information in a full-featured database without the trouble of importing files from a foreign database. On-File is more of a file manager than a genuine database, but it will let you code and index your records in several ways, sort and select a variety of records, and print information in lists as well as on labels.

On-File differs in two distinct ways from the word-processing part of the program. First, it is *screen-driven,* as opposed to *menu-driven.* Everything that you can do with the On-File program is displayed on screens with instructions and a list of all the function keys that can affect the screen being displayed. On-File uses the concept of index cards to record and display information, and it even displays a picture of a card on the screen that you work with. This allows you to organize any type of information typically found in an office.

The second distinction is that there is no limit to the number of records in a data file, or a card box, nor is there a limit to the number of boxes you can create, except the space available on the disk where the records and card boxes are being recorded.

Using the On-File cards, you can perform the following usual database functions:

- Create and add cards to card boxes
- Search cards by subject, index word, color, and date
- Sort any three of these fields at any one time, in ascending or descending order
- Print reports, lists, and labels using the information on the cards
- Combine the information on cards directly with a Merge document to create a series of Result documents

In addition to the usual database features, On-File provides:

- Tickler/Action date feature for dated cards
- Perpetual calendar
- "Scan and match" feature for words and phrases on cards

There are only three basic steps for working with On-File:

1. Set up On-File.
2. Open a box and create your first record by designing a template.
3. Add additional records and organize and print them in a variety of ways.

SETTING UP ON-FILE

The On-File database comes on two disks: the On-File System/Boot Diskette and the On-File Utilities Diskette. If you are using a dual-floppy system, place the On-File System Boot Diskette in your floppy drive, and at the system prompt type

SETUP

and press Return.

If you are using a hard disk, and you have already loaded the files from the On-File Utilities Diskette onto the hard disk, proceed to type the Setup command at the system prompt and press Return.

The Setup screen will appear, offering you three choices:

F1 Setup system defaults

F2 Set color monitor

F3 Set monochrome monitor

If you press F1, the Set System Defaults screen, shown in Figure 13.1, will appear. The three categories you can change are default drives, installed drives, and whether you want the sound turned on. Default drives refer to the drive where you want to record your *card box,*

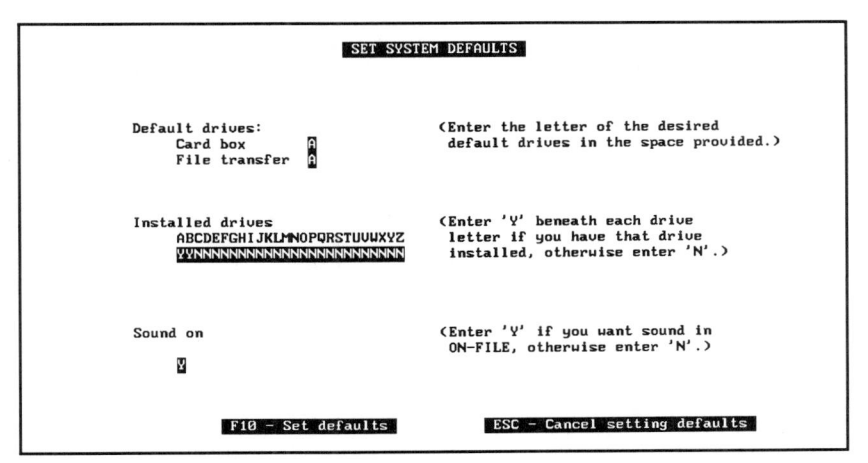

```
                    ┌─────────────────────────────────────────────────────┐
                    │              SET SYSTEM DEFAULTS                    │
                    │                                                     │
                    │  Default drives:          (Enter the letter of the desired
                    │       Card box    A        default drives in the space provided.)
                    │       File transfer A
                    │
                    │  Installed drives         (Enter 'Y' beneath each drive
                    │    ABCDEFGHIJKLMNOPQRSTUVWXYZ   letter if you have that drive
                    │    YYNNNNNNNNNNNNNNNNNNNNNNNN   installed, otherwise enter 'N'.)
                    │
                    │
                    │  Sound on                 (Enter 'Y' if you want sound in
                    │                            ON-FILE, otherwise enter 'N'.)
                    │       Y
                    │
                    │      F10 - Set defaults        ESC - Cancel setting defaults
                    └─────────────────────────────────────────────────────┘
```

Figure 13.1: Set System Defaults screen

or database file, and the *file transfer,* or the drive to which you want to transfer the database file. You will perform a file transfer when you place a card box of selected records onto the same disk that contains the Merge document. These two files will then combine during a merge print to issue a series of Result documents.

The *installed drives* category allows you to instruct On-File which drives you are using in your computer, including hard disks and RAM disks. *Sound on* refers to an audible prompt that On-File uses to warn you of certain conditions, such as when you are at the text limit of a single card. When you begin to add, edit, and organize many cards in a single box, you might find that you can move at such a rapid pace that listening for a prompt instead of looking for it is handier.

Press F10 when you are finished with the Set System Defaults screen. You will see the prompt

> System defaults set ...
> Press any key to continue

Pressing any key will take you back to the Setup screen.

Pressing F2 from the Setup screen will set your monitor (or screen display) for a color system, and pressing F3 will set it for a monochrome monitor. You can continue pressing these keys to see which setup actually gives you better resolution.

After you have adjusted the Setup settings, you have completed the first step for working with On-File. Press Escape to leave the Setup screen and return to the system prompt.

CREATING RECORDS

At the system prompt, enter On-File by typing

ONFILE

and pressing Return. The first screen to appear in the program is the copyright screen. Press the Space bar to exit from this screen and move on to the On-File title screen, shown in Figure 13.2.

When you see this title screen for the first time, the demonstration files DEMO and MLLIBRARY should be listed in the directory display in the middle of the screen, under the prompt

Available Boxes:

Boxes refer to your database files, which hold a collection of records. A record is displayed as a card, and you can handle information on it in the same way that you do to maintain a card file. When you begin to create and use many boxes, you might want to place them in a

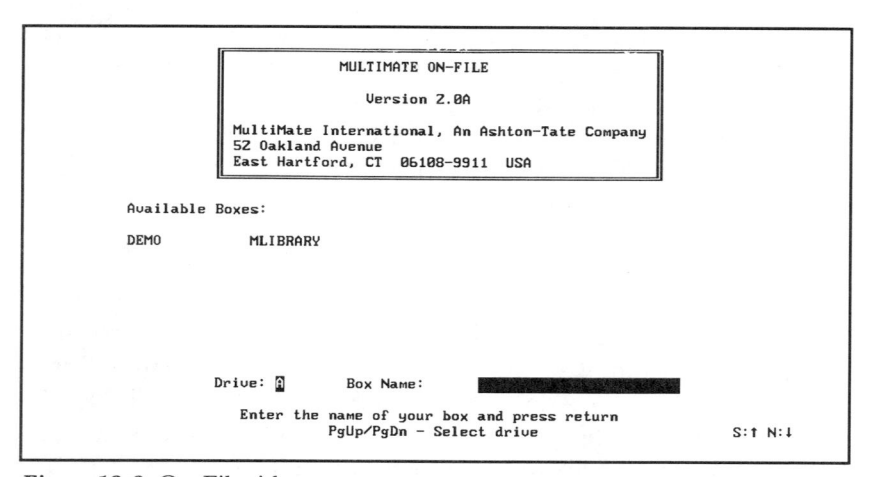

```
                    MULTIMATE ON-FILE
                       Version 2.0A
             MultiMate International, An Ashton-Tate Company
             52 Oakland Avenue
             East Hartford, CT  06108-9911  USA

   Available Boxes:
   DEMO        MLIBRARY




                Drive: A    Box Name: ▉▉▉▉▉▉▉▉▉▉▉▉▉
                  Enter the name of your box and press return
                      PgUp/PgDn - Select drive            S:↑ N:↓
```

Figure 13.2: On-File title screen

different subdirectory. Pressing PgUp and PgDn on the title screen allows you to flip through the available subdirectories to pick the box that you want to work with. At the bottom of the screen, you'll see two prompts

    Drive:_ Box Name:_____

where you can enter the drive designation that will contain the records and card boxes, as well as the name of the card box you want to start working with.

The box name you enter here can be for a box that has already been created, or for a box you want to create. To create a box for the first time, you can enter any combination of up to 25 characters for a card box name. The name cannot include any spaces, and the first 12 characters must always be unique to each file.

For the box name, type *Wineries* and press Return. Immediately, the name of the box will appear in all uppercase letters, regardless of how you typed the name. The prompt

    Start a new box?(y/n)

will appear at the bottom of the screen, to which you should reply by pressing y (or Y). As soon as you do, the prompt

    New box is being created...

will appear, and then the On-File main menu, shown in Figure 13.3, will be displayed. It is from this menu that you can access all the features of On-File.

In addition to the five selections on the On-File main menu, two categories of information are also displayed on this screen. The first, located in the upper left corner of the screen, shows the file drive designation, the card box opened, and the number of records (or *cards*) currently in the box. The second category of information on this screen, located in the upper right corner, displays current time and date information. You might find this information helpful for scheduling your work within On-File. The current date will always be entered onto cards when you create them. At the bottom of the screen, the information you entered when you branded the On-File

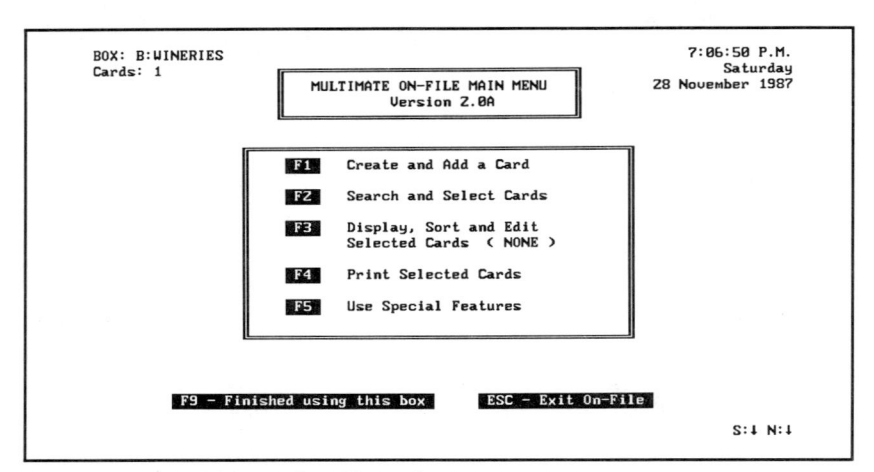

```
BOX: B:WINERIES                                    7:06:50 P.M.
Cards: 1                                              Saturday
           ┌─────────────────────────────┐       28 November 1987
           │ MULTIMATE ON-FILE MAIN MENU │
           │       Version 2.0A          │
           └─────────────────────────────┘

              ┌──┐
              │F1│  Create and Add a Card
              └──┘
              ┌──┐
              │F2│  Search and Select Cards
              └──┘
              ┌──┐
              │F3│  Display, Sort and Edit
              └──┘  Selected Cards  ( NONE )
              ┌──┐
              │F4│  Print Selected Cards
              └──┘
              ┌──┐
              │F5│  Use Special Features
              └──┘


       ┌──────────────────────────┐  ┌──────────────────┐
       │ F9 - Finished using this box │  │ ESC - Exit On-File │
       └──────────────────────────┘  └──────────────────┘
                                                      S:↓ N:↓
```

Figure 13.3: MultiMate On-File main menu

program appears—that is, your name and the serial number of your program.

Press F1 to create your first card. The Create and Add a Card screen will appear on your screen, which looks like Figure 13.4. The picture of an index card occupies the center of this screen, while the area around this index card contains instructions for entering information on the card.

Beginning at the upper left corner, *subject line* refers to the subject category of the card you are creating. What you enter in this area will determine what subjects you can search, as well as sort, on your cards. The subject line should be the largest subcategory inside the card box Wineries.

At the lower left corner of the card, *index line* refers to the words or numbers on which you want the cards sorted. Once you've entered data for the card, you can enter up to three categories here. You enter the categories by placing the cursor on the word or number within the card that you wish to appear on the index line, and then press F5. The word or number will then appear on the index line. To index all categories on all the cards in the current box, press F8 for automatic indexing.

Table 13.1 describes these features in greater detail.

When the Create and Add a Card screen appears, the current date should appear in the upper right corner of the card, next to the marker *action date.* This date will remain on the card unless you want to change it during the editing process. The cursor should be blinking in the first

```
                    ┌─ CREATE AND ADD A CARD ─┐
                    
   subject line ─────┌──────── BLUE ────────┐── action
                     │                       │    date
       [F4]  Color   │                       │   Row
                     │                       │    1
       [F5]  Index   │                       │   Column
                     │                       │    1
       [F6]  Flip    │                       │
                     │                       │
       [F7]  Center  │                       │
                     │                       │
   index line ──────└───────────────────────┘
                        (No template selected)
                   [F3 - Template Selection]  [F8 - Automatic Indexing]

   [F10 - Add card]  [F2 - Add and copy]   [ESC - Cancel card]  S:↓ N:↓
```

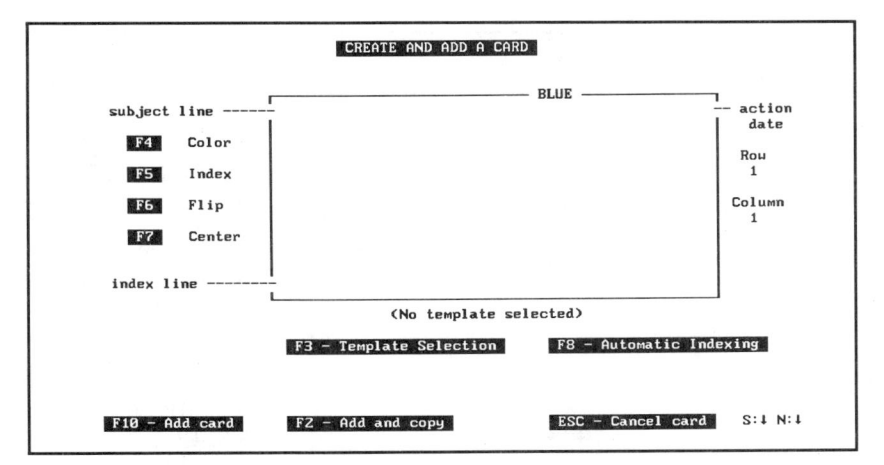

Figure 13.4: Create and Add a Card screen for On-File

position on the card, as noted by the current cursor *row* and *column* markers on the right side of the screen. There are 12 rows and 50 columns on a card. When the cursor gets to the last column in the first row, the cursor will jump to the first column of the second row. When the cursor gets to the last column of the bottom row, the cursor will jump to the first column of the first row. (Instead of word wrap, on a card you'll see "character wrap.") You will not lose any text when the cursor jumps—unless you continue typing after the cursor reaches the last column of the bottom row, and you've already entered text into the *subject line* of the card.

Now you can begin to fill in the card. Type the following information:

```
Davis Bynum Winery: Dave Bynum
8075 Westside Road
Healdsburg, CA 95448
707-456-7890
```

Press Return to end the last line of the address, and then press F6 to flip the card over. This is where you can add the selection of wines you buy from Dave Bynum, as well as other wines you might be interested in. For this example, type:

```
Wines we buy: Pinot Noir 1982,1983; Merlot 1981
Interesting wines: Cabernet Sauvignon 1982,1983
```

Key	Name	Function
F1	Add date	Adds date to card.
F2	Add and copy a card	Adds displayed card to box and remains in current card.
F3	Template selection	Cycles through selection of customized templates already created in the Special Features selection on the main menu.
F4	Color	Cycles through the colors BLUE-BROWN-GREEN-PINK-PURPLE-RED-WHITE-YELLOW in order. A card can be color coded. Color code appears in upper right corner. Blue is the default.
F5	Index	Selects first text unit (contiguous numbers and letters surrounded by spaces) on current cursor line and places it on index line for future indexing. Index line can contain up to three selected text units.
F6	Flip	Flips current card over. You can use both sides of a card.
F7	Center	Centers text on current cursor line when in editing mode.
F8	Automatic indexing	Indexes cards automatically in current card box according to text units on index line.
F10	Add card and exit	Adds current card to box and leaves card.

Table 13.1: Functions on the Create and Add a Card screen

Press Return after you finish entering these wines. Press F6 to flip the card back to its front side and check for mistakes. Then press F2 to add the card as the first card in the box *Wineries*, and the prompt

Add in progress

will appear below the card. In a few moments, the prompt will disappear, and an empty card will await your next entry. You could create as many cards as you wanted, following the same steps. For this example, though, do not create a second card. (If you did enter any text, you could delete it using the Delete key, and press F10 to cancel the card.) A prompt

Abandon card?(Y/N)

would appear directly above the instructions for F10. Press Y to abandon the card and return to the On-File main menu. Press F10 on this screen to exit from On-File, and the prompt

Are you sure?(Y/N)

will appear directly above the instructions for F10. Press Y, and the message

Closing A:WINERIES box...

will appear blinking in reverse video in the middle of the screen for a few moments. Finally, the system prompt will appear on the screen.)

To use any of the other procedures on the main menu, it is advisable to work with more than one card in a box. Load the On-File program a second time, enter *Wineries* in the field for box name, and press Return. You will return to the main menu for this box. Press F1 to create and add three more records. Create them the same way you did the card for Dave Bynum. You can use the three examples shown in Figure 11.3, or make up your own examples.

You can always return to the previous screen by pressing Escape. Pressing Escape will return you from any screen to the On-File main menu.

SEARCHING AND DISPLAYING CARDS

Once cards have been created and added to a box, you can search through these cards and display them on the screen for viewing or editing purposes. You must select cards before you can display them. To do this, press F2 on the On-File main menu, and the Search and Select Cards screen, shown in Figure 13.5, will appear.

Once you pick your search category, a list of the cards in the current box arranged by search category will appear, and you can scroll through the search category with a light bar by using the ↑ and ↓ keys. Each time a category is highlighted, it will also appear in a field at the top of the screen. As an example, if you search the contents of *Wineries* now, there is only one search category: *Domestic*. After you enter cards for imported wineries, and label the search index *Imported,* then you can choose to search all Domestic or all Imported cards. Once the search is complete, the number of cards found that matched the search category will be displayed on the screen.

You can now select one of the following options:

    F1   To select cards and release (or unselect) prior selection

    F2   To add cards to prior selection

    F3   To remove duplicate cards from prior selection

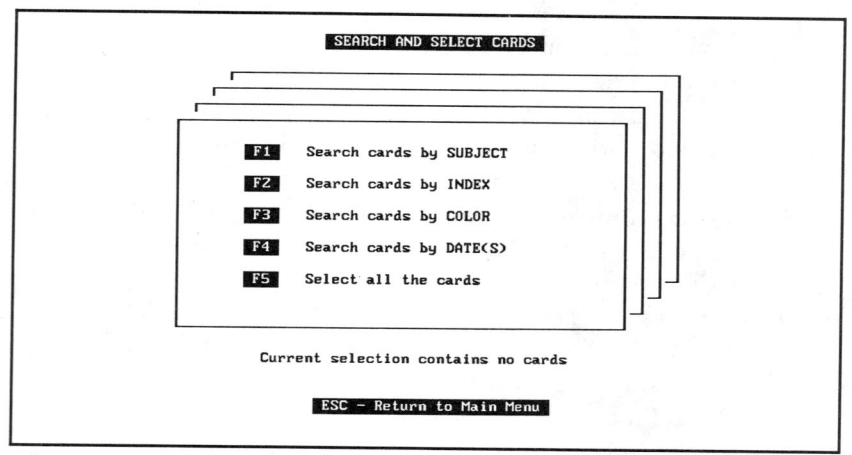

```
          ┌──────────────────────────────────────┐
          │      SEARCH AND SELECT CARDS         │
          │                                      │
          │                                      │
          │   F1   Search cards by SUBJECT       │
          │   F2   Search cards by INDEX         │
          │   F3   Search cards by COLOR         │
          │   F4   Search cards by DATE(S)       │
          │   F5   Select all the cards          │
          │                                      │
          │                                      │
          │   Current selection contains no cards│
          │       ESC - Return to Main Menu      │
          └──────────────────────────────────────┘
```

Figure 13.5: Search and Select Cards screen

F4   To keep any cards that are also in prior selection

F5   To display new cards

If you press F5 to display the new cards, you will be able to select them individually by going forward or backward through the stack of cards matching the search category. Once you have selected one or more cards, and you return to the above list of choices, a sixth choice will appear. This allows you to choose

F6   To match selected cards for word or phrase

WORKING DIRECTLY FROM THE DOS PROMPT

With Advantage II, you can create boxes, cards, and search and select cards, working directly from the DOS prompt. This allows you to bypass the title screen and main menu, thus speeding up your work with On-File.

CREATING A BOX FROM THE DOS PROMPT

To create a box from the DOS prompt using a floppy-disk system, type at that prompt

    A>onfile *newboxname*

Note the space between the word *onfile* and the box name. As with all DOS files, you are limited to 11 characters for the name of the new box. After you enter this information, press Return. You will be taken directly to the main menu for this new box.

ADDING A CARD FROM THE DOS PROMPT

To add a card to an existing box using a floppy-disk system, type at the DOS prompt

    A>onfile *boxname*,A.

Again, note the space between the word *onfile* and the box name. The comma comes directly after the box name, followed by the letter *A* (for add) and a period. Pressing Return will take you into the Add a Card screen for the box you specified.

SEARCHING AND SELECTING CARDS FROM THE DOS PROMPT

You can go directly to the Search and Select Cards screen for a specific box by typing at the DOS prompt

    A>onfile *boxname*,S.

The letter *S* stands for search and select.

MOVING THROUGH A CARD BOX

While you are working with cards in a box, you can move to any specific card. You can go forward through the box using the F1 key and backward using the F2 key. First enter the number of the card you want to see, then push the appropriate function key for the direction. For example, if you are working with card number 8 and you want to go to card number 250, type 250 first and then press F1 to move forward. (This is the reverse order of the Go To procedure for working with documents.)

DISPLAYING, SORTING, EDITING, AND DELETING CARDS

Once you have selected cards, you should return to the On-File main menu to declare what you want to do with these cards. After the third option on the On-File main menu—Display, Sort, and Edit Selected Cards—you should now see a number in parentheses. This number reflects the total number of cards selected. You can press F3 on the On-File main menu to see the Display of Current Card Selection screen. This screen allows you to display, edit, sort, and delete selected cards, and it is shown in Figure 13.6. (If you have not yet selected any cards, the prompt

No cards have been selected

will appear at the bottom of the screen. You must select at least one card to display, edit, or delete, and you must select more than one card to sort.)

The first card of the stack will then appear on the screen. To the right of this card, the number of the card in the stack will be displayed. You have the following choices:

- F1   To move forward through the stack of selected cards
- F2   To move backward through the stack
- F3   To sort the selected cards
- F4   To print, edit, or delete cards; or to view them under templates already created in Special Features (see next section)
- F6   To flip the card over
- F10 To finish with the current card

If you decide to print a card after pressing F4, only the current card will print, and it will be printed as it appears on the screen.

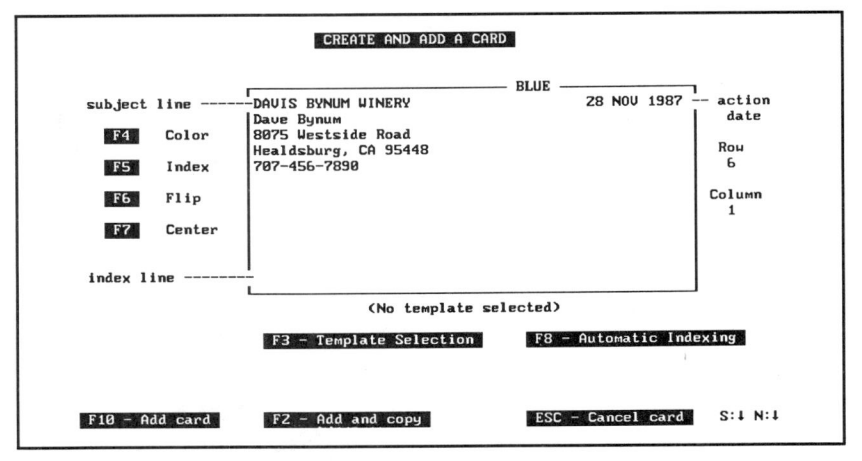

Figure 13.6: Display of first card

PRINTING CARD INFORMATION

Once you have selected and edited cards to your satisfaction, you can print them several ways. Press F4 on the On-File main menu to view the Print Selected Cards screen, which is shown in Figure 13.7.

As with the previous On-File main menu selection, if you have not selected any cards yet, a prompt will appear telling you of this. You must select cards before you can print them.

Templates have to be created in Special Features, which I'll discuss shortly. If you want to print On-File cards as they have been created, you can adjust only the line spacing between cards. If you want to create custom label formats, you will again have to create templates first in Special Features.

You can print labels directly from cards by pressing F4 to obtain the print labels screen, and then pressing one of the following:

←, →	To position card correctly for label
F1	To start printing
F2	To test printer (this will print a blank card)
F3	To select front of card, back of card, or both sides
F4	To toggle between printing cards on 11-inch paper or as separate labels
F10	To cancel printing

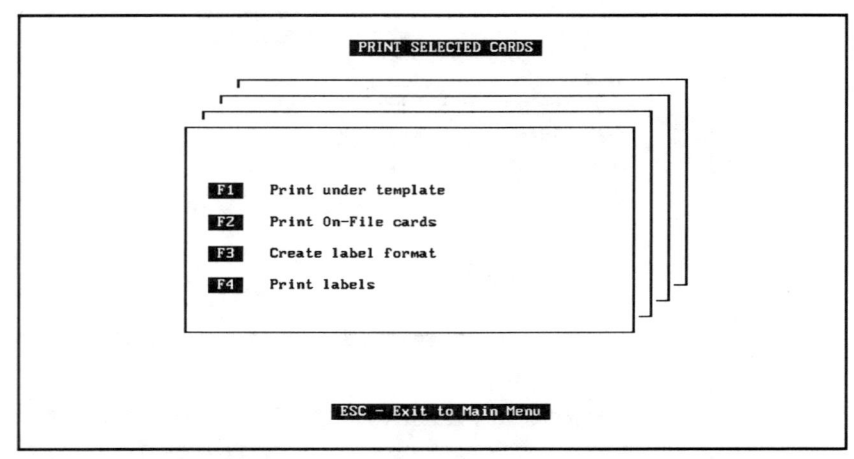

Figure 13.7: Print Selected Cards screen

SPECIAL FEATURES

From the On-File main menu, press F5 to access the Use Special Features screen. You'll see five choices, shown in Figure 13.8.

Display calendar cards will place a selected calendar month on the screen, showing on which days of the week the dates of the month fall. If your system has an internal calendar in it, the current month will display when you first enter this screen. In any case, you can cycle back or ahead one month at a time, as well as a year at a time.

Assign color identification allows you to change the color coding of any cards already created.

Delete selected cards allows you to delete a stack of selected cards.

Read and write cards allows you read and write cards to a file, write cards to a MultiMate merge data file, and write cards under a template to an ASCII file.

The techniques for handling cards in these screens are explained on each appropriate screen.

TEMPLATES

The most important function in Special Features is the ability to create and edit templates. You do not need to create a template to handle and manage information in On-File, but templates can

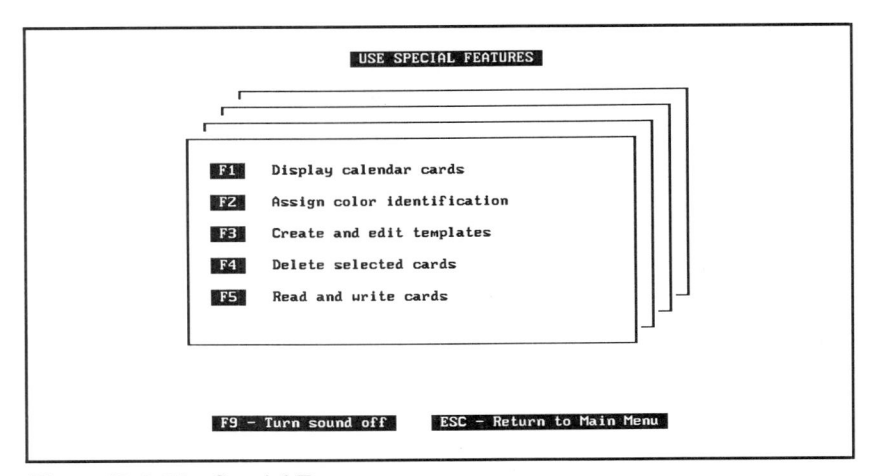

Figure 13.8: Use Special Features screen

make your work easier. In this respect, templates in On-File are similar to the templates you used with merge data files. They organize information graphically on a card, and they provide fields to which the cursor can jump quickly and accurately.

CREATING TEMPLATES

Creating templates in On-File is markedly different from the techniques you used to create templates in merge data files. Begin by pressing F3 on the Use Special Features screen. The Create and Edit Templates screen will appear with four choices:

    F1   To create a new template

    F2   To delete an existing template

    F3   To edit an existing template

    F4   To copy an existing template

If you haven't created a template, the prompt

    A:WINERIES has no templates

will appear at the bottom of the screen. When you have created templates, the number of templates attached to the box you are working with will appear here, so you know how many you can edit, copy, or delete.

Press F1 on the Create and Edit Templates screen, and the Create a New Template screen will appear. This screen displays a blank card with a prompt at the bottom that will guide you through the steps of creating a template. The first prompt

    Enter a name for this template
    and press return

asks you to give a name to this first template. Later, in other screens, when you wish to select a special template to work with, you will press the appropriate key and cycle through the templates you have created so far.

For this template, type the name *Domestic* and press Return. Several new features will appear on the Create a New Template screen. First of all, the name of the template will appear above the top of the card. Second, three cursor markers will appear on the right side of the card: *row* and *column,* with which you are already familiar, and *length,* which displays the length of the field you are creating. You will find this third marker useful when you create a field that isn't flush with the left margin.

The prompt

> **Press any alpha key to define desired
> template area length
> F10 - Set this template area**

will appear below the card. You should position the cursor where you want the first field to begin. For the template Domestic, you can begin the first field in the first position on the card. You define the length of the field before you assign it a label. The card you are going to create is shown in Figure 13.9. To begin, press any letter key, and the letter *A* will appear at the cursor position. The letter *A* will appear regardless of which letter key you press, since *A* stands for the first field. (Each subsequent field will be marked by *B, C,* and so forth, regardless of which letter key you press to begin the field.) To define

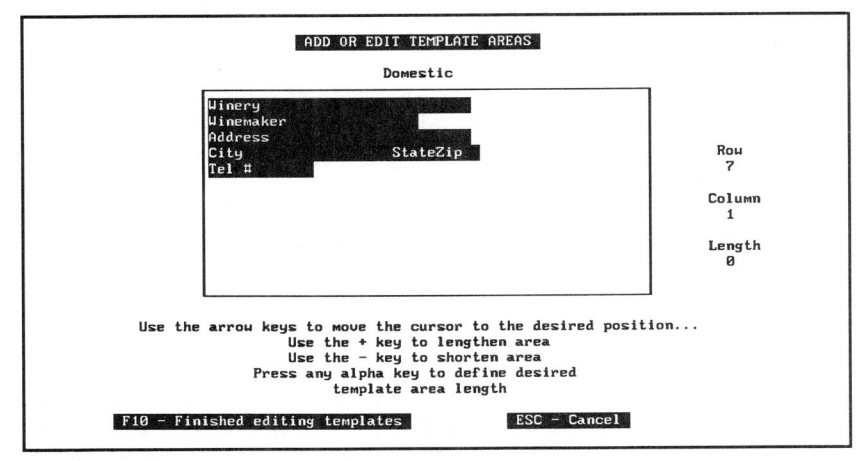

Figure 13.9: Add or Edit Template Areas screen

the length of the first field, press the key 30 times. You can keep track of the movement of the cursor by watching the markers. A field 30 spaces long will show *Row* 1, *Column* 31, and *Length* 30. The 30 spaces for this first field will be filled with *A*s. The maximum number of spaces allowed for the field on the first line of the card is 35. All the other lines on the card will allow you to use the maximum space count of 50. Fifteen spaces are reserved on the first line to display the date. The field length does not include the length of the label.

Press F10 to set this field length. The prompt

> Enter a title for the area designated A:
> and press return

will appear below the card, along with a shaded area 30 spaces long. It is in this space that you should now type the title of this first field. Type *Winery:*, which will appear in the shaded section. When the title is complete, press Return, and the title will appear on the first line of the card.

You could continue to create fields on the first line, but you've used up 30 spaces. Press Return, and the cursor will jump down to the first column of the second line. This is where you press any letter key and begin the second field by marking the length with the letter *B*. Give this second field the title *Winemaker:*. Press Return and on the third line create a third field labeled *Address:*, 25 spaces long. Press Return and on the fourth line create a fourth field labeled *City:*, 22 spaces long. Now, on the same line, create the fifth field, *State:*, using 5 spaces. Ideally, you would use only 2 spaces for this field, but the field has to be at least as long as the title. You could use the two-letter title *St* to signify the state, but you lose a measure of clarity. One of the advantages of using a template is that someone unfamiliar with your card can still fill it in with information based on the field names, which will appear as prompts when you use the template.

In this case, using a six-space field for State will make the template more balanced. When you enter the sixth field, *Zip:*, using five spaces, this field will end in the same column as the field above it, *Address*. Because a template displays information graphically, the visual balance is important.

Create the seventh field, *Tel#:*, using 12 spaces on the fifth line. Then, complete the template Domestic by pressing F10 to return to the Create and Edit Templates screen.

Now when you use this template to fill in the fields with information, each field name will appear at the bottom of the screen, prompting you to type in the proper information.

EDITING TEMPLATES

To edit the features in a template, return to the Use Special Features screen shown in Figure 13.8. Then press F3 to edit the template Domestic. You are given three functions on the editing screen, but the function keys attached to them will not appear until you select a template to edit. Press F9, and when the function keys appear, choose one of the following:

- F1   To add or edit a template area, or field name
- F2   To rename template or field names
- F3   To delete or resequence template areas

Press F1 to view Domestic for editing. The prompt at the bottom of the screen provides instructions for editing the fields. To shorten or lengthen a field, place the cursor on the space just after the end of the field, or area name, you want to change. You cannot place the cursor inside the field. That is why the marker position shows the cursor to be in *Row* 1 *Column* 31. Pressing the Minus key on the keypad will shorten the field the cursor is next to, and the cursor will trail the shortening field. Pressing the Plus key will lengthen the field, up to the line limit, and the cursor will precede the lengthening field.

The third option on the Add or Edit Template Areas screen allows you to delete a template or template area, which is self-explanatory, or resequence template areas. Using screen instructions, you can reorganize the sequence of the fields on the template, and delete those you no longer want.

ON-FILE UTILITIES

On-File provides three utilities. To use them, first place the files from the On-File Utilities Diskette on your hard disk, or place the On-File Utilities Diskette in drive A. At the system prompt, type

OFUT

The copyright screen will appear first. You can press the Space bar to move into the main menu, or you can wait a couple of moments, and the main menu will appear.

The main menu offers four functions:

    F1 MultiMate Document Cataloging
    F2 MultiMate Merge Data File Conversion
    F3 On-File Conversion Utilities
    F4 On-File Box Recovery

MultiMate Document Cataloging allows you to reorganize MultiMate files recorded on disk, both documents and card boxes, including moving files between subdirectories. Additionally, the number of files is displayed, as well as the amount of disk space used to contain the files.

MultiMate Merge Data File Conversion allows you to create an On-File box of cards from a merge data file created in the word processor. One page in the merge data file will match one card in the new box.

On-File Conversion Utilities allow you to convert other information files to On-File cards, and vice versa, and copy cards from one box to another (as described below). You can also transfer templates between card boxes.

On-File Box Recovery allows you to attempt to restore the data in an On-File box that has become corrupted. Because there are many different kinds of corruption, this utility may or may not work.

COPYING FILES FROM ONE BOX TO ANOTHER

Although Table 13.1 lists F2 as the Add and Copy a Card key, it does not actually perform a card copying function. To copy cards from one box to another, you must work through both the On-File and the On-File Utilities programs.

As an example, we'll copy the cards from our Wineries box into a new box named Cawines (for California wines). Follow these steps:

1. From the On-File main menu, press F2 to select the Search and Select Cards option.

2. Press Escape to return to the main menu, then press F5 for Special Features.

3. Press F5 for Read and Write Cards.
4. Press F1 to select Write Cards to an On-File Format. When the screen appears, enter the file name *Cawines*.
5. Press Escape several times to exit the On-File program.
6. Enter On-File Utilities and press F3 to select On-File Conversion Utilities.
7. Press F1 to select Convert from an On-File Format. When the screen appears, enter the drive letter and file name for Cawines, then press F10.
8. When the conversion is complete, press Escape three times to exit On-File Utilities.
9. Reenter On-File and press F5 twice.
10. Press F2 to select Read Cards from an On-File Format to a Box. When the screen appears, enter the drive letter and file name for Cawines.
11. Press F10 to complete the procedure.

You now have a new box called Cawines that contains copies of the cards in your Wineries box.

Appendix A

Installing the Program

TO RUN MULTIMATE ADVANTAGE II, YOU WILL NEED PC-DOS or MS-DOS version 2.0 or later, and at least 384K of RAM (random-access memory). Earlier versions of MultiMate needed only 256K or 320K, so if you have used MultiMate and are upgrading to the Advantage II package, you should make sure you have enough memory to run Advantage II.

MultiMate Advantage II will work well with most monitors and printers. You can use either a monochrome screen or a color screen, with or without enhanced graphics capability. Certain features in the word-processing program are enhanced by color, such as screen instructions and highlighting. On the other hand, monochrome monitors give a much better resolution, and if you are going to spend a lot of time at your screen, you will probably find the higher resolution of the monochrome screen less fatiguing.

Printers always present problems, but Advantage II has almost 400 printer files on a separate disk. This covers most of the printers available, and Multimate International Corporation releases new printer files to keep up with the market. For instructions on installing the proper printer files for the printers you intend to use, see Appendix B.

MULTIMATE ADVANTAGE II DISKETTES

Your MultiMate Advantage II package contains 11 diskettes:

- System Diskette
- Boot Diskette
- Dictionary/Speller Diskette
- Thesaurus Diskette
- Advanced Utilities Diskette
- Conversions 1 Diskette

- Conversions 2 Diskette
- Printer Tables Diskette
- Beginning Diskette
- On-File Boot/System Diskette
- On-File Utilities Diskette

If any disks are missing from your package, you should contact the place where you bought it and obtain a complete package.

If you intend to use the technical support provided with Advantage II, and to take advantage of subsequent updates, you will have to register your purchase with Ashton Tate.

Also in the package is a keyboard layout, which you can put on the wall near your computer, and which is detailed enough to provide you with all the information you need to perform routine procedures with MultiMate Advantage II. You should keep several reference books close by, however, because the keyboard layout sheet does not include some advanced techniques.

DOS PRELIMINARIES

After you make sure your package is complete, you need to make copies of all the program diskettes. It is crucial that you create archival copies of all the diskettes you bought. You will find it expensive and time-consuming to replace original diskettes if you damage them.

You can only copy files to a disk formatted for the system you are using. When you format a disk, the system divides the new disk into sectors that DOS is familiar with. This allows the system to place files on the disk and keep track of where they are located.

FORMATTING DISKETTES

The easiest method for copying the files from the program diskettes is to format the same number of blank floppy disks and then transfer the files disk to disk. If you want to economize on the number of disks you use, you can pack all the files onto less than the original number of disks, but I do not recommend that you do this. All the program files have been collected into related groups, and although each file can be copied and transferred independently of all other files, you may damage or lose a file if you handle it too often.

To format a disk, use the FORMAT command at the DOS prompt. If your system uses a hard disk, the system prompt will most likely be C>; with a two-floppy system, A>. Place the blank unformatted disk in drive B (drive A for hard disk) and at the DOS prompt type the FORMAT command

FORMAT B:

for floppies (or *FORMAT A:* for a hard disk) and press Return. The following message will appear on the screen:

Insert new diskette for drive B:
and strike any key when ready

(or *drive A:* for a hard disk). Follow these instructions, and the message

Formatting...

will appear. This means that DOS is formatting the blank disk. When the formatting is complete, you will see the message

Formatting...Format complete

Almost immediately, the message

362496 bytes total disk space
362496 bytes available on disk

will appear, showing you how much of the total disk space is available for you to use. When you are formatting a new disk for the first time, the maximum amount of space will usually be available.

For double-sided, double-density 5¼-inch diskettes, you'll usually have 362,496 bytes available. For 3½-inch diskettes, you'll have twice that amount—730,112 bytes. When less than the maximum space is available, parts of the disk are incorrectly formatted. Sometimes repeating the FORMAT command can clear up the problem. If a new disk does not yield the maximum amount of space for use, return it; most new disks come with this kind of guarantee.

A third message will appear after each formatting:

Format another (Y/N)?

You can format another disk by answering Y for yes and placing a new blank, unformatted disk in the appropriate drive. Strike any key in answer to the second prompt, and the system will format the new disk.

When you have formatted all the new disks, return them to their sleeves. Take special care when handling floppy disks. You may find it helpful to place a blank label on the formatted disks so you can easily distinguish them from unformatted disks. You should always format a few more disks than you plan to use, in case something goes wrong with the disks you expect to use. For instance, you could find yourself in a bind if you wanted to download files from your computer and all you needed was a blank formatted disk, but you didn't have one— and you couldn't format one because the computer's RAM was full.

Specific instructions for using 5¼-inch or 3½-inch disks in your computer should be available from the manufacturer of the computer.

Before you begin to copy files from the original diskettes, place a read/write protection sticker over the read/write protect notch on the original diskette. (This notch is on the upper right edge of the disk when you are looking at the side of the disk showing the manufacturer's label.) Covering this notch prevents inadvertent erasure of the files on the disk, although your computer can still read the files on the disk.

If you would like to learn more about DOS and the commands available to you in it, you can refer to the following books:

- *The MS-DOS Handbook,* by Richard Allen King (SYBEX, 1985)
- *MS-DOS Power User's Guide,* by Jonathan Kamin (SYBEX, 1986)
- *Mastering MS-DOS,* by Judd Robbins (SYBEX, 1987)

INSTALLING ON A TWO-FLOPPY SYSTEM

With two floppy drives, all you need do is make copies of the program disks, and you'll be ready to use the program. Simply place each original program diskette in drive A and a blank, formatted disk in drive B. Type

    COPY A:*.* B:

and press Return to begin the copying procedure. This command means, "Copy every file from the disk in drive A to the disk in drive B." Make sure to press the Space bar only twice: once after COPY and again before B:. The asterisks are *wild card* characters: *.* means every file, *.DOC means every file with the extension .DOC, and CHAP*.* means every file beginning with *CHAP* (CHAPTER, CHAP1, and so on).

    The files on the original disk in drive A will be copied to the disk in drive B in the order they appear in the disk directory. Each file will be listed on the screen as it is copied. When the COPY command is finished, you will see the complete list of files copied, with information on the file size and the date each file was loaded onto the original disk. You'll also see the amount of disk space available.

    To confirm that the program files do indeed exist on the new disk, you can view the disk directory. Change the directory by typing *B:* at the A> prompt, then use the DOS command DIR, for directory, to see the list of files on the disk:

    DIR

This list should match the one from the COPY command. You can proceed in this manner, copying and checking disks, for all 11 original diskettes.

INSTALLING ON A HARD DISK

    You can just load all the files onto your hard disk, and the word-processing program will work fine. To improve the performance of MultiMate Advantage II on your hard disk, you may want to do one of the following:

- Decide which files you want to load, based on what you want to do with the program

- Create subdirectories to organize all the files on the hard disk

WHICH FILES TO LOAD

You will need to use all the files on the following diskettes:

- System Diskette
- Boot Diskette
- Dictionary/Speller Diskette
- Thesaurus Diskette

These are the basic files necessary for operating the word-processing program. You will also need to load selected printer action table files from the Printer Action Tables Diskette. Which files you load depend upon the printers you intend to use (see Appendix B).

If you intend to edit key procedure files or custom dictionaries often, you might want to load the files from the Advanced Utilities Diskette onto your hard disk. They take up over 350K of space, so you have to weigh the advantage of immediate access to the advanced utilities. If you plan to use all the file-conversion programs, you will also have to load the files on the Conversions Diskettes. These are very useful files—when you want to use them—but disk space can become tight when you start to load many programs and then keep files created from these programs on the same disk.

You might find it more advantageous to access the lesser used files, such as those on the Advanced Utilities and the two Conversions Diskettes, by placing these diskettes in your floppy drive when you need to use them. They work fine in the floppy disk drive, and they don't take up precious space on your hard disk.

The question of which files to copy onto the hard disk, and which ones to leave out, depends on your use of MultiMate Advantage II. I recommend you load only the basic files first, and then after you become more familiar with the program, you can expand your file selections as you find you need them.

In any case, creating archival copies of your original diskettes is a crucial step for the diskettes you don't load onto the hard disk. If you have only one floppy drive, you can create duplicate diskettes only by loading all the program files onto your hard disk and then transferring them to floppies. (With two floppy drives, simply follow the copying procedure in the section on installing on a two-floppy system.)

INSTALLING MULTIMATE ADVANTAGE II IN A SUBDIRECTORY

Placing your Advantage II files in a subdirectory will help you keep track of your files. Advantage II offers full path support. To create a subdirectory, you must first go to the root directory. If your DOS files are not on the hard disk, place your DOS disk in drive A and turn your computer on. When the system prompt C> appears, type

CD

and press Return. The backslash (\) denotes the root directory. You must now create the subdirectory and give it a name. Let's call it MM, for MultiMate Advantage II. The DOS command for creating a subdirectory is MKDIR or MD, for *make directory*. Type the command

MD MM

and press Return. The next step is to change the default directory from \ to MM. When the system prompt returns, you can make MM the current directory by using the command CD (or CHDIR), which stands for *change directories*. Type

CD MM

and press Return.

Now remove the DOS disk, if you are working with one. And now, if you copy files from the floppy disk drive onto the hard disk, all the files can be in the same subdirectory. This way you can view them and copy them with much less trouble than if they were scattered among other files on the hard disk.

For reference, you may want to make a list of the files on each original diskette before you copy them to the hard disk. You can do this by placing an original diskette in the floppy drive, displaying a list of the files on the screen using the DIR command, and then making a Quick Print of the screen by pressing Shift-PrtSc. (If your printer is not connected to your computer, you can write down the list of files by hand.) Figure A.1 illustrates the contents of the System Diskette.

You should not load files that are not going into a subdirectory onto the hard disk without knowing the exact names of the files. The files won't be lost, but you can waste a lot of time trying to go back through the directory of all files on your hard disk to find them and re-record them to floppies for backup.

To copy files from the original diskettes into the subdirectory on the hard disk, simply place each diskette in the floppy drive (drive A) and repeat the following COPY command for each original diskette at the C> prompt:

COPY A:*.* C:

and press Return. You still can select only certain files for copying, if you want to save space on your disk and in your subdirectory. All document files that you create while using MultiMate Advantage II will also be recorded to the MM subdirectory.

Once your system files and your document files are in a subdirectory, you will have to enter the drive designation and subdirectory name in certain prompts—for instance, to edit or delete a custom dictionary, or to edit a key procedure file.

MODIFYING CONSOLE DEFAULTS

A utility file on the Advanced Utilities Diskette allows you to change the appearance of your display screen. If you are using a

```
A:\>dir
    Volume in drive B has no label
    Directory of  B:\

WP       OVL    140848    3-20-87    9:03p
WPSYSD   SYS      1069    3-20-87    9:10p
WPSYSD   CMP      1069    3-20-87    9:10p
WPSYSD   STB      1069    3-20-87    9:10p
WPSYSD   XXX      1069    3-20-87    9:10p
WPMSG    TXT     10106    3-15-87   12:03a
WPHELP   TXT     42784    3-15-87   12:04a
TTYCRLF  PAT      1920   10-14-84    5:28a
CLAMCONV EXE     66000    1-07-87    2:54p
         9 File(s)      91136 bytes free

A:\>_
```

Figure A.1: List of files on System Diskette

monochrome monitor, you can change the intensity of the black-and-white contrast as well as the shades of gray. If you are using a color monitor, you can change the colors used for various screens. You will find this change in colors particularly helpful with certain editing functions, such as highlighting, as well as with underlining and boldfacing. You should be aware, however, that a monochrome monitor has a much higher resolution than does a color screen. This is an important distinction for people who spend long hours in front of the monitor. The higher the resolution, the less fatiguing it is to your eyes.

To modify the console defaults, place your copy of the Advanced Utilities Diskette in the disk drive and type *MM* at the DOS prompt. When you press Return, the MultiMate Advantage II Boot-Up menu (Figure 8.5) will appear on your screen. Select

3) Utilities and Conversions

The Advanced Utilities main menu (Figure 8.6) will then appear. Press the Space bar to highlight

Modify Console Defaults

and press F10 to move into the Console Defaults Select Utility screen (Figure A.2).

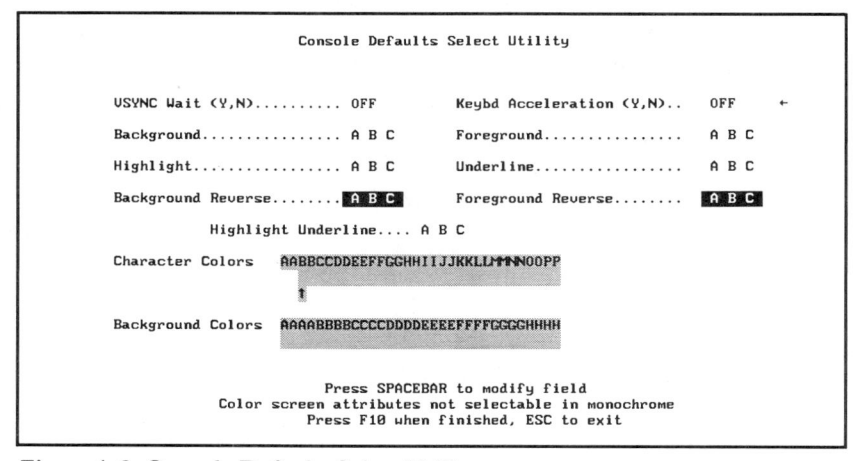

```
                    Console Defaults Select Utility

    VSYNC Wait (Y,N).......... OFF      Keybd Acceleration (Y,N).. OFF
    Background............... A B C     Foreground............... A B C
    Highlight................ A B C     Underline................ A B C
    Background Reverse....... A B C     Foreground Reverse....... A B C
              Highlight Underline.... A B C
    Character Colors   AABBCCDDEEFFGGHHIIJJKKLLMMNNOOPP

    Background Colors  AAAABBBBCCCCDDDDEEEEFFFFGGGGHHHH

                    Press SPACEBAR to modify field
              Color screen attributes not selectable in monochrome
                    Press F10 when finished, ESC to exit
```

Figure A.2: Console Defaults Select Utility screen

This is a fairly tricky screen to play with. It has two parts: the list of nine defaults you can change in the top half, and two rows of colors (or varying shades of gray if you are using a monochrome monitor) in the bottom half.

To change the default settings, move the cursor to the default you want to change by pressing the arrow keys, and change the color or shading scheme of that default by pressing the Space bar. Immediately, the cursor will jump to the bottom half of the screen, to one of the two color bars, depending upon which default you are changing. An arrow in the top half of the screen will mark the default you are changing. Press the Space bar to choose a color or shading, then press any arrow key to move the cursor back to the top half of the screen and on to the next default.

Controlling the Speed of Console Functions

The two defaults in the top row of the screen control two functions of speed on the screen. When you place the cursor on either and press the Space bar, the field value will toggle between yes and no.

VSYNC, which stands for *video synchronization,* refers to synchronization between DOS and a color board, if your computer has one. (If you are using a monochrome monitor, then this default has no effect on your display.) With some color boards, there is a chance that visual static, or *snow,* will appear when a screen image changes radically, and when there is insufficient time for the color board to redraw the screen the way the system wants it to. Answering yes to this default causes the system to wait for synchronization with the color board. This wait might cause a slight delay in the operation of Advantage II, but then there will be no snow to distort the screen image.

The *Keybd Acceleration* default enables you to change the speed with which your keystrokes are displayed on the screen. The actual speed is controlled from a field named Acceleration Rate in the Edit System Defaults screen, but you can only change the speed on that screen if you have answered yes to activate the keyboard acceleration here.

Controlling Colors on the Console

The next seven fields on the Console Defaults screen control the various features on your screen that can be viewed in color or in different shadings. Table A.1 defines these fields.

FIELD	DEFINITION
Background	The color of the screen when it is blank
Foreground	The color of standard text
Highlight	The color of highlighted text
Underline	The color of the bar used to underline words
Background Reverse	The color of the screen appearing behind characters in reverse video
Foreground Reverse	The color of the characters appearing in reverse video
Highlight Underline	The color of highlighted text that is underlined

Table A.1: Fields controlling video display

When you use the arrow keys to place the cursor next to any of these seven fields and press the Space bar, the cursor will jump to the bottom half of the screen, beneath one of the two color bars. (If you do not have a color monitor with a color card in your computer, these bars will appear as shadings increasing in darkness from left to right.)

Pressing the Space bar will move the cursor along the color bar. Play with this feature to get the feel of it. You can only move the cursor in one direction, toward the right, but when you get to the right end of the color bar the cursor will jump to the left end and start all over again.

You select the color or degree of shading for the default you've chosen, which is marked with an arrow in the top half of the screen, by pressing any arrow key. This will return the cursor to the top half of the screen, and you can continue to make more changes. When the settings have been changed to suit you, press F10 to fix these default settings in the WPSYSD.SYS file on your Advanced Utilities Diskette. You will see what effect these changes have on your screen when you return to the MultiMate Advantage II Boot-up menu. After viewing these changes, you can return to the Console Defaults Select Utility screen and modify the defaults again, if you wish.

After you have exited from the Advanced Utilities Diskette, you will have to transfer a copy of the file WPSYSD.SYS back to the System Diskette, if you are using dual floppy drives and no hard disk.

CONVERTING CUSTOM DICTIONARIES

If you have created custom dictionaries with earlier versions of the MultiMate word-processing program, excluding MultiMate Advantage, you need to convert them to accommodate the Dictionary/Speller program in MultiMate Advantage II version 1.0. To protect your original custom dictionary, make a copy of it on a separate disk before you try to convert it.

DUAL-FLOPPY SYSTEM

If you are working with a dual-floppy system, place the Dictionary/Speller Diskette in drive A, and place the disk that contains your original custom dictionary in drive B. At the A prompt, type

> CLAMCONV B:(original custom dictionary name)

and press Return. If you didn't give a special name to your custom dictionary, it will have been recorded as CLAMFL.UH. The new version of your custom dictionary will be given the same name as the original.

You can double-check the accuracy of this conversion by printing a list of all the words in this new converted custom dictionary. You can do this because the conversion process creates two files: the new custom dictionary, and an ASCII file containing all the words in the original custom dictionary. You print the list from the ASCII file. Place your DOS disk in drive A and the disk that contains your new custom dictionary in drive B. Type at the A prompt

> PRINT B:(new custom dictionary name)

and press Return. If you have never used the PRINT command before, the prompt

> Name of list device [PRN]

will appear. Pressing Return will cause the listings in your new custom dictionary to print out on the first printer device connected to your computer.

To make room on your Dictionary/Speller Diskette for more new entries into the custom dictionary, you should now erase the file that converted your old custom dictionary. You do this by typing at the A prompt

DEL CLAMCONV.EXE

and pressing Return. Check to make sure this file has been deleted by typing at the A prompt

DIR

and pressing Return.

HARD-DISK SYSTEM

If you are using a hard disk, make sure to make a backup copy of the original custom dictionary before you try to convert it. You can convert a file that is on the same disk as the conversion program CLAMCONV.EXE by typing at the C prompt

CLAMCONV (original custom dictionary name)

and pressing Return. After the conversion, use the DOS command DEL to erase CLAMCONV.EXE from the disk to make room for more custom dictionary entries.

OTHER UTILITIES

You can specify all the drive designations for the Advantage II word-processing program as well as improve the performance of certain features such as insert mode. To do this, select

7)System and Document Defaults

from the main menu. You'll see the System and Document Defaults menu (Figure A.3).

```
          SYSTEM AND DOCUMENT DEFAULTS


             1) Edit System Format Line
             2) Edit Drive Defaults
             3) Edit System Defaults
             4) Edit Document Defaults






                  Press desired number
                  Press ESC to exit
```

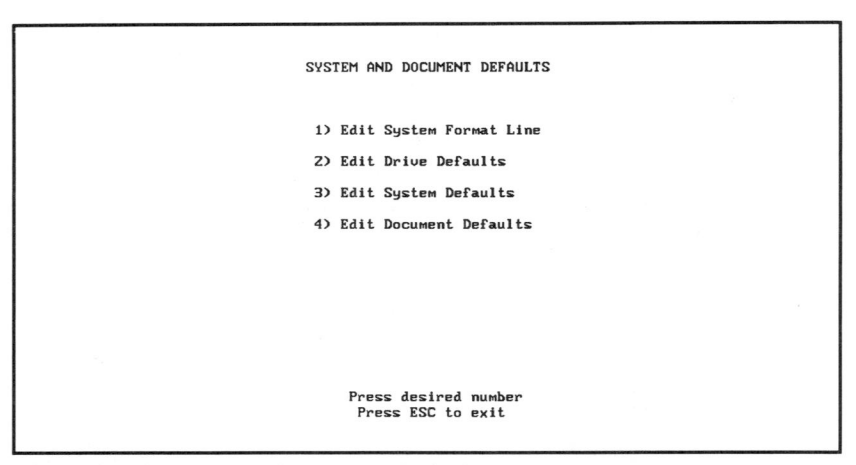

Figure A.3: System and Document Defaults screen

EDITING THE SYSTEM FORMAT LINE

The first option on the System and Document Defaults menu allows you to reset the format line that appears when you create any document. The Edit System Format Line screen is shown in Figure A.4. The number in the column field shows which column the cursor is in on the format line, the right margin field shows the right-margin setting, and line spacing is defined in the text line. Change the format line as you wish, then press F10 to save the new settings.

EDITING DRIVE DEFAULTS

The second option on the System and Document Defaults menu allows you to change disk-drive designations so that Advantage II knows where to look for such things as the system programs, documents, and library files. There are six fields on the Drive Defaults screen (Figure A.5).

The cursor will appear in the first setting, System Drive. The next three fields are for the Document, Library, and Dictionary drive designations. As you pass through each field by pressing Return, the cursor will move to the next field. If you are using a hard disk, then you will probably want to change the first four settings from A to C.

The next setting also has 16 settings to specify whether the installed drives are floppy disks or hard disks. Enter F for floppy disk drives, or

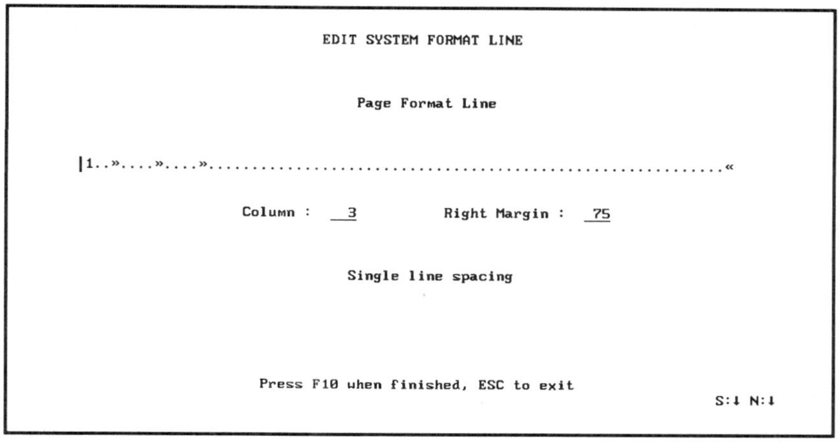

```
                    EDIT SYSTEM FORMAT LINE

                         Page Format Line

|1..»....»....»..........................................«

                Column :  _3_      Right Margin :  _75_

                         Single line spacing



                Press F10 when finished, ESC to exit
                                                          S:1 N:1
```

Figure A.4: Edit System Format Line screen

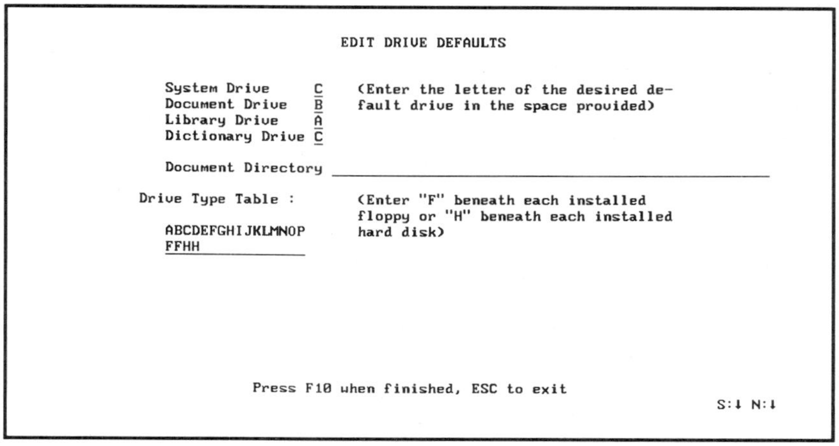

```
                         EDIT DRIVE DEFAULTS

          System Drive     C    (Enter the letter of the desired de-
          Document Drive   B     fault drive in the space provided)
          Library Drive    A
          Dictionary Drive C

          Document Directory _____

          Drive Type Table :    (Enter "F" beneath each installed
                                 floppy or "H" beneath each installed
          ABCDEFGHIJKLMNOP       hard disk)
          FFHH


                Press F10 when finished, ESC to exit
                                                          S:1 N:1
```

Figure A.5: Edit Drive Defaults screen

H for a hard disk. Leave all other letter designations blank if you are not using them. If you enter an incorrect letter, you can delete it by pressing the Delete key (the Minus key will not work). Press Return to go to the next field.

The last field is the Document Directory default. Use this field to enter the name of the directory where you store most Advantage II documents, if you have more than one subdirectory installed.

When you've specified all the fields to your satisfaction, press F10 to set these designations. If you have entered an unacceptable setting, some or all of the settings will blink, depending upon what errors you have made. Pressing F10 returns you to the System and Document Defaults menu, and pressing Escape will return you to the main menu.

EDITING SYSTEM DEFAULTS

The third option on the System and Document Defaults menu allows you to modify the nine features that appear on the Modify Document Defaults screen that you see when you first create a document, as well as 14 other features that can affect a document. Most of these other features are discussed in the main body of the book. We'll review those that have not been described in detail earlier.

The Insert Mode setting allows you to specify where text following the cursor will go when you press the Insert key. The default setting is P for Push.

The Destructive Backspace setting allows you to use the Backspace key either to delete as you backspace (Y) or to move without erasing (N).

The Backup Before Editing Document setting is N in the default mode. You can change it to Y, and a backup document will be created each time you enter a document to work on it. This provides you with a copy of the document you are working on in case it becomes corrupted for some reason.

The (D)ocument Mode or (P)age Mode setting allows you to determine which mode Advantage II should use to handle your documents. Document mode is the default setting.

The default setting for Display Directory is Y. Normally, Advantage II displays the directory of files on the default drive in the document portion of such screens as Edit a Document, Create a Document, and Print a Document. Press N if you don't want to see the file directory.

The Display Spaces as Dots [.] setting controls what you see on the screen when you press the Space bar. In the default setting (N), you'll see spaces. Press Y if you want to see a dot (.) instead. Dots as spaces will not appear outside the boundaries of an Indent, Tab, or hard carriage-return symbol.

The Speed Up Movement Between Pages setting can be used to increase the speed at which Advantage II moves to the next page.

The default setting is Y. Entering N slows down the movement, but it ensures that all the data on the previous page has been saved to disk before you can enter new text on the next page.

The Strikeout Character setting simply allows you to choose a strikeout character. The slash mark (/) is the default character, but you can use any character that your printer can print.

The System Date Standard setting allows you to specify a different date standard than the one you want printed.

The Acceleration Rate [0–9] setting controls the speed at which your keystrokes are processed. The higher the number, the faster your keystrokes are entered. The default setting is 5. This setting is particularly useful if you're a fast typist and you want the screen display to keep up with you.

The Acceleration Responsiveness [0–9] setting controls how long you have to press any key before it autorepeats. The higher the number, the quicker the response. You can have any key autorepeat.

The Main Dictionary and Custom Dictionary settings allow you to specify which dictionaries you want the spelling check to use.

HELPFUL HINTS FOR TROUBLESHOOTING

It is practically inevitable that you will encounter problems and frustrations when you start using a new and unfamiliar program. MultiMate Advantage II is a powerful and versatile program, but it will do only what you ask it to. When you encounter a problem, it could come from:

- Computer malfunction
- DOS system glitch
- Software bug
- Your error

The most frequent cause of computer problems is human error, so follow these rules when you encounter a problem:

1. Double-check all the mechanical connections: make sure the

computer is turned on, connected to the printer, and connected to the external drive, if you are using one.

2. Double-check the instructions, and keep reference material close to your computer.

3. Try to perform the procedure a second time, paying closer attention to what you are telling the computer to do.

In addition to these general rules, you should remember to:

1. Keep your floppy disks clean and free from dirt and damage.

2. Mark your floppy disks correctly so you don't lose track of their contents.

3. Make backup copies of all your files on a regular basis, and store these backups in a safe place.

4. Read as much as you can on the programs you use most often. Others' experience and advice can save you from repeating their mistakes.

5. Resort to the technical support of the program manufacturer last. The manufacturer is generally glad to help you out, but customer-service lines are busy, and the time you spend waiting could often be better spent searching for your own solution. There is no better teacher than your own experience. The number for technical support for MultiMate Advantage II in Hartford, Connecticut, is 203-247-3445. Hours are 9 A.M. to 7 P.M. EST weekdays.

Appendix B

Printer Installation

INSTALLING A PRINTER MEANS CONNECTING A printer correctly to your computer so that you can print all the features in your MultiMate Advantage II files. Obtaining this correct connection between your computer and the printer can be as simple as copying a single file from one disk to another, or as complicated as writing a custom program. You'll find the simple steps described completely in this appendix, and an overview of the more complicated procedures.

For a printer to print correctly, it must receive clear instructions from the program operating on the computer. In a sense, each printer speaks its own language, so there must be a translator between the program and the printer so that the printer can understand the program commands. This translation is done by special printer files. In most cases, you need to use only one file, although there are cases where you will need to use two and (rarely) three. Files for all popular printers can be found on the Printer Action Tables Diskette.

To choose the proper printer action table, you need to know what kind of printer you are going to use, and its brand and model. With MultiMate Advantage II, you can use all the printers on the market, including impact printers, sheet-feeder printers, and laser printers. You also need to keep in mind what effects you expect to obtain from the printer.

VIEWING FILES ON THE PRINTER ACTION TABLES DISKETTE

You select the file or files you need to use from a long list on the Printer Action Tables Diskette. This diskette contains three kinds of files:

- Printer action table files
- Sheet feeder action table files
- Character width/translation files

The largest category of files is the printer action table (PAT) files, which are designated with the file extension .PAT. A PAT file for a particular printer contains all the codes needed to interpret Multi-Mate Advantage II's word-processing instructions to drive that printer. As an example, the PAT file that drives an Epson FX-80 printer appears as EPSONFX.PAT. Almost all printers are driven by PAT files. The exception is sheet-feeder printers, which are driven by sheet-feeder action tables, or SATs. These too can be found on the Printer Action Tables Diskette, and are the equivalent of PATs for sheet-feeder printers.

A third category of files is called character width/translation files. These are given the extension .CWT only when they are not contained within a PAT file, which is where they usually reside. You can call up individual CWT files when special conditions apply. You can even create your own CWT file, once you become familiar with their purpose. A character width/translation file defines two things: the width of each character (in 1/120ths of an inch), and the translation of a character sent to the printer. The first condition changes the appearance of the printed characters with such features as bold and shadow print. Modifications in these files can make bold print a bit bolder. The effect is more dramatic with laser printers, which can take advantage of such fine settings.

The translation of a character sent to a printer refers to the file's ability to assign alternative characters to keys and symbols. As an example, you can design a custom character width/translation file to instruct the printer to print a section symbol, which doesn't normally get printed. You can even change the appearance of this section symbol to a standard asterisk.

The files on the Printer Action Tables Diskette are arranged in alphabetical order, according to the brand name of each printer. Because of the eight-character DOS limitation on file names, these brand names and model numbers are abbreviated, although you should be able to decipher them. All the files are in a single subdirectory on this disk called PRINTERS. To see the complete list of files available to you, place the Printer Action Tables Diskette in drive A, and type

CD\PRINTERS

and press Return. When the system prompt reappears, type

DIR

and press Return. The complete list of printer files will begin to scroll down your screen, as shown in Figure B.1.

If you want to stop this scrolling and check a file or batch of files more closely, press Ctrl-S. To start scrolling again, press any key. You can print a list of all the files on a screen by first pressing Ctrl-S to freeze the screen. Next, print a Quick Print of the screen by pressing Shift-PrtSc. The complete list of printer files takes up several screenfuls.

Some printers require only one printer file to print correctly. Others require a CWT file as well to provide the highest quality of print the printer can produce. In particular, you need to use two files for laser printers, along with some other printers that can produce high-quality graphics.

Once you have located the proper files to copy, you must place them either on your System Diskette, if you are using a dual-floppy system, or onto your hard disk. You should try to determine beforehand exactly which files you need to use, but this is not always possible. Because of the variety of printers and their needs, as well as the possible difficulty of determining exactly which LaserJet PAT files

```
        .              <DIR>         3-19-87   11:17a
        ..             <DIR>         3-19-87   11:17a
        5201PS   PAT    1824         1-01-80   12:16a
        ASTLASR  PAT    3361         2-06-87    4:45p
        BDSLASER PAT    3031         1-22-87   12:50p
        BLASER   PAT    3757         2-28-87   12:38p
        BROIF100 PAT    1920        11-01-85    3:08p
        BROTHR1  PAT    1920        10-14-84    4:06a
        CANLBPL  PAT    3955         1-08-87    3:19p
        CANLBPP  PAT    3955         1-08-87    2:28p
        CITOH310 PAT    2899         3-03-87    5:00p
        CITOHF10 PAT    1920        10-27-85    1:36p
        DAISYWRT PAT    1920        10-27-85    1:31p
        DECLA100 PAT    1920        10-29-84    6:07p
        DECLN03  PAT    1824         6-18-86    1:23p
        DIABL150 PAT    1824        11-01-84    2:32p
        DIABL620 PAT    1920         1-16-87    3:21p
        DIABL630 PAT    1824         1-16-87    3:21p
        DMP2100  PAT    1840        11-25-86   12:06p
        DWII     PAT    1920         7-05-84    3:29p
        DWIIB    PAT    1840        11-12-84   11:16a
        EPFXLINE PAT    2767         1-21-87    2:42p
        EPSON           1716        10-28-85    1:05p
        Strike a key when ready . . .
```

Figure B.1: Beginning of list of printer files

you need to use (there are 23 of them), and LaserJet CWT files (there are 52 of these), you might have to experiment with different combinations. (If this seems like too much trouble, call the MultiMate technical-support numbers given at the end of Appendix A.)

Almost 400 printer files are provided on the Printer Action Tables Diskette, but more are always being produced by the manufacturer to keep current with the new printers coming on the market. If the printer files necessary for your printer are not available on the disk that came with your package, you can order the appropriate files from the company.

COPYING THE RIGHT FILES

Before you try to copy any files from the Printer Action Tables Diskette, make sure you have entered the subdirectory PRINTERS. If you try to copy files from that disk before you enter the subdirectory, you will obtain the following error message:

```
Volume in drive A has no label
Director of A:\

PRINTERS  <DIR> 3-28-86 3:22p
       1 File(s)       0 bytes free
```

(This assumes the Printer Action Tables Diskette is in drive A.) Thus, first type *CD\PRINTERS* at the A> prompt. The next step is to specify the correct file.

To copy the EPSONLQ file to a hard disk, at the A> prompt type

```
COPY EPSONLQ.PAT C:
```

and press Return. (To copy any other file, replace EPSONLQ.PAT with the name of the file you want to copy.) If you are using a dual-floppy system, place the System Diskette in drive B, and at the A> prompt type

```
COPY A:EPSONLQ.PAT B:
```

and press Return.

If you want to copy all printer files for Epson printers, you can save time by using wild-card characters. For example, if you want to copy all Epson files to your hard disk, type the command

COPY EP*.* C:

which instructs the system to copy every file that begins with the letters EP. Some of the Epson files are marked EPSON, but others are marked EP only. EP* covers them all. Furthermore, the .* copies all extensions of EP* files. Although there are no CWT files for Epson printers, there is one EPSON file with no extension, and this one will be copied as well.

Now, when you view the Document Print Options screen, all the PAT, SAT, and CWT files that you transferred from the Printer Action Tables Diskette to the System Diskette, or to the hard disk, will be displayed at the bottom of the screen. If you transfer more than 16 of these files, you will have to scroll through the list to see them all. Before you can print a document, you will have to enter the name of the PAT file you want to use in the Printer Action Table field, the name of the SAT file you want to use in the Sheet Feeder Action Table field, and the name of the CWT file you want to use in the Char Translate/Width Table field.

CONNECTING TO A SERIAL OR PARALLEL PORT

The two forms of communication between a printer and a computer are parallel and serial, and each requires its own kind of port into the computer. Most printers communicate with the computer through a parallel port, but a few communicate through a serial port. The easiest way to find out which method of communication your system uses is to connect the printer to your computer and see which connection works. You will have to print through the Document Print Options screen (for a shortcut, use Hot Print, Ctrl-PrtSc), and in most cases you can quickly discover the communications method appropriate to your printer by experimenting with the P and S settings in the (P)arallel/(S)erial/(F)ile/, (L)ist/(A)uxiliary/(C)onsole field.

If you have just one port on your computer marked *printer*, then you should only have to switch between P and S to find the right one. If you have ports marked *serial* and *parallel*, then you will have to switch printer cable connections as you try the P and S settings. If you still cannot get your printer to print, you should check your system settings. You can do this at the system prompt. Place your System Diskette in drive A and type

    MODE LPT3: = COM1

and press Return. If the screen message is

    LPT3:redirected to Com1

or

    LPT3: = COM1...Resident portion of MODE installed

then your printer communicates in parallel with your computer.

If you see the message

    Illegal Device Name

or

    Bad command or file name

then your printer probably communicates serially with your computer. Double-check this possibility by typing the command

    LPT3: = COM2

and pressing Return. If the command is redirected, or MODE is installed, then the printer does communicate serially with the computer.

DESIGNING PRINTER FILES

You can also design your own printer files. I do not recommend that you do this if you have no experience with programming. You need to know what ASCII and hexadecimal files contain, as well as other printer terms such as tokens. Using these and other tools, it is possible to create custom PAT, SAT, and CWT files.

Begin at the MultiMate Advantage II Boot-up menu (Figure 8.5), and select

3)Utilities and Conversions

The light bar should appear over the first option

Printer Tables Editor

so just press F10. The Printer Tables Editor screen should appear, which looks like Figure B.2. Pressing F10 on this screen will take you into the Printer Action Tables screen that allows you to edit, create, or delete a file, as shown in Figure B.3.

If you press F10 when the light bar is on the first selection, the Edit an Old File screen will appear, as shown in Figure B.4. It is on this screen that you select a PAT file to edit by moving the light bar over the appropriate PAT file and then pressing F10. As an example, if you highlight EPSONLQ and then press F10, it will move you into the Edit Printer Action Table screen for EPSONLQ, as shown in Figure B.5. You can move the light bar using the cursor keys to select any feature listed on this screen for editing.

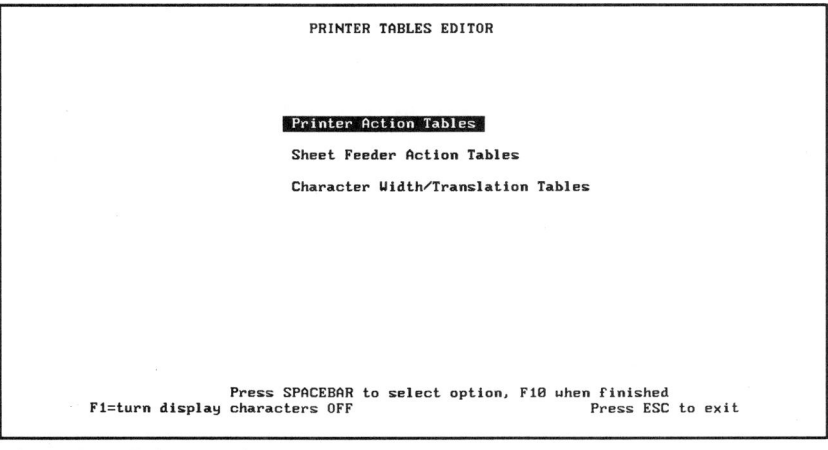

```
                      PRINTER TABLES EDITOR



                      Printer Action Tables
                    Sheet Feeder Action Tables
                  Character Width/Translation Tables






               Press SPACEBAR to select option, F10 when finished
         F1=turn display characters OFF                  Press ESC to exit
```

Figure B.2: Printer Tables Editor screen

The options on this screen serve up additional screens that apply to editing PAT, SAT, and CWT files. The instructions on these screens are self-explanatory, and you can navigate through them without further instruction, provided you already know the effects of various printer codes.

Creating Printer Files

If you select Create a New File, you will enter the Create a New File screen, as shown in Figure B.6. In the field after FILE:, enter the

```
                        PRINTER ACTION TABLES




                        Edit An Old File
                        Create A New File
                        Delete A File




            Press SPACEBAR to select option, F10 when finished
                        Press ESC to exit
```

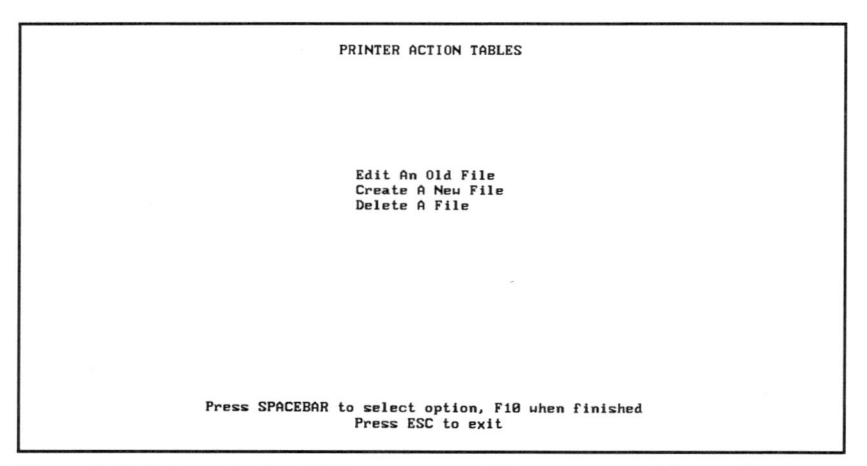

Figure B.3: Printer Action Tables screen to edit, create, or delete a file.

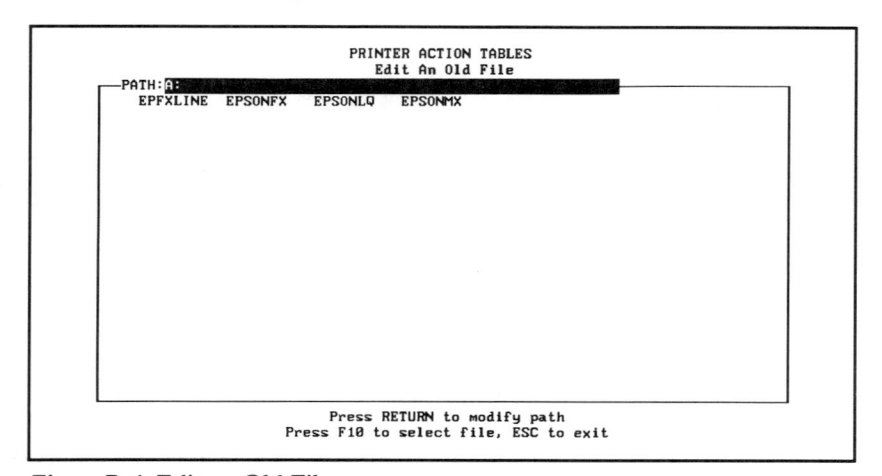

```
                        PRINTER ACTION TABLES
                            Edit An Old File
  ─PATH: A:
         EPFXLINE   EPSONFX    EPSONLQ    EPSONMX











                    Press RETURN to modify path
                 Press F10 to select file, ESC to exit
```

Figure B.4: Edit an Old File screen

name of the PATs that you want to create. Note that creating a PAT file from scratch requires a high level of programming skill.

DELETING PRINTER FILES

If you select Delete a File on the Printer Action Table screen shown in Figure B.3, the screen shown in Figure B.7 will appear. The first file name will be highlighted, but you can move the highlighting over other file names using the cursor keys. When the file

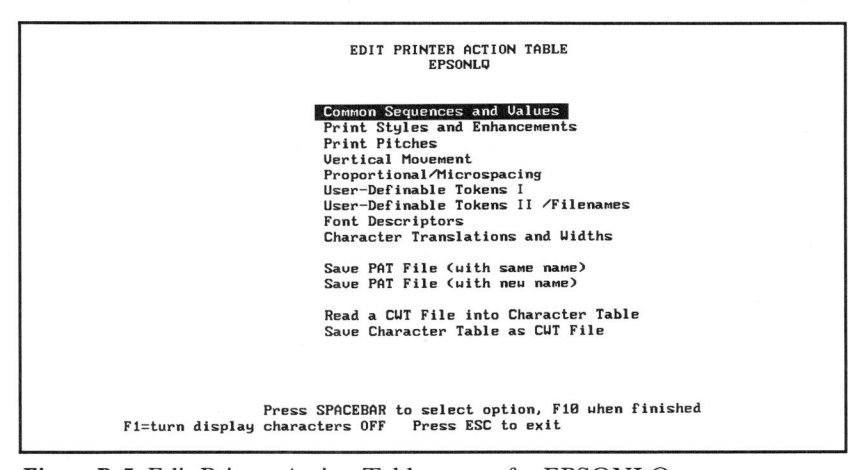

```
                    EDIT PRINTER ACTION TABLE
                            EPSONLQ

                    Common Sequences and Values
                    Print Styles and Enhancements
                    Print Pitches
                    Vertical Movement
                    Proportional/Microspacing
                    User-Definable Tokens I
                    User-Definable Tokens II /Filenames
                    Font Descriptors
                    Character Translations and Widths

                    Save PAT File (with same name)
                    Save PAT File (with new name)

                    Read a CWT File into Character Table
                    Save Character Table as CWT File


             Press SPACEBAR to select option, F10 when finished
       F1=turn display characters OFF   Press ESC to exit
```

Figure B.5: Edit Printer Action Table screen for EPSONLQ

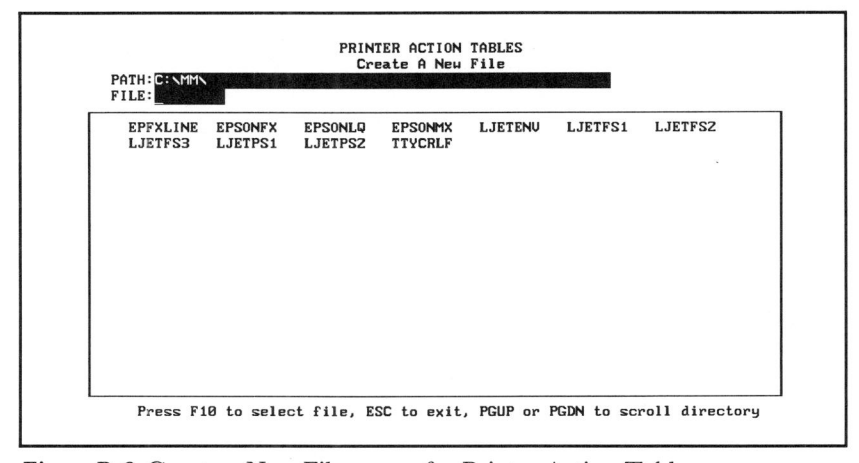

```
                         PRINTER ACTION TABLES
                           Create A New File
       PATH: C:\MM\
       FILE:

         EPFXLINE   EPSONFX   EPSONLQ   EPSONMX   LJETENV   LJETFS1   LJETFS2
         LJETFS3    LJETPS1   LJETPS2   TTYCRLF











         Press F10 to select file, ESC to exit, PGUP or PGDN to scroll directory
```

Figure B.6: Create a New File screen for Printer Action Tables

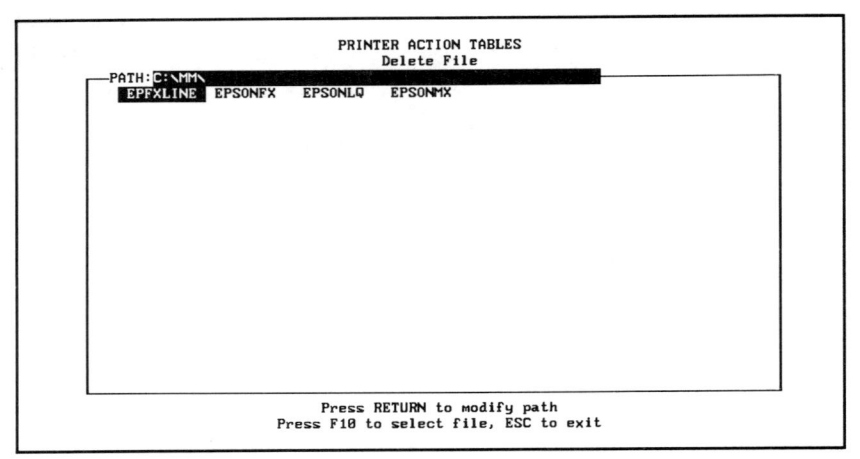

```
                       PRINTER ACTION TABLES
                            Delete File
   ┌PATH: C:\MM\
   │  EPFXLINE   EPSONFX    EPSONLQ    EPSONMX




                    Press RETURN to modify path
                 Press F10 to select file, ESC to exit
```

Figure B.7: Delete File screen for Printer Action Tables

you want to delete is highlighted, press F10. The prompt

> **ARE YOU SURE YOU WANT TO DELETE FILE?**
> **YES NO**

will appear at the bottom of the screen. YES will be highlighted as the default, and if you press F10, the file name highlighted will be deleted. If you do not want to delete that file, highlight NO with the Space bar and press F10 to return to the Printer Action Tables screen menu.

Appendix C

Summary of Command and Key Functions

THIS APPENDIX LISTS ALL THE COMMANDS AVAILable to you in MultiMate Advantage II and the keys that generate them. Table C.1 lists the commands in alphabetical order and shows the key or keys matched to them. Table C.2 lists the keys in alphabetical order and shows the commands that they generate.

COMMANDS AND THEIR KEYS	
COMMAND	KEY(S)
Alternate Keyboard	Alt-K
Backspace	← or Backspace key
Backwards Function key, On-File	F2
Bold Print	Alt-Z
Case Significance	Alt-G
Center	F3
Column Calculations	Ctrl-F4
Column Mode	Shift-F3
Column Sort	Shift-F3, then F5
Comments, add	Ctrl-[
Copy	F8
Copy External	Shift-F8
Create Document	Alt-2
Cursor Change Rate, decrease	Shift-(Hyphen)
Cursor Change Rate, increase	Shift- +
Cursor Down	↓
Cursor Left	←
Cursor Right	→
Cursor Up	↑

Table C.1: Commands and Their Keys

Command	Key(s)
Decimal Tab	Shift-F4
Delete	Delete
Delete Character	Minus (–) on keypad
Document Handler	Alt-6
Document Reorganization	Ctrl-F2
DOS Access	Ctrl-2
Double Underscore	Ctrl –
Draft Print	Alt-D
Edit a Document	Alt-1
End of Page	Ctrl-End
End of Screen	End
Endnotes	Ctrl-J
Enhanced Print	Alt-N
Escape	Escape key
Footer	Alt-F
Footnote	Alt-V
Footnote separator, change	Alt-H
Footnote separator, edit	Alt-F
Format Change	F9
Format Current	Shift-F9
Format Page	Alt-F9
Format System	Ctrl-F9
Forwards Function key, On-File	F1
Go To (Page #)	F1
Go To Place Mark	Ctrl-F1
Hard Space	Alt-S
Header	Alt-H
Help	Shift-F1

Table C.1: Commands and Their Keys (continued)

Command	Key(s)
Home	Home key
Horizontal Addition	Ctrl-F3
Hot Print	Ctrl-PrtSc
Hyphen	Shift-F7
Hyphenation, automatic	Ctrl-F2, then Alt-2
Indent	F4
Insert	Insert key
Insert Character	Plus (+) key on keypad
Key Procedure, create	Ctrl-F5
Key Procedure, execute	Ctrl-F8
Key Procedure, pause	Ctrl-F6
Key Procedure, prompt	Ctrl-F7
Key Procedure, replay	Alt-R
Library	F5
Library Attachment	Shift-F5
Library Copy	Alt-J
Line Draw	Alt-E
Line Highlight	Alt-F6
Merge	Alt-M
Merge Print	Alt-5
Move	F7
Next Page	Ctrl-PgDn
Next Word	Ctrl-→
Page Break	F2
Page Combine	Shift-F2
Page Down	PgDn
Page Length	Alt-F2

Table C.1: Commands and Their Keys (continued)

Command	Key(s)
Page Up	PgUp
Paragraph Highlight	Alt-F8
Pause Print	Alt-P
Place Mark, clear	Alt-Y
Place Mark, set	Alt-F1
Preview Mode, current page	Alt-I
Preview Mode, multiple pages	Alt-3
Previous Page	Ctrl-PgUp
Previous Word	Ctrl-←
Print Bold	Alt-Z
Print Control	Alt-4
Print Current Document	Alt-3
Print Enhanced	Alt-N
Print Font	Alt-C, then A to Z
Print Pitch	Alt-C, then 1 to 9
Print Shadow	Alt-X
Printer Cancel	Ctrl-Break
Printer Control Codes	Alt-A
Printer Pause	Alt-P
Pull-Down Menus	Alt-L
Repagination	Ctrl-F2, then Alt-1
Replace	Shift-F6
Return	Return key
Return to DOS	Alt-9
Required Page Break	Alt-B
Row Calculations	Ctrl-F3
Save	F10
Screen Print	Shift-PrtSc

Table C.1: Commands and Their Keys (continued)

Command	Key(s)
Scroll Left	Alt-F3
Scroll Right	Alt-F4
Search	F6
Section Numbering	Ctrl-F2, then Alt-3
Sentence Highlight	Alt-F7
Shadow Print	Alt-X
Spell Check	Ctrl-F10
Spell Edit	Alt-F10
Strikeout Character	Alt-0
Subscript	Alt-W
Superscript	Alt-Q
System and Document Defaults	Alt-7
System Print Commands	&command&
Tab	Tab key
Tab, decimal	Shift-F4
Table of Contents, create	Ctrl-F2, then Alt-4
Thesaurus	Alt-T
Top of Page	Ctrl-Home
Underline	Shift –
Underline, alphanumerically	Alt – (equal sign)
Underline, double	Ctrl –
Underline Text	Alt –
Undo Delete	* (asterisk on keypad)
Word Highlight	Alt-F6

Table C.1: Commands and Their Keys (continued)

KEYS AND THEIR FUNCTIONS	
KEY(S)	**COMMAND**
* (on keypad)	Undo deletion
←	Backspace
↓	Cursor down
←	Cursor left
→	Cursor right
↑	Cursor up
Alt- = (equal sign)	Underline text alphanumerically as the text is entered
Alt- -(hyphen)	Underline text, but not spaces or punctuation marks, as the text is entered
Alt-1	Edit a document by going directly from current document
Alt-2	Create a document by going directly from current document
Alt-3	Preview multiple pages
Alt-4	Access print control menus directly from current document screen
Alt-5	Begin merge print from current document screen
Alt-6	Access document handling screens from current document
Alt-9	Return to DOS from current document screen
Alt-A	Insert printer control codes
Alt-B	Insert required page break
Alt-C	Change print pitch (followed by a number) or change print font (followed by a letter)

Table C.2: Keys and Their Functions

Key(s)	Command
Alt-D	Change document print mode to draft print
Alt-E	Begin to draw lines
Alt-F	Insert a footer
Alt-G	Change case significance
Alt-H	Insert a header
Alt-I	Preview current page
Alt-J	Copy a section of text from a document into a library as an entry
Alt-K	Access alternate keyboards
Alt-L	Access pull-down menus
Alt-M	Insert merge code
Alt-N	Change document print mode to enhanced print
Alt-O	Insert strikeout characters
Alt-P	Cause the printer to pause at a specified point inside a document
Alt-Q	Begin superscript text
Alt-R	Replay a key procedure
Alt-S	Insert a hard space
Alt-T	Access thesaurus information
Alt-V	Insert a footnote
Alt-W	Begin subscript text
Alt-X	Change document print mode to shadow print
Alt-Y	Clear a place mark
Alt-Z	Change document print mode to bold print
Alt-F1	Set a place mark
Alt-F2	Set page length

Table C.2: Keys and Their Functions (continued)

Key(s)	Command
Alt-F3	Place cursor on first character of current text line
Alt-F4	Place cursor on last character of current text line
Alt-F5	Highlight a complete word
Alt-F6	Highlight a complete text line
Alt-F7	Highlight a complete sentence
Alt-F8	Highlight a complete paragraph
Alt-F9	Insert a copy of the current page format line in the text of the current page
Alt-F10	Begin spell edit
Backspace key	Move cursor backwards
Ctrl –	Insert double underline beneath text
Ctrl-[	Add comments
Ctrl-←	Move cursor to first character of previous word
Ctrl-→	Move cursor to first character of next word
Ctrl-Break	Cancel printing
Ctrl-End	Move cursor to end of current page
Ctrl-2	Access DOS directly
Ctrl-F1	Go to specified place mark
Ctrl-F2	Reorganize a document
Ctrl-F3	Perform calculations on row of numbers
Ctrl-F4	Perform calculations on column of numbers
Ctrl-F5	Create a key procedure
Ctrl-F6	Insert a pause in a key procedure
Ctrl-F7	Insert a prompt in a key procedure
Ctrl-F8	Begin to execute a key procedure

Table C.2: Keys and Their Functions (continued)

KEY(S)	COMMAND
Ctrl-F9	Insert a copy of the system format line in the text of the current document
Ctrl-F10	Begin to check spelling
Ctrl-Home	Move cursor to top of current page
Ctrl-J	Insert an endnote or footnote
Ctrl-PgDn	Move cursor to top of next page
Ctrl-PgUp	Move cursor to bottom of previous page
Ctrl-PrtSc	Print current screen while remaining in document
Delete key	Delete text
End key	Move cursor to end of current screen
Escape key	Escape various functions and procedures
F1	Go to a specified page number, or (in On-File) Forwards Function key
F2	Insert a page break, or (in On-File) Backwards Function key
F3	Center text
F4	Indent text
F5	Begin to use a library
F6	Search for specific features within a document
F7	Move text within a document
F8	Copy text within a document
F9	Change features of any format line
F10	Save current document and exit to the main menu
Home key	Move cursor to top of current screen
Insert key	Insert space or character
Minus (−)/keypad	Delete space or character

Table C.2: Keys and Their Functions (continued)

APP. C

Key(s)	Command
PgDn	Move down 19 lines of text
PgUp	Move up 19 lines of text
Plus (+)/keypad	Insert space or character
Return key	Insert hard carriage return
Shift –	Underline text character by character
Shift-F1	Access help information and context-sensitive help instructions
Shift-F2	Combine two adjacent pages
Shift-F3	Begin column mode
Shift-F4	Insert a decimal tab
Shift-F5	Attach a library to a document
Shift-F6	Replace selected features in a document
Shift-F7	Insert soft hyphen
Shift-F8	Copy text to an external document
Shift-F9	Insert a copy of the current format line within text
Shift-PrtSc	Print screen
Tab key	Insert a tab mark

Table C.2: Keys and Their Functions (continued)

Appendix D

Comparing Program Versions

MULTIMATE ADVANTAGE II IS AN ENHANCED VERsion of its predecessor, MultiMate Advantage. Both are direct descendents of the MultiMate line of word-processing programs. The most recent version of plain MultiMate was 3.30. The name Advantage was added in late 1985 for version 3.50, and many significant features were added to the program. The memory requirement was increased from 256K for MultiMate 3.30 to 320K for MultiMate Advantage. For MultiMate Advantage II, it has been increased to 384K.

As a step up from plain MultiMate Advantage, Advantage II includes several important new features, plus many smaller enhancements. The new features are listed in Table D.1, and the enhancements are listed in Table D.2.

Readers who are upgrading from a version of plain MultiMate to MultiMate Advantage II should be aware of the changes that were added to the original version of Advantage. These features and enhancements are listed in Tables D.3 and D.4.

Editing Features

    Automatic and adjustable hyphenation from keyboard

    Bidirectional search

    Column manipulation (sorting and math)

    Cursor movement rate adjustable from keyboard

    Document reorganization

    Footnote separator, setting and editing

    Maximum line count per page increased

    Math

        division

        multiplication

        exponents

Table D.1: New features in MultiMate Advantage II

    percentages
    Program speed increase

On-File Features
    Card count per box increased
    Go to card
    Write card to MultiMate document

Printing Features
    Font support increased
    Change fonts within document
    Print Document Summary screen with document
    Number of printer tables increased

Utility Features
    Document cataloging increased
    Faster file conversions
    ASCII file direct import
    Bypass Startup Screens
    Comments
    DOS Access
    dBASE Direct Merge
    Document Mode
    Endnotes
    ID Program
    Full Path Support
    Preview Printing Mode
    Pull-Down Menus
    Quick Start
    Undo Delete

Table D.2: Enhancements in MultiMate Advantage II

Thesaurus
Section Numbering
Line and Box Drawing
Table of Contents
On-File Information Handling
GraphLink

Table D.3: New features in MultiMate Advantage

Editing Features
    Adjustable cursor speed
    Search case-sensitive text
    Automatic footnotes
Text Formatting
    Column mode for text
Print Features
    Hot Print one-page document
    Typewriter mode
    Keyboard merge
Spelling Dictionary
    Legal terms added
Custom Dictionary
    Edit, reorganize, view, and delete
Library
    Copy text from separate document into library
Merge with Other Software
    Sequential ASCII data file merge

Table D.4: Enhancements in MultiMate Advantage

APPENDIX E

DISK UTILITIES

MULTIMATE ADVANTAGE II CAN SHARE INFORMAtion with all the popular software programs. The two Conversion Diskettes supplied with the program contain the files to be used for file conversion.

If one of your files becomes damaged, you can try to retrieve the lost information through Advantage II's Document Recovery utility. To protect your files from such data loss, you should have the program create document backup copies automatically, as described in this appendix. Then if an original file is damaged, you can retrieve the backup copies.

CONVERTING FILES

Incorporating information from files in other software programs is an important capability for a program that operates in the modern office, where there might be half a dozen software programs in frequent daily use. These programs include spreadsheets and databases, as well as other word-processing programs creating documents of their own. It is possible, using the Advanced Utilities Diskette, to exchange file information between these other programs and MultiMate Advantage II. Such an exchange can occur in both directions, importing foreign files for use in Advantage II documents, and exporting information from Advantage II documents into foreign files.

All computer files are written in a format that is specific to the manufacturer of the program. MultiMate Advantage II is written in such a specific format, and you have to follow several steps when you import or export files. To start the import or export process, you must start at the MultiMate Advantage II Boot-up menu (Figure 8.5). Select

3)Utilities and Conversions

This will move you into the Advanced Utilities menu (Figure 8.6). The third option on this screen is File Conversion, so press the Space

APP. E

bar twice to highlight this option. Press F10 to move into the File Conversion screen (Figure E.1), which will appear next.

The first of two options on this screen, Convert Document(s), should be highlighted. Press F10 to begin the conversion procedure, and the Convert a Document screen, shown in Figure E.2, should appear. It is on this screen that you will perform all your conversions. This screen is divided into three sections: a top section where you designate source and destination file information; a middle section that displays convertible files according to file designations; and a bottom section offering a list of formats you can convert files from or to.

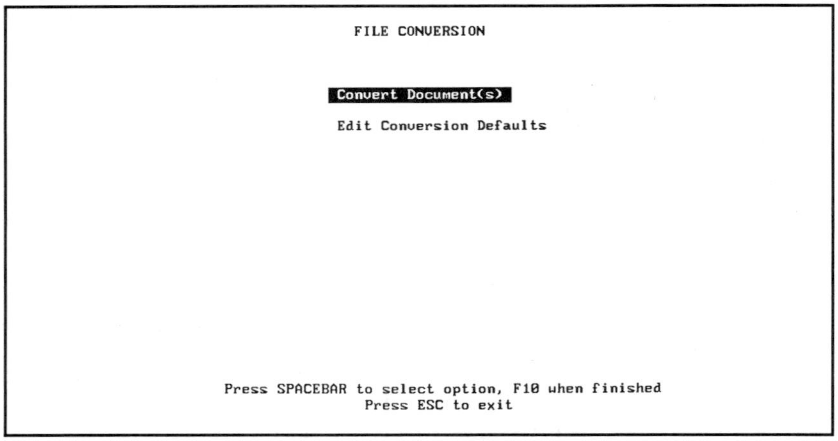

Figure E.1: File Conversion screen

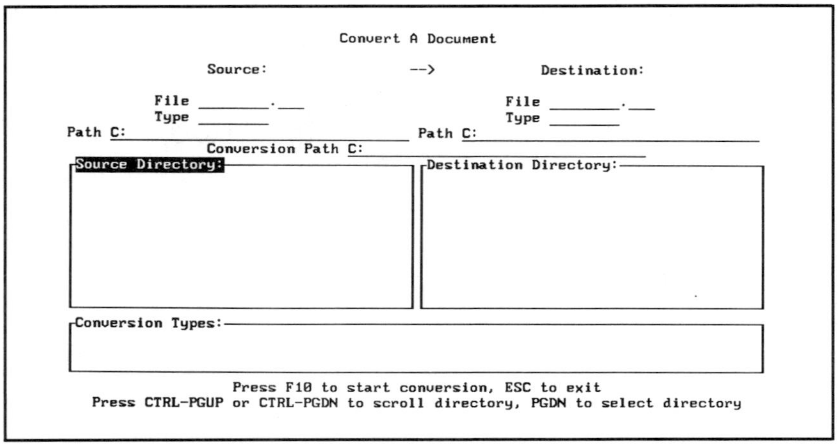

Figure E.2: Convert a Document screen

These three sections provide you with all the prompts and information you need to specify three things:

1. The name and location of the file you want to convert (the *source* file)
2. The name and location of the file you want the source file converted to (the *destination* file)
3. The type of format you want for the destination file

File names consist of up to 12 characters: the eight characters before the dot separator, and the three-character extension. You can see the file LETTER1.DOC as one of the documents listed in the Source Directory window in Figure E.2. The first seven characters are the name you gave the document, and the file extension .DOC was added by MultiMate Advantage II. Most formats require a special extension. When you convert files from one format to another, you will usually have to specify the correct extensions for both files. Some formats, such as ASCII, will accept any extension.

You can convert files on the same disk or on different disks. If you convert a file on the same disk, you will have to give the destination file a different name, if only a different extension, than the source file, or else the source file will be copied over with the converted file.

SOURCE AND DESTINATION FILES

When the Convert a Document screen first appears, the cursor will be blinking in the Source File field. This field is divided into two parts, separated by the dot, where you enter the first part of the file name and the extension. You must select a file name that is showing in the Source Directory window. If you enter the name of a file that does not exist on the Source drive and fill in the rest of the information as indicated, the error message

    ERROR: Source file does not exist

will appear. The Source Directory window can display up to 24 file names. If your source disk holds more than that, you can scroll through the complete list by first pressing the Space bar, and when

Source Directory is highlighted, pressing Ctrl-PgDn or Ctrl-PgUp to move through groups of 24 file names.

After you type the name of the file to be converted, if it is less than eight characters long, space over to the first position after the dot. This is where you enter the file extension. Once you've entered a complete source file name, press Return, and the cursor will move down to the Source Type field. This is where you enter the abbreviation for the format of the source file. In most cases, the file extension will match the conversion type, or at least suggest which conversion type it is. Conversion types are explained later in this appendix. Once you've entered the proper conversion type, press Return to move the cursor down to the Source Path field.

The path can consist of only the drive designation, or a drive and subdirectory name, if you are working with a file located in a subdirectory. You will probably use subdirectories only if you are working with a hard disk (see Appendix A). In any case, first enter the drive designation: A, B, or C. Advantage II automatically adds the colon. If you are going to access a subdirectory, enter a backslash (\) immediately after the drive designation, and then type the name of the subdirectory.

Pressing Return moves the cursor to the Destination File field. Enter information regarding the destination document here. Since you are going to be creating this file, you should make sure that a file with the same name does not currently exist on the disk in the destination drive. You can scroll through the list of files on the destination disk the same way you scrolled through the source directory list—with the Space bar and Ctrl-PgUp or Ctrl-PgDn.

As an example, if you wanted to convert the file LETTER1.DOC to an ASCII format, you would fill in the following information:

    Source:

FileLETTER1.DOC
Type.MM
PathA:

and then enter the information for the destination file in this manner:

    Destination:

FileLETTER1.DOC

>   TypeASCII
>   PathB:

The Destination Type field is blank because converting to ASCII format does not require an extension.

Conversion Path

Pressing Return after entering B for the Destination Path will place the cursor in the Conversion Path field. This is where you enter the drive designation where your conversion overlay files are maintained. As soon as you enter the correct drive and press Return, the conversion files available to you on that drive will appear in the window called Conversion Types at the bottom of the screen. You can convert files only to one of the formats in this window. These files are also showing in the Destination Directory window, since the Advanced Utilities Diskette is in drive A. Conversion files have the extension OV1 or OV2. If your system has two floppy disk drives and a hard disk, you can specify drives A, B, and C in the three path fields on this screen.

For the example, enter A:ASCII in the Conversion Path field. When all the information in each field has been entered, you are ready to begin the conversion process. Press F10 to begin, and the prompts

>   * * *SOURCE CONVERSION BEING LOADED* * *
>   * * *DESTINATION CONVERSION BEING LOADED* * *
>   * * *CONVERSION IN PROGRESS* * *

will be displayed as the procedure moves through the steps described. It can take up to a minute or more to convert a long file. When the conversion is complete, the message

>   Use F10 to start conversion
>   Use ESC to escape

will appear at the bottom of the screen. This is the same message that was in place before you started the conversion.

Converting a file from a foreign format into the Advantage II document can be handled in an identical manner. Make sure that you use an acceptable Advantage II extension name, such as .DOC (documents) or .TOC (table of contents).

CONVERSION FORMATS

A variety of conversion format files are included with MultiMate Advantage II. Because of the large file sizes of these conversion programs, they are distributed among the several diskettes you received in your MultiMate Advantage II package. A brief description of each type will help you to understand when to use each one.

ASCII

ASCII stands for American Standard Code for Information Interchange. All microcomputers can convert their files into straight ASCII code, but the converted files will lose all formatting codes. No extension is necessary for ASCII files. This is the most common format for exchanging information between differently formatted programs. You can convert files from ASCII to Advantage II format, as well as convert Advantage II documents into ASCII.

COMM

COMM files, with the extension .CMM, are used to send files over communications links, such as the telephone system. You can convert Advantage II files to and from the COMM format.

DIF

DIF stands for Data Interchange Format, and such files have the .DIF extension. Most spreadsheet programs, such as SuperCalc3 and SuperCalc4 and some Lotus 1-2-3 files, use this format for presenting their statistical and financial data. You can only convert DIF files to Advantage II documents, not vice versa.

DCA

DCA stands for Document Content Architecture, and such files have the .RF or .RFT extension. This format was designed by IBM to standardize the interchange of information between microcomputers and its minicomputers and mainframes. You can convert Advantage II documents both to and from documents in DCA format.

GSA

The GSA format was created by the General Services Administration for standardizing files used by branches of the U.S. government. This format has been adopted by the U.S. Navy as Navy DIF files. Advantage II files can import GSA files and be exported to them. No file extension is necessary for GSA files.

Just Write

Just Write refers to an abbreviated word-processing package designed by MultiMate International Corporation. The format extension is .JW, and you can convert Advantage II documents to and from this format.

Lotus WKS

Lotus 1-2-3 files have the extension .WKS or .WK1. You can only convert a 1-2-3 file into an Advantage II document, not vice versa. Since a Lotus spreadsheet can contain many complicated symbols, you might experience some data loss or distortion, and I recommend that you first convert 1-2-3 files to ASCII format, then into MultiMate Advantage II format.

Wang WPS

Wang word processors create files with the extension .WPS. Advantage II documents can import these files as well as be exported to them.

EDITING FORMAT CONVERSION DEFAULTS

Some of the conversion files provided with Advantage II can be modified for features such as line length, end-of-page markers, line spacing, page numbering, and other features that affect the format of the printed page. You can select the second option on the File Conversion screen by pressing the Space bar once and highlighting

Edit Conversion Defaults

and then pressing F10. The Edit Conversion Defaults screen (Figure E.3) will appear. This screen will display the conversion files resident on the disk in the drive shown. You can change this drive designation, and enter a subdirectory name if necessary, to access the conversion files in a different drive. Press the cursor arrow keys to move a light bar over the conversion file you want to edit, and then press F10. With some conversion files, the message

> No Defaults for Selected Conversion

will appear. This means that the conversion file cannot be edited. Press Escape to return to the Edit Conversion Defaults screen.

If the file can be edited, the appropriate list of features and the default settings will appear on the screen. You should be familiar with the results of each setting before you begin to change them. An incorrect setting can create havoc with the file it tries to convert incorrectly.

DOCUMENT RECOVERY

The fifth utility listed on the Advanced Utilities menu is called Document Recovery. This utility, which is not as comprehensive as similarly named programs in Norton Utilities and Mace Software, can help you resurrect some, if not all, of the data in a damaged file.

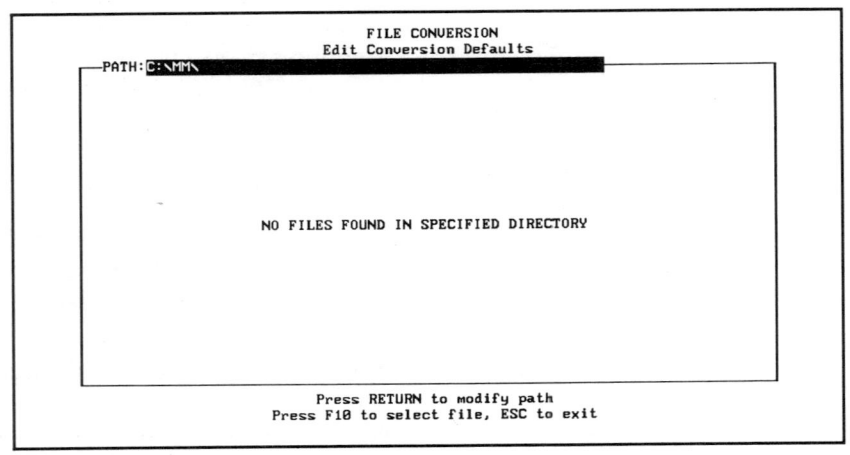

Figure E.3: Edit Conversion Defaults screen

Actually, Advantage II's Document Recovery utility may be more useful than these other more popular recovery programs because MultiMate Advantage II files are stored in a unique fashion; each page is a separate file within the larger file that contains all the pages of a single document. This makes it possible to lose individual pages in the middle of what appears to be a single file. The MultiMate Advantage II recovery utility is designed to work with the program's special storage system. Mace Utilities provides a special recovery procedure for MultiMate files, but you have to resurrect the file page by page. These pages, if created and edited at various times, might not be sequentially ordered.

To access the Document Recovery utility in Advantage II, bring up the Advanced Utilities main menu and press the ↓ four times so that the light bar is over Document Recovery. Press F10, and the Document Recovery screen, shown in Figure E.4, will appear.

The cursor won't appear on this screen until you press Return. Then it will appear blinking under the drive designation in the Path field. Enter the drive and any pathnames to direct this utility to the directory or subdirectory that contains the file you want to restore. After you've entered this information, press Return. The list of files on that drive and directory will be displayed, with the first file now showing in reverse video. Move the reverse-video bar onto the name of the file you want to restore using the appropriate arrow keys, and

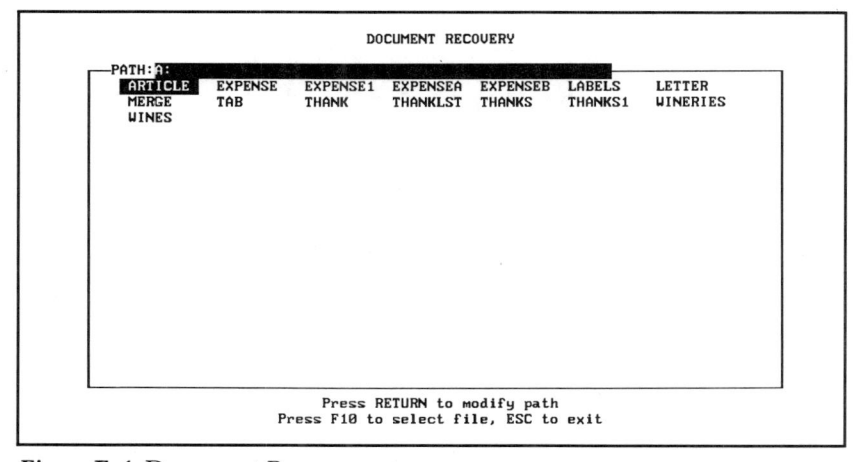

Figure E.4: Document Recovery screen

press F10 to begin the restoration process. The prompt

> **WORKING**

will appear at the bottom of the screen. When the process is complete (usually in a few moments) the prompt

> Document Recovered
> Press any key to continue

will replace the previous prompt.

This second prompt doesn't always mean that the document is in fact recovered. It may be only partially recovered, or not recovered at all. This utility does what it can, and then calls the process complete. Files can become corrupted in many different ways, and it takes a full-fledged recovery program to check all the possibilities. The files that are most easily restored are those that bring up these two prompts:

> -ERROR: UNABLE TO LOAD ENTIRE PAGE
> - End of File Has Been Encountered - Data May Have Been Lost

when you try to edit a file.

AUTOMATIC BACKUP FILES

One way to avoid having to try to recover a file is to keep automatic backups of your important work. You can create backups for all files by changing the setting in the Backup Before Editing Document field on the Edit System Defaults screen, or you can backup selected files by changing the same setting on individual Modify Document Defaults screens.

Restoring Backup Files

The seventh selection on the Document Management screen (Figure 3.5) allows you restore a backup file and make it an original file by changing its file name extension. You can make this change by using the Restore a Backed-Up Document screen, shown in Figure E.5.

An original MultiMate document file has the extension .DOC, and a backup copy has the extension .DBK. All you have to do is

```
                    RESTORE A BACKED-UP DOCUMENT
        Drive:C               Document:
        Path: \MM\


        Approximately 13299712 characters [05319 Page(s)] available on C:









          Press F10 when finished, ESC to exit, PGDN to switch drives
          Press CTRL-HOME to select default path, CTRL-END for next path
                  Press F6 to display document directory           S:↓ N:↓
```

Figure E.5: The Restore a Backed-up Document screen

enter the name of the file you want to restore, without the extension, and Advantage II will make the changes for you.

You can also change a backup copy to an original by using the RENAME command at the DOS prompt. Using this procedure, you must enter every character in the backup file name.

INDEX

Acceptable decimal tab, 91
Access DOS, 192–193
Additional Print Functions menu, 278
Advanced Utilities
  file conversion, 390–396
  to create key procedures, 201–203
  to delete key procedures, 203–204
  for document recovery, 396
  to edit key procedures, 194–201
  modifying console defaults, 348–352
Advanced Utilities menu, 195
Alphanumeric underlining, 115
Alternate keyboards, 282–284
Arrow keys, 20–22
ASCII file, creating, 394
Automatic backup files, 398–399
Automatic page breaks, 91

Background printing, 150
Backspace, destructive, 5, 356
Backup before editing, 91
Backup files, 398–399
Boot-up menu, 194
Bound columns, 228–232
  format line, 229
Boilerplate, 157
Bold print, 107
Bypass Document Summary screen, 42
Bypassing main menu, 278–279

Calculations
  addition, 249–250
  division, 254–255
  exponents, 255
  multiplication, 252–254
  percentages, 255–256
  subtraction, 250–252
Caps Lock key, 3
Case-sensitive searching, 59
Case Significance keys, 59
Centering, 99
Character Translate/Width Table field, 150
Character width/translation files, 364–365
Colors on console, 350–352
Columnar text
  copying, 236–238
  creating, 227–234
  deleting, 244–245
  editing, 235
  highlighting, 235–236
  inserting, 237–238
  moving, 241–242, 243–244
Column mode, 234
Columns
  bound, 228–232
  calculating math, 248
  cursor movements, 229
  decimal tab, 245–248

end column group symbol, 234
hard column break symbol, 232
line and box drawing, 256-260
snake, 233-234, 242-243
snake, balancing, 242-243
Command summary, 373-377
Comments, 129-132
Converting files, 389-393
Converting formats, 394-395
Copying columns, 236-237
Copying text
  of entire document, 52-54
  externally, 48-51
  within a document, 45-46
Counting words misspelled, 71
Create a New Document screen, 9-12
Currency symbol, 93
  Pound symbol, 284
Current format line, 101
Cursor acceleration, 350, 357
Cursor indicators
  in documents, 18
  in On File cards, 325
Cursor movement, 20-23
  in columns, 229
  in merge data files, 300
Cursor speed, 23-24
Custom dictionaries
  adding a new word, 83-84
  building, 77
  creating, 80-81
  converting, 352-353
  deleting, 81
  deleting words, 78-79, 85
  editing, 82-85
  modifying, 82-83
  reorganizing, 85
  viewing a word, 84-85

Date and time indicators, 152

Date standard, printing, 92-93
dBASE merge, 311
Decimal tabs, 91
  in columns, 245-248
  with section numbering, 220-222
Delete key, 6
Deleting text and screen symbols, 25-26, 46-47
Deleting documents, 55-56
Deleting words from dictionary, 78-79
Destination document, 48
Destination files, 391-393
Dictionaries, 77-85
  adding words, 76, 83-84
  deleting words, 78-79
  see also Custom dictionaries
Direct dBASE merge, 311
Displaying spaces as dots, 356
Document Management screen, 51-57
Document mode, 38, 356
Document Print Options screen, 141
Document recovery, 396-398
Document screen, 17-19
Document startup screens, 92
Document Summary screen, 12-14
DOS commands
  CD, 347
  COPY, 345, 348, 364-365
  DEL, 353
  DIR, 345, 353
  FORMAT, 343-344
  MD, 347
  PRINT, 352
  using wild-card characters, 345
Double underscore, 107-108
Draft print, 106-107, 147

Edit a Document screen, 42
Edit System Defaults screen, 78
Editing custom dictionaries, 82-85

Editing drive defaults, 354–356
Editing format conversion defaults, 395–396
Editing key procedure files, 193–201
Editing library entries, 164–170
Editing system defaults, 356–357
Editing system format line, 354
End of page, 23
End of screen, 23
End column group symbol, 234
Endnotes, 93, 121–126
   changing to footnotes, 126
   creating, 125–126
Enhanced print, 107, 147
Escape key, 4
Escaping changes, 29
External copy, 48–51

Fields, 10
File conversion, 390–396
Flags. *See* Place marks
Fonts
   default, 152
   print, 144–146
Footers, 126–129
   empty, 128
   first page number in, 150
   page numbers, 128
   text- and page-associated, 92
Footnotes, 93, 121–126
   changing to endnotes, 126
   creating, 121–125
   deleting, 125
   editing, 125
   format line, 125
   numbering, 124
Foreground printing, 150
Format conversions, 389–393
Format lines, 18–19, 95–104
   in bound columns, 229

current, 101–102
deleting, 102
for library entries, 167–168
page, 101–102
replacing, 103–104
searching for, 102–103
in snake columns, 229, 234
system, 97–101
Formatting disks, 342–344
Function keys, 2

Germanic keyboard, 282
Go to page number, 118–119
Go to place mark, 114
Graphic keyboards, 282–284

Hard carriage-return symbol, 9
Hard spaces, 109
Headers
   canceling, 128
   creating, 126–128
   empty, 128
   first page number in, 150
   page numbers, 128
   text- and page-associated, 92
Help
   context-sensitive, 32
   exiting, 33
   from main menu, 30–32
Highlighting, 43–44
Hot Print, 137–138
Hyphenation
   automatic, 112–113
   case-by-case, 110
   user selected, 111–112
   zone width, 110–112
Hyphens, soft, 109–110

ID program, 6
Importing non-MultiMate files, 389–393

Indenting text, 100
Inserting characters and words
   in column mode, 237-238
   in standard document, 26-29
Insert key, 5, 356
   protected mode for columns, 237
Installing MultiMate Advantage, 344-348

Justification, 151

Keyboard, 1-6
   special characters, 282-284
Key procedures
   building, 178-182
   building without text, 188-189
   Create a New File screen, 202
   creating in Advanced Utilities, 201-203
   deleting, 200, 203-204
   Edit an Old File screen, 196
   editing, 193-201
   error messages in, 181-183
   executing, 182-183
   executing during pause, 185-186
   file display, 198-199
   File Edit Utility screen, 197
   File Utility menu, 195
   pausing, 183-186
   prompting, 187-188
   renaming, 190-192
   replaying, 189
Key summary, 378-382

Layout option, 37
Libraries
   adding entries, 170-171
   attaching to documents, 162-163
   changing entry names of, 168-170
   copying entries in same document, 171-172
   copying from one document to another, 173
   creating, 157-162
   deleting, 173-174
   editing entries in, 164-170
   entries, 158-162
   format line for, 167-168
   inserting, 163-164
   names, 160-161
   printing copies of entries, 170
   status line for, 159
Line and box drawing
   in columns, 256-260
   in merge data files, 296-297
Line spacing, 97-98
Lines per page, 91
List documents, 266-269

Main menu, 7-9
   bypassing, 278-279
Margins
   left, 147-148
   right, 98-99
Math keyboard, 282
Memory requirements, 341
Menu-driven, 8
Merge data files
   adding records, 304-305
   creating records in, 298-299
   cursor movements in, 300
   data fields, 294-295
   default data fields, 295
   designing a template for, 291-293
   editing, 299-305
   labels, 294, 301-303
   line and box drawing, 296-297
   printing, 309-311
   prompts, 296
   renaming labels, 301-302
   selecting and unselecting, 308-309

INDEX

sorting records, 307–308
templates, 291–298
text entries in, 293–294
Merge documents, 264–266
Merge item names, 263
Merge printing
  canceling, 271
  from keyboard, 271–272
  of List documents, 266–269
  of merge data files, 309
  of Merge documents, 264–266
  with merge item names, 263–266
  of Result documents, 269–271
  symbol for, 313
Merge printing special commands in, 272–276
  End Repeat, 274
  Next, 274–276
  Omit if Blank, 272–273
  Repeat, 274
Merging with other databases, 311–316
  using random files, 314–315
  using sequential files, 311–314
Micro justification, 151
Mode of operation, 37
Modify console defaults, 348–352
Moving a document, 54–58
Moving text, 48
  in column mode, 241–244
MS-DOS command symbols, 10

Normal keyboard, special character set for, 282–284
Num Lock key, 3
Number of lines per page, 91
Number of original copies, 147
Numbering pages, 119–120
Numeric keypad, 2
Numeric section numbering, 93–94, 218–220

On File database
  Create and Add a Card screen, 325
  creating records, 322–327
  deleting cards, 330
  displaying cards, 330
  editing cards, 330
  index line, 324
  main menu, 324
  moving through card box, 330
  printing card information, 332
  searching and displaying cards, 328
  setting up, 320–322
  sorting cards, 330
  subject line, 324
  templates, 333–337
  utilities, 337–339
  working from DOS prompt, 329–330
Orphans, 90
Overwriting text, 25

Page, go to, 118–119
Page breaks, 91, 117
  automatic, 91
Page format line, 101–102
Page length, 152
Page numbering, 119–120, 146–147
  arbitrary, 120
  automatic, 119–120
Page formatting, 115–121, 356
Pages
  break, 118–119, 121
  combining, 117–118
  go to, 118–119
  length, 116
  numbers, 119–120
Paths, 347–348
Path field, 10
Pausing
  of printer, 141–143

while executing key procedures, 183–186
Place marks
  clearing, 76, 114
  go to, 114
  removing, 76
  setting, 72, 113
Pound symbol, 284
Preview printing, 138–139
Print commands, 151
Print date standard, 92–93
Print Document Summary screen, 140
Print fonts, 144–146
Print modes, 104–107
Print Parameters for Document screen, 146–152
Print pitch, 144
Printer action tables, 361–370
  copying, 364–365
  deleting, 369–370
  designing, 366–369
Print a Document screen, 140
Print date standard field, 152, 357
Print delay, 152
Print Document Summary screen, 151, 284–286
Print This Screen, 151
Print time and date, 92–93, 152, 357
Printer, how to stop, 141–143
Printing
  background vs. foreground, 150
  control codes for, 105–106
  Document Summary screen during, 284–286
  Hot Print, 137–138
  of merge data file records and templates, 309
  of On File card information, 332
  preview, 138–139

queue, 152
Quick Print, 136
stop, 141–143
typewriter modes in, 279–282
Productivity records, 13–14
Proportional spacing, 151
Pull-down menus, 8, 35–37
  for spell check, 72

Queue printing, 276–285
Quick Print, 136
Quit, 34

Recovering damaged documents, 396–398
Removing place marks, 76
Renaming documents, 57
Repaginating
  of standard documents, 120
Replacing text
  discretionary mode, 63–66
  escaping, 66
  format lines, 103–104
  global mode, 62–63
  showing changes, 66
Result documents, 269–271
Return key, 5
Return symbol, 19
Roman section numbering, 93, 209–218
Romance keyboard, 282

Saving documents, 34
Screen-driven, 319
Screen symbols, 105–106, 108
  revising and canceling, 109
Scroll Lock key, 3
Scrolling in DOS (Ctrl-S), 363
Searching
  of cards in On File, 328
  case-sensitive, 59

INDEX 407

Document Summary screen for, 286–288
format lines, 102–103
for text, 59-61
Section numbering
  assigning numbers, 214
  decimal tabs, 220–222
  editing, 218
  flush left, 212–215
  Numeric, 93–94, 218–220
  Roman, 94, 209–218
  symbol, 212
  tab indents, 215–218
Setting place marks, 72, 113
Setting up On File, 320–322
Shadow print, 107
Sheet feeder parameters, 150
Snake columns, 233–234, 242–243
Sorting text and numbers, 239–241
Source files, 391–393
Spaces as dots, 356
Spaces, hard, 109
Special keyboards, 282–284
Specialized fields, 150
Speed up movement through documents, 356–357
Spell Check a Document screen, 70
Spell Edit menu, 73
Spelling check, 69–72
  counting words misspelled, 70
  editing, 72–75
  escaping from, 71–72
Status lines
  for library entries, 159
  for standard documents, 18–19
Strikeout character, 108, 357
Strings, 59
Subdirectories, 10–11, 347–348
Subscripts, 108–109

Superscripts, 108–109
System format line, 97–101

Tab stops, 20, 98
Tab symbol, 20
Tables of contents
  creating, 222–229
  Document screen, 223
  editing, 224–225
Templates
  for merge data files, 291–298, 299–303
  for merge data files printing, 309–311
  for On File, 333–337
Text
  replacing, 59–61
  searching, 61–66
Thesaurus, 85–87
Time and date indicators, 129
Troubleshooting, 357–358
Typewriter printing modes, 279–282
  lines of text, 282
  single characters, 281

Underlining, 115
  double, 107–108
Undo Delete, 6, 29–30

Video synchronization, 350

Widows, 90
Wild-card characters, 365
Word wrap, 20
Words
  replacing, 61–66
  searching, 59–61

Character Set (00–7F) Quick Reference

DECIMAL VALUE →		0	16	32	48	64	80	96	112
↓	HEXA DECIMAL VALUE	0	1	2	3	4	5	6	7
0	0	BLANK (NULL)	►	BLANK (SPACE)	0	@	P	`	p
1	1	☺	◄	!	1	A	Q	a	q
2	2	☻	↕	"	2	B	R	b	r
3	3	♥	‼	#	3	C	S	c	s
4	4	♦	¶	$	4	D	T	d	t
5	5	♣	§	%	5	E	U	e	u
6	6	♠	▬	&	6	F	V	f	v
7	7	•	↨	'	7	G	W	g	w
8	8	◘	↑	(	8	H	X	h	x
9	9	○	↓	)	9	I	Y	i	y
10	A	◉	→	*	:	J	Z	j	z
11	B	♂	←	+	;	K	[	k	{
12	C	♀	∟	,	<	L	\	l	|
13	D	♪	↔	−	=	M	]	m	}
14	E	♫	▲	.	>	N	^	n	~
15	F	☼	▼	/	?	O	_	o	△

Character Set (88–FF) Quick Reference

DECIMAL VALUE → ↓ HEXADECIMAL VALUE		128 8	144 9	160 A	176 B	192 C	208 D	224 E	240 F
0	0	Ç	É	á	▓	└	╨	∝	≡
1	1	ü	æ	í	▒	┴	╤	β	±
2	2	é	Æ	ó	▓	┬	╥	Γ	≥
3	3	â	ô	ú	│	├	╙	π	≤
4	4	ä	ö	ñ	┤	─	╘	Σ	∫
5	5	à	ò	Ñ	╡	┼	╒	σ	∫
6	6	å	û	ª	╢	╞	╓	µ	÷
7	7	ç	ù	º	╖	╟	╫	τ	≈
8	8	ê	ÿ	¿	╕	╚	╪	Φ	°
9	9	ë	Ö	┌	╣	╔	┘	Θ	•
10	A	è	Ü	¬	║	╩	┌	Ω	·
11	B	ï	¢	½	╗	╦	█	δ	√
12	C	î	£	¼	╝	╠	▄	∞	n
13	D	ì	¥	¡	╜	═	▌	φ	2
14	E	Ä	₧	«	╛	╬	▐	∈	∎
15	F	Å	ƒ	»	┐	┘	▀	∩	BLANK 'FF'

Technical Reference Manual, pp.7-12–7-13, © 1984 International Business Machines Corporation

SYBEX Computer Books are different.

Here is why . . .

At SYBEX, each book is designed with you in mind. Every manuscript is carefully selected and supervised by our editors, who are themselves computer experts. We publish the best authors, whose technical expertise is matched by an ability to write clearly and to communicate effectively. Programs are thoroughly tested for accuracy by our technical staff. Our computerized production department goes to great lengths to make sure that each book is well-designed.

In the pursuit of timeliness, SYBEX has achieved many publishing firsts. SYBEX was among the first to integrate personal computers used by authors and staff into the publishing process. SYBEX was the first to publish books on the CP/M operating system, microprocessor interfacing techniques, word processing, and many more topics.

Expertise in computers and dedication to the highest quality product have made SYBEX a world leader in computer book publishing. Translated into fourteen languages, SYBEX books have helped millions of people around the world to get the most from their computers. We hope we have helped you, too.

For a complete catalog of our publications:

SYBEX, Inc. 2021 Challenger Drive, #100, Alameda, CA 94501
Tel: (415) 523-8233/(800) 227-2346   Telex: 336311